Analyzing Language and Humor in Online Communication

Rotimi Taiwo
Obafemi Awolowo University, Nigeria

Akinola Odebunmi
University of Ibadan, Nigeria

Akin Adetunji
Emmanuel Alayande College of Education, Nigeria

I0868867

A volume in the Advances in Linguistics and Communication Studies (ALCS) Book Series

Information Science REFERENCE
An Imprint of IGI Global

Published in the United States of America by
Information Science Reference (an imprint of IGI Global)
701 E. Chocolate Avenue
Hershey PA, USA 17033
Tel: 717-533-8845
Fax: 717-533-8661
E-mail: cust@igi-global.com
Web site: http://www.igi-global.com

Copyright © 2016 by IGI Global. All rights reserved. No part of this publication may be reproduced, stored or distributed in any form or by any means, electronic or mechanical, including photocopying, without written permission from the publisher. Product or company names used in this set are for identification purposes only. Inclusion of the names of the products or companies does not indicate a claim of ownership by IGI Global of the trademark or registered trademark.

Library of Congress Cataloging-in-Publication Data

Names: Taiwo, Rotimi (Dr.) editor. | Odebunmi, Akinola, 1967- editor. | Adetunji, Akin.
Title: Analyzing language and humor in online communication / Rotimi Taiwo, Akinola Odebunmi, and Akin Adetunji, editors.
Description: Hershey, PA : Information Science Reference, [2016] | Includes bibliographical references and index.
Identifiers: LCCN 2016006154| ISBN 9781522503385 (hardcover) | ISBN 9781522503392 (ebook)
Subjects: LCSH: Wit and humor in social media.
Classification: LCC PN4565.W58 A53 2016 | DDC 809.7--dc23 LC record available at https://lccn.loc.gov/2016006154

This book is published in the IGI Global book series Advances in Linguistics and Communication Studies (ALCS) (ISSN: Pending; eISSN: Pending)

British Cataloguing in Publication Data
A Cataloguing in Publication record for this book is available from the British Library.

All work contributed to this book is new, previously-unpublished material. The views expressed in this book are those of the authors, but not necessarily of the publisher.

For electronic access to this publication, please contact: eresources@igi-global.com.

Advances in Linguistics and Communication Studies (ALCS) Book Series

Abigail G. Scheg
Western Governors University, USA

ISSN: Pending
EISSN: Pending

Mission

The scope of language and communication is constantly changing as society evolves, new modes of communication are developed through technological advancement, and novel words enter our lexicon as the result of cultural change. Understanding how we communicate and use language is crucial in all industries and updated research is necessary in order to promote further knowledge in this field.

The **Advances in Linguistics and Communication Studies (ALCS)** book series presents the latest research in diverse topics relating to language and communication. Interdisciplinary in its coverage, ALCS presents comprehensive research on the use of language and communication in various industries including business, education, government, and healthcare.

Coverage

- Discourse Analysis
- Graphic Communications
- Computational Linguistics
- Forensic Linguistics
- Semantics
- Language acquisition
- Non-Verbal Communication
- Cross-Cultural Communication
- Youth Language
- Interpersonal Communication

IGI Global is currently accepting manuscripts for publication within this series. To submit a proposal for a volume in this series, please contact our Acquisition Editors at Acquisitions@igi-global.com or visit: http://www.igi-global.com/publish/.

The Advances in Linguistics and Communication Studies (ALCS) Book Series (ISSN Pending) is published by IGI Global, 701 E. Chocolate Avenue, Hershey, PA 17033-1240, USA, www.igi-global.com. This series is composed of titles available for purchase individually; each title is edited to be contextually exclusive from any other title within the series. For pricing and ordering information please visit http://www.igi-global.com/book-series/advances-linguistics-communication-studies/78950. Postmaster: Send all address changes to above address. Copyright © 2016 IGI Global. All rights, including translation in other languages reserved by the publisher. No part of this series may be reproduced or used in any form or by any means – graphics, electronic, or mechanical, including photocopying, recording, taping, or information and retrieval systems – without written permission from the publisher, except for non commercial, educational use, including classroom teaching purposes. The views expressed in this series are those of the authors, but not necessarily of IGI Global.

Titles in this Series

For a list of additional titles in this series, please visit: www.igi-global.com

Discourse Analysis as a Tool for Understanding Gender Identity, Representation, and Equality
Nazmunnessa Mahtab (University of Dhaka, Bangladesh) Sara Parker (John Moores University, UK) Farah Kabir (Action Aid, Bangladesh) Tania Haque (University of Dhaka, Bangladesh) Aditi Sabur (University of Dhaka, Bangladesh) and Abu Saleh Mohammad Sowad (University of Dhaka, Bangladesh)
Information Science Reference • copyright 2016 • 323pp • H/C (ISBN: 9781522502258) • US $185.00 (our price)

Revealing Gender Inequalities and Perceptions in South Asian Countries through Discourse Analysis
Nazmunnessa Mahtab (University of Dhaka, Bangladesh) Sara Parker (John Moores University, UK) Farah Kabir (Action Aid, Bangladesh) Tania Haque (University of Dhaka, Bangladesh) Aditi Sabur (University of Dhaka, Bangladesh) and Abu Saleh Mohammad Sowad (University of Dhaka, Bangladesh)
Information Science Reference • copyright 2016 • 286pp • H/C (ISBN: 9781522502791) • US $185.00 (our price)

Interdisciplinary Perspectives on Contemporary Conflict Resolution
Paulo Novais (University of Minho, Portugal) and Davide Carneiro (University of Minho, Portugal)
Information Science Reference • copyright 2016 • 363pp • H/C (ISBN: 9781522502456) • US $185.00 (our price)

Handbook of Research on Effective Communication, Leadership, and Conflict Resolution
Anthony H. Normore (California State University Dominguez Hills, USA & International Academy of Public safety, USA) Larry W. Long (Illinois State University, USA & International Academy of Public Safety, USA) and Mitch Javidi (North Carolina State University, USA & International Academy of Public Safety, USA)
Information Science Reference • copyright 2016 • 733pp • H/C (ISBN: 9781466699700) • US $315.00 (our price)

Handbook of Research on Cross-Cultural Approaches to Language and Literacy Development
Patriann Smith (University of Illinois at Urbana-Champaign, USA) and Alex Kumi-Yeboah (University at Albany–State University of New York, USA)
Information Science Reference • copyright 2015 • 567pp • H/C (ISBN: 9781466686687) • US $305.00 (our price)

Communication and Language Analysis in the Corporate World
Roderick P. Hart (University of Texas - Austin, USA)
Information Science Reference • copyright 2014 • 435pp • H/C (ISBN: 9781466649996) • US $215.00 (our price)

Communication and Language Analysis in the Public Sphere
Roderick P. Hart (University of Texas - Austin, USA)
Information Science Reference • copyright 2014 • 580pp • H/C (ISBN: 9781466650039) • US $190.00 (our price)

Digital Rhetoric and Global Literacies Communication Modes and Digital Practices in the Networked World
Gustav Verhulsdonck (University of Texas at El Paso, USA) and Marohang Limbu (Michigan State University, USA)
Information Science Reference • copyright 2014 • 398pp • H/C (ISBN: 9781466649163) • US $205.00 (our price)

IGI GLOBAL
DISSEMINATOR OF KNOWLEDGE
www.igi-global.com

701 E. Chocolate Ave., Hershey, PA 17033
Order online at www.igi-global.com or call 717-533-8845 x100
To place a standing order for titles released in this series, contact: cust@igi-global.com
Mon-Fri 8:00 am - 5:00 pm (est) or fax 24 hours a day 717-533-8661

Editorial Advisory Board

Adeleke Fakoya, *Lagos State University, Nigeria*
Christian Mair, *University of Freiburg, Germany*
Alleen Nilsen, *Arizona State University – Tempe, USA*
Don L. F. Nilsen, *Arizona State University – Tempe, USA*
Babatunde Opeibi, *University of Lagos, Nigeria*
Tope Omoniyi, *University of Roehampton, UK*
Victor Raskin, *Purdue University, USA*

Table of Contents

Detailed Table of Contents

The humorous depiction of Nazism and Holocaust by some American sitcom writers is the focus of this chapter. Demsky demonstrates the visibility of this depiction in shows such as South Park, Family Guy, and Robot Chicken. Many of the writers associated with these comedies are of Jewish heritage; but the joking has stirred only limited controversy. The author examines the messaging, delivery, and impact in Holocaust humor and attempts to answers questions such as: What are American comedy writers signaling with these absurd stories? How does their comedic employment contribute to a wider process of misremembering distorting, or diluting known Holocaust accounts? It also analyzes how computer-mediated communication - website like Hulu and Youtube - have transferred these accounts beyond American audiences.

This chapter discusses the use of wits in selected Facebook jokes based on a Nigerian joke character called Akpos. The authors analysed six out of fifteen sampled jokes within the theoretical perspectives of Istvan Kecskes' Socio-Cognitive Approach (SCA), aspects of the common ground theory, aspects of conversation analysis and elements of selected humour theories. The authors argue that the joke characters' situationally adaptive orientation to apriori or emergent common ground and intention demonstrates the Akpos jokes' recontextualisation of particular Nigerian social and cultural experiences through the characters' socio-cognitive designs in the mediated encounters. They conclude that while these designs offer the relaxant effects jokes are naturally meant to yield, their negotiation mechanisms provide resources for the application of Kecskes' SCA in Facebook humour and produce sarcasm with a wing of moral lessons.

This chapter discusses how humor is generated in a puppet political satire program featuring prominent actors on the Nigerian political scene. The programme is tagged Oga at the Top series (OATT). The author, Olubode-Sawe focuses on the socio-political context of the nation to explicate the videos by exploring how other texts and contexts are incorporated and how viewers receive them. The author shows from the 25 videos from Season One that humor creation mechanisms in OATT were found to include the use of puppet doubles of national leaders, re-interpretation of contemporary happenings, musical parody, verbal humor, inter-texuality and physical humor. Though the stated function of the series was to exploit the Nigerian political climate for humor, the analysis shows that the audience has appropriated the videos for their own ends based on the functions they felt the videos could serve. The author concludes by explicating the significance of online distribution of the videos.

Applying the mechanisms of conversational humour to interactional processes in blogs, Idowu-Faith in this chapter demonstrates how a popular Nigerian blogger, Linda Ikeji creates humorous keys to induce humorous turns from her readers. The author investigates how the readers respond to and sustain humour in Linda Ikeji's blog. The author also discusses the undermining of the seriousness of posts lacking keyed humour by readers. As humour occurs from both author's and readers' ends, the chapter clearly establishes the fact that conversational humour is a collaborative effort that strengthens social bonds and acts as a tool for sustaining entertainment and for motivating blog users.

This paper socio-critically analyses some visual constructions of humour on Facebook. Based on 17 visual data, gathered through the method of extensive Internet Ethnography, the paper indicates that members of the Facebook networking site are informal misogelasts, who through the methods of digital cloning, image cropping and digital impersonation, generate or appropriate visual materials and post such to generate social/communicational humour. Using insights from Visual Social Semiotics and Critical Social Semiotics, analyses reveal that constructed visual humour incorporates and interrogates such social phenomena as religion, education, morals, love, health and politics. The paper concludes that Facebook is not just a site for meeting new faces and interacting with them but also a medium for obtaining information on these social phenomena and how they are represented in the minds of individuals.

This chapter examines the rhetoric of visual humor on Facebook with the goal of developing a conceptual framework for understanding uses of humor on Facebook, and demonstrating that humorous texts on this social networking site are argumentative in focus. Using ideas from Aristotelian rhetoric, Barthian semiotics, and Saidian discourse analysis, the work contends that Facebook visual humor tends to perform four main functions. They can be gubernatorial, institutional, cultural, or grotesque, and often ridicule societal problems in either overt or covert ways. The findings are useful for developing a conceptual framework for studying the complexities of human culture in digital spaces.

This chapter looks at the creative and innovation humorous ventures in the famous Nigerian online talk show comedy - Klint Da Drunk. The comedy show, tagged "Alcoholic Talk Show" (ATS) by the author, features simulated alcoholic utterances, whose distortions produce humour. The data for the study were sourced from selected YouTube recordings of Klint da Drunk Show. They were subjected to visual and perceptual analysis. Analysis of the video recordings was guided by insights from Bergson's Theory of Comedy. The analysis revealed that ATS manifests lingual distortions, speech dysfluencies and gestural patterns that are characteristics of utterances rendered in a state of drunken stupor such that they produce humour and laughter. The study concluded that thespians do not only dramatise actions but also mime speech styles.

This chapter explores the forms of linguistic humour in Cameroon e-mail, Facebook, Yahoo Messenger and mobile telephone SMS. The author, using the incongruity and the incongruity-resolution theory of humour perception to analyse 270 electronic chats and messages, demonstrates that humour on these spaces flout Gricean maxims, exhibit spelling variations and sound devices. The author also demonstrates that Cameroonians employ humour for pleasure, intimacy and maintenance of cultural values. Humour markers like emoticons, special repetition of letters and some punctuation marks were prominent features in the social media humour. Others such as real-life anecdotes and oral naming patterns were peculiar to Cameroon, thus making the author to observe the independent nature of linguistic humour in Cameroon social media. The author demonstrated that humour thrives on the Facebook than the other social media platforms.

This chapter explores the ramifications of having race-based "dirty laundry" aired through humor, without necessarily being dirty jokes. The author interrogates the uncensored public broadcast of humor based on racial prejudices. He observes how racial humor online in forms of jokes, vines, videos and memes elicit comments and responses that likely would not be uttered within a formal, public forum. Citing three case studies the author teases out the implications of the continued sharing online of racial humor, with those both in and outside of the original joke. The author concludes that despite the virtual closeness the Internet encourages, the popularising of racial prejudices through online jokes makes at risk for growing even further apart.

Humor produces laughter, but beyond the laughter, producers of humor sometimes use it expresses social power. This representation of power in humor is the focus of this chapter. The author argues that a close reading of humour can provide an insight into how power is discursively produced and expressed by humorists online. This chapter examines Nigerian humour, which is gradually gaining popularity in the digital space. Twenty-five jokes from Naijabookofjokes.com, a Facebook forum for sharing jokes, were critically examined for the discursive elements that signal power relations. The chapter concludes that jokes are used to contest social and symbolic order among the people, thereby expressing power, especially through stereotyping and Otherness.

In this chapter, Onwu develops an elaborated Pragmatic Act Model (ePAM) and applies it to humorous interactions in students' chat room interactions in a Federal University of Technology in Nigeria. Drawing insights from Giora's Graded Salience Hypothesis (GSH), Mey's Pragmatic Act theory, four humour types – canned jokes, punning/wordplay, question and answer jokes, and hyperbole/overstatement were analysed. Findings show that four pragmatic acts are performed in the identified humour, namely, eliciting laughter, electioneering, teasing and overstating. In each of the humour types, the pragmatic mechanism drawn upon to comprehend the joke and to perform the pragmatic acts is indicated.

In this chapter, Adetunji highlights the linguistic value of addressivity in two Youtube videos of Joan Rivers' stand-up comic performance, Live at the Apollo. Joan Rivers' comic performance foregrounds the deployment of certain salient linguistic elements, such as: repetition, disfluencies, formulaicity, paralanguage, parenthetical expressions, figurative language, direct address, discourse markers. These forms are located within and interpreted with Bakhtin's notion of 'addressivity'. Significantly, her ubiquitous use of parenthetical expressions confers on her a unique rhetorical voice. The author argued that Rivers' overt audience interaction and her thematic preoccupation with social, biographical and autobiographical issues is one macro act of addressivity, foregrounding the complex intersection of the speaker (comedian), the listener (present audience), and the third person/superaddressee (non-present audience/previous discourses).

Visual verbal texts can be interpreted from the perspective of multimodality and intertextuality. This chapter investigates the manner in which visual-verbal code-pairing in texts becomes humorous within specific contexts and the role of incongruity as a major ingredient of humour. Adopting a combination of visual

Foreword

A good sense of humour ranks high among the qualities that many people expect of their spouses, friends and acquaintances – a 'requirement' that people be acquainted with jokes, quips, one-liners, humorous quotations, and any talk that could liven up dull moments especially unexpectedly. As of two decades ago, the 'provision' and availability of humour had been limited to the print and electronic media – that is, books, newspapers, the radio and television – but the advent of the Internet has endowed the present century with other possibilities for the creation, dissemination and consumption of humour.

In addition, humour these days is both composite and multimodal: humour providers can combine any number of devices and strategies to make others chuckle, laugh or guffaw. This reality is enhanced by the various outlets available to the humour provider: blogs, chat-forums, and platforms like the *Facebook*, *WhatsApp*, *Instagram*, *WeChat*, *etc*. What with the growing popularity of blogs and similar websites, the society is able to evaluate humour through comments and also increase existing stock by providing further humour in all computer-mediated communication. Thus, one can assertively say that humour and its provision are both enjoying unprecedented societal acceptance and appreciation.

The digital age is effectively the 'crown-prince era' of all that gives mirth, whether this be text, image or face-to-face interaction. The availability of the Internet immediately guarantees the institutionalization of a format that encourages both the study of humour on the Internet and the generation of online humour. So, for the researcher as well as the visitor to the sites providing 'humour services', there are resources that fulfil everyone's desire.

The present book is a marker of that fulfilment, judging by the vastness and appeal of its contents. Adopting diverse analytical, theoretical and methodological perspectives, the contributors offer exceptional descriptions of the nature and character of humour from such sources as politics, journalism, interpersonal relationships, religious worship, ethnic affiliations, trade and commerce, activism, gender, identity and equality, and education. More importantly, the contributors approach their descriptions from diverse analytical orientations: Multimodal Discourse Analysis, Discourse Stylistics, Critical Discourse Analysis, Pragmatics, Conversation Analysis, Semiotics, Ethnography, Ethnolinguistics, and Computer-mediated Discourse Analysis. Part of the appeal of the book, in fact, is the comprehensiveness and relevance of all these approaches to the analysis and description of the subject matter – whether humour is used to amuse us, criticise authorities, highlight issues or resolve conflict.

In tune with the overall goal of its authors, this book will be a landmark reference compass in regard to issues relating to humour in all its forms and characterizations, and although it's all about humour, its contents and concerns are not a laughing matter by any manner of means.

Adeleke A. Fakoya
Lagos State University, Nigeria

Preface

Analysing Language and Humour in Online Communication brings together a group of articles which address the current and important issue of humour in online platforms. Its motivation derives not only from the relaxant effects humour generates in the virtual communities, but also from the progressive transactional significance humour is gaining in a multitude of global cyber settings.

There are 15 chapters in the book, written by scholars from America and Africa. Their thematic engagement scope transcends their geographical spaces, courtesy of the Internet which has collapsed world boundaries and shrunk dispersed societal differences. This translates into cross-boundary humour sharing, a clear feature of the digital age, which of necessity, gets tracked and accounted for in a number of the chapters.

The jokes in the volume are sourced from *Facebook*, blogs, *YouTube*, chat rooms, emails, *Yahoo messenger*, Short Message Service (SMS) and online video distribution programmes which typify the virtual space. Twenty contributors, some of whom are co-authors, develop the central theme of humour from several experiential and theoretic perspectives. These give the chapters a taste of variegation and appeal, dwelling on issues from a number of American, Nigerian, and Cameroonian socio-cyber encounters.

In Chapter 1, Jeffrey Demsky in the article "Searching for Humour in Dehumanization: American Sitcoms, the Internet, and the Globalization of Holocaust Parodies" focuses on the humourous depiction of Nazism and Holocaust by selected American sitcom writers. His search in and analysis of *South Park*, *Family Guy*, and *Robot Chicken* shows demonstrate the comic writers' construction of absurd historical realities, how this enhances disremembering, and how *Hulu* and *YouTube* have globalised the accounts. Akin Odebunmi and Simeon Ajiboye handle the use of wits in selected *Facebook* jokes (tagged Akpos Jokes) largely shared within, but obviously not restricted to, Nigerian virtual communities. Their analysis, conducted with a number of theoretic traditions, shows that characters in the jokes orient to a priori or emergent common ground and intention to recontextualise particular Nigerian social and cultural experiences such as fraud, materialism and mischief.

In Chapter 3, "More Than a Joking Matter: Humour and Political Engagement in *Ogas at the Top*," Funmi Olubode-Sawe discusses the generation of humour in a puppet political satire programme, tagged *Oga at the Top series* (OATT), which feature prominent personalities in the Nigerian political space. Olubode-Sawe notes the deployment of such humour creation mechanisms as the use of puppet doubles of national leaders, re-interpretation of contemporary happenings, musical parody, verbal humour, inter-textuality and physical humour in the contextualisation of puppetry and corruption in the series. She points out the humorous and satirical dimensions to the series and comments on the societal and academic value of online distribution of videos. In a study of the language of blogs, Bimbola Idowu-Faith conducts a stylistic exploration of the nature and mode humourous conversations in selected blogs.

She reports on the way humour is initiated and created, and how the humourist constrains the responses of the audience in a symmetrically discursive manner, which strengthens social bonds, by sustaining entertainment and motivating blog users.

Ibrahim Esan Olaosun studies the social and communicative content of selected visual constructions of humour on *Facebook* from a visual semiotic perspective. His findings indicate that constructed visual humour embeds and interrogates religion, education, morals, love, health, politics and a number of other social phenomena. In another contribution on visual humour, Wincharles Coker and Stephen Kwame Dadugblor examine a rhetoric of online visual humour premised on interpretive netnography. They develop a framework for the exploration of rhetorical functions of humour in virtual spaces. Arguing from a function-loaded perspective on humour, they identify four basic rhetorical arguments or rhetographs: gubernatorial, institutional, cultural, and grotesque.

Chapter 7 examines the linguistic features of Klint Da Drunk's 'Alcoholic' Talk Show (ATS) sourced from *Youtube*. The features include lingual distortions, speech dysfluencies and gestural patterns, observed to characterise stupor-tainted utterances that generate humour and laughter. In Chapter Eight, "Language and Humour in Cameroon Social Media", Camilla Arundie Tabe investigates the forms of linguistic humour in Cameroon e-mail, *Facebook*, *Yahoo Messenger* and mobile telephone SMS. The author, using the incongruity and the incongruity-resolution theory of humour perception, shows that humour in the sampled data flouts Gricean maxims, and displays variation in spelling and sound devices. His findings also indicate three discourse functions of Cameroonian online humour: pleasure, intimacy and maintenance of cultural values, achieved through the use of markers of humour such as emoticons, special repetition of letters and punctuation marks, real-life anecdotes and oral naming patterns with peculiar connection to Cameroon

In Chapter 9, the contribution, "'Can I Get in on the Joke, Too?' Analysing Racial Humour within the Public/Private Realm of the Internet" investigates the strategic management of online race-sensitive jokes. The author, Fredrick Gooding, interrogates the uncensored public broadcast of humour based on racial prejudices. In Chapter 10, "Discursive Representation of Power in Humour in *Naijabookofjokes.com*," Rotimi Taiwo is concerned with the way power is exercised in humour in an online discursive context. He argues that humour in *Naijabookofjokes.com* contests social and symbolic order among the subscribers to the site, thus demonstrating power through stereotyping and display of Otherness. The next contribution, by Inya Onwu, addresses the pragmatics of humour in a Nigerian university's departmental chat rooms. With a mix of theoretical insights, Onwu identifies four humour types - canned jokes, punning/wordplay, question and answer jokes, and hyperbole/overstatement. He connects these humour types with four pragmatic acts: eliciting laughter, electioneering, teasing, and overstating.

In Chapter 12, Akin Adetunji analyses the properties of addressivity in Joan Rivers stand-up comedy. He identifies markers such as repetition, disfluencies, formulaicity, paralanguage, parenthetical expressions, figurative language, direct address, discourse markers as theoretic descriptions of the comic events. The distinction of the rhetorical voice is marked off by the ubiquitous use of parenthetical expressions. He argues that Rivers' overt audience interaction and her thematic preoccupation with social, biographical and autobiographical issues, which are macro acts of addressivity, foreground the complex intersection of the speaker (comedian), the listener (present audience), and the third person/superaddressee (non-present audience/previous discourses). Tayo Lamidi, in Chapter 13, "Humour in Visual-Verbal Code-Pairing in Selected Comments on the Facebook Forum," explores the potential of interpreting visual verbal texts from the perspective of multimodality and intertextuality. He investigates how visual-verbal code pairing in the texts becomes humorous within specific contexts and the role of incongruity as a major ingredient of humour. He presents the view that the two parts to the visual-verbal humour have the tendency to constitute a composite whole, forming the unexpected portion, while the background to the joke serves as the expected.

In "Socio-semiotics of Humour in Ebola Awareness Discourse on *Facebook*," Chimuanya Lilly and Ajiboye Esther examine humorous graphics, texts and memes posted on *Facebook* during the heat of the Ebola virus epidemic that was experienced in parts of West Africa in 2014. Using Kress and Leeuwen's approach to multimodal discourse analysis, the authors argue that the posts both indexicate humour and informal awareness campaign cues. The contribution on contextual beliefs and pragmatic strategies of humour in Akpos Jokes by Oluwatomi Adeoti and Ibukun Filani identifies shared knowledge of language and knowledge of situation and events in Nigeria as the assumptions upon which humour in the jokes are based. It also picks out the use implicature and stereotyping of the character of *Akpos* as strategies for the achievement of humorous effects in the jokes.

The methodologies and analytical approaches employed by the contributors generate a clear alignment with humour research procedures and genre expectations in the discipline. These place the book, *Analysing Language and Humour in Online Communication,* on a competitive pedestal, and readily recommend it to readers who are interested in how online humour gets lexicalised and unpacked in a professionally incisive and impressive manner.

Rotimi Taiwo
Obafemi Awolowo University, Nigeria

Akinola Odebunmi
University of Ibadan, Nigeria

Akin Adetunji
Emmanuel Alayande College of Education, Nigeria

Chapter 1
Searching for Humor in Dehumanization:
American Sitcoms, the Internet, and the Globalization of Holocaust Parodies

Jeffrey Demsky
San Bernadino Valley College, USA

ABSTRACT

During the last two decades, to varying degrees, some American sitcom writers have depicted Nazism and the Holocaust humorously. This sort of activity is visible on such shows as South Park, Family Guy, and Robot Chicken. Many of the writers associated with these comedies are of Jewish heritage; but the joking has stirred only limited controversy. This chapter examines the messaging, delivery, and impact in Holocaust humor. It answers questions such as: What are American comedy writers signaling with these absurd stories? How does their comedic employment contribute to a wider process of misremembering distorting, or diluting known Holocaust accounts? It also analyzes how computer-mediated communications—website like Hulu and Youtube—have transferred these false accounts beyond American audiences.

INTRODUCTION

During the last two decades, to varying degrees, some American sitcom writers have depicted Nazism and the Holocaust humorously. This sort of activity is visible on such shows as *South Park*, *Family Guy*, and *Robot Chicken*. Many of the writers associated with these comedies are of Jewish heritage; but the joking has stirred only limited controversy (Eshman, 2013; Holm, 2011, p.10). Such parodies encapsulate a unique variant of Holocaust post-memory, the process by which modern observers commemorate the traumas of those who came before (Hirsch, 2012, p. 4). The iconoclasm also offers a comedy lesson, notably Woody Allen's witticism about humor being the combination of tragedy plus the passage of time. The reasons provoking this type of levity are not altogether clear; also uncertain is its effects on the genocide's global memory. Americans have a long tradition of belittling Adolf Hitler (Wisse, 2013,

DOI: 10.4018/978-1-5225-0338-5.ch001

Copyright © 2016, IGI Global. Copying or distributing in print or electronic forms without written permission of IGI Global is prohibited.

p.179). Lampooning his victims, however, is something new. In this regard, American sitcom writers have razed a boundary, pushing into unknown artistic and commemorative spaces (Kaplan, 2002, p. 343).

American scholars have explored Holocaust humor for more than a decade. In 2001, an organization called the Conference on the Holocaust and the Churches published John Morreall's paper, "Humor in the Holocaust: Its Critical, Cohesive, and Coping Functions." His was a theoretical study, referencing Greek and Shakespearean writers, which argued that comedy is not "time out" from real world grittiness. Jokes are simply another vehicle of human expression (Morreall, 2001). Humor is a sign of emotional intelligence; it is a powerful communication strategy. Nothing in life, including the Nazis' genocide, forever eludes mockery (Muller, 2012). Humor can also help hear trauma (Kaplan, 2002, p. 341). It was very much part of camp life (Lipman, 1991). The concern, however, that some current commentators maintain is whether or not laughing at the dead blurs the line between the degeneracy of the mocker, from that of the mocked (Wisse, 2013, p. 234).

This chapter does not consider whether or not Holocaust humor is amusing, or appropriate. Rather, I am studying its messaging, delivery, and impact. What are American comedy writers signaling with these absurd stories (Critchley, 2002, p. 75)? How does their comedic emplotment contribute to a wider process of misremembering, distorting, or diluting known Holocaust accounts (Lipstadt, 1993, p.14)? With regard to its broadcast, I want to analyze how computer-mediated communications—website like Hulu and Youtube—have transferred these false accounts beyond American audiences. According to Katayama (2009), humor brings people together under shared laughter. However, since humor requires highly sensitive linguistic and cultural competence, expressing and appreciating humor is often a challenge in cross-cultural communication (p.125). Whether American sitcom writers intended to engage global Holocaust memory is unknown. My study examines the parodies less for their intention, than for the ways they might help to reshape the discourse.

Since the 1950s, the program of murder that came to be known as the Holocaust has been part of the American cultural experience (Garber and Zuckerman, 1989, p. 202). On television and in theatres and films, successive generations of postwar citizens have internalized its lessons and legacies (Shandler, 1999, p. 44). What differentiates this tradition, however, from humor-based appropriations, is that earlier works promoted vigilance. When shows such as *Star Trek* and *Twilight Zone* represented the Holocaust to ordinary citizens, they did so to teach. This was also the case with the 1970s American mini-series *Holocaust*, which attracted hundreds of millions of viewers. These artifacts laid out what might be called responsible fictions, helping people born after the genocide to learn who did what to whom (Hilberg, 1992, p. 215).

Schindler's List (1993) is the best-known example of this cultural pedagogy. It opened the same year as the US Holocaust Memorial Museum, reinforcing Americans' duty to the memory. *Schindler's* reached beyond a Jewish reference group, chronicling a non-Jewish protagonist on his path to forgiveness and redemption, traditionally Christian leitmotifs (Loshitzky, 1997, p. 107). Owing to its compelling story, heavy marketing, and various delivery platforms, the film had a huge impact. Tens of millions of consumers screened the film in theatres. Countless millions more have watched it on television, DVD, Blu-Ray, or online. At the time of its release, the head of Walt Disney film studios remarked that the picture will "end up being more than a movie…it will affect how people on this planet act and think" (Rosenfeld, 2011, p. 82). *Schindler's* profitability cleared a path for additional Holocaust themed productions such as *Life is Beautiful* (1997) and *The Pianist* (2002). Director Steven Spielberg also allocated a portion of his profits from *Schindler's* to establish a video archive that catalogs online thousands of survivors' oral histories (USC).

While such commemorations have strengthened remembrances, not all observers see pure altruism. Critics note that Holocaust-inspired productions also connote substantial revenue streams. *Schindler's List* grossed over three hundred million dollars at the box office. Theatre owners, vendors, lawyers, publicists, and others profited from the tale of Jewish suffering (Horowitz, 1997, p. 119). This fiscal reality has led to the appearance of what some commentators call "*Shoah* business," and others term the memory's "industrialization" (Cole, 1999, p. 76; Finkelstein, 2000, p. 161). The issue of whether economic, or scholarly, factors drive representations is provocative. However, I am more focused on the ways these dominating remembrances, as prevalent, are susceptible to revision. I am not referring to so-called deniers, but rather to farcical tales steeped in fantasy, escapism, and comedy. Some of these renditions are so far removed from fact that they are not only incapable of being anchored within factual accounts, but they also have the potential to undermine them. Particularly in a streaming, online environment the existence—and, indeed persistence—of alluring counter-narratives may contribute to forgetting.

The closing scene to *Inglorious Basterds* (2009) highlights this possibility. The action depicts Jewish American soldiers assassinating Adolf Hitler and the SS high command in a Paris movie theatre. The film's implication is this faux event ended World War II and the Holocaust. For susceptible viewers, the slick, noir, sensationalist images have the potential to form false values (Zelizer, 1998, p. 6). Where *Schindler's* story bolstered scholars' research-based findings, *Inglorious*' plot undermines traditional truths. The end result is a more likable trope. *Inglorious* shows us Nazi gullibility, Jewish courage, and a non-collaborative picture of the French (Wolf, 2004, p. 63; Jungius and Seibel, 2008, p. 441). Such narrative alternatives may appeal to people born after the genocide, who do not want to approach the trauma. It could also appeal to older witnesses, once close to the memory, but now desiring of release (Funk, 2015).

These processes speak to a subtler truth. Despite the many books that are written about it, the many museums devoted to perpetuating its memory, and the many films and media artifacts that continue to draw large audiences, knowing about the Holocaust is not the same as upholding its validity. Vague banalities about the imperative to "never forget" are not analogous to remembering (Mintz, 2001, p. 174). As commemorations take on distinctive characters, the tale is reshaped and reconstituted to ensure that it is remembered at all (Dumitru, 2008, p. 49; Pinnock, 2007, p. 516; Kansteiner, 2006, p. 121; Ivanova, 2004, p. 402). It is in this shifting terrain that American comedy writers, aided by computer-mediated communications, can operate. Repackaging the received wisdom with humor is not necessarily a gateway to social amnesia. Instead, tweaking dominant beliefs might help to sustain their continued relevance. Joking about the Holocaust, for those whose tastes permit, is only funny if the humor first validates the sinister nature of the reality it is attempting to demystify.

PART ONE: UNLIKELY MEMORIES: AMERICA AND THE HOLOCAUST

To understand why some sitcom writers have arrived at the point where they now see in the Holocaust a muse, we must review America's relationship to the Nazis' war on Jews. Of course, the genocide occurred in Europe. No Jewish Americans were killed. This does not mean, however, that the program of murder was unknown. On December 17, 1942, President Franklin Roosevelt forcefully condemned the Nazis' "bestial policy of cold-blooded extermination" (Medoff, 2009, p. 9). Two years later, with the pace of the killings unimpeded, he declared, "These acts of savagery shall not go unpunished. All who knowingly take part in the deportation of Jews to their death are equally guilty as the executioner.

All who share the guilt shall share the punishment" (State, 1944). In October 1945, just months after the Nazis' capitulation, these promises became policy. Allied jurists convened an International Military Tribunal in Nuremberg, Germany. Two-dozen Nazi leaders were indicted under a new statute termed "crimes against humanity." Half received capital sentences (Ball, 1999, p. 60).

The swiftness with which the Allies enforced justice indicated their abhorrence. It also hints at a larger question of why, then, leaders did so little to blunt the killings as they occurred. Despite detailed knowledge of what Hitlerism denoted for European Jews, and countless pleas for help, American government officials did not act. During the 1930s and 1940s, policymakers strengthened the "paper walls" limiting Jewish immigration (Wyman, 1968, p. 209). Proposals to resettle European Jews on the US Virgin Islands fell through (Breitman and Lichtman, 2013, p. 137). Calls for the Army Air Force to bomb the death camps garnered mixed support (Neufeld and Berenbaum, 2000, p. 113). The postwar discovery that some wartime officials held anti-Jewish opinions, a sentiment experts locate across thirties America, gave rise to sweeping conclusions that Americans had "abandoned" Europe's Jews (Wyman, 1984, p. 341). This view has proved resilient. For thirty years, into current times, the judgment has set the context for American Holocaust memory (Medoff, 2013, p. 195).

Whether the US could have, and should have, taken more steps to end the genocide is a valid issue. However, rather than directly engaging this literature, I am asking how the perception—that not enough was done—has set the contours of memorialization. Rather than rejecting the "failure to rescue" criticisms, such critical findings have spurred a process in which Americans now prominently uphold Holocaust memory. In 1979, President Jimmy Carter speechified to this point. "Although the Holocaust took place in Europe," he explained, "the event is of fundamental significance to Americans." "It was American troops who liberated many death camps, and who helped to expose the horrible truth of what had been done there." "We feel compelled to study the systematic destruction of the Jews so that we may seek to learn how to prevent such enormities from occurring in the future" (J. Young, 1999, pp. 72-73).

While honorable, this claim to stewardship also puzzles. The German writer Henryk Broder (2001) has observed, "What is it with Americans and the Holocaust?" They have two national Holocaust museums, with a third in the works, and almost every major city has its own memorial… from the fervor with which America commemorates the event, a naive observer might reasonably conclude that the Nazi Holocaust took place in the United States, and that Americans feel obliged to come to grips with this dark chapter of their history" (p. 74). This "Americanization" of Holocaust memory concerns many others as well (Dochartaigh, 2006, p. 459). Scholars wonder if the retelling of European memories through an English second language confuses more than it enlightens (Rosen, 2005, p. 36)? They want to know if Western preferences for so-called welcome narratives have silenced voices (Reich, 2006, p. 464)? Perhaps, the thorniest issue is whether or not current onlookers are actually remembering the Holocaust, or are instead recalling what experts have come to say the genocide represented (Novick, 2003, p. 32). It is from this unlikely wellspring that American Holocaust comedy traces its roots. Sitcom writers may simply be laughing at what others have already pointed out is a contested claim to memory.

PART TWO: UNLIKELY HUMOR: AMERICA AND THE HOLOCAUST

American daughters and sons of Holocaust survivors, the so-called second-generation witnesses, possessed a unique purchase on the question of post-Auschwitz Jewish identity (Berger, 1995, p. 24). "Baby

Boomers" overwhelmingly embraced their parents' traumas. Many dedicated their lives to drawing out usable past from the catastrophe. Second generation Jewish witnesses built museums, erected memorials, and codified a standardized curriculum of global Holocaust lessons (Fallace, 2006, p. 80). Members of this cohort also saw in the catastrophe a call to arms against perceived Jewish powerlessness. During the late 1960s and early 1970s, as Israeli forces battled Arab enemies, survivors' progeny proclaimed "Never Again" (Oren, 2003, p. 332) Some American youth left the US to join the Middle East fight. Others supported domestic groups such as the Jewish Defense League, exhibiting both vigilance and vigilantism against anti-Semitism.

Forming an active identity against prejudice betrays closeness to the trauma. To second-generation witnesses, the lesson of their parents' misfortune was the need for constant watchfulness against bigotry (Heller, 2015). While an ironclad belief to "Baby Boomers," some of their children, members of the third generation, possess different judgments, based on differing experiences (Landsberg, 1997, p. 64). It is this cohort that produces and consumes Holocaust humor. Such steps do not necessarily repudiate their ancestors' suffering, but might instead signal a deeper set of challenges that postwar Jewish Americans have encountered with the memory (Wiesen, 2009, p. 11).

As Holland (2012) reminds us, each generation must "enter into a history that is literally not their own." In terms of its descent, the events and their meanings "belong to someone else" (p. 20). Added to this distance is the variable of changed social norms. People born in the US after 1970 had a very different experience with anti-Semitism than their grandparents. It seems likely they would have encountered discussions of anti-Semitism and the Holocaust more within their families, then on the schoolyards (Blakeslee, 2000, p. 41). This difference has the potential to deflate the stories, as the lessons appear more a parent's urging than a practical life tool. It is also possible some unwillingness has formed within this cohort to approach communal memories rooted in themes of victimization. What makes this process compelling is that third generation witnesses enjoy a mastery of online technologies that allows them to re-message those aspects of the legacy they find problematic.

Take for example Anne Frank's story. Since its publication during the late 1940s, her diary has introduced tens of millions of people to the Holocaust (Holligan, 2014). During the 1950s, a theatrical adaptation of her writings was performed in the US and elsewhere. By the decade's end, the story was a Hollywood motion picture screened in such lands as West Germany, Soviet Union, France, and Israel. The narrative's universality, mourning social hatreds, taught a transnational lesson. Numerous groups have come to stake "ownership" of her legacy (Rosenfeld, 2011, p. 50; Ozick, 1997, p. 76). Anne Frank helps white South Africans to negotiate Apartheid; it forgives Germans for their Nazi past (Gilbert, 2010, p. 36; Sackett, 2002, p. 243). Anne even holds current pop culture status. In 2013, following a visit to her Amsterdam memorial, Canadian musician Justin Bieber shared his judgment that Anne was a "great girl" (Weinstock, 2013). In their song "Fresh and Clean," American rap group *Outkast* imagines her a reclusive siren with whom they hoped to "hit the attic to hide out for 'bout two weeks" (Benjamin, Patton, & Sheats, 2001).

It is this tradition American sitcom writers have joined. References to Anne Frank abound in their work. The episodes are currently broadcast in America, Europe, and Asia. They stream online, via multiple websites. In terms of repackaging Anne and the wider Holocaust, *South Park* has been poking fun the longest. Its debut season featured a show in which a youngster wore a Hitler Halloween costume to school (Stone & Parker, 1997). Over the last two decades, its writers have consistently probed the war on Jews for humor. They also engage other taboos, depicting females as inferior, making fun of impov-

Figure 1. Eric Cartman as Adolf Hitler
South Park courtesy of Comedy Central. © 1997, Comedy Partner. All rights reserved. Used with permission.

erished people, lampooning pedophilia, and once threatening to cartoon the Islamic prophet Mohammed (Julian, 2010; Khodasevich, n.d.). To analyze how this brash cultural style has had impact on Holocaust remembrances, some fuller discussion of the show's production is required.

South Park depicts the lives of four grade-schoolers, and their neighbors, living in a quiet Colorado town. One of the boys, Kyle Broflovski, is Jewish. The show's co-creator, Matt Stone, reportedly fashioned the Broflovski family as autobiographical. Kyle struggles to negotiate his inherited ethnic identity, a process complicated by the cascade of harassment he receives from his bigoted classmate, Eric Cartman. Although just a fourth-grader, Eric is a hardened anti-Semite. He is also, unflinchingly, a swindler, liar, hypocrite, and even an accomplice to murder (Parker, 2001). In this sense, he represents humanity's seedier impulses, and mature viewers might situate his anti-Jewish beliefs as part of that more sinister spirit (W. Young, 2013, p.11).

Major Boobage (2008) is the episode during which writers have Cartman deliver a snide wink to Anne Frank (Parker & Stone, 2008). Ostensibly, the story's plot involves children huffing cat urine. To discourage them, authorities decided to round up and deport the town's cats. Nothing overt about this narrative suggested a looming Holocaust joke. However, when authorities arrived at Eric Cartman's home, searching for cats, a doorway to genocide humor opened. The anti-Semite Cartman now channels Meip Gies, frustrating the officers' search. After it was safe, as plangent, minor-mode background music crescendos, Cartman ascends a staircase to his attic. He is hiding a cat. Cartman explains the danger to the feline. Before closing the attic's latch, he slips the animal a book and says, "Here, write a diary."

By relating Anne's tale to that of a stray cat, *South Park* writers might be satirizing any number things. Of course, the real-life Anne began her diary entries by writing "Dear Kitty." Such homage demonstrates writers' familiarity with the canon, and might strike informed viewers as droll. For those simply enamored of the Cartman character, such advice betrays his greed-driven personality. It is also possible that the show's writers enjoying blaspheming, and at this particular time Anne just happened to be in their crosshairs (Murtagh, 2013, p. 113). Other American sitcoms, however, also find Anne Frank's story comedic. The *Family Guy* episode *If I'm Dyin', I'm Lyin* (2000) had nothing to do with the Holocaust. Nevertheless, writers embedded a black-and-white "cut away" scene that featured the show's main character, Peter Griffin, seated in an attic. He is set to the side, looking at a huddled group of men, women, and teens, drawn as observant Jews. In the center sits a girl with braided hair. She is clutching a book marked "Diary" (Sheridan, 2000).

After setting up the joke's premise, the punch line arrives via three interlocking images. First, viewers witness the Nazis kicking down a door and storming into the house. Next, the camera pans upward to show those hiding in the attic. It is at this most dramatic point that *Family Guy* writers unveil their final frame, as Peter munches on potato chips. His crunches are very loud (Sheridan, 2000). While the soon-to-be victims stare in horror, his countenance is blank. He continues to snack. The inanity of this scene, from Peter being in the attic, to the availability of potato chips, renders the clip so clearly at odds with reality that writers might well have concluded it was unlikely any viewer would mistake the rendition for fact.

However, writers may also have been offering additional commentary. Selecting the obese, ignorant Peter Griffin for the joke's vehicle might be a larger commentary of Americans' intellectual fatigue (Marc, 1997, p. 132). Clearly, Peter Griffin and his ilk are incapable of properly upholding Holocaust memory. They are not going to acts as stewards. This does not mean, however, their jocularity, what Kaplan (2002) would term a "transgressive mode" of expression, damages remembrances (p. 345). Matters such as why Peter was eating potato chips next to Anne Frank during the early 1940s are less important than how these restorations, in this case comedic, rejuvenate existing narrative frameworks (Holm, 2011, p. 31). This course of thought asks people to consider how joking about Anne Frank—and, ultimately her murder—nevertheless renders her a continued part of collective memory.

PART THREE: UNKNOWN IMPACTS: THE GLOBALIZATION OF AMERICAN HOLOCAUST HUMOR

Irrespective of whether or not people enjoy these parodies, American Holocaust humor is entrenched in global discourse. Computer-mediated communications enable fresh iterations—e.g. Photoshopping, GIFs, memes, and re-dubbed movie dialogue—that continually reassign the humor. Holocaust jokes air in Germany, Ireland, Holland, France, England, and New Zealand. Such cross-cultural transfers raise various questions. For Europeans, generally, anti-Semitism remains a persistent social challenge (Goldberg, 2015). According to scholars at Tel Aviv University's Kantor Center, during 2014 France led European nations with the most number of reported attacks against Jews and their property. (Kantor Center, 2014, p. 83). Such evidence supports a more pervasive trend; anti-Jewish violence is surging around the world (Chaouat, 2013, p.118).

Similar reports dot the landscape of American society (Markoe, 2015). Despite such flare-ups, however, Jews in the US are more positively integrated to the culture than at anytime in their history (Jaher, 1994, pp. 186-187). Since the postwar years, creedal categories, rooted in shared reverence for civic ideals, have provided Jewish citizens a bridge to the American mainstream (Herberg, 1960, pp. 76-77). The differing social experiences known to American and European Jewry separates their Holocaust perspectives. It may also disconnect their views about its proper commemoration. With regard to sitcom parodies, these divergences can complicate the messages that writers in the US fashion, and the cues Europeans are receiving (McLennan, 2012).

An example of this uncertainty is visible in some Holocaust humor from the sitcom *Robot Chicken*. The show debuted in 2005 and remains in current production. Joining *South Park* and *Family Guy*, its third generation Jewish American writers also worked up an Anne Frank skit. Youtube hosts the clip, outfitted with French subtitles, which has attracted more than thirty thousand viewers. The episode is *Toy Meets Girl* (2005). In this repurposing, Anne is happy to live in an annex behind her father's business. She confides to her dairy that she is "awesome" because "everything I want is right here." Following her jubilance, the camera pans across a tastefully decorated room to reveal her companion, Peter Van Dann, wearing Tallit and reading from torah (Allen-Duton et al., 2005).

When the Nazis finally arrive, Anne is ferocious. Equipped with a full complement of *Home Alone* (1990) traps—paint can on rope and ice puddles—she stymies the Storm Troopers. *Robot Chicken* writers close their fantasy with Anne and Peter, now wearing modern couture, embracing atop an Amsterdam river crossing. Peter assures her, "You're really something, Anne Frank." "I'm just me," she replies, tossing back her hair and curving her leg (Allen-Duton et al., 2005). Comments posted to the clip's chat board are mixed. Some viewers indicated their support via digital acronyms like "LOL" (McCann, 2015). Others, however, rejected the irreverence. "Can't believe how awful that was," exclaimed one woman, uploading her comments in both English and French (Saint-preux, 2013). In response, another French viewer shared their hope this skit would be the "first and last" (Zéro, 2013).

In this sense, the contexts supporting Holocaust humor seem to determine if they are harmless or hurtful. Of course, it also matters who is reconfiguring the memory. Artists, for example, are charged with the task of engaging social discourses. They possess a license to provoke. The Italian artist AleXsandro Palombo engages received memory via "humor chic," a method in which he assigns well-known American cartoon images to unfunny things. To encourage breast cancer awareness, Palombo fashioned images of Betty Boop, Jessica Rabbit, Snow White, and the Little Princess, all with double hysterectomy scars. In a similar vein, hoping to draw attention to the scourge of domestic violence, he portrayed Olive Oil, Wilma Flintstone, and Wonder Woman with blackened eyes (Palombo, 2014).

Palombo's Holocaust series is *The Simpsons*-NEVER AGAIN. He devised these images as a way to educate new generations about Holocaust trauma (Denham, 2015).

Figure 2. The Simpsons-NEVER AGAIN
© 2015, Alexsandro Palombo. Used with permission.

In his renderings, Homer, Marge, and the kids are shown imprisoned and emaciated. They are set behind barbed wire; Stars of David are sewn to their garb. A number of drawings in this collection are recreations of actual photographs. The implied notion, that persecuted *Simpsons* characters may elicit greater familiarity from modern observers than black-and-white shots of nameless people, may be less a matter of fault than it is fact. Palombo is attempting memory modernization. He is trying to close off distance between bygone events and contemporary times. Others around the globe are producing un-orthodox imaginings; evidence of what Alvin Rosenfeld has termed the Holocaust's new plasticity (Rosenfeld, 2011, p. 45). In 2015, a British high school student made global news after submitting various Lego-based creations depicting Hitlerism and the Holocaust As with Palombo, the student's rationale for depicting the genocide unorthodoxly was to spark continued interest in the killings (B'Ayin, 2015).

However, what if people laying claiming to Holocaust humor are not promoting artistry? What if the memory they stoke glorifies aspects of Nazism? In these cases, does existing lightheartedness provide bigots an unintended doorway to intolerance? Take for example PEGIDA chief Lutz Bachmann. PEGIDA is a German anti-immigration and anti-Muslim movement. In January 2015, Bachmann joined some twenty thousand supporters at a Dresden rally. Owing to similarities in PEGIDA and Nazi rationales, the event provoked significant global commentary (Connolly, 2015a). Further inflaming the episode was Bachmann's subsequent claim to Holocaust humor. Shortly after the march, various online media outlets obtained "screen grabs" of a "selfie" in which Bachmann had configured himself to look like Adolf Hitler. The photo soon went "viral," reposted on Facebook, Twitter, and splashed across the front pages of dozens of newspapers.

While his spokesperson insisted the photo was satire, a chorus of outrage forced Bachmann's retreat (McLaughlin 2015). This type of scandal, however, is not just about one person's poor taste. Understanding Bachmann's "just kidding" defense speaks directly to the unknown impacts of computer-mediated Holocaust humor. It is an uncharted field, and those fashioning irreverent renditions have no way to ultimately control how their work is appropriated (Norrick, 2010, p. 237).

Figure 3. Hitler in Legos
© 2015, John Denno. Used with permission.

Figure 4. Lutz Bachmann As Hitler
(2015, January 21). Sein Hitler-Selfie kennt jetzt die halbe Welt. Bild.

Bachmann's buffoonery was tone deaf, but perhaps more complex than onlookers recognize. Born during the 1970s, he is part of the third generation of German Holocaust witnesses. Along with other third generation inheritors, across Germany and elsewhere, he is renegotiating the memory (Eder, 2012; Kansteiner, 2003, p. 142). Owing to the fact that Bachmann came of age in the former East Germany, he learned relatively little of the Holocaust through popular culture (Wolfgram, 2006, p. 57). Compared to West Germans, where the memory was central, Bachmann may perceive the war on Jews as less critical to national identity. Such diminution, combined with his firebrand rhetoric, certainly lends itself to the perception of bigotry. However, the core question remains who may, or may not, fête Nazism.

As far back as the 1960s, British rock stars massaged this boundary. While in Munich, Rolling Stones' guitarist Brian Jones posed for portraits with the West German magazine *Stern*. He was wearing an SS uniform (Tyrnka, 2014, p. 192, 209). During the 1970s, David Bowie, Sid Vicious, and Keith Moon paid similar homage (Spiardi, 2013). Some British rockers went so far as to appropriate Nazi mindsets. In 1976, Eric Clapton delivered a drunken rant to his Birmingham, England audience. "Stop Britain from becoming a black colony," he exclaimed. "Get the foreigners out. Get the wogs out. Get the coons out. Keep Britain white. I used to be into dope, now I'm into racism. It's much heavier, man." (Street, 1986, pp. 74-75).

Of course, Germans' claims to this wellspring are more problematic. German law proscribes showing or displaying Nazi symbols. Shops and websites may not sell Nazi paraphernalia. It is forbidden to glorify the Third Reich, or its ideology. However, *Bundesrepublik* statutes permit cultural engagement with these things. It is a primary way that Germans approach the history. Indeed, Lutz Bachmann's decision to pose as Hitler, he claims, was tied to a contemporary German parody of Adolf Hitler (McLaughlin, 2015).

The work is Timur Vermes' *Er ist wieder da /He's Back Again* (2012). In this fiction, Adolf Hitler reawakens on Earth during the early twenty first century. As it did during his life, multiculturalism repulses Hitler. However, rather than expressing his vitriol in beer halls, the reanimated Adolf—and his rants—become Youtube celebrity. The sway of social and online digital networks eventually facilitates his re-entry to politics (Connolly, 2013b). Vermes' fiction sold over a million copies. It has been translated into dozens of languages. Whether Hitler is an appropriate figure for comedic reexamination remains contested (Evans, 2013). What is clearer, however, is that someone like Lutz Bachmann saw in

Figure 5. Brian Jones as Nazi
(1966). Børge.

the discourse a license for Holocaust humor. Speaking of the story, he is reported to have told German journalists, "You need to be able to joke about things now and then" (McLaughlin, 2015).

Owing to his affinity for such parodies, it seems probable that Bachmann has consumed American Holocaust humor through German media sources. And this is the unlikely point where computer-mediated communications connect Jewish American writers with German xenophobes. *Family Guy* is very popular in Germany. It airs on the *ProSeiben* channel, whose website houses the show's complete catalog. *Family Guy* writers repeatedly employ Hitler and Holocaust jokes, with differing levels of intensity. Sometimes they merely reposition Hitler. *Death Is A Bitch* (2000) depicts him as a talk show host, angling to see his guest's posterior (Blitt, 2000). *Untitled Griffin Family History* (2006) has "Addy" as a henpecked brother (Viener, 2006). In *Road to Germany* (2008), Stewie Griffin dresses up as Hitler. He eventually encounters the leader, and the two engage in Chaplin-esque miming (Meighan, 2008).

Other times, however, *Family Guy* depictions are not so cheerful. This tends to be the case when writers stop lampooning Hitler and barb the Holocaust, which is a distinctive form of comic framing (Muller, 2012). *Fighting Irish* (2015) features gratuitous Holocaust denying as Peter Griffin, in a complete non sequitur, declares that the show's lesson was that "Oskar Schindler wasn't real and neither was anything in that movie" (Samuels, 2015). *Long John Peter* (2008) has a *Kristallnacht* joke. The show's Jewish character, Mort Goldman, shrieks the term after a pirate gang smashes through his storefront's window (Wild, 2008a). *Mc Stroke* (2008) features a Dachau quip, made by a talking cow, voiced by *Fantasy Island*'s Ricardo Montalban (Wild, 2008b). In *Family Goy* (2009), the show's writers spoof *Schindler's List*. Re-imagining Amon Goeth as Peter, he is drawn shirtless, cigarette dangling from his mouth, aiming a rifle out of his bedroom window. He shoots at Mort Goldman. This is also the episode in which Peter "becomes" Jewish. Notably, he stakes immediate ownership to Holocaust memory, sauntering down a synagogue's aisle cheering, "I'm Jewish, now. Oh, yeah, number one! Holocaust! (Hentemann, 2009).

Perhaps *Cool Hand Peter* (2011) is the best example of American humor, streamed into a European context, having the potential to deflate Jewish victimization. This show finds Peter and his friends traveling in a car. To help pass time, they play a game called "what would you rather be?" Peter asks, "Would you rather be a hobo with a five percent chance of getting inherited by a rich guy, or be Hitler two years before the end of World War II? Cuz you know you gonna have to shoot yourself, but you still got two more years as Hitler." A friend works through the predicament. "As Hitler," they ask, "can I change certain policies so that maybe I'm looked on more favorably at the end of the war?" At first appearance, this dialogue is palliative. It betrays sensitivity and awareness of Hitler's crimes. But it was all just a comic device. Peter blurts out, "You already screwed up, big time. 'Lotta dead Jews" (Johann and Ries, 2011).

Some people find this sort of back-and-forth amusing. Understandably, others do not agree. Outside of this debate, however, rests the larger question of how the humor draws new witnesses to the memory. According to Desilet and Appel (2011), comedy and tragedy, as dramatic productions, echo each other in the warnings they offer audiences (pp. 349-352). Their shared goal is to help people recognize, and combat, social threats. Of course, teasing tragedies may also have the exact opposite impact, as people might take from the joke the lesson that humanity is inexorably baneful, and as such is comedic. In this mindset, the Holocaust would be no more, nor any less, tragic than countless others instances of man's cruelty. This is the combustible foundation upon which the search for Holocaust humor rests. It is a risky business, but a flourishing one.

CONCLUSION

In January 2015, German talk show host Markus Lanz recalled an anecdote in which the Jewish American comedian Mel Brooks is reported to have quipped, "make fun of Hitler, otherwise he will haunt you guys [Germans] forever" (Lanz, 2015). Indeed, humor has the potential to deflate the Nazis' power, providing modern observers agency. Rather than passively receiving accounts of the crimes, infusing comedy makes people stakeholders in refashioned realities. Humor serves additional ends. As Morreall (2001) has argued, Holocaust humor might even play a role in physical and emotional healing.

Of course, humor also possesses a political valence, whereby it functions as a social aesthetic and identity marker (Holm, 2011, p. 2). It is in this form that iconoclastic representations can reshape long-standing attitudes about the genocide. Computer-mediated communications have a primary role in this process. Internet websites broadcast massive amounts of genocide information. The US Holocaust Memorial Museum is a pioneer in this regard. Other online collections include Israel's Yad Vashem archives, the Raoul Wallenberg Institute, Simon Wiesenthal Center, and David S. Wyman Institute for Holocaust Studies. Such repositories offer patrons open access to primary documents, oral histories, photographs, private videos, and other credible pieces of evidence. Such digitization permits anyone with interest the chance to learn about, and cite from authority, aspects of the legacy.

However, on the Internet, misinformation also thrives. It is possible for well meaning people to err when selecting their research links. In these cases, the results can be disastrous. In 2014, for example, Rialto, California teachers directed their students to research neo-Nazi websites before writing Holocaust essays. As a result of these online interactions, dozens of students concluded that the Holocaust was a hoax, devised to further economic and political ends (Yarbrough, 2014). In this instance, the joining of Holocaust studies with online technologies confounded knowledge. Whether such mishaps came about as a result of poorly trained teachers, a confusing curriculum, or an effort to subvert Holocaust memory remains unknown. All that is clear is online information will continue to play a pivotal, if unpredictable, role in this discourse. Digital delivery platforms have the power to broadcast factual genocide accounts globally, bolstering their significance. They also possess the ability, however, to disperse false narratives, reminding us that the elimination of accurate memory may well represent the last stage of genocide.

REFERENCES

Allen-Dutton, J., Fasolo, M., Goldstein, D., Green, S., McCallum, P., Root, T., & Senreich, M. (Writers), & Senreich. M. (Director). (2005). Toy Meets Girl [Television series episode]. In M. Senreich & S. Green (Producers), Robot Chicken. Los Angeles, CA: ShadowMachine Studios.

B'Ayin. Z. (2015, January 14). This Chronological History Of The Holocaust Was Done Entirely With Legos. *Heeb*. Retrieved from http://heebmagazine.com/chronological-history-holocaust-done-entirely-legos/53985

Bachmann, R. (2015, January 22). Sein Hitler-Selfie kennt jetzt die halbe Welt. *Bild*. Retrieved from http://www.bild.de/politik/inland/pegida/presseecho-ruecktritt-lutz-bachmann-39447360.bild.html

Ball, H. (1999). *Prosecuting War Crimes and Genocide: The Twentieth-Century Experience*. Lawrence, KS: University Press of Kansas.

Benjamin, A., & Patton, A., & Sheats, D. (2001). So Fresh, So Clean [Recorded by Outkast]. On *Stankonia* [CD]. New York: NY: Arista, RCA Records.

Berger, A. (1995). The Holocaust, Second-Generation Witness, and the Voluntary Covenant in American Judaism. *Religion and American Culture:Journal of Interpretation*, *5*, 23–47.

Blakeslee, S. (2000). *The Death Of American Anti-Semitism*. Westport, CT: Praeger.

Blitt, R. (Writer), & M.D. DiMartino (Director). (2000). Death Is A Bitch [Television series episode]. In S. MacFarlane (Producer), Family Guy. Los Angeles, CA: Fox Broadcasting Company.

Breitman, R., & Lichtman, A. (2013). *FDR and the Jews*. Cambridge, MA: The Belknap Press of Harvard University Press. doi:10.4159/harvard.9780674073654

Chaouat, B. (2013). Anti-Semitism Redux: On Literary and Theoretical Perversions. In A. Rosenfeld (Eds.), Resurgent Anti-Semitism: Global Perspectives (pp. 118-140). Bloomington, IN: Indiana University Press.

Cole, T. (1999). *Selling the Holocaust: From Auschwitz to Schindler: How History Is Bought, Packaged, and Sold*. New York: Routledge.

Connolly, K. (2015, January 6). German Leaders Condemn Xenophobia After Pegida Protests. *The Guardian*. Retrieved from http://www.theguardian.com/world/2015/jan/06/germany-pegida-protests-dresden-immigration

Connolly, K. (2015, February 5). Adolf Hitler Novel Tops German Bestseller List But Divides Critics. *The Guardian*. Retrieved from http://www.theguardian.com/world/2013/feb/05/adolf-hitler-novel-german-bestseller

Critchley, S. (2002). *On Humour*. New York: Routledge.

Denham, J. (2015, February 5). The Simpsons in Auschwitz: Harrowing aleXsandro Palombo Cartoons Mark 70th Anniversary of Death Camp Liberation. *The Independent*. Retrieved from http://www.independent.co.uk/arts-entertainment/art/news/the-simpsons-in-auschwitz-harrowing-alexsandro-palombo-cartoons-mark-70th-anniversary-of-death-camp-liberation-10025606.html

Desilet, G., & Appel, E. C. (2011). Choosing a Rhetoric of the Enemy: Kenneth Burke's Comic Frame, Warrantable Outrage, and the Problem of Scapegoating. *Rhetoric Society Quarterly*, *41*(4), 340–362. doi:10.1080/02773945.2011.596177

Dochartaigh, P. (2006). Americanizing the Holocaust: The Case of "Jakob the Liar. *Modern Language Review*, *101*(2), 456–471. doi:10.2307/20466794

Dumitru, D. (2008). The Use and Abuse of the Holocaust: Historiography and Politics in Moldova. *Holocaust and Genocide Studies*, *22*(1), 49–73. doi:10.1093/hgs/dcn002

Eder, J. S. (2012). *West German Reactions to American Holocaust Memorial Culture*. Paper presented at the Benelux American Studies Association Conference: American Responses to the Holocaust, Transatlantic Perspectives, Middleburg, The Netherlands.

Eshman, R. (2013, February 25). Seth MacFarlane: Not An Anti-Semite. *Jewish Journal*. Retrieved from http://www.jewishjournal.com/rob_eshman/article/seth_macfarlane_not_an_anti_semite/

Evans, S. (2013, May 2). Timur Vermes' Hitler Novel: Can the Führer be funny? *BBC News*. Retrieved from http://www.bbc.com/culture/story/20130417-is-it-okay-to-laugh-at-hitler

Fallace, T. D. (2006). The Origins of Holocaust Education in American Public Schools. *Holocaust and Genocide Studies*, *20*(1), 80–102. doi:10.1093/hgs/dcj004

Finkelstein, N. G. (2000). *The Holocaust Industry: Reflections On The Exploitation Of Jewish Suffering*. New York: Verso.

Funk, T. (2015, April 10). With Holocaust Survivors Aging, Keeping Memories Alive Falls To Their Children, Grandchildren. *Charlotte Observer*. Retrieved from http://www.charlotteobserver.com/living/religion/article18142778.html#storylink=cpy

Garber, Z., & Zuckerman, B. (1989). Why Do We Call the Holocaust "The Holocaust?": An Inquiry Into the Psychology of Labels. *Modern Judaism*, *9*(2), 197–211. doi:10.1093/mj/9.2.197

Gilbert, S. (2010). Jews and the Racial State: Legacies of the Holocaust in Apartheid South Africa, 1945-60. *Jewish Social Studies*, *16*(3), 32–64. doi:10.2979/jewisocistud.16.3.32

Goldberg, J. (2015, April). Is It Time For The Jews To Leave Europe? *The Atlantic*. Retrieved from http://www.theatlantic.com/features/archive/2015/03/is-it-time-for-the-jews-to-leave-europe/386279/

Heller, A. (2015, April 13). Children of Holocaust Survivors Inherit the Role of Witness. *The Times of Israel*. Retrieved from http://www.timesofisrael.com/children-of-holocaust-survivors-inherit-the-role-of-witness/

Hentemann, M. (Writer), & J. Purdum (Director). (2008). Family Goy [Television series episode]. In S. MacFarlane (Producer), Family Guy. Los Angeles, CA: Fox Broadcasting Company.

Herberg, W. (1960). *Protestant, Catholic, Jew*. Garden City, NY: Anchor Books.

Hilberg, R. (1992). *Perpetrators, Victims, Bystanders: The Jewish Catastrophe, 1933-1945*. New York: Aaron Asher.

Hirsch, M. (2012). *The Generation of Postmemory: Writing and Visual Culture after the Holocaust*. New York: Columbia University Press.

Holland, S. P. (2012). *The Erotic Life of Racism*. Durham, NC: Duke University Press. doi:10.1215/9780822395157

Holligan, A. (2014, May 8). Anne Frank Keeps Memory Alive For New Generation. *BBC News*. Retrieved from http://www.bbc.com/news/entertainment-arts-27308964

Holm, N. (2011). Reassessing the Right to Laughter: Humour, Dissent and the Liberal Imagination. *AntePodium: Online Journal of World Affairs*. Retrieved from http://www.victoria.ac.nz/atp/articles/pdf/Holm-2011.pdf

Horozitz, S. (1997). But Is It Good For The Jews? Spielberg's Schindler and the Aesthetics of Atrocity. In Y. Loshitzky (Eds.), Spielberg's Holocaust: Critical Perspectives On Schindler's List (pp. 119-140). Bloomington, IN: Indiana University Press.

Ivanova, E. (2004). Ukrainian High School Students' Understanding of the Holocaust. *Holocaust and Genocide Studies*, *18*(3), 402–420. doi:10.1093/hgs/dch086

Jaher, F. C. (1994). A Scapegoat. In *The New Wilderness: The Origins and Rise Of Anti-Semitism In America*. Cambridge, MA: Harvard University Press.

Johann, A., & Ries, S. (Writers), & B. Iles (Director). (2011). Cool Hand Peter [Television series episode]. In S. MacFarlane (Producer), Family Guy. Los Angeles, CA: Fox Broadcasting Company.

Julian, H. L. (2010). *South Park* Writers Warned Not to Say 'M' Word 'Mohammed'. *Israeli National News*. Retrieved from http://www.israelnationalnews.com/News/News.aspx/137187#.VV_s4qbyBnR

Jungius, M., & Seibel, W. (2008). The Citizen As Perpetrator: Kurt Blanke and Aryanization In France, 1940-1944. *Holocaust and Genocide Studies*, *22*(3), 441–474. doi:10.1093/hgs/dcn040

Kansteiner, W. (2003). Entertaining Catastrophe: The Reinvention of the Holocaust In the Television of the Federal Republic of Germany. *New German Critique, NGC*, *90*(90), 135–162. doi:10.2307/3211113

Kansteiner, W. (2006). Losing the War, Winning the Memory Battle: The Legacy of Nazism, World War II, and the Holocaust In the Federal Republic Of Germany. In R. N. Lebow & W. Kansteiner & C. Fugo (Eds.), The Politics of Memory In Postwar Europe (pp. 102-147). Durham, NC: Duke University Press.

Kantor Center for Study of Contemporary European Jewry. (2014). *Anti-Semitism Worldwide 2014*. Tel Aviv: Dina Porat.

Kaplan, L. (2002). It Will Get a Tremendous Laugh: On the Problematic Pleasures and Politics of Holocaust Humor. In H. Jenkins & T. McPherson & J. Shattuc (Eds.), Hop on Pop: The Politics and Pleasures of Popular Culture (pp. 343-357). Durham, NC: Duke University Press.

Katayama, H. (2009). A Cross-cultural Analysis of Humor In Stand-up Comedy In the United States and Japan. *JoLIE*, *2*, 125–142.

Khodasevich, V. (n.d.). *The Debasement of Females in South Park*. Retrieved from Lecture Notes Online Web site: http://www.brooklyn.cuny.edu/pub/departments/bcurj/pdf/khoidasevich.pdf

Landsberg, A. (1997). America, the Holocaust, and the Mass Culture of Memory: Toward a Radical Politics of Empathy. *New German Critique, NGC*, *71*(71), 63–86. doi:10.2307/488559

Lanz, M. (Producer). (2015, January 27). *Markus Lanz* [Television Broadcast]. Mainz, Germany: Zweites Deutsches Fernsehen.

Lipman, S. (1991). Laughter. In *Hell: The Use of Humor during the Holocaust*. Northvale, NJ: J. Aronson.

Lipstadt, D. (1993). *Denying the Holocaust: The Growing Assault On Truth and Memory*. New York: Free Press.

Loshitzky, L. (1997). Holocaust Others: Schindler's List versus Lanzmann's Shoah. In Y. Loshitzky (Eds.), Spielberg's Holocaust: Critical Perspectives On Schindler's List (pp. 104-119). Bloomington, IN: Indiana University Press.

Marc, D. (1997). *Comic Visions: Television Comedy and American Culture* (2nd ed.). Malden, MA: Blackwell Publishers.

Markoe, L. (2015, February 28). Anti-Semitism Is A Big Problem At American College Campuses, According To New Report. *Huffington Post*. Retrieved from http://www.huffingtonpost.com/2015/02/28/anti-semitism-college-cam_n_6775238.html

Mc Cann, B. (2015, January). *LOLZ* [Msg 1]. Message posted to https://www.youtube.com/watch?v=gjm8iMRkfFQ

McLaughlin, E. C. (2015, January 21). Anti-Islamization Leader Steps Down Amid Uproar Over Hitler Selfie. *CNN*. Retrieved from http://www.cnn.com/2015/01/21/europe/germany-pegida-hitler-pose-bild/index.html

McLennan, R. (2012). *American and European Representations of Anne Frank*. Paper presented at the Benelux American Studies Association Conference: American Responses to the Holocaust, Transatlantic Perspectives, Middleburg, The Netherlands.

Medoff, R. (2009). *Blowing the Whistle On Genocide: Josiah E. Dubois, Jr., and the Struggle For A U.S. Response To the Holocaust.* West Lafayette, IN: Purdue University Press.

Medoff, R. (2013). *FDR and The Holocaust: A Breach of Faith.* Washington, DC: David S. Wyman Institute for Holocaust Studies.

Meighan, P. (Writer), & G. Colton (Director). (2008). Road To Germany [Television series episode]. In S. MacFarlane (Producer), Family Guy. Los Angeles, CA: Fox Broadcasting Company.

Mintz, A. (2001). *Popular Culture and the Shaping of Holocaust Memory in America.* Seattle, WA: University of Washington Press.

Morreall, J. (2001). Humor in the Holocaust: Its Critical, Cohesive, and Coping Functions. In *Proceedings of the Conference on the Holocaust and the Churches, Hearing The Voices: Teaching the Holocaust to Future Generations.* Retrieved from http://www.holocaust-trc.org/humor-in-the-holocaust/

Muller, A. (2012). *Have a Holly Jolly Holocaust: Humor, Genocide, and the Moral Imagination.* Paper presented at the International Network Of Genocide Scholars: Third Global Conference on Genocide, San Francisco, CA.

Murtagh, K. J. (2013). Mary's Menses and Morality: Blasphemy in South Park. In R. Arp and K. Decker (Eds.), The Ultimate South Park and Philosophy: Respect my Philosophah! (pp. 108-119). West Sussex, UK: Wiley-Blackwell.

Norrick, N. R. (2010). Humor in Interaction. *Language and Linguistics Compass, 4*(4), 232–244. doi:10.1111/j.1749-818X.2010.00189.x

Novick, P. (2003). The American National Narrative of the Holocaust: There Isn't Any. *New German Critique, NGC, 90*(90), 27–35. doi:10.2307/3211105

Nuefeld, M. J., & Berenbaum, M. (2000). *The Bombing of Auschwitz: Should the Allies Have Attempted It?* New York: St. Martin's Press.

Oren, M. (2002). *Six Days Of War: June 1967 and the Making Of the Modern Middle East.* Oxford, UK: Oxford University Press.

Ozick, C. (1997, October 6). Who Owns Anne Frank? *The New Yorker Magazine*, 76-88.

Palombo. (2014, March 3). *What Kind Of Man Are You?* [Web log comment]. Retrieved from http://humorchic.blogspot.it/2014/03/humor-chic-art-social-campaign.html

Parker, T. (Writer), & Stough, E. (Director). (2001). Scott Tenorman Must Die [Television series episode]. In T. Parker & M. Stone (Producers), South Park. Ft. Worth, TX: Braniff Productions.

Parker, T., & Stone, M. (Writers), & Parker, T. (Director). (2008). Major Boobage [Television series episode]. In T. Parker & M. Stone (Producers), South Park. New York, NY: Comedy Partners.

Parker, T., Stone, M., & Stark, P. (Writers), & Parker, T., & Stone, M. (Directors). (1997). Pinkeye [Television series episode]. In T. Parker & M. Stone (Producers), South Park. Denver, CO: Celluloid Studios.

Pinnock, S. (2007). Atrocity and Ambiguity: Recent Developments in Christian Holocaust Responses. *Journal of the American Academy of Religion*, *75*(3), 499–523. doi:10.1093/jaarel/lfm038

Postman, N. (1985). *Amusing Ourselves to Death: Public Discourse in the Age of Show Business*. New York: Viking Press.

Reich, W. (2006). Unwelcome Narratives: Listening to Suppressed Themes in American Holocaust Testimonies. *Poetics Today*, *27*(2), 463–472. doi:10.1215/03335372-2005-014

Rosen, A. (2005). *Sounds of Defiance: The Holocaust, Multilingualism, and the Problem of English*. Lincoln, NE: University of Nebraska Press.

Rosenfeld, A. (2011). *The End of the Holocaust*. Bloomington, IN: Indiana University Press.

Sackett, R. (2002). Memory by Way of Anne Frank: Enlightenment and Denial Among West Germans, Circa 1960. *Holocaust and Genocide Studies*, *16*(2), 243–265. doi:10.1093/hgs/16.2.243

Saint-preux, S. (2013). *Can't believe how awful that was. C'est terrible! le journal d'Ann Frank* [Msg 20]. Message posted to https://www.youtube.com/watch?v=gjm8iMRkfFQ

Samuels, J. (Writer), & B. Iles (Director). (2015). Fighting Irish [Television series episode]. In S. MacFarlane (Producer), Family Guy. Los Angeles, CA: Fox Broadcasting Company.

Shandler, J. (1999). Aliens in the Wasteland: American Encounters With the Holocaust on 1960s Science Fiction Television. In H. Flanzbaum (Ed.), The Americanization of the Holocaust (pp. 33-45). Baltimore, MD: Johns Hopkins University Press.

Sheridan, C. (Writer), & Scott, S. O. (Director). (2000). If I'm Dyin', I'm Lyin' [Television series episode]. In S. MacFarlane (Producer), Family Guy. Los Angeles, CA: Fox Broadcasting Company.

Spiardi. (2013, August 18). *Heil, Heil, Rock-n-Roll. What's with Brit Rockers and the Third Reich?* [Web log article]. Retrieved from http://hipquotient.com/heil-heil-rock-n-roll-whats-with-brit-rockers-and-the-third-reich-part-two/

State Department. (1944). *Department of State Bulletin*. Washington, DC: Government Printing Office.

Street, J. (1986). *Rebel Rock: The Politics of Popular Music*. New York, NY: Blackwell.

Tyrnka, P. (2014). *Brian Jones: The Making Of the Rolling Stones*. New York, NY: Viking.

USC Shoah Foundation. The Institute For Visual History and Education, 2007-2015. (2015). Retrieved from http://sfi.usc.edu/

Viener, J. (Writer), & Z. Moncrief (Director). (2006). Untitled Griffin Family [Television series episode]. In S. MacFarlane (Producer), Family Guy. Los Angeles, CA: Fox Broadcasting Company.

Weinstock, M. (2013, April 17). Anne Frank, Belieber? *The New Yorker Magazine*. Retrieved from http://www.newyorker.com/books/page-turner/anne-frank-belieber

Wiesen, J. (2009). Service Above Self? Rotary Clubs, National Socialism, and Transnational Memory in the 1960s and 1970s. *Holocaust and Genocide Studies*, *23*(1), 1–25. doi:10.1093/hgs/dcp017

Wild, W. (Writer), & D. Polcino (Director). (2008). Long John Peter [Television series episode]. In S. MacFarlane (Producer), Family Guy. Los Angeles, CA: Fox Broadcasting Company.

Wild, W. (Writer), & B. Iles (Director). (2008). McStroke [Television series episode]. In S. MacFarlane (Producer), Family Guy. Los Angeles, CA: Fox Broadcasting Company.

Wisse, R. R. (2013). *No Joke: Making Jewish Humor*. Princeton, NJ: Princeton University Press. doi:10.1515/9781400846344

Wolf, J. (2004). Harnessing the Holocaust: The Politics of Memory. In *France*. Palo Alto, CA: Stanford University Press.

Wolfgram, M. A. (2006). The Holocaust Through the Prism Of East German Television: Collective Memory and Audience Perceptions. *Holocaust and Genocide Studies*, *20*(1), 57–79. doi:10.1093/hgs/dcj003

Wyman, D. (1968). *Paper Walls: America and the Refugee Crisis, 1938-1941*. Amherst, MA: University of Massachusetts Press.

Wyman, D. (1984). *The Abandonment of the Jews: America and the Holocaust, 1942-1945*. New York: Pantheon.

Yarbrough, B. (2014, July 31). Rialto Unified Panel Wrestles With Accountability For Holocaust Essay Assignment. *San Bernardino Sun*. Retrieved from http://www.sbsun.com/social-affairs/20140731/rialto-unified-panel-wrestles-with-accountability-for-holocaust-essay-assignment

Young, J. E. (1999). America's Holocaust: Memory and the Politics of Identity. In H. Flanzbaum (Ed.), The Americanization of the Holocaust (pp. 68-83). Baltimore, MD: Johns Hopkins University Press.

Young, W. (2013). Flatulence and Philosophy: A Lot of Hot Air, or the Corruption of Youth. In R. Arp & K. Decker (Eds.), The Ultimate South Park and Philosophy: Respect my Philosophah! (pp. 7-19). West Sussex, UK: Wiley-Blackwell. doi:10.1002/9781118607442.ch1

Zelizer, B. (1998). *Remembering to Forget: Holocaust Memory Through the Camera's Eye*. Chicago: University of Chicago Press.

Zéro, E. T. (2013). *Firts et last je crois?* [Msg 19]. Message posted to https://www.youtube.com/watch?v=gjm8iMRkfFQ

Chapter 2
Negotiation of Wit in *Facebook* Humour

Akin Odebunmi
University of Ibadan, Nigeria

Simeon Ajiboye
Federal University of Technology, Nigeria

ABSTRACT

This chapter unpacks the humorous contents of selected Facebook-based Akpos jokes which have received inadequate attention in the scholarship with respect to wit negotiation which mostly indexes the jokes. Six out of fifteen sampled jokes have been analysed with the theoretic aid of Istvan Kecskes' Socio-Cognitive Approach (SCA), aspects of the common ground theory, aspects of conversation analysis and elements of selected humour theories. The analysis shows three forms of wit negotiation: negotiation of mis-oriented twists, negotiation of dis-preference and negotiation of un-designed twists. In the respective cases, the talk initiating speakers have their logic flawed by recipient speakers, usually Akpos, and consequently get outsmarted; earlier sequentially dispreferred social choices are re-negotiated as preferred options in the light of new discursive realities; and the interactive designs or expectations of talk initiating participants receive undersigned or unexpected sequential responses in symmetrical or asymmetrical relationships. The paper argues that the joke characters' situationally adaptive orientation to apriori or emergent common ground and intention demonstrates the Akpos jokes' recontextualisation of particular Nigerian social and cultural experiences through the characters' socio-cognitive designs in the mediated encounters. It concludes that while these designs offer the relaxant effects jokes are naturally meant to yield, their negotiation mechanisms provide resources for the application of Kecskes' SCA in Facebook humour and produce sarcasm with a wing of moral lessons.

INTRODUCTION

The *Facebook* is a veritable Internet host of visual and verbal texts designed to boost rapport among its users. Part of the resources for establishing the rapport is the posting and sharing of humorous discourses which may be short, witty statements or extended, conversation-styled exchanges. Among other foci, the humours exploit pictures and words to generate laughter and consequently keep *Facebook* friends

DOI: 10.4018/978-1-5225-0338-5.ch002

Copyright © 2016, IGI Global. Copying or distributing in print or electronic forms without written permission of IGI Global is prohibited.

bonded. Their value as a social media network resource for emotional therapy and contact maintenance is, therefore, inestimable.

A particular joke type that is popularly shared among most *Facebook* users in Nigeria, and that constitutes the data source for the present study, is the Akpos stories. Created around the funny but highly intelligent character named Akpos, the jokes, often in dialogic form, centre on the characters' social, administrative, cultural, political and emotional experiences. They typically present encounters where Akpos enters into wit battle with others, often with the skills to outwit the other parties. This scenario means that the wits of the parties get negotiated in the mediated context of the jokes, and the punch line often develops at the point where the superior wit emerges. Thus, the characters orient to apriori and emergent common ground and intentions (Kecskes, 2014), which put into operation their pre-encounter and in-encounter goals. Often, what are negotiated in the jokes are emergent cues as apriori common ground and intentions typically work to provide communicative facility between the parties but not to offer negotiable salience which often occurs as a twist undersigned by at least one of the parties.

Apparently, wit negotiation, defined in this study as the strategic interchange of clever propositions between characters in the mediated context of Akpos jokes, constitutes an important factor in processing the interpretation of the *Facebook*-based Akpos humour and by extension several other humours presented in conversation formats in Computer-mediated Communication (CMC). Yet, previous studies on CMC have explored other concerns than the negotiation of wit in the humour, and have utilised other instruments than the Kesckeskian (2014) socio-cognitive approach (SCA) which accounts for apriori and emergent common ground and intention, relevant as they are to the discourses.

A number of extant studies have examined the functions or roles of humour in online communication (Marone (2015); Hubler and Bell (2003); Baym (1995); Schnurr and Rowe (2008); Norrick and Kelvin (2008); Taylor (2009); and Stoll (2015)). Others have given attention to humour markers in online communication (Adams (2012) and Holcombs (1997)). Studies in the former group have explored such context-shaped functions of humour in online communication as veiling capability, mitigating negativity and boosting participation to ensure community cohesion. Research in the latter group has identified as markers of humour punctuation marks, formatting, emoticons, laughter, capitalisation and spacing, adapted effectively to CMC interaction to show users' orientations to rapport building, identity creation, power relation, face alignment or disalignment and offensiveness. Of all these studies, only Stoll (2015) focuses on the roles of humour in *Facebook* posts. While it investigates humour in *Facebook* within the frame of credibility and social attraction, its engagement of the issues neither utilises the socio-cognitive approach nor considers the participants' negotiation of wit in the humour.

The fact is that while previous studies have reported on discourse and pragmatic features of Internet-based humour, and have demonstrated how participants use them within their affordances to conduct personal and group communicated socio-emotional activities, their non-consideration of the wit elements in the jokes, a quality which accounts for most punchline-characterised jokes, points to a neglect of a major pragmatic feature of *Facebook* (and to a large extent most online) jokes, leaving several chunks of the jokey interactions unexplained. In addition, the non-use of SCA limits the depth of earlier research to account for the pragmatic dynamism of the interactions, which should reveal more clearly the design of the joke constructor and the goals of the joke characters.

In the light of the foregoing argument, the present study identifies the witty contents of selected *Facebook*-based Akpos jokes and discusses the characters' orientation to apriori and emergent strategies in negotiating wits. These enable a cognitive entry into the discursive space of the texts and provide a context-shaped account of the interactive structure of the encounters. For data, six Akpos humorous conversations with eminent wit negotiation contents, chosen to instantiate the negotiation categories raised from the overall selected jokes, were selected from a total of fifteen conversations purposively sampled from the current authors' *Facebook* accounts. The conversations were examined for argumentative logic which demonstrates a display of witty and outwitting acts. They were further subjected, in the main, to the principles of Kecskes' (2014) socio-cognitive approach, showing their revelation of apriori and emergent common ground and intentions. Complementary insights were deployed from aspects of the general common ground theory and conversation analysis. The Nigerian Pidgin in the analysed samples is italicized, the Americanisms are in bold font and the Standard English is rendered recte.

THEORETICAL BACKGROUND

Common ground and intention are central to accessing strategic communication. In other words, what constitutes interactants' shared knowledge prior to their encounters and their goals predating the interaction take a significant place in the design and interpretations of participants' utterances during encounters. However, while this thesis presents a sound theoretic basis for unpacking strategic cues in interaction, it throws up a difficulty to accommodate new interactive cues. Hence, Kecskes (2014) presents SCA which takes as a part of its engagements, the apriori and emergent nature of common ground (see also Allan 2013) and intention.

Kecskes (2014) identifies as components of common ground, common knowledge, assumed familiarity and presumed background information. Like earlier researchers such as Clark et al. (1983), Clark, (1996, 2000) and Stalnaker (2002), Kecskes discusses two categories of common ground: prior context or a prior/ core common ground and emergent common ground, considered significant in interactive encounters (Kesckes 204:153; see also Odebunmi 2006 and Odebunmi and Alo 2010). These two categories of common ground produce two approaches in the scholarship, namely, the pragmatic view and the cognitive view. The pragmatic view developed in Stalnaker (1978); Clark and Brenna (1991); Clark (1996); and Odebunmi, (2006) presents common ground as a "category of specialized mental representations that exists in the mind apriori to the actual communication process' (Kesckes, 2014:155). It emphasises the importance of cooperation in the process of communication, and the interactants' mutual processing of expressed intentions (cf. Clark 1996). The cognitive view, unlike the pragmatic view, conceives of common ground as "a dynamic, emergence-through-use" interactive mechanism which relies on the emergent experiences of interlocutors in the participation space to negotiate intentions (Kecskes, 2014:155). It thus aligns with the joint co-constructional view of interaction (cf Arundale, 1999, 2008)..

The socio-cognitive approach combines the pragmatic and cognitive perspectives of common ground as a tool to gain entry into interactants' communicative goals. This theoretic standpoint provides a convenient pedestal for the examination of interlocutors' prior shared knowledge and their accommodated knowledge during interaction, and thus enables the participants to orient to both past and current knowledge to process intentions. While these two dimensions of common ground do not necessarily occur together on all interactive occasions, SCA's conceptualisation of both offers a single, well integrated theoretic package that facilitates access into intention negotiations utilising interactive resources indexing apriori and emergent perspectives as demonstrated by the *Facebook* humour unpacked in the current chapter. The choice of SCA is thus contingent upon its ability to show the dynamism of the context of *Facebook* humour in terms of the characters' orientation to wits and outwitting which of necessity requires the use of both shared and unshared interactive cues

In addition to the specific resources of SCA, this paper utilises such aspects of the general common ground theory as salience (the interactively grounded common belief that appeals to discourse participants), including perceptual salience (gestural or prosodic common ground resource), scripts (patterns of information constituting participants' shared knowledge), and private goals (a personal agenda not declared to other participants). The resources of conversation analysis (CA) deployed include sequences (an utterance constituting a speaker's turn in a conversation), turn (a time when a participant in a conversation speaks), turn construction unit (TCU) (a speaker's sequential contribution) and footing ("switches in the mode and frame of a conversation" (Goffman, 1981: 124))

To situate the jokes in the scholastic traditions of humour, aspects of three humour theories have been considered: conventional, violation, and sociology theories. Conventional theories are divided into three basic theories, namely, superiority, relief and incongruity theories. Derived from the works of Plato, Aristotle and Hobbes, the superiority theory deals with the assumption that people laugh about the misfortune of others, thus emphasising the superiority of some individuals over others. In his three-part thesis, Gruner (1997) identifies the following components:

- All humorous situations demonstrate winners and losers.
- There is incongruity in all humours.
- Surprise is integral to humour.
- The concept of superiority constitutes a first part of a humour thesis.

The relief theory, largely attributed to Sigmund Freud (Mulder & Nijholt, 2000) explains the place of laughter in the discharge of tension and energy in the psychic region. Freud observes that the release of the energy inspires laughter (Mulder & Nijholt, 2000). The theory of incongruity associated with Kant (1911) captures a situation where a concept initially connected to two objects becomes applicable to only one of them in the progression of a joke. And this attracts laughter. The violation theory, credited to Thomas Veatch, offers three conditions for the perception and occurrence humour: the violation (V) of a perceiver's commitment with respect to the regular forms of things; the normalcy (N) a perceiver predominantly associates with particular situations; V and N are required to be present in a joke concurrently (simultaneity) for the humour of the joke to be perceived (Mulder & Nijholt, 2000). Sociology theories of humour give attention to the sociocultural context of a joke or any humorous episode. By Rutters' (1997) account, the theory trifurcates into maintenance theories, negotiation theories, and frame theories. Maintenance theories focus on jokes as a tool for maintaining social roles and structures. Negotiation theories handle humour in dyadic or multiparty interactions. Frame theories present jokes as a venture into the relaxation part of life, a shift from the solemn everyday human experience. In each of the sociological theories, what constitutes humour are the contexts evoked between the parties in interaction.

The theories have the mechanisms to systematically explain, in conjunction with the resources of SCA and conversation analysis, the incongruity, surprise, socio-culturally-driven interpretations and relaxant effects that characterise Akpos jokes. In the analysis that follows, while the major focus is placed on negotiation types and strategies through the application of SCA and CA features, elements of humour theories work to complement this application by their resourcefulness in providing genre-based information on the episodes of the jokes analysed.

ANALYSIS AND FINDINGS

The selected Akpos jokes demonstrate three categories of wit negotiation, namely, negotiations of mis-oriented twists, dis-preference and undesigned twists. In each case, the joke participants rely on apriori and emergent discursive resources to access the intentions of co-participants (co-characters) and then react appropriately or otherwise to the salience generated. Mostly, the salience to which reactions are directed bears a participant's wit and sometimes their design to outwit the co-participant. The appropriate reaction is sometimes the co-participant's outwitting of the talk-initiating or recipient speaker by an orientation to a largely emergent common ground-based logic, and the inappropriate reaction is the talk-initiating or recipient speaker's failure to process the co-participant's intention correctly, leading to their being outwitted. In large measure, the point where the outwitting or out-smarting occurs demonstrates the punch line of the jokes.

Below, each of the wit negotiation categories is handled. Relevant samples are selected to exemplify the negotiation types and the strategies by which they have been achieved.

Negotiation of Mis-Oriented Twists

The negotiation of mis-oriented twists captures a situation where the logic of a talk-initiating interactant gets flawed by recipient speakers, and the latter consequently outwits the former. In most cases, interactants' encyclopedic knowledge constitutes apriori common ground at the initial stage, and interactive power gets assumed by the talk-initiating speaker on most of the occasions which are asymmetrical in nature, causing them not to notice the flaw of logic resident in their presentation. Twists often occur where recipient speakers take the advantage of the fallible logic of the talk-initiating speaker to side-step asymmetrical power to outsmart the talk-initiating speaker and attack their face (Brown & Levinson, 1987) in the punch line of the joke. The joke below exemplifies these features.

Excerpt 1

In this joke, a teacher and two students, namely Emeka and Akpos, discuss the logic of existence of some things, initiated by the teacher. While Emeka responds to the teacher's questions establishing the logic, Akpos responds to the portion requiring another example, an opportunity used by Akpos to fault the teacher's logic, leading to the punch line of the joke.

1. TEACHER: Anything you cannot see, touch and feel does not exist. Example, Can u
2. see God?
3. EMEKA: NO
4. TEACHER: Can you touch God?
5. EMEKA: NO
6. TEACHER: Can you feel God?
7. EMEKA: NO
8. TEACHER: This means. There is no God. Can anybody give me any other example?
9. AKPOS: Yes Ma,
10. TEACHER: Go ahead AKPOS
11. (AKPOS faces the teacher)

12. AKPOS: Can you see your brain?
13. TEACHER: NO,
14. AKPOS: Can you touch your brain?
15. TEACHER: NO,
16. AKPOS: Can you feel your brain?
17. TEACHER: NO
18. AKPOS: Therefore, YOU HAVE NO BRAIN.

The lesson begins with the teacher introducing three premises of the logic of existence: seeing, touching and feeling. She moves to the second level of his premise structuring, building on the first, by asking Emeka to confirm each of the premises. Emeka affiliates with her regarding the logics that God cannot be seen, touched or felt. Up to this point, the teacher's arguments align with the parties' apriori knowledge of God as an abstract entity. Her conclusion, though in agreement with her initial premise, goes against the concept of God known to the other party, thus yielding an emergent common ground, which the party has to accommodate within the frame of the teacher's apriori intention of teaching the subject matter of logic and existence.

The asymmetrical nature of the encounter apparently prevents the other party from expressing a counter position. However, the teacher's invitation of additional contributions offers Akpos the opportunity to negotiate the teacher's wit, itself a discursive cue of reaction against the teacher's view. This reaction is indexed by Akpos directing his question at the teacher, not Emeka, as the teacher does. Like the teacher, he builds his initial logic on their apriori knowledge of abstractions, but tactically side tracks the teacher's original premise that "anything you cannot see, touch and feel does not exist", as a ploy to gain entry into the participation space from a suspicious and overtly impolite angle. His choice of "your" tallies with the teacher's as a generic direct address pronominal reference, but its implications are power-neutralising. Thus, it both serves as a marker of apriori common ground of the impossibility of humans to see, touch and feel their brains and a power-levelling indicator to discursively prepare the teacher for the face threat in line 18. The affiliative 'no response' from the teacher responds to the logic of Akpos, the teacher apparently unsuspecting the emergent intention of Akpos, perhaps clinging on to her asymmetrical power as teacher. Akpos' logical conclusion, "Therefore you have no brain" offers the following interactive achievements:

a. It presents the punch line of the joke as it subjects the reader to humorous laxative action, coming within the ambits of relief theory of humour.
b. It suddenly introduces Akpos' emergent intention to demonstrate the fault of the teacher's logic in the earlier sequences.
c. Its display of unshared knowledge and its unexpectedness, given the power differential between Akpos and the teacher, facilitate its effectiveness as a resource for outwitting the teacher, demonstrating a principle of superiority theory.
d. Implicatively, it provides a hit-back response to the teacher's logic-based position on the inexistence of God, which is opposed to the belief of the larger Nigerian setting in which the joke is situated. Thus, "you have no brain" derives from Akpos'built up premises, and also insults the teacher's seeming unintelligent dismissal of God's inexistence, derived from her original absolute first premise.

The extract below further explains the issue of negotiation of mis-oriented twists.

Excerpt 2

In this joke, Akpos, who is taking bread and jam, has an encounter with an American who is chuckling a chewing gum. His excellent application of logic outwits the American who had earlier communicated to Akpos a disparaging discursive content over the part of bread eaten by African and Americans.

1. American: You African folks eat the whole bread??
2. Akpos (*in a bad mood*): Of course.
3. American: We don't. In the States, we only eat what's inside. The crusts we collect
4. in a container, recycle it, transform them into croissants and export them to Africa.
5. (The American has a smirk on his face).
6. (Akpos listens in silence).
7. (The American persists): *D'ya* eat jelly with the bread??
8. Akpos: Of Course.
9. American: We don't. In the States we eat fresh fruit for breakfast, then we put all
10. the peels, seeds, and leftovers in containers, recycle them, transform them into
11. jam and export them to Africa.
12. Akpos *(pissed of)* then asks: "Do you have sex in America ?"
13. American: "Why of course we do", the American says with a big smirk.
14. Akpos: And what do you do with the condoms once you've used them ?"
15. American: We throw them away, of course.
16. Akpos: We don't. In Africa, we put them in a container, recycle them, melt
17. them down into chewing gum and export them to America!!

Each question of the American (lines 1 and 7) is based on the current experience of Akpos: eating bread with jam. This event constitutes shared knowledge indicated by Akpos' affiliative response: "of course". However, each of the comments by the American displays emergent common ground and intention as it is not shared between the parties. The first (lines 3-4) relates to the claim of the American that the crusts of bread, not eaten by Americans, are processed into croissants and exported into Africa; whereas Africans eat the whole bread, not just its inner part eaten by Americans. The emergent intention of the American to disparage Africans for wastefulness, which becomes salient through the smirk on the face of the American, is accommodated by Akpos' silence, itself a possible sequential strategy by Akpos to conceal his anger. The next turn of the American (line 7) is another inquirer derived both from the current eating experience of Akpos and the snacks eating manners of the entire African race. The affiliative "of course" by Akpos again signals apriori common ground, which indicates the dyad's shared knowledge of Africans' "eat[ing] jelly with bread". The comment that follows in the next turn of the American, which mocks Africans as consumers of Americans' waste in an emergent intention scenario, invites the initiation of a discursive twist from the angered Akpos. His sequence: "Do you have sex in America", which receives an affiliative turn from the American, produces apriori common ground which assumes the interactants' shared orientation to the proposition in Akpos inquirer, and sets up the premise for Akpos' interactive reprisal. He negotiates his emergent intention, beginning from line 14, first by modifying the wit-building strategy deployed by the American in earlier sequences. He achieves this by inserting another inquirer which assumes protective sex among Americans and ventures to know the Americans' disposition to sex instrument wastes i.e. used condoms. Unsuspecting Akpos's emergent intention, the American eagerly responds to the inquirer, treating Akpos' sequence as a rudimentary, predictable logic: "We throw them away of course. At this point (lines 16-17), in a surprise-laden move, consistent with the humour theory of superiority, Akpos hits the American's face with disparagement bordering on his consumption of chewing gum made of condoms used by Africans. This sequence by Akpos obviously:

a. Produces the punch line as it presents the actual joke-indicative, incongruous object of the interaction.
b. Negotiates the emergent intention by drawing on the same rhetorical structures deployed by the American to outwit and outsmart him.
c. Utilises the waste concept initiated by the American more degradingly, in a twisty turn, by presenting him as a consumer of Africans' sex instruments processed into chewing gums.

Negotiation of Dis-Preference

Social choices sometimes sequentially dispreferred by participants at the early stage of a conversation are sometimes renegotiated in the later part of it in the light of emergent realities. This discursive situation is shown in Excerpt 3 below:

Excerpt 3

In this excerpt, a boy attempts to woo a girl who is materialistically minded. She inquires about the boy's assets, and given his negative responses, she decides to turn down his marriage proposal only for her to realise that the boy is very wealthy. Her efforts to align with the new situation however prove impossible.

1. Boy: I like u [you] dear, pls marry me.
2. Girl: Hmm, do you have a house?
3. Boy: No
4. Girl: Do you have a B.M.W car?
5. Boy: No
6. Girl: How much is your salary?
7. Boy: No salary.... but butt !
8. Girl: Shut up there *joor[please]*, what is but... just imagine, you have nothing... how can I
9. marry you?? *Abeg shift one side [*Please, get off], just leave me alone please.
10. Boy: OMG (Oh my God, but i have one villa, 3 land properties, 3 Feraris, 2 Lambogini..
11. so what will i still need a B.M.W car for?? And how can I get salary
12. while am the boss??
13. Girl: woow, I really wanna get married ooh??
14. Boy: Hell no, park well joor... too late I wish some people [Hell no, leave me alone… it is too late]
15. will learn something from this cus NO BE SMALL THING! [because it is a serious matter]

The encounter begins with the expression of love and marriage proposal by the boy. This is received with a series of questions from the girl. While the inquirers constitute a potential shock to a non-Nigerian, they are demonstrated to be apriori common ground elements by the boy whose "no" responses cut through all the sequences by the girl. In point of fact, the interrogatives bordering on the boy having a house and a BMW car, and the amount he receives as salary come from the background of a typical young material-minded Nigerian lady who believes in financial comfort as a condition for getting engaged with a man. The boy's response at line 7: "No salary… but butt" demonstrates an attempt to negotiate the girl's condition from an emergent angle. Its approbation nature (Levinson, 1983) shows some level of sincere interest in spite of the dyad's played script of the recipient speaker's materialistic perspective. However, the lady's thorough commitment to overtly expressed materialism or no relationship blocks the success of the initiated negotiation.

The lady's insult directed at the boy between lines 8 – 9, which aptly summarises her earlier propositions, and which concludes the premise that material wealth is her only condition for marriage, generates a jointly co-constructed salience of failed proposal and impossibility. The boy orients to this salience by:

a. First introducing his superior wealth status (one villa, three landed properties, three Feraris, two Lamborghinis and being a rich self-employed personality) which places him far above the standard of the lady, a situation that displays the boy's emergent intention to both downgrade the girl and show off his substantial affluence in a surprise-suffused move.
b. His emergent intention in 'a' above is calculated at teasing out a reconsideration of the lady's dispreference given the apriori knowledge of the script of materialism being played by her.

The boy's private goal design (see Clark, 1996) gets achieved as the girl immediately shifts her position to accepting the boy's proposal. Her prosodic design ("woow") at line 13, indicating her surprise and impressiveness, contrasts with that of the boy (OMG [Oh! My God]), which expresses his disappointment and ties in with the salience of impossibility earlier generated by the girl. The girl's attempt at renegotiating her earlier dispreference at line 13 deploys the following strategies:

a. It assumes an apriori script of many Nigerian men's gullibility, often leading to the rescinding of their positions once a lady does, especially considering, in this instance, the boy's seeming sincere commitment at line 7 where he attempts to negotiate the girl's choice and decision.
b. Its use of "really", a marker of attitudinal stance (cf Keisannen. & Karkkanen, 2014), shows her sudden commitment and illustrates her emergent accommodation of the new realities
c. Its choice of "wanna" a colloquial American English word works to change the footing of the interaction to an encounter between people who are already in intimate relationship to influence the boy's final decision.

Between lines 14 – 15, the boy, utilising a mix of his apriori knowledge of Nigerian women's materialistic tendency and his emergent common ground knowledge of the girl's condition-influenced sudden change of stand, upholds the dispreference earlier embraced by the girl. His strategies to achieve this include:

a. An emphatic negative decision which is consistent with the mode adopted by the girl.
b. A footing change with the instrument of Nigerian English (Park well joor… too late), parodying the girl's in earlier sequences as a device to disgrace her as a shameless gold digger.
c. An insertion of a morality-infused sequence, itself a blend of the voice of the boy and an overlaid voice of the original creator of the humour, in a combination of Standard English and Nigerian Pidgin, to stigmatise the girl as a point of reference for wrongful material-based partner choices.

The extract below further demonstrates the negotiation of dispreference in the jokes.

Excerpt 4

In this encounter, when Akpos' daughter who has just returned from Vietnam informs her father about her job as a prostitute, she is ordered out of the house. But Akpos rescinds this order the moment her daughter mentions the huge material benefits that accrue to him from the prostitution.

1. AKPOS the Father (angry): Where the hell have you been all these years???
2. Girl: I was working as a Prostitute in the Vietnam.
3. AKPOS the Father: What!!?..... Get out of my house, You Whore;
4. I don't want to see your face Again do you understand!!!!! !????
5. Girl(crying): Before I go Dad, I came to give you $10million cheque,
6. and here is $2 million for my brother. I have bought a big house in
7. UK for you with everything in it including a Ferarri and a Bugati, bye Dad
8. AKPOS (smiling): What kind of work did you say you
9. were doing in Vietnam??
10. Girl (crying out loud): A Prostitute Dad!!!
11. Akpos: Come and give Daddy a hug, I thought you
12. said you were a "prosecutor".

Akpos' inquirer in line 1 about his daughter's absence from home goes with exasperation and firmness. The situation gets worse between lines 3 – 4 after the daughter tells him she has been involved in prostitution as a profession (line 2). Akpos' reaction, seated in the apriori common ground of the dyads, negotiates African cultural responsibility which demands that the father dissociate from a child's misdeeds especially, in this context, prostitution, a highly stigmatised tendency in Nigeria. This shared cultural question is interactively salient and informs the daughter's response in line 5a. Her "before I go [leave])" implicatively orients to the cultural question and admits her wrongness. However, the second bit of the turn contributing unit introduces emergent common ground and intention. The daughter declares the largesse she has brought for Akpos and her brother together with the property, including a house in the UK and two ultramodern cars (Ferrari and Bugari) she has acquired for Akpos. By this contribution, the daughter designs to try out the general Nigerian script of materialism against the cultural position of his father to retain her bio-social space in the home. The effort becomes emergent in that it is not automatic within the Nigerian cultural context for the positive disposition such as the one obtained based on the daughter's design to be achieved as some conservative men, in spite of the substantiality of the material gains would not review their stand. Thus, Akpos' changed position, humorously renegotiated between lines 8-12, achieving the punch line at lines 11-12, in a series of surprise-demonstrated insertions, is not consistent with most cultural expectations in Nigeria.

After the mention of the assets at line lines 5-7, Akpos' sequence at lines 8 – 9 feigns a wrong uptake of the daughter's turn contributing unit at line 2 in an emergent strategic move to renegotiate his earlier declared dispreference. His daughter, not sure of the success of her sequential design, displays purgation ("crying out loud") as a culturally-ingrained gender-based act to demonstrate regret, and orients to accentual salience ("A prostitute Dad!!!) as a strategic resource to influence Akpos' favourable decision, Akpos' inquirer at lines 8 -9 not being committal about his final disposition. Thus, Akpos' twisty next turn (line 11a) becomes salient as it changes the footing of the preceding sequences completely. It smartly plays on the purgative action of the daughter and his own materialistic inclination to negotiate preference implicatively. This preference, inclusive reversing his earlier quit order and approving the daughter's prostitution job, is implicatively achieved in lines 11b and 12 where he deploys mishearing as a strategy to negotiate acceptability.

Negotiation of Un-Designed Twists

There is an undersigned twist when the fraudulent design of a discourse initiator gets suspected or when either of the parties receives unexpected revelations. These interactive events are negotiated by the participants within the apriori and emergent contexts. The two excerpts below, taken in turn, exemplify the negotiation forms.

Excerpt 5

This excerpt shows an encounter between a fraudster and Akpos, who, sensing that his caller is a fraudster, plays along with him until it becomes clear to the former that he has lost the bid to defraud Akpos.

1. Mr 419: Hello, how are you?
2. Akpos: Fine! Pls, who am i speaking with?
3. Mr 419: Ha, don't u remember me, who do u know in London dat culd be calling?
4. Akpos: (Sensing a scam & throwing in a trap) Ejiro! Is dat u?
5. Mr 419: Of course, of course, this is Ejiro, i am Ejiro,
6. how come u didn't recognise my voice?
7. Akpos: Ejiro! Chei, you are a bad boy o. Your Father died, you didn't even show
8. up or send a letter. O boy, ur children go pay you back. You no hear of him death, (This boy, your children will pay you in return. You didn't hear of his death?)
9. he was so bitter and full of curses for u. (he was so bitter that he cursed you to the fullness)
10. Mr 419: (Obviously subdued)I didn't hear o!. I would have come.
11. Akpos: Did u hear your Mother had leprosy?. U didn't hear about dat too abi?.
12. Mr 419: (Now uncomfortable) No, i didn't hear.
13. Akpos: Na wa o! Your wife foolish too? I neva hear from her since d two of una (That's unfortunate! Is your wife foolish too? I have not heard from her since both of youy got

14. marry without our blessings!. If Husband no wise, wife no go wise?. (married without our blessings. If the husband is not wise, is the wife too foolish?)
15. Mr 419: She is fine! I'm sure she'll get across to u.
16. I have an issue to discuss with u.
17. Akpos: Enhen! Ejiro, you offend me. I send u money make you buy me Hummer (I sent you money to buy Hummer)
18. Jeep, u disappear. When am i having my money back?. U want make i curse you (Jeep for me but you absconded (Do you want me to curse you?)
19. like ur Father. I go pronounce wicked curses on you o. As your father did. I will curse you greatly)
20. Mr 419: Dis issue dat i want to say is very important.
21. Akpos: Shut up!. When u go send money come home?.We sent u to school, (when will you send money home.)
22. clothed you & sent u abroad. U don become 419?. Wey won steal from me, ur (You have turned a fraudster who wants to defraud me your
23. own friend?. O boy, ur Father was right to curse you, you can't escape it if u (own friend? This boy)
24. continue like this.
25. Mr 419: Don't worry, i will repay you ur (your) money. For now, i have an issue to
26. discuss with u (you).
27. Akpos: Hahahahaha, look here Mr 419, i no know any Ejiro or anybody 4 (I don't know any Ejiro or anybody in)
28. London, i jus wan teach u lesson.
29. (London, I'd just wanted to teach you a lesson)
30. Mr 419: Whaat! Mad man, and you have been insulting and wasting my credit
31. since morning. God go judge u (God will judge you)

The call from the fraudster, Mr [1]419, opens the encounter, with Akpos demanding to know the identity of the caller. Mr 419's response in line 3 where he introduces an unwarranted rapport with Akpos provides a cue of fraudulence script. The apriori common ground that signals Akpos' suspicion is this script of fraud displayed in the response of Mr 419:

a. He does not declare his identity to Akpos, rather he evokes familiarity with him by challenging Akpos' recollection competence with respect to who he is (line 3a)
b. He evades Akpos' question again in line 3b by further evoking apriori common ground of his location through a cleverly constructed familiarity-toned inquirer
c. Additionally, in the same part of the line in 'b' above, he both mentions London as his location and implicates his person as Akpos' only contact in London with whom Akpos has a sufficient familiar relationship to warrant a call.

'C' above picks out the quintessential 419 scam script as most of the fraudsters of this orientation prefers a London, or United States location, often calling through a hidden caller identity, which is believed to constitute an attraction to Nigerians, especially those who are West-worshipful. This spatial association concept and Mr 419's construction of self as Akpos' sole link in the West in particular generate the apriori salience of fraud which Akpos orients to in his next contribution.

Akpos' mention of Ejiro (line 4), an arbitrary pragmatic choice which is a response to Mr 419's personal goal design in line 3, is consistent with the 419 interactive response cue. For Akpos, who is initiating a strategic script, this demonstrates a local context independent belief[2]. The same independent belief applies to Mr 419 who, following his professional fraud script, connects the mention of Ejiro with the pragmatic success of his interactive design. However, while Akpos is initiating an emergent intention, Mr 419 is sticking with an apriori intention, which his fraud design affords.

Akpos' "Ejiro, is dat u?" in line 4 instigates Mr 419's disclosure of his pretended close relationship with Akpos (lines 5–6). Right from this point, Akpos inserts series of offensive turns with the emergent intention to pique and outwit Mr 419. To do these, he constructs Ejiro, the 419, in the following frames, which demonstrate Akpos' perception of him as a bastard, a social misfit and of course, a criminal:

a. An irresponsible, culturally poorly brought up child whose untoward attitude to the father and his death has attracted the father's curses to him (lines 7 – 9). Playing along, Mr 419, in spite of his unease, accommodates the pique and admits his irresponsibility (line 10).
b. A member of a family of outcasts (as lepers are not permitted to live among the people in the Nigerian societies) who has married an unintelligent wife, who cares as less for her mother in-law's leprous situation as the husband does (lines 11 – 13a). Mr 419 uncomfortably admits irresponsibility as he does in line 9 above (line 12).
c. An irresponsible shirker of traditional rights of marriage, who is in unacceptable marital union with an unintelligent woman (lines 13b – 14). Mr 419's contribution at line 15 flouts relevance (Sperber and Wilson 1986). "She is fine" (line 15) addresses no part of Akpos' earlier sequence, thus showing Mr 419's confusion and uncomfortability with Akpos. In a way, it demonstrates his orientation to an emergent common ground with Akpos as he seems to get somewhat disoriented with the deeply offensive trend of Akpos' piques, partially losing track of his fraud script. However, he quickly picks up the apriori script in the 'b' part of the same line so as to prevent his emotion from catching up with his current game. Thus by saying, "I'm sure she'll get across to you", he orients to the relevance of Akpos' earlier turn: "I neva hear from her since d two of una marry without our blessing".
d. A fraudster who neither delivered a Hummer Jeep for which he had been paid nor returned the money taken (lines 17-19). This sequence, narrowed down to the actual identity role of Mr 419, has a direct emergent intention to, in addition to piquing him, bring him to Akpos' awareness of his fraudster identity in their current encounter. Again, rather than connect with this common ground, Mr 419 sticks with the script apriori intention of defrauding a bitter client who had mistaken him for a real world individual with whom he had had a business encounter. His sequence at line 20 is an attempt to further initiate a fraudster script which fails as Akpos' accentual salience (line 21a) stalls the TCU as he demands the return of his paid money, charging him with ingratitude, fraud and betrayal (line 21b – 23a) and confirming his curse-prone personality (lines 23b-24). However, partly by Akpos' design and partly by interactive accident, his sequence generates again, at least as interpreted by Mr 419 in lines 25-26, the salience of a bitter client.

Finally, Mr 419's attempt to insert another fraudster script – an insincere promise and then a scam design – in lines 25 -26 where the punch line of the joke resides receives an undersigned twist from Akpos who, at lines 27 – 28, now discloses his actual emergent intention by:

a. directly addressing Mr 419 as a fraudster (line 27a)
b. disclosing his creation of the fraudster's name, Ejiro, as an interactive ploy (lines 27b-28a)

c. announcing his discursive design to outsmart his addressee – Mr 419 (line 28a)

Mr 419's final sequence (lines 29-30) confirms the achievement of Akpos' personal goal in the interaction and demonstrates the dispreferred nature of the twist he experiences in the encounter with Akpos. His labeling Akpos "Whaat Madman" (line 29a) confirms his being outsmarted perhaps with no precedence. His regret and curse pronouncement in lines 29b – 30) establishes his apriori common ground and intention played throughout the encounter against Akpos' emergent common ground and intention.

The interaction below is another instantiation of the negotiation of undersigned twists.

Excerpt 6

In this short jocular encounter, Akpos enters his female boss's room without knocking. The woman disapproves of this action, arguing that it could expose her nudity to Akpos were she yet to get dressed or getting dressed. Akpos' response is that he always peeps first to be sure his boss is not in any of the states feared by her before he enters.

1. MADAM: Akpos, this is wrong, what if I was naked or dressing up?
2. AKPOS: That can never happen, Madam.
3. MADAM: How can you be so sure?
4. AKPOS: I always peep first and if you are naked,
5. I'll just wait and watch until you have dressed up before I enter.

The opening of the encounter reveals Akpos's female boss' anger with him with respect to his entering the room without knocking as she might be naked or getting dressed. This sequence exploits the script of privacy shared with Akpos. The apriori knowledge gets partly confirmed in Akpos' next turn by the use of the demonstrative "that" which connects with the boss' turn, and which, when combined with the rest of the sequence, denies the possibility of the occurrence of the proposition of the sequence. This contribution brings in an emergent common ground and signals an emergent intention. The new common ground is indicated with the boss' inquirer in line 3: "How can you be so sure"? where she expresses her curiosity to connect with Akpos' emerging cognitive construction. Akpos' final sequence between lines 4 -5, which bears the punch line of the joke, demonstrates his emergent intention, constructed from an angle of his independent belief. Its emergent nature demonstrates the following discursive orientations:

a. It sequentially connects with the boss' turns in lines 1 and 3 and clears her fears of Akpos' physical presence while she is naked or dressing up, but it does not preclude his intrusion into her boss' privacy (line 4).
b. It expressly confirms the woman's fear regarding Akpos' access into her nudity as he peeps first to be sure it is safe to enter the room (line 4 - 5). This emergent perspective points to the source of Akpos' contextual confidence not to knock before entering the boss' room. Thus, it indicates a

dispreferred twist in the encounter as the action is naturally ruled out both in the asymmetrical relationship in which the two participants are found and in the larger inter-gender interactions.

c. Akpos' emergent intention to explain away his boss' worry at line 3 unveils the unethical nature of his action, itself a clear interactive index of irresponsibility.
d. Ultimately, the verbalisation of his action implicates his utter stupidity and slow wit often possessed by many Nigerian house helps.

CONCLUSION

In the foregoing, three forms of negotiation have been identified in the *Facebook*-based Akpos humour: negotiations of mis-oriented twists, dis-preference and un-designed twists. In the respective cases, the talk initiating speakers have their logic flawed by recipient speakers, usually Akpos, and consequently get outsmarted; earlier sequentially dispreferred social choices are re-negotiated as preferred options in the light of new discursive realities; and the interactive designs or expectations of talk initiating participants receive undersigned or unexpected sequential responses in symmetrical or asymmetrical relationships. The negotiations, seated in the theoretic frames of Kecskes' socio-cognitive approach, aspects of the larger common ground theory, aspects of conversation analysis together with elements of selected humour theories have demonstrated the adaptability of apriori and emergent perspectives to the mediated encounters of *Facebook* humour. Their provisions for context-shaping and context-determined cues offer the strategic instruments for unpacking layers of wits and outwitting that ultimately yield the punch lines of the jokes.

The paper argues that the characters' situationally adaptive orientation to apriori or emergent common ground and intention demonstrates Akpos jokes' recontextualisation of particular Nigerian social and cultural experiences through the characters' socio-cognitive designs in the mediated encounters. While these designs offer the relaxant effects jokes are naturally meant to yield, their negotiation mechanisms provide resources for the application of Kecskes' SCA in *Facebook* humour, an attempt yet to be made in pragmatics scholarship; and produce sarcasm with a wing of moral lessons.

REFERENCES

Adams, A. (2012). On the identification of humour markers in computer –mediated communication. *Association for the Advancement of Artificial Intelligence.*, *2*, 1–3.

Allan, K. (Forthcoming). What is common ground? In Perspective on Pragmatics and Philosophy. Berlin: Springer Verlag. doi:10.1007/978-3-319-01014-4_11

Arundale, R. B. (1997). *Against (Grice's) intention.* Paper presented at LSI Preconference on Language and Cognition, International Communication Association Conference, Montreal, Canada.

Arundale, R. B. (2008). Against (Gricean) intention at the heart of human interaction. *Intercultural Pragmatics*, *5*(2), 229–258. doi:10.1515/IP.2008.012

Attardo, S., & Raskin, V. (1991) Script theory revis(it)ed: joke similarity and joke representation model. HUMOR, the International Journal of Humor Research, 4(3-4), 293-348. doi:10.1515/humr.1991.4.3-4.293

Attardo, S. (1994). *Linguistic theories of humour.* Berlin: Mouton de Gruyter.

Baym, Nancy, K. (1995). The performance of humour in computer-mediated communication. *Journal of Computer-Mediated Communication.*

Brown, P., & Levinson, S. (1987). *Politeness: Some Universals in Language Usage.* Cambridge, UK: Cambridge University Press.

Clark, H. H., & Brennan, S. E. (1991). Grounding in communication. In *Perspective on Socially Shared Cognition* (pp. 127–149). Washington, DC: American Psychological Association.

Clark, H. H., Schreuder, R., & Buttrick, S. (1983). Common ground and the understanding of demonstrative reference. *Journal of Verbal Learning and Verbal Behavior, 22,* 245–258. doi:10.1037/10096-006

Clark, H. H. (1996). *Using Language.* Cambridge, UK: Cambridge University Press. doi:10.1017/CBO9780511620539

Dynel, M. (2011). *The Pragmatic of Humour aross Discourse Domain.* Amsterdam: John Benjanmin Publishing. doi:10.1075/pbns.210

Edward, C., Bresnahan, K., & Krystal, A. (2008). The influence of humorous positive computer-mediated word-of-mouth communication on student motivation and affective learning. *Texas Speech Communication Journal, 53*(1), 1–8.

Goffman, E. (1981). *Forms of Talk.* Philadelphia: University of Pennsylvania Press.

Gruner, C. (1997). *The Game of Humor: A Comprehensive Theory of Why We Laugh.* New Brunswick, NJ: Transaction Publishers.

Hubler, M. T., & Bell, D. C. (2003). Computer-mediated humor and ethos: Exploring threads of constitutive laughter in online communities. *Computers and Composition, 20*(3), 277–294. doi:10.1016/S8755-4615(03)00036-7

Holcomb, C. (1997). A class of clowns: Spontaneous joking in computer assisted discussions. *Computers and Composition, 14*(1), 3–18. doi:10.1016/S8755-4615(97)90035-9

Kant, I. (1911). *Critique of Judgment.* Oxford, UK: Clarendon Press. (Original work published 1790)

Keisannen, T., & Karkkanen, E. (2014). Stance. In K. Schneider & A. Barron (Eds.), *Pragmatics of Discourse* (pp. 295–322). Berlin: Mouton de Gruyter. doi:10.1515/9783110214406-012

Knight, N. (2008). "Still cool…and american too!": An SFL Analysis of Deferred Bonds in Internet Messaging Humour. *Language & Communication.*

Lanineste, L. (2013). Funny or Aggressive? Failed humour in Internet comment. Electronic. *Journal of Folklore, 53,* 29–46.

Levinson, S. C. (1983). Pragmatics. Cambridge, UK: Cambridge.

Marone, V. (2015). Online humour as a community- building cushioning glue 3,1. Cognitive Constraints on Communication.

Mulder, M. P., & Nijholt, A. (2002). Humour Research: State of the Arts. Centre for Telematics and Information Technology.

Norrick, N. R. (1993) Repetition in canned jokes and spontaneous conversational joking. HUMOR, The International Journal of Humor Research, 6(4), 385-402.

Odebunmi, A. (2006). *Meaning in English: An Introduction*. Ogbomoso: Critical Sphere.

Odebunmi, A., & Alo, M. (2010). Belief in GSM Text Messaging Among Academics in Two Nigerian Universities. In Handbook of Research on Discourse Behavior and Digital Communication Language Structures and Social Interaction (vol. 1, pp. 468-478). New York: Information Science Reference. doi:10.4018/978-1-61520-773-2.ch029

Rutter, J. (1997). *Stand-Up as Interaction: Performance and Audience in Comedy Venues*. University of Salford.

Schnurr, S., & Rowe, C. (2008). The 'dark side' of humour. An analysis of subversive humour in workplace emails. *Lodz Papers in Pragmatics*, *4*(1), 109–130. doi:10.2478/v10016-008-0010-6

Sperber, D., & Wilson, D. (1986). *Relevance: Communication and Cognition*. Oxford, UK: Blackwell Publishing.

Stalnaker, R. C. (1978). Assertion. In C. P. Pragmatics (Ed.), *Syntax and Semantics 9* (pp. 315–332). New York: Academic Press.

Stalnaker, R.C. (2000). Common ground. *Linguistics and Philosophy*, *25*, 701-721.

Stoll, B. A. (2015). The Effects of Humorous *Facebook* Posts on Messenger Credibility and Social Attractiveness. *The Hilltop Review*, *7*(2), 3–18.

Taylor, C. (2009) 'Laughter' in L2 computer-mediated discourse. In Advances in discourse approaches. Cambridge Scholars Publishing.

KEY TERMS AND DEFINITIONS

Apriori Common Ground/Intention: Interactants' shared assumptions/discursive goals that predate interaction.

Emergent Common Ground/Intention: Interactants' assumptions/goals that come up/emerge during interaction.

Facebook: This is operationally defined as a veritable host of visual and verbal texts shared among its subscribers.

Outwitting: A situation where the wits of the involved parties get negotiated in the (mediated) context of jokes, and the punch line often develops at the point where superior wit emerges.

Negotiation of Dis-Preference: Deals with social choices that are sometimes sequentially dispreferred by participants at the early stage of a conversation but that are sometimes renegotiated in the later part of it in the light of the emergent realities.

Negotiation of Mis-Oriented Twists: Captures a situation where the logic of talk-initiating interactants gets flawed by recipient speakers, and the latter consequently outwits the former.

Negotiation of Un-Designed Twists: A situation where the fraudulent design of a discourse initiator gets suspected or when either of the parties receives unexpected revelation.

Wit Negotiation: This is the strategic interchange of clever propositions between characters which constitutes an important factor in processing the interpretation of humours presented in conversation format in online jokes.

ENDNOTES

1 419 is the code used to symbolise advanced fee fraud or scam in Nigeria. It is commonly used as a generic noun or an adjective, but sometimes as a nominal head as used in this joke.

2 Odebunmi (2006), in developing a model of contextual beliefs, discusses independent beliefs (interactants' independent or exclusive experience and perception of the world) and shared beliefs.

Chapter 3
More Than a Joking Matter: Humor and Political Engagement in *Ogas at the Top*

Funmi Olubode-Sawe
Federal University of Technology Akure, Nigeria

ABSTRACT

This chapter discusses how humor is generated in Oga at the Top series (OATT), a puppet political satire program featuring prominent actors on the Nigerian political scene. The question of how multimodal phenomena in humor bearing texts combine to create a humorous political commentary has not been addressed within the Nigerian context. This chapter therefore explores how different semiotic resources are combined to create humor in OATT. From the 25 videos selected from Season One, the humor creation mechanisms in OATT were found to include caricature of national leaders, re-interpretation of contemporary happenings, musical parody, script opposition in conversation, inter-texuality and physical violence. Though the stated function of the series was to exploit the Nigerian political climate for humor, the analysis shows that the audience has appropriated the videos for their own ends based on the functions they felt they could serve. The chapter concludes with the significance of the online distribution of the videos.

The views and content expressed in this chapter are those of the author but not necessarily of the publisher and may contain some explicit ideas and concepts.

INTRODUCTION

Humor is an interesting phenomenon that suffuses many aspects of human interaction, both in the private and public spheres. One such sphere is politics, where the use of political humor is thought to date from antiquity, in ancient Greece and Rome. As Sorensen (2014) demonstrates, research on political humor frequently approaches the subject from a historical perspective or as a certain type of genre (satire,

DOI: 10.4018/978-1-5225-0338-5.ch003

Copyright © 2016, IGI Global. Copying or distributing in print or electronic forms without written permission of IGI Global is prohibited.

cartoon) presented in a certain medium (TV or the Internet). This chapter discusses humor as a form of social engagement during a period of political transition in Nigeria through an analysis of Season One of the satirical Oga at the Top series (OATT), a puppet political satire program featuring prominent actors on the Nigerian political scene.

It is an expository chapter, focusing on the language and visual content of the videos, how other texts and contexts are brought in and how viewers receive them. English is the language most frequently used by the puppet characters, although a few code-switch into Nigerian Pidgin. Expletives and interjections in some indigenous languages of Nigeria, namely Hausa, Yoruba and Ijaw The series is produced by Buni Media, a Kenyan company and distributed on Buni Media's video-on-demand platform Buni TV, and are also available on SaharaReporters.com, YouTube, Afrinolly, and MTN Play.

Humor commodities such as cartoons and jokes are regularly created and disseminated in Nigeria, with the political space and players therein sometimes being the focus of these jokes. There are professional comedians; comedy shows are a staple fare of festive seasons; and television programming includes comedy shows in English and indigenous languages. However, not much attention has been given to why the commodities are deemed to be funny or what makes a particular 'joke' or other humor commodity funny. A corollary of this is the question of how the various elements in a supposedly humorous text combine to create humor. Specifically, the question of how the various elements of spectacle, speech and music in the Oga at the Top puppet TV series combine to create a humorous political commentary has not been addressed. To the best of my knowledge, there is no previous research on the political satirical humor featuring puppet characters in the Nigerian political environment

The objectives of the study reported in this chapter are as follows:

- To identify and describe the various types of humor used in OATT;
- To identify and describe the humor creation strategies in OATT;
- To analyze the mechanisms employed within the identified strategies;
- To determine the significance of the online transmission of the videos; and
- To describe the functions that the audience sees the texts as performing.

The study therefore attempts to proffer answers to the following research questions:

- Which types of humor are used in OATT?
- By which strategies are these types of humor created?
- What mechanisms are employed within the identified strategies?
- What functions are the texts seen as performing?and
- What significance, if any, does online transmission of the videos have?

The study is significant in that the Oga at the Top series provide the first example of political humor using puppet characters on the Nigerian humor scene. Here we have multimodal phenomena,a blend of the semiotic resources of image, gesture,speech and music; appealing to the visual and auditory sensory modalities.This genre of humor lends itself to a multimodal analysis. The findings will therefore provide a systematic account of humor creation across a variety of modes. In addition, the study shows, via an audience reception analysis, that humor is not necessarily merely for laughter, and documents the social functions of a particular genre of humor, i.e., puppet political TV.

Methodology

The 49 videos of Season One were published online between March 9 and July 13, 2014 and downloaded from YouTube, between January 21 and 22, 2015. 25 of the 49 videos were purposively selected to represent the different interaction types: those involving dyads/triads, small group interactions and crowds, interviews and musicals. This sample is considered an adequate representation of the series. Thevideos were played back slowly and the speech carefully transcribed. Screen shots of relevant frames of the videos were also captured to show details of physiognomy, costume and props/ artefacts. The lyrics of musicals parodied are taken fromwww.azlyrics.com/lyrics/.Data for audience reception are taken from the comments to the videos.

Wherever necessary in these analyses, explanations will be provided for a relevant feature of context or a significant topical allusion so that readers unfamiliar with the narrower cultural reference points will still be able to disambiguate the basic humor mechanism.

BACKGROUND

Humor Theories

Humor is that psychological state which tends to produce laughter. The tendency to produce laughter rather than the actual production is critical here, for as Veatch (1998) shows, not all perceptions of humor actually produce overt laughter. This definition allows for laughter with or without humor and vice versa. Humor theories are mainly of three kinds: those which focus on some kind of incongruity, inconsistency or contradiction; those which see humor as an expression of aggression, superiority, disparagement, or criticism; and then those theories which see humor as a way of experiencing release or relaxation. This categorization is for convenience only: humor can be an expression of aggression while highlighting incongruity, and may also cause the audience to experience relaxation.

According to Krikmann (2006) incongruity theories are based on the assumption that every such act involves two different and mutually incompatible planes of content, with a common part which makes the shift from one to another possible. Incongruity involves a conflict between what the joke teller leads the hearer to expect and what actually occurs in the joke. Humor is therefore seen as primarily being "the result of cultural perceptions, both individual and collective, of incongruity, exaggeration, distortion, and any unusual combinations of the cultural elements in external events" (Apte, 1985, p. 16).

Two of the better known humor-as-incongruity theories are Raskin's (1985) Semantic-Script Theory of Humor (SSTH) and Attardo's General Theory of Verbal Humor (GTVH). In SSTH, humor is seen as a violation of Grice's cooperative principle. In Raskin's conceptualization, humor is created from the opposition between two overlapping semantic scripts and the backtracking that occurs when the hearer consults his/her world knowledge to process the contrast and re-interpret the utterance as a joke. (Attardo&Raskin, 1991). In the revision of Raskin's script-based semantic theory of humor, Attardo and Raskin collaborate to put forth a "General Theory of Verbal Humor" (GTVH). The GTVH is based on six knowledge resources from which the joke-teller must choose to create the humorous incongruity: script opposition, logical mechanism, situation (which includes the audience and the props), target (butt of the joke), narrative strategy, and language (Attardo&Raskin, 1991, p. 313).

Aggressiveness theories focus on the negative attitude of the producer and/or user of humor towards its target (the butt of the joke). Raskin (1985) identifies three main kinds of "aggressive" humor – sexual, ethnic and political. Of special interest to this chapter are political jokes which are usually intended to show that the life or actions of a political figure or group are at variance with some societal expectation or perception. The jokes allude to a particular series of events, slogans or mannerisms, for which reasons Raskin suggests that some jokes might be more easily accessible to contemporaries living in a certain geographical area and who may have internalized the scripts to which the allusions are made. This might be true of mannerisms, slogans and routine government business. However, occurrences of political significance in any corner of the globe might be accessible to interested watchers elsewhere if news of such gets online.

Political jokes are subdivided into two: denigration jokes and exposure jokes. Denigration jokes may have as their target political figures, political groups or institutions or political ideas. Exposure jokes are typically targeted at political regimes and contain a reference to an incident or a series of events which are not well publicized. This is not an exclusive categorization; "some exposure may actually occur in a denigration joke, and the purpose of all exposure is usually denigration (Raskin, 1985, p. 222). Both types of political jokes are pertinent to this analysis.

Satire and Parody as Humor

One vehicle for presentation of aggressive humor is satire, the use of wit, especially irony, sarcasm, and ridicule, to criticize faults. The impetus for satire emanates from a perceived disapprobation, by the satirist, of some aspect of a potential satirical target. Though OATT is marketed as a humor commodity, the focus on the perceived shortcomings of the Nigerian political elite makes their work an exercise in political satire. Political satire usually involves the replication and exaggeration of some elements of a real-world situation or persons to convey political messages. Employing techniques such as caricatures and impersonation, credibility is achieved by placing characters in situations derived from real world politics, with portrayals "accurate enough for the audience to accept the humor as credible while still accepting their exaggeration" (Crines 2014, p. 152).

An echoic dimension in textual formation exists that imbues satirical discourse with its "spoof" or parodic quality, or the "quality of inter-textual mediation" (Simpson, 2003, p. 93). Inter-textuality occurs when a text makes reference to some other identifiable text or stretch of discourse (Norrick, 1989, p.117). Berger (n.d.) cites parody as an example of inter-textuality, which relies on the addressee recognizing the original text in order to get the most out of the humor, though in some parodies, the exaggeration and absurdity of the text itself is enough to please audiences. Parody functions principally as a discourse of allusion to other genres and registers (Nash, 1985); with "certain memorable phrases, certain grammatical constructions, certain principles of versification and certain propositions" being mentioned (Carstyn& Noh, 1995, p. 4). While Berger suggests that many kinds of parody involve ridiculous imitation, joke bearing texts which involve parody are not necessarily constitutive of an attack on the particular individual whose discourse is echoed (Simpson, 2003, p. 121).

A related concept is that of recontextualization, where the original text is not just alluded to, but parts of it are purposely selected and resituated in another context (Chandler &Munday, 2011). When meanings (or discourses, genres and styles) are moved from one field to another, they are transformed by being decontextualized (taken out of their contexts) and recontextualized (put in new contexts) (Fairclough, 1988: 26). Both inter-textualityand recontextualization are important humor generation devices in OATT, especially in the musical parody videos.

Humor TV

Political satire can take the format of many humor commodities – stand-up comedy, plays, cartoons, spoof journalism and puppet TV. Simpson developed his model of satirical discourse by analyzing spoof newspaper articles published in *Private Eye*, a British satirical publication while Crines (2014) uses three examples of British political comedy: *The Thick of It, Private Eye* and *Spitting Image* to present an introductory account of the relationship between the satirist and the audience.

Spitting Image which ran in the U.K. from 1984 to 1996 was one of the first puppet TV shows primarily for political commentary. Using latex puppets, it satirized politicians, TV personalities, and the royal family in sketches that featured caricature and other modes of symbolic aggression: mimicry, defacement, belittlement, exaggeration, and deformation utilized in carrying out its political agenda (Brillenburg, 2011). Crines (2014), however, suggests that *Spitting Image* sketches merely manipulated pre-existing media-constructed images to tap into the mood of the audience and were therefore reflective of what the writers believed the audience (or at least parts of it) already felt.

African television puppet shows have grown within the last decade. The XYZ Show (produced by Buni Media) uses humor and satire to illustrate political and controversial issues in Kenya. Inspired by *Spitting Image* and *Les Guignols,* the XYZ Show has been hailed for using puppets to battle corruption in Kenya, poking relentless fun at Kenyan politicians (Rogers, 2009). The show which was conceived as a forum of social and political debate to contribute to civic education in Kenya had its producers receiving threats from the Kenyan government in its early days (Ochwada, 2012): 208, 209). A comparable show is South African Puppet Nation ZA which has been produced in South Africa since 2009. Both the XYZ Show and Puppet Nation had difficulties in getting broadcast houses to host their shows. According to informationactivism.org, Puppet Nation ZA was broadcast wholly online until 2011, and then began airing on a satellite TV service.OATT created in Kenya for a Nigerian audience is the latest entrant into the field.

Being in form of video, the OATT series requires a multimodal discourse analysis to explicate the combination of the meaning-making events in the videos. A multimodal analysis involves taking cognizance of semiotics other than language-in-use, e.g. image, music, gesture, as found in OATT.

The ubiquity of sound, image, film, through TV, the computer and the internet is undoubtedly behind this new emphasis on and interest in the multi-semiotic complexity of the representations we produce and see around us (Iedema 2003, p 33). MDA is suited to the analysis of language together with other semiotic resources, such as images, scientific symbolism, gesture, action, music and sound. 'Semiotic resource' here refers to the resources (or modes) (e.g. language, image, music, gesture and architecture) which integrate across sensory modalities (e.g. visual, auditory, tactile, olfactory, gustatory, kinesthetic) in multimodal texts, discourses and events, collectively called multimodal phenomena (O'Halloran, 2011).

HUMOR CREATION IN OATT

The humor creation strategies in the OATT videos differ according to the type of comedy presented. Therefore, the strategies are discussed under the types of humor in which they are used. First of all, the targets of the jokes are clearly identified as the ruling class, and the designation of the group, "*ogas*at the top" meaning the bosses or the high and mighty highlights this. The jokes in OATT combining exposure and denigration are realized by fivestrategies: caricature in visual comedy, re-interpretation of real-world politics, musical parody, phonological and conversational patterning in verbal humor, and comic exploitation of violence. Inter-textuality as a device is used within many of these strategies and a separate section is devoted to it.

Denigration Strategies in Visual Comedy

The focus of visual comedy is what is seen. In OATT therefore, one humor generation strategy is denigration through caricature, that is, comic exaggeration of some physical features of the puppet characters that feature in the videos. Though there is no gross defacement or deformation, some physiognomic features and items of clothing are highlighted to give realistic identity to the puppets. The most significant government figure is Dr. Goodluck Jonathan. His puppet double has very dark skin, a prominent nose and cheeks bunched up in a permanent smile. He wears a dark grey Ijaw suit and a black felt top hat. Even when wearing other costumes, the top hat is a must. Figure 1 shows a GEJ Puppet Double (left) in *Personally* and Dr. Goodluck Jonathan. As the composed picture in the figure shows, details from the real-life physiognomy and dress are incorporated into the creation of the puppet to make the audience identify the fictional creation with the real deal.

Other government figures portrayed are the President's wife, Dame Patience Jonathan (DPJ), Finance Minister Dr. NgoziOkonjo-Iweala (NOI), Minister of Petroleum Resources Diezani Allison Madueke (DAM) and Information Minister LabaranMaku. NOI has dark skin and a chubby face, wears a head gear

Figure 1. GEJ Puppet Double (left) in Personally and Dr. Goodluck Jonathan

of the same wax print material as her dress sitting low on her forehead. General SaniAbacha (GSA) wears a smart military uniform with cap insignia of skull and crossbones, dark sun glasses and has extra-large ears.DAM is fair-skinned, has prominent eyes, loves diamond rings and always wears a shawl over her right shoulder. (See Figure 2 below.)

The identity of public figures with the caricature puppets, using details by which the real-life personalities can identified (e.g. items of dress), plus the exaggeration of some details of physiognomy: Abacha's large ears, GEJ's large nose and DAM's bulbous eyes all serve to evoke humor at the expense of the said public figures.

Apart from identity-marking visual cues in the videos, gesture, body position and movement are also highlighted for the viewer's notice.In *Shut Up and Fly*, DAM has the President under her thumb (tells him to shut up and pilot her plane, which he does) and might be having an affair with him. Figure 2 is a Screen Shot from *Shut Up and Fly featuring DAM*, showing GEJ ogling DAM. Note the angle of his gaze and his hand scratching his chin as if he would rather be holding the lady. The DAM puppet is also placed to display the 'diamond' necklace, rings and earrings.

Costuming and movement are other visual phenomena used for humor. Here again, the purpose is for denigration. The *Ogas* music videos highlight incongruity in the real life personality and puppet double behavior, with the performance subverting or compromising the characters by casting them as entertainers rather than as community leaders. Apart from the humor involved in the re-wording of the songs (which will be taken up later), the costumes and the movements of the characters contribute to the humor. In *Anything for the Vote* (Buni TV, 13 July 2014), the usually sedate GMB is transformed into Hari-Bubu, the youth-friendly alternative, 'hanging out' at a night club with his young friends in gangsta rapper attire (or an approximation of it) tee-shirt, baseball cap and heavy necklaces (See Figure 3, Screen Shot from *Anything for the Vote*). The background shows walls with indecipherable graffiti, and the hand positions all contribute to the 'gangsta attitude'. Dance movements in the videos include head jerking, finger snapping, jumping and waving their hands, sudden changes of direction and back and forward movements. The puppet doubles of responsible and highly regarded citizens are generally seen making a fool of themselves, and this can be humorous for many.

Figure 2. Screen shot from Shut Up and Fly featuring DAM, showing GEJ ogling DAM

Figure 3. Screen shot from Anything for the Vote

It must be noted that the happenings, as distinct from characters, depicted as elements of denigration humor in visual comedy may or may not have any semblance to real-life historical events. The focus is to poke fun at the butt of the joke by showing him/her looking foolish or doing foolish things.

Re-Interpretation of Real-World Politics

This strategy is used when the general context presented in the joke has a real-life existence. Factual incidents and personalities that have a real-life basis are presented, though a (different) version that serves the purpose of the humorist is composed. In other words, the audience is told: "Recall incident X that you heard/read about? This is what actually happened". These are exposure jokes that ostensibly reveal what the powers that be would keep hidden.This strategy involves recontextualizing the event and may therefore alter the meanings.

In OATT, the background events alluded to include the political processes leading up to the 2015 general elections in Nigeria, and the Boko Haram insurgency. The first video, published on March 9, 2014 is *Jonathan Undecided speaks to Christiane Amanpour*. The real-world background to this is that early in 2013, there were widespread speculations whether or not the sitting President would seek re-election. Some party operatives claimed he would but others, including the Presidential spokesperson and the Chair of the Peoples Democratic Party claimed at different fora that President Goodluck Jonathan was yet to decide whether or not to seek re-election, because he was too busy focusing on the task before him. And as matter of fact, President Jonathan was interviewed by CNN's Anchor, Christiane Amanpour on January 23, 2013. Below is OATT's version of what transpired.

Presenter: *Hello and welcome to Amanpour Live. My guest tonight is President Goodluck Ebele Jonathan, hosting us at his Presidential Villa in Abuja. Our viewers can contribute by following the hash tag Jonathan Undecided. Mr. President, thank you for inviting us.*
President: *You are welcome, Christine*
Presenter: *Let us get right to it right away. Will you be running for a second term in 2015?*
President: *....hmn... I have said it before that it is too early to heat up the polity with a declaration. I am too busy trying to transform Nigeria. At the appropriate time, I will make my decision known.* (*Jonathan Undecided*, 00:14 – 00:51)

The rest of the interview showed the hesitant President parrying questions, and asking the international community for help and prayers in combating Boko Haram menace. The bona fide script of a busy president delivering the "dividends of democracy" to his people is suspect because it is unbelievable that a president would invite a global news outlet only to announce that he was yet to decide to run for a second time. The opposing script is that the president is an incompetent liar who cannot even tell convincing lies. When Amanpour raised the issue of electricity, the President's proof of improved power supply was that there was uninterrupted supply at the presidential residence, and that the Minister of Power who confessed that power generation had not increased must have been misquoted, even though the interviewer experienced two power cuts at the airport. Then the lights started to flicker, and the following exchange ensued.

Amanpour: *Excuse me, Mr. President? (Lights continue to flicker on and off) O dear! Er, Mr. President, is everything alright here? It looks that this power problem is bigger than we thought.*
President: *It's okay, it's okay, everything is under control; (nervous laughter) I can assure you, it's the work of my enemies who are trying to bring me down... Suleman! Can't you see we are having an interview here?*
Amanpour: *Mr. President? Mr....-Mr. President?* (Total blackout)
President: *Put on the generator!* (*Jonathan Undecided*, 04:41 – 05:02)

The President's evidence was disproved; even the Presidential Villa runs on generator.

Nigerian Ministry of Information Boko Haram and the Abuja jailbreak (Buni TV, 6 April, 2014) mocks the incompetence and lack of coordination of the nation's information management mechanism with regard to an attempted escape of Boko Haram detainees from the Directorate of State Security, and the official statement about the incident released by the DSS spokesperson, Ms Marilyn Ogar. In the puppet video, a press conference was being addressed by Marilyn Ogar, Information Minister Labaran-Maku, and an unnamed army spokesperson. Mr. Maku was glibly holding forth on the successes of the Federal Government against the Boko Haram insurgents in superlative terms: 2000 insurgents killed in one attack, 700 vehicles seized and (as the army spokesperson reminded him) 70 Boko Haram camps overrun. He wanted photographs of the seized vehicles projected, but the projector did not work. Asked about the attempted jailbreak of 30 March, 2014, the government representatives were vey disorganized.

Journalist: *How many people died in the incident on both sides, that is the DSS and the suspects*
Maku: *I'm not aware we lost any of our officers the attempt was quickly quelled, and with heavy casualties for the perpetrators*
Ogar: *(first leans over to whispers to LM, then to the audience)A quick clarification. A few DSS officers did not make it. Otherwise, we were quickly able to contain the incident and neutralize the enemy, down to the last man.*

...

Maku: *In summary, this is the story. On Sunday, evil insurgents overpowered one of our DSS operatives who went to feed them, attacking him with the plate and taking his gun.*
Ogar: *(leaning over to Maku and whispering) It was really with a toilet seat, sir.*
LM: *Oh, ok.Er, a small correction there: the insurgents attacked the helpless officer in the toilet using a ripped off toilet seat after he had accompanied one of them who said he was pressed...*

Ogar: *Actually...both versions are correct...The insurgents attacked using every weapon at their disposal. What is most important is that our gallant DSS boys neutralized them with the help of the army. So that is the real story here. Nigerian Ministry of Information:*(2.12-2.41...3.06-3.47)

First Maku refused to answer questions, then decided to allow questions which he wanted Ogar to answer but she declined. She kept correcting the minister on factual details. Prompted by her, Maku presented several versions of how the attempted jailbreak occurred, without batting an eyelid even when he controverted himself. The DSS spokesperson finally concluded that the different versions were correct. The army spokesperson merely polished his sidearm throughout the interview.

Another issue re-interpreted include the response of public functionaries to the kidnapping of over 200 secondary school girls from Chibok in North-eastern Nigeria on April 14, 2015. In *Anywhere but Chibok* (Buni TV, May 25, 2014), the president chooses to address the Chibok issue from Paris rather than visit the village as he had been scheduled to. The protesting Chibok villagers were being calmed by a patriotic lady expressing faith in the Commander-in-Chief and the indivisibility of the nation. At that same moment, we see Mr. President having to escape from his wife.

President: *Chai! Na God dey save person o. Which kind woman be dis one? You know, even as we were still running into the jet, I could hear her voice all the way from the villa.*
Maku: *Your Excellency, me too o.*
President: *That woman na winch o.*
Maku: *We barely escaped.*
President: *Wo! Anyway, back to the matter... Labaran, between you and I, I dey fear dis Boko boys o.*
Maku: *Ah... but er... I understand with you, Sir but, but Sir, you know cannot say that in public, Your Excellency.*
President: *I know, I know, I know but you see, er..er..Nigerians, demtink say me I be superman, but I'm a family man too. I have family issues to handle.* (*Anywhere but Chibok*, 00:45 – 01:20)

We see here the mismatch between the great expectation of the people for a commander who will lead them to war yet who has to escape from his wife and confesses that he is afraid of the enemy. In his private moments, he faces issues that the common man may face, speaks Nigerian Pidgin and refers to his wife as 'winch' which may mean 'termagant' or 'woman having evil powers'.

Maku finally gets him to rehearse his speech

President: *True, true, true. Ok, er... Ok. Em...how do I start this now? Em... (clears his throat) I have here come to show that we stand with Chibok and we will defeat the enemy by standing together. How does that sound?*
Maku: *Ah You read speeches far better than Obama, Your Excellency, Sir. Ten thousand times better, Sir. ... May be you say a greeting in the local language when we arrive. I know they will love that.* (*Anywhere but Chibok*, 01:25 – 01:52)

Maku's flattery generates laughter, since the President rehearses his speech in a sing-song voice reminiscent of a child reciting a nursery rhyme. That night, the waiting Chibok villagers see Mr. President and the Minister on TV in Paris. The script opposition is resolved as the viewer realizes that the President never intended to go to Chibok. After saying, "Me go to Chibok, I dey mad?", the president raps the rest of his message under bright lights with the Eiffel Tower in the background. An interesting verse from his song is "What's 200 girls to a leader like me, can you please remind me?" whileMaku provides back-up: 'Emperor, yes my king, yes my lord… Amen, Amen, yes my king, yes my lord.'

The Chibok saga and the Nigerian Government's responses to it provide inspiration for two other videos. In real life, following the abduction, an advocacy group, Bring Back Our Girls emerged on April 30, 2014. They organized marches and online advocacy campaigns which drew global attention to the abduction, to the embarrassment of the Nigerian government. The Bring Back Our Girls campaign caught the imagination of the nation. *#BringBackOurGirlsForTheSakeOf2015* (Buni TV, 25 May, 2014) focuses on politicians trying to get political mileage out of it.

President: *Eh-heh, So, this paper we are talking about, you said it is what exactly?*
Aide: *Sir, It is Bring Back Our Girls. It is a social media campaign for the girls of Chibok.*
President: *Ah-ah, I see. Even Tinubu and Atiku have carried. Buharinko?* (*#BringBackOurGirlsForTheSakeOf2015*, 00.08 – 00:20)

The President was quite primitive and 'local' in his glee about those who "have carried"; he did not seem unduly distressed about the kidnapped girls but just 'wanted in'. It transpired that even his wife had "shot a video" as her contribution to the campaign. The import of this might be lost on any but the viewers of Nigerian local news as the video in question was of the First lady breaking down at a public function. Uploaded on May 4, 2014 by Channels Television, the video went viral, and phrases from it have become a staple of Nigerian humor discourse, as will be discussed later.

Mr. President also wants to hop on the Bring Back Our Girls bandwagon, but has no idea of what to do, confirming the allegations of his detractors that he was "Jonathan clueless, Jonathan sleeping, Jonathan this, Jonathan that." The buildup leads the audience to expect a stellar performance from the president. Still acting the "Jonathan clueless" script, his ideas of appropriating the campaign for his own ends were too transparent to be useable, and he went from bad to worse.

President: *Okay. Oya, wetin make I write?..What about erm… what was that er…what was that thing you said?*
Aide: *Hash tag*
President: *#BringbackourgirlssothatwecanshameAPC*
Aide: *Sir, don't you think it's a bit too long?*
President: *Huhn. okay, okay. What about #Bringbackourgirlsbecausetheyareneededtovoteformein2015*
Aide: *Er, Sir, Sir, you see, not only is that long, but Sir, that the message is very, very…*
President: *Then why don't you think? Everything I am bringing out you are just attacking me. All the good ideas… are you not the professional? I am just the president. What do I know about…* (*#BringBackOurGirlsForTheSakeOf2015*, 00.47 – 02:47).

'Clueless' takes on another meaning at the president's evaluation of his suggestions as 'good ideas', and his claim that being "just a president" means he should be a know-nothing. Similarly, in *National Security Priority* (Buni TV, 22 June, 2014), the President's definition of the nation's problems runs counter to common sense.At a high-level meeting with the security chiefs, the President and Commander-in -Chief is dressed for the part in military fatigues and felt top hat. He was visibly upset and talking tough.

President: *Er... Gentlemen, as you can see, I am now ready for battle...*
Police chief: *Finally, Sir?*
President: *Yes, finally. We cannot continue to treat these terrorists with kid gloves. They have done too much to damage me and the nation in such a short time.*
Army chief: *They are nothing but a bunch of miscreants.*
President: *To be honest, I know that they are politically motivated but it is time for them to be forcefully and immediately exterminated.* (*National Security Priority*, 00.08 – 00:38)

Predictably, the security bosses were very happy to cooperate since they (and the viewers) know who the terrorists were. Both groups were, however, rudely disabused of this misconception when Mr. President identifies the national security priority.

Army chief: *Just give the go-ahead, Sir...Boko Haram must be defeated.*
Police Chief: *Boko Haram must be defeated, Your Excellency.*
President: *Ah-ah? What are these men saying? Boko who? That is not who I am referring to o. I am talking about the number one threat to national security today. It is this 'bring-back-our-girls' protestors now. They are the one giving us sleepless nights.*
Security Chief: *Pardon us, Your Excellency, for not realizing.*
President: *Those protestors, they are terrorizing me. Every time I close my eyes, that is all I see and hear.* (*National Security Priority*, 00.39 – 01:24)

When the Army Chief suggested that the campaigners did not qualify as terrorists, Mr. President lectures him on the distinguishing characteristics of a terrorist.

President: *...You mean to tell me that a group that has a common goal of embarrassing my government, calling us to account, urging me to man up and do my job, demanding that the Chibok girls be returned now and alive, does not qualify as a terrorist group? What nonsense are you talking? What are you vomiting? ... Do you know who is funding them? Can you not see they have foreign support? Were you sleeping when the hash tag was trending on Twitter? And they were receiving support from all over the country including international celebrities, and people who do not want to mind their own business? Were you not there? Were you sleeping?* (*National Security Priority*, 01.33 – 02:10)

The joke here is that a demand for good governance is treated as terrorism by the government. The Army Chief makes one last feeble effort to turn the President's attention to the real problem: Boko Haram. The President handles this dismissively, identifying the insurgents almost fondly as "Boko". All the security bosses promised to do was to ban the 'Bring Back Our Girls' terrorists and disrupt their peaceful sit-ins and marches.

The President was not the only one being held up to ridicule here: the security chiefs who could not insist on pushing forward their expert advice were also being lampooned. As the short movie wound to a close, it was revealed why they could not afford to antagonize the President.

President: *That is what I want to hear. That is what I pay you for. Now I can sleep easy and remove this nonsense khaki uniform. Now on to more important things... Which of you would like to follow me* *to watch the Super Eagles play in the World Cup? (All of them chorus their desire to go.) I thought you would like that. #TheCupIsOurs. Brazil, here we come. Super Eagles all the way* (*National Security Priority*, 02.37 – 03:09)

The joke involves some deflation of the expectations of the audience who have been set up to expect drastic far-reaching actions from the Commander-in- Chief dressed for battle. First we find the security priority is not Boko Haram as one would expect but civilians marching and tweeting; and the forceful extermination would be effected by disrupting peaceful demonstrations, a classic case of much ado about nothing.

This section has presented the generation of humor through the fictionalization of events that have or could have happened. As a matter of historical fact, President Jonathan was interviewed by Amanpour, there was an Abuja jailbreak incident and a press conference addressed by Ogar and Maku. The humor is created by recontextualizing the events, so that the audience perceives the events and actors in a particular manner.

Musical Parody

A very effective method of humor generation in OATT is musical parody, with tunes of popular songs presented with new lyrics and sung by the Ogas. As earlier mentioned, joke bearing texts which involve parody are not necessarily constitutive of an attack on the particular individual whose discourse is echoed (Simpson 2003: 121). This means that the musical videos are not a commentary, for good or ill, on the parodied music. Rather, they serve to define the humor community, the group of people who access the humor commodity. As Table 1 shows, with the exception of 'Imagine', all the Ogas remixes are of songs released in the last ten years, and will be familiar to young adults. They might have heard the songs and would be attracted by the tunes. If they also know the lyrics (available online), they would appreciate how each remix differs from the original and find that humorous.

As suggested above, if the lyrics of the popular songs are known to the humor community, they can better appreciate the re-wording. Usually, the new *Ogas* lyrics rhyme with the original, with words and sometimes whole verses lifted. *Personally* (Buni TV, 18 May 2014) sticks very closely to the wording of the P-Square original. In verse 2 (Table 2 below), in addition to "Personally, professionally", "radically" and "Emotionally, psychologically" which are repeated wholly, "internationally" rhymes with "intentionally", and "politically" with "biologically". However, the concerns of the two texts are different. While

Table 1. Date of release of some original songs remixed on OATT

OATT Remix	Original Song /Artiste/ Year Released
'Imagine' By Jonathan	Imagine (John Lennon), 1977
Drop It Like It's Hot by APC	Drop It Like It's Hot (Snoop Dog Feat. Pharell Williams), 2004
Shut And Fly Feat. DAM	Shut Up and Drive (Rihanna), 2007
Personally	Personally (P-Square), 2013
Happy - Ogas at The Top Version	Happy (Pharell Williams), 2013
Drunk in Power by G.E.J. and Dame Patience	Drunk in Love (Beyoncé Feat. Jay Z), 2013

Table 2. Lyrics of Ogas lyrics compared with the original

P-Square's Personally	OATT's Personally
[Verse 1] Personally I rock your body I promise you go home You won't tell your daddy I'll give it to you like you've never had it Swimming chin chin like speaking Chinese Ehnnawetin be this Baka boom boomnawetin I see Saga! And she no wan greee She talk say no wan leave *[Verse 2]* Personally, professionally I see what you're doing intentionally Girl, me want it physically So give it to me give it to me radically Emotionally, psychologically You're turning me on biologically Sexually, dramatically And she talk say she no wan leave Eh – I no go lie The things weydey my mind When I see you dancing, girl you got me high And if you want to try, Gbege go dey tonight Cos I'm in the mood As long as you feeling the groove I go deal with you www.azlyrics.com/lyrics/psquare/personally.html	*[Verse 1]* Personally I tell you, Peshy You don't have to cry silly I tell you, baby I'll give it to them like they've never had it Send out the army to rescue the kids Ehnnawetin be this Boko boom boomnawetin I see Saga! Dey wan me to leave Tell them we cannot leave *[Verse 2]* Personally, professionally They wanna wreck me internationally I won't go there physically To give it to them give it to them radically Emotionally, psychologically They just wanna end me politically Ah-eh, dramatically Boko say they no wan leave Eh – I no go lie The things weydey my mind When I sleep, I dream about their dynamite And if they wanna try, I go show dem tonight Cos I'm in the mood Me and my crew Go deal with you (Author's transcription)
Drop It Like It's Hot by Snoop Dogg	**Drop It Like It's Hot by APC**
when the pimp is in the crib, ma Drop it like it's hot Drop it like it's hot Drop it like it's hot when the pigs try to get at ya Park it like it's hot Park it like it's hot Park it like it's hot and if a nigga get a attitude Pop it like it's hot Pop it like it's hot Pop it like it's hot I got the rolly on my arm and I'm pouring Chandon And I roll the best weed cause I got it going on www.azlyrics.com/lyrics/snoopdogg/dropitlikeitshot.html	If the cap dey tight you for head Drop it like it's hot Drop it like it's hot Drop it like it's hot If your post dey overwhelm you Drop it like it's hot Drop it like it's hot Drop it like it's hot If your peeps are showing attitude Drop it like it's hot Drop it like it's hot Drop it like it's hot It's clear you are definitely not the best man So make way for the General and the Jagaban[1] (Author's transcription

the persona in the P-Square duet claims to be a sexual virtuoso intent on personally giving a woman an exhilarating time, Mr. President is promising to personally give the Boko Harom terrorists a hard time.

Some popular songs are appropriated for electioneering, as in *Drop It Like It's Hot by APC*, shown above, in which the opposition APC advise the ruling PDP to hand over the reins of government.

While the opposition message comes across very clearly, the government party is mercilessly mocked. In *Shut and Fly feat. DAM* (Buni TV, 1 June, 2014), President Jonathan is portrayed as being under the control of Diezani Allison Madueke (DAM), and being her personal pilot. The remix of Rihanna's *Shut Up and Drive* contains a sexual sub-text, especially noticeable for those who know the original. The remix is of course a snide reference to the scandal following the discovery that the Minister for Petroleum Resources had a publicly-funded private jet for which infraction the President did not call her to account. Well, in this performance, DAM rubs it in:

Yeah, Commander in Chief of all Naija magnificent
When you have Goodluck, you fly first class.
Haters, go and die.
I don't give a damn.
(Shut And Fly Feat. DAM)

In the remix of Pharell Williams' '*Happy*', the singers: GEJ, DPJ, NOI, GMB and GSA, appear to be out of touch with reality: claiming to be winning the war against Boko Haram (and electoral victory in Lagos) when the facts suggest otherwise. The first hook is sung by NOI, thumping a copy of *Reforming the Unreformable*, with GEJ interlacing it with his own commentary.

Because I'm happy

NOI: *Happy 'cause I know that I can rule and rule and rule*
(**GEJ:***Tell them again, my sister*)
Because I'm happy
NOI: *Happy 'cause I know that Boko Haram can't stop me too*
(**GEJ:***They still think this is Bayelsa*)
Because I'm happy
NOI: *Happy 'cause I know that APC can kiss my shoes*
(**GEJ:***Shoes are no longer a problem*)
Because I'm happy
NOI: *Happy 'cause I know the PDP will win Lagos too*
(**GEJ:***It's GEJ, y'all*) Happy - Ogas At The Top version

Even the late General SaniAbacha is happy "… because a poisoned apple could not put me away/ And I'm happy I made all the money before they tried to take me down /And I'm happy to show Nigeria that my power forever lives/ And finally I'm happy to come back down if you are ready for the military rule". His propositions are ludicrous. For a dead man to claim that he has everlasting power is obviously false. It would seem that just as Abacha is in denial, so are the rest of the "happy" team.

Apart from what the audience hears in the music videos, one can also see the puppets dance. As earlier mentioned, the sight of presidents, past and serving, and ministers also creates a humorous effect.

Verbal Humor Strategies

Verbal humor is generated by the speech of the characters. One strategy used is the highlighting of phonological errors. Apart from humor which arises from the overall presentation of the OATT videos, there are ethnic jokes, for example, contrasting GMB's pronunciation with ABT's in *APC Wedding Planners* and *Drop It Like It's Hot by APC*. For GMB, /p/ and /f/ are in free distribution, and the phoneme /p/ is pronounced as /f/ in such words as 'impeachment', 'part' and 'I-phones', as may be found in the speech of many speakers of English of Northern Nigerian extraction. ABT speaks with a cadence that is typical of the Yoruba of South-western Nigeria, especially those who are not well-educated. Both speakers code-switch, ABT using such phrases as *bẹ̀ẹ̀ni* (Yes) *kílódé* (what is it) and nítoríỌlọ́'un (for God's sake), and GMB says *wallahi* (By God!) and *Kobahakaba?* (Isn't it?), lending authenticity to their speech.Maku's speech is full of insincere hyperbole as earlier noted in *Nigerian Ministry of Information Boko Haram and the Abuja jailbreak*, in which video he also promises not to "leave any turn unstoned".

Memorable phrases used by GMB in *Anything for the Vote* include: "I usually go clubbing and I drink *fa,* imagine. Please, Barman,... two shots of *fura de nono*" (asking for a milkshake in a nightclub); of a selfie taken with young nightclubbers, "I'll photo-shop a smile into it later" and to give his night clubbing companions a slogan to remember: "harsh tag young at heart, harsh tag youths want change, harshest of the tags why shouldn't I run again. Harsh tag Haribubu". Some one-liners include ABT to Amanpour: "No, no, no. I am not a Nigerian leader. I am a Nigerian opposition leader. There is a difference" and "I should have emerged poorer? Is that the point of politics?" (*Tinubu Washington DC Interview*). In *The Madueke Massage*, DAM says, "If they get rid of me like Stella, I'll still have a few friends to see me through... Give me diamonds any day. Diamonds are girls' best friends".

Some of these humorous phrases can be explained by Raskin's script opposition framework. When ABT says, "No, no, no. I am not a Nigerian leader", the hearer might initially take the statement as a lie. But when he explains, "I am a Nigerian opposition leader. There is a difference", the hearer re-interprets "Nigerian leader" to mean a leader in power in Nigeria rather a respected member of society. Similarly, in *Anything for the Vote,* GMB "I usually go clubbing and I drink, *fa*, imagine" also sounds like another lie. The real General Buhari is reputed to be abstemious. And when he calls the barman to ask for a drink, the expectation is that the 'holy man' will sacrifice his virtues to fit in. that is, until we hear what his choice drink is: *fura de nono.* The hearer is forced to change his interpretation of the complement of the verb "drink" from "alcohol' to "any beverage"

ABT and GMB, the leading opposition figures frequently converse at cross purposes, and this generates a lot of humor. While GMB mounts a moral high horse with regard to the state wedding of the President's adopted daughter, ABT was all for using the presidential strategy to enrich the opposition war chest. GMB is especially irritated by the golden I-phones distributed to guests at the wedding.

GMB: *Sha, me I won't get involved in gold I-phones o. You know I am a simple man, wallahi.*
ABT: *General, you... you... know, don't worry., I have told you. Let me handle the gold I-phones.*
...
(ABT's phone rings
GMB: *Ah-ah Bola, answer your phone now; answer.*
ABT: *Ah, General, not to worry, it's not important.*
GMB: *You never know, It can be very, very important for the election.*
ABT: *Awon ta lo tun n pe mi? Awonwo lo tunfekoba mi bayi? Awon ta l'eleyibayi?* [2]
GMB: *Ah –ah, jesubwa? Ha!*
ABT: *General, what is it?*
GMB: *Wayo Allah na* [3] *? So you mean you have the I-phone, you are using the golden I-phone?* (*APC Wedding Planners*, 02.52 – 03:06; 03:35 – 04.03)

The speaking at cross purposes is nowhere more evident than on an interview program on OATT TV, in the video, *End of the Affair* (Buni TV, 11 May, 2014). As the interview progressed, it was clear that they did not have much in common.

Presenter: *My first question is this: what exactly do the two of you have in common?*
GMB: *First of all, we are going to sweep corruption…*
ABT: Beeni, under the carpet
GMB: *And away from Nigeria*
ABT: *Yes, that is what I mean to say.*
Presenter: *Because it does not seem that anything in common except that you are both…*
ABT: *Er- er no need to throw the air mud around carelessly*
GMB: *The parochial sentiments are what our party is fighting for.*
ABT: *Beeni, Fighting against*
GMB: *Yoowa* (*The End of the Affair*, 00:21 – 00:47)

The contrariety of their outlooks on life became more pronounced as the interview progressed.

Presenter: *So, in essence, you are promising to take on corrupt public officials?*
GMB: *Anybody who has at all who has stolen public money, in or out of office, I will attack and deal with them; those who have built private media empires with public funds, and massive hotels and established airlines with our money. Ah, my anti-corruption policies will not continental or regental or like those of the past nations. I will put the nation first, and break the backs of those looters, Wallahi, inshaallah* [4]
Presenter: *What is your reaction to that, Chief*
ABT: *Er…my record is not been impeachable. I have fought tyrants and dictators to a standstill. I have risked my life to make sure that no military man who has seized power through the barrel of a gun can ever return and pretend to be a born-again democrat, beeni.*
Presenter: *Are you in any way referring to people like the General?*
ABT: *Er…I did not mention any names, beeni. I did not men*tion any name *beeni, kini? ki lo de*?[5] (*The End of the Affair*, 03:21 – 04:27)

The two political comrades are engaged in verbal jousting, as each presents his stand on corruption, democracy and ethnicity. The interview ends unceremoniously, with the two comrades-in arms turning on each other and each beating his erstwhile partner with brooms, the symbol of their 'sweep Nigeria clean' slogan.

This section on verbal humor has identified two main strategies: highlighting of phonological errors and conversational failure. Interlocutors who seem to be cooperating in conversation are made to speak at cross purposes, leading

Physical Violence in Physical Comedy

Physical comedy, dependent on clownish exploitation of movement is not used in OATT. There are no pratfalls, no walking into walls or making funny faces. However, a video where a significant part of the humor relies on physicality is *GEJ Meets Boko* (Buni TV, 22 June, 2014). Mr. President has a private meeting with Shekau, leader of the Boko Haram insurgents. After some chit-chat, Mr. President convinces Shekau to take a lie detector test and the first question was on the motivation for the atrocities committed by the insurgents. The machine slaps Shekau when he claims the group is merely fighting western education. The President is deeply gratified by this, but when he begins to hold forth about how he loves the Nigerian people, the impartial machine slaps him hard, twice. The President's exclamations, "Tamuno!" and "Jeeesus!!!" were the high points of the joke, as well as the slap that disproved the President's story of his not having shoes as a school boy. Other slap-generating lies were that Boko Haram's war was ordained by allah himself, and that the group had some special explosives. As noted, the slapping is certainly funny, but the conversation also carries the burden of the humor.in End of the Affair, there is some physical violence as GMB and ABT beat each other when they had a disagreement.

Inter-Textuality

An important humor device used in OATT is inter-textuality, involving the strategies of allusion and verbal parody. It features in visual comedy via the incorporation of recognizable features into the look of the puppets. Its use in musical parody has already been discussed. The focus of this section is on words, memorable phrases and grammatical constructions with established humor credentials, so that repeating them in other circumstances tends to generate laughter. To this we may add non-verbal signs that convey particular meanings to members of a humor community: gestures, items of clothing and similar artifacts. This kind of humor-generating texts/signs might be more accessible to people living in the environment where the original humor-generating texts were produced. The original texts might not have been intended as jokes; the examples here were produced in serious, highly valued public social intercourse, one at a television interview; the other a meeting that was covered by the press. However, since the audience reacted with laughter, the texts became humor-generating texts.

The first text is from an interview of the NSCDC PRO on the March 12, 2013 edition of 'Sunrise Daily' a breakfast program on Channels Television. Videos of the interview were uploaded on YouTube and short clips shared to friends. The text of a segment relevant to this discussion is transcribed below, with words/gestures that came to be frequently reproduced highlighted in bold.

PRO: *(pointing with his left fore-finger) The one we are going to make use of is going ... is going to be made known by (* ***raising up his right fore-finger*** *)* ***my oga at the top*** *, yes. I can't...* ***I can't announce one now and my oga says it's another one*** (NSCDC PRO on Channels TV, 00:20 – 00:33).

The second is a 2.40 video clip of the Mrs Patience Jonathan's emotional outburst on the some developments on abduction of over 200 girls from Chibok. The video was uploaded on YouTube by Channels Television and was widely circulated on cellphones. An excerpt is transcribed below and important portions highlighted.

DPJ: *Do you come with two teachers?*
Voice: *No, Ma.*
DPJ: *You were not informed too? Heh? Continue. No problem. God will see us. There is god. There is god in everything we are doing.* ***Those bloods that are sharing in Bornu will answer.*** *(3s) What*

of two teachers, WAEC, two teach...er..two ...teachers, what of two teachers ***that can tell us that dem conducted that exam? Do you come with any (2s) Preespal?***

Voice: *Ma?*

DPJ: *No too?* ***You only you waka come*** *, okay. ... Now the First Lady is calling, come, I want to help you, come to find yer... bless... yer child, yer missing child, will you keep quiet?*

Voices: *No*

DPJ: ***Chai, chai, dere is god o. Dere is god o. The bloods we are sharing, dere is god o. Dere is god o, dere is god o, dere is god o.*** *(Voice cracking) Dere is god o, dere is god o.* (Clip of Mrs. Jonathan Weeping on TV, 01:03-2.25)

Below, phrases from the two texts incorporated into OATT videos are highlighted in bold. The first 56 seconds of the *Personally* video, before the music, was a private scene in the bedroom of the first family: DPJ crying and GEJ comforting her.

DPJ: *(In between sobs) Imagine!* ***Na only one person waka come.***

GEJ: *I heard.*

DPJ: *Only one person waka come.*

GEJ: *Calm down, it's all right. Calm down, it's not that serious.*

DPJ: *I don dey tell dis people...*

GEJ: *Chai*

DPJ: *All dis things weyunadey do us.* **Dere is god o.** (*Personally*,00:29 – 00: 56)

This brief introduction incorporates the real life incident of Mrs. Jonathan breaking down and crying on TV. Similarly, GEJ says "*chai*" in this family incident and several other occasions while Marilyn Ogar says, with right forefinger raised, at 2.48 – 2.55 in *Nigerian Ministry of Information Boko Haram and the Abuja jailbreak* "I'll have to seek authorization to disclose this operational detail. I do not want to **say one number and my oga at the top say another**". In *'Imagine' by Jonathan*, GEJ imagines "there's no Boko, no **bloods to share**".

There are several references to Peshy's language proficiency or lack thereof. Though OATT provides no actual data on any grammatical blunders, the internet provides a lot of anecdotal evidence. The Channels clip of 'Mrs. Jonathan Weeping on TV' attests sentences that suggest that there may be some truth in the allegations. Such sentences include "Those bloods that are sharing in Bornu will answer... what of two teachers that can tell us that dem conducted that exam? Do you come with any? Preespal? ... The bloods we are sharing, dere is god o." It is to such blunders that the following allude: GEJ singing "Imagine my wife Peshy/A Professor of English (well, **dere is God**)" (in *'Imagine' by Jonathan*, 1.00-1.12) and Peshy herself singing "Jump along if you know there's beauty in my English too" (*Happy - Ogas At The Topversion*, 1.33-1.38).

Of artefacts, we can name four. Gold i-phones, which were allegedly shared among guests at the wedding of President Jonathan's adopted daughter, are used by some of the characters. Mr. President and his wife hold such phones in *Anywhere but Chibok, Drunk in Power* and *Happy;* and ABT was caught with one in *APC Wedding Planners* and Peace won one on the quiz show, *Who wants to be the President's Daughter. Reforming the Unreformable* is visible in *The Diplomatic Chat, Finance Minister Speaks, Happy* and *GEJ meets Boko.* Brooms identify opposition figures GMB and ABT. In locations in Nigeria, they hold brooms made of natural fibers (sometimes to beat one another with), but when

ABT appeared on Amanpour Live, (*Tinubu Washington DC Interview*, Buni TV, 30 March, 2014), he held a brush with a head of bristles attached to a long thin handle, as would be used in the United States.

The humor creation strategies in the OATT videos have been used to realize three types of humor: visual, verbal and physical. Caricature through the use of puppets was the significant strategy in visual humor, though elements of posture, gesture and costuming strategy denigration were also important. In musical parody, humor was generated by the changed new lyrics as well as the performanceof the musicians: their costumes as well as their dance. Phonological errors and conversational patterning were exploited in verbal humor in verbal humor, and, to a very limited extent, physical comedy was presented in one video; two antagonists being slapped in turn by a machine. Inter-textualitywas found to be an overarching device, used in visual as well as verbal humor types, and even serving to lend credence to fictional recreation of historical events.

The subject of puppet videos is the basis of the audience's political engagement with them. Many of the videos in the OATT series are intended to show that the life or actions of a political figure or group are at variance with their society's expectation or perception. Season One focuses on the Boko Haram insurgency and in episodes like *Nigerian Ministry of Information Boko Haram and the Abuja jailbreak, Anywhere but Chibok, BringBackOurGirlsForTheSakeOf2015, and National Security Priority,* the Nigerian Government was shown as being incapable of decisive action. Time and again, the incompetence of leaders as depicted by their puppet doubles was highlighted. Even in *Personally* where he vows to deal with Boko Haram personally, the bravado remains unconvincing, especially when the third verse contains phrases like "AsoRockatically/ Grammar, and your dictionary".

The forthcoming 2015 general elections were also foregrounded as the one overriding interest of the incumbent administration. In fact, GEJ says in *Happy*, "All I care about is 2015". The major contenders are allowed to speak for themselves (or rather their puppet doubles are made to speak for them. If GMB comes out as not being sophisticated, at least he is allowed to present himself as Mr. Clean. However, GEJ is shown as the dreaming, singing, drinking, dancing and lying president, obsessed with his re-election bid. It would therefore seem that the OATT videos do have a political agenda. The intro to *Anything for the Vote* has 61 seconds of unmistakable opposition political propaganda asking for change,[6] just before fading in to the promised savior who turns out to be GMB.

Not a Joking Matter: Audience Reception and Engagement with OATT

Having considered how humor is created in OATT videos, this section now briefly highlights some of the responses of the humor community to them. If, as Benton (1988) suggests, the political joke will change nothing…its impact is as fleeting as the laughter it produces, it is of interest to see whether humor consumers feel that the OATT videos change anything. Aside from the issue of impact, audience response is also significant, first for identifying what the humor community finds humorous, and then for providing insight into the functions that the videos are perceived as serving.

For some joke consumers, it was not enough to watch the videos; they also commented on them online and interacted with other members of the online humor community. Conversations about OATT are classified into three on the basis of the functions allocated to OATT videos as described below.

Type 1 comments state whether the viewer liked a video or not. The majority of commenters delighted in the uproarious hilarity of the videos without actually indicating the cause of their mirth. Some others (here identified by initials) indicated the high or low points of a particular video they liked or disliked. Table 3 presents some examples.

Table 3. Examples of evaluative comments on OATT

Video	Comment
Personally	LMAO Who the hell did this…The hand snapping part tho (AT)
	grammar I'm your dictionary, lool (AA)
Anything for the Vote	'the hashest of the tags' haha (XC)
	Hahahaha, harshest of the tag 'Why shouldn't i run again (DY)
	2 shots of fura da nonolol (AK)
Drop It Like It's Hot	The best music yet of all, i like that you have localized the accent! GREAT JOB GUYS (W007)
	make more like recurrent expenditure, that was good, forget the songs (KM)
Finance Minister speaks	I just can't get over NOI's voice!! Best voice impersonation on your videos (PT)
Jonathan Undecided	@3:53"HAVE YOU SEEN THE LIGHT BLINK?" LOOL (AMO)
Drunk in Power	Well, the animation is not bad but more work on the lip sync. The lips syncs are very bad and annoying, especially GEJ lips (SA)

Some commenters generated new jokes from the videos. From EX: 'All this video you are doing with our president "There is God O". Him go soon deal with you personally. You funny jawe!' and AB: 'Who else noticed GEJ's personal cabinet for girls arranged in alphabetical order... Dat Nigga a pimp... Lol'. A few comments requested for certain humor commodities, asking for a particular character to be created or a song to be used. For commenters quoted above, the function of the humor videos does not seem to go beyond entertainment. They enjoy the videos, and may generate jokes from them. Conversely, they may dislike other videos because they did not satisfy a humor requirement.

Type 2 comments link the humor videos to contemporary socio-political realities. Perhaps because the viewers feel the videos mirror reality or may affect perception, a few viewers found some videos unsettling or disrespectful. *Drop It Like It's Hot*, AM wrote, "is quite disrespectful" while AA had unprintable expletives for the producers of *Drunk in Power* and "everyne …in nigeria" (sic) for their disrespect and childishness in mocking the President. Type 2 comments also show that some viewers feel the video have a salutary effect on the political situation. An example: '…Until all our leaders… respect us as citizens n give us all our rights to electricity, good roads…, I want more of dis video to roll out…' (EA) Some comments are reflective, the videos having provided food for thought. The following string is from comments on *Drunk in Power*:

jonz April 15, 2014 at 10:17 pm

This guy deserves no attention, not even for humorous purposes.
200 kidnapped today
70-100 dead yesterday
tomorrow…..
my bad…..continue joking.

Kilipot April 15, 2014 at 11:04 pm

He sincerely deserve no attention whatsoever.

ao April 16, 2014 at 12:43 am

You are correct. There is nothing to laugh about.

God'schosen April 16, 2014 at 1:27 am

Just what I thot…I'm very sure our president ain't smiling right now…some folks be like, i kuku don't live in the north…smh

Fatimah April 16, 2014 at 11:38 am

Unfortunately, our President is laughing shamelessly. From birthday party to rallies, Jona no send us o. This is really a funny skit but yesterday when I saw his rally pictures etc, I just felt helpless. How can a President be so unfeeling? How could he shrug off all that happened and just go on merrymaking with no concrete, visible action to at least assuage our fears if anything. Right now, I am this close to being officially tired of this country.

One commenter (SYE) read an ethnic dimension into the videos and posted similar comments in response to *#BringBackourGirlsForTheSakeOf2015, Drunk in Power* and *Who Wants to Be the President's Daughter.* I quote SYE at some length below.

…What I have noticed is that it is mostly Yoruba people are the ones that make most of these videos. This is because they hate the president because they see them as a threat to their political pursuits and he is a South South and his wife is Igbo. This is the first time ndi Igbo have come back to power after our unjust treatment in the Biafra War And with reference to the "there is God oh" video: Honestly, she is just simply communicating to the common woman in that video who are most probably illiterate…Just because she wasn't speaking in a western accent people are going bananas. Nigerians don't use their brain. I can't wait for oil money to reduce substantially so we can reconstruct Nigeria into the confederate system and go back to FARMING…

Commenters in this second group see the videos as facilitating political discourse by highlighting issues requiring attention, defining problems and calling leaders to account or persecuting the President, depending on their political conviction.

Type 3 comments request for a modification of function for the jokes. For this group, it is not just enough for the videos to be funny and highlight problems; they should also proffer solutions or be a medium for civic education. In other words, some humor consumers believe that humor videos can be a driver of change. On *Happy,* SA writes: 'I really enjoy the various videos but now i have to ask is there a purpose for them? Cus you talk about the issues facing Nigeria but can this be a medium to a solution? Think about it!!' while AB, on *Personally*suggests, 'but please can you advance your handwork by educating children with SOME moral Education'.

Types 2 and 3 comments suggest that some see political humor as more than a joking matter, but as a site for political engagement. They feel it has the capacity to change how people think and what people do.

CONCLUSION

This chapter has explored the humor creation strategies in OATT. These are the use of puppet doubles of national leaders, re-interpretation of contemporary happenings, musical parody, phonological and conversational have been used to create visual, verbal humor and physical humor. Though the stated function of the series was to exploit the Nigerian political climate for humor, the chapter shows that the audience has appropriated the videos for their own ends based on the functions they felt they could serve.

That access to the videos is through private viewing, whether online or downloaded and shared with friends on their devices, is significant. Though Nigeria has been under democratic governance since 1999, 'the socio-political environment influences press freedom; with adverse implications for education, information, entertainment and surveillance' (Akinwale 2010: 47). Therefore, though some viewers would like the videos on domestic TV, it is quite doubtful whether television stations in Nigeria will air OATT videos anytime soon. How much of a limitation is this?

In 2011 while their show was broadcast only online, the promoters of Puppet Nation considered their reach limited because only 10% of the South Africa had access to the Internet. In Nigeria, Internet penetration rose from 0.06% (78,749 users) in 2000 to 24% (38,329,867) in 2010. 2014 estimates put the number of internet users at 67,101,452 or 37.59% of the population (www.internetlivestats,com/internet-user/nigeria/), with internet user being defined as 'an individual who can access the internet at home, via any device type or connection'. Other users may use shared computing at work or at cyber cafés. Online access and offline sharing may therefore provide enough access to these joke videos, and considering the potential danger to producers and broadcasters, may present be the only safe access to a humor commodity which many viewers consider to be more than a joking matter.

It may be of research interest to determine how much impact humor videos may have on voter education and electoral behavior, especially in light of the outcome of the 2015 general elections in Nigeria.

REFERENCES

Akinwale, A. A. (2010). Repression of press freedom in Nigerian democratic dispensations. *Africa Development. Afrique et Developpement*, *35*(2), 47–70.

Apte, M. (1985). *Humor and laughter: an anthropological approach*. Ithaca, NY: Cornell University Press.

Attardo, S., & Raskin, V. (1991). Script theory revis(it)ed: Joke similarity and joke representation model. Humor: International Journal of Humor Research, 4(3-4), 293-347.

Berger, A. A. (n.d.). *Signs of Humor: On the Structure of Laughter*. Retrieved from www.culturestudies.pbworks.com/f/Semiotics+of+Humor+AAB.doc

Brillenburg, K. (2011). Spitting Image and pre-televisual political satire: Graphics and puppets to screens. *Image and Narrative*, *12*(3), 113–136.

Carstyn, R., & Noh, E. (1995).A truth-functional account of metalinguistic negation with evidence from Korean. *UCL Working Papers in Linguistics, 7*, 1–26

Chandler, D., & Munday, R. (2011). *A dictionary of media and communication*. Oxford. doi:10.1093/acref/9780199568758.001.0001

Crines, A. S. (2014). Rhetoric and Satire – Spitting Image And Political Comedy. In *Rhetoric in British politics and society*. Basingstoke, UK: Palgrave Macmillan.

Drop it like it's hot. (n.d.). Available atwww.azlyrics.com/lyrics/snoopdogg/dropitlikeitshot.html

Fairclough, N. (2006) semiosis, ideology and mediation. In Mediating ideology in text and image: ten critical studies (pp.19-36). Amsterdam: John Benjamins.

Iedema, R. (2003). Multimodality, resemiotization: Extending the analysis of discourse asmulti-semiotic practice. *Visual Communication*, *2*(1), 29–57. doi:10.1177/1470357203002001751

Krikmann, A. (2006). *Contemporary Linguistic Theories of Humour*. Retrieved 20 January 2015 from http://www.folklore.ee/folklore/vol33/kriku.pdf

Nash, W. (1985). *The language of humour*. Harlow: Longman.

Nigeria Internet Users. (n.d.). Retrieved 23 May 2015 from www.internetlivestats.com/internet-user/nigeria/

Norrick, N. R. (1989). Intertextuality in humor. *Humor: International Journal of Humor Research*, *2*(2), 117–139. doi:10.1515/humr.1989.2.2.117

Ochwada, H. (2012). From Kamiirithu to XYZ-Show: Between cultural "flaws" and democratic change in independent Kenya. In A. Agwuele A (Ed.), Development, modernism and modernity in Africa (pp. 196-211). New York: Routledge.

Ogas at the Top. (n.d.). Available at http://buni.tv/shows/ogas-at-the-top/; http://www.youtube.com/ogasatthetop

O'Halloran, K. L. (2011). Multimodal discourse analysis. In K. Hyland & B. Paltridge (Eds.), *Companiontodiscourse analysis* (pp. 120–137). London, New York: Continuum.

Personally. (n.d.). Available at www.azlyrics.com/lyrics/psquare/personally.html

Puppets take on politicians in South Africa. (n.d.). Retrieved 15 May, 2015 from https://informationactivism.org/en/puppets-take-politicians-south-africa-za-news

Raskin, V. (1985). *Semantic mechanisms of humor*. Dordrecht: Kluwer Academic Publishers.

Rogers, R. (2009). *TV puppet satire torments Kenyan elite*. Available at www.theguardian.com/world/2009/nov/22/xyz-kenya-tv-puppets-satire

Simpson, P. (2003). *On the discourse of satire: Towards a stylistic model of satirical humour*. Amsterdam: John Benjamins. doi:10.1075/lal.2

Veatch, T. (1998). A theory of humor. *Humor: International Journal of Humor Research*, *11*(2), 161–215. doi:10.1515/humr.1998.11.2.161

ADDITIONAL READING

Alexander, R. J. (1997). *Aspects of verbal humour in English.* Tubingen: Günter NarrVerlag.

Alves, J. (1997). The thin end of the wedge: Jokes and the political socialization of children. *Humor: International Journal of Humor Research, 10*(3), 301–331. doi:10.1515/humr.1997.10.3.301

Apte, M. L. (1985). *Humor and laughter: An anthropological approach.* Ithaca, NY: Cornell University Press.

Attardo, S. (1994). *Linguistic theories of humor.* Berlin, New York: Mouton de Gruyter.

Attardo, S. (1997). The semantic foundations of cognitive theories of humor. *Humor: International Journal of Humor Research, 10*(4), 395–420. doi:10.1515/humr.1997.10.4.395

Attardo, S. (2001). *Humorous texts: a semantic and pragmatic analysis* [Humor Research Monographs 6]. Berlin: Mouton de Gruyter. doi:10.1515/9783110887969

Attardo, S. (2011). The general theory of verbal humor, twenty years after. *Humor: International Journal of Humor Research, 24*(2), 123. doi:10.1515/HUMR.2011.007

Berger, A. A. (1999). *An anatomy of humor.* Edison, NJ: Transaction Publishers.

Bex, A. (1996). Parody, meaning and literary genre. *Journal of Literary Semantics, 25*(3), 225–244. doi:10.1515/jlse.1996.25.3.225

Carrell, A. (1993). Audience/community, situation, and language: A linguistic/rhetorical theory of verbal humor. Unpublished doctoral dissertation, Purdue University.

Carrell, A. (1997a). Humor communities. *Humor: International Journal of Humor Research, 10*(1), 11–24. doi:10.1515/humr.1997.10.1.11

Carrell, A. (1997b). Joke competence and humor competence. *Humor: International Journal of Humor Research, 10*(2), 173–185. doi:10.1515/humr.1997.10.2.173

Carstyn, R. (1981). Irony and parody and the use-mention distinction. *Nottingham Linguistic Circular, 10*(1), 24–35.

Chapman, A. J., & Foot, H. C. (Eds.). (1977). *It's a funny thing, humour.* Oxford: Pergamon Press.

Consalvo, C. (1989). Humor in management: No laughing matter. *Humor: International Journal of Humor Research, 2*(3), 285–297. doi:10.1515/humr.1989.2.3.285

Gross, E. G. (1987). The form and function of humor in the Liège puppet theater. In *D. Sherzer, & J. Sherzer, Humor and comedy in puppetry: Celebration in popular culture* (pp. 106–126). Bowling Green: Bowling Green University Popular Press.

Epskamp, K. P. (1993). The political exploitation of the clown figure in traditional and popular theater in Asia. *Humor: International Journal of Humor Research, 6*(3), 271–284. doi:10.1515/humr.1993.6.3.271

Gray, J. Jones, Jeffrey, P., & Thompson, E. (2009).Satire TV.Politics and Comedy in the Post-Network Era. New York: New York University Press.

Gruner, C. (1997). *The game of humor: a comprehensive theory of why we laugh*. New Brunswick, NJ: Transaction Publishers.

Lippitt, J. (1994). Humour and incongruity.*Cogito8* (2) 147-153.

Mbangwana, P. (1993). Some instances of linguistic and literary resource in certain humorous Camerooni-anisms. *Humor: International Journal of Humor Research, 6*(2), 195–222. doi:10.1515/humr.1993.6.2.195

McGhee, P. E., & Goldstein, J. (Eds.). (1983). *Handbook of humor research*. New York, NY: Springer-Verlag.

Meinhof, U., & Smith, J. (2000).Spitting Image: TV genre and intertextuality. In U. Meinhof& J. Smith (Eds.), Intertextuality and the media: From genre to everyday life (43-60). Manchester: Manchester University Press.

Meyer, J. C. (2000). Humor as a double-edged sword: Four functions of humor in communication. *Communication Theory, 10*(3), 310–331. doi:10.1111/j.1468-2885.2000.tb00194.x

Morreall, J. (1983). *Taking laughter seriously*. Albany, NY: State University of New York Press.

Morreall, J. (1987). Funny ha-ha, funny strange, and other reactions to incongruity. In J. Morreall (Ed.), *The philosophy of laughter and humor* (pp. 188–207). Albany, NY: State University of New York Press.

Morreall, J. (Ed.). (1987). *The philosophy of laughter and humor*. Albany, NY: State University of New York Press.

Morreall, J. (1989). Enjoying incongruity. *Humor: International Journal of Humor Research, 2*(1), 1–18. doi:10.1515/humr.1989.2.1.1

Nilsen, D. L. F. (1993). *Humor scholarship: A research bibliography*. Westport, CT: Greenwood.

Olubode-Sawe, F. O. (2015). Aspects of error analysis in some Nigerian jokes. In B. Ekanjume-Ilongo, A. Hala-Hala, & L. Dunton (Eds.), *Recent developments in linguistics and literature: A florilegium for FrancinaMoloi* (pp. 182–201). New York: David Publishing.

Oring, E. (2003). *Engaging humor*. Urbana, IL: University of Illinois Press.

Palmer, J. (1994). *Taking humour seriously*. London: Routledge. doi:10.4324/9780203380154

Speaight, G. (1990). The history of the English puppet theatre (3rded.). Carbondale and Edwardsville: Southern Illinois University Press

Sherzer, D., & Sherzer, J. (Eds.). (1987a). *Humor and comedy in puppetry: Celebration in popular culture*. Bowling Green: Bowling Green University Popular Press.

Sherzer, D., & Sherzer, J. (1987b). Verbal humor in the puppet theater. In D. Sherzer & J. Sherzer (Eds.), *Humor and comedy in puppetry: Celebration in popular culture* (pp. 47–65). Bowling Green: Bowling Green University Popular Press.

Sosa-Abella, M., & Reyes, M. R. (2014). Political humor in comic strips: A comparative analysis between Oriental and Occidental approaches. *International Journal of Cultural Studies, 18*(2), 243–259. doi:10.1177/1367877914520894

Thai, A. (2014, February 6). Political satire: Beyond the humor. The Harvard Crimson. Available at www.thecrimsom.com

Tsakona, V., & Popa, D. E. (2011). *Studies in political humour: In between political critique and political entertainment.* Amsterdam: John Benjamins. doi:10.1075/dapsac.46

Zimbardo, Z. (2014). Cultural politics of humor in (de)normalizing Islamic stereotypes.*Islamophobia Studies Journal 2* (1).59-81.

KEYWORDS AND DEFINITIONS

Humor Commodity: A text created for the purpose of generating humor and distributed through personal interaction, public performance, publishing or communication technologies. Examples are jokes, comic cartoons, parodies, TV sitcoms, stand-up comedy, comic videos, clown shows and spoof journalism (print and electronic).

Humor Community: A group of people who have access to a particular humour commodity, whether that group is restricted to a physical location or geographically dispersed but interacting and maintaining group identity through publishing and communication technologies.

Humor Credential: Funniness, the acceptance by a humor community that a text is a valuable humor commodity.

Parody (noun): A piece of writing or music that deliberately copies another work of the same genre to achieve a particular effect.

Verbal Humor: humor that focuses on words: wisecracks, double entendre, jokes, pun, verbal allusion, etc.

Visual Humor: humor that focuses on spectacle or what can be seen rather than words.

ENDNOTES

1 A traditional chieftaincy title of the real-life Asiwaju Bola Tinubu.

2 Who are those calling me? Who are those trying to get me into trouble again? Who on earth are these?

3 Oh, my God!

4 I swear. By God's grace.

5 Yes. What? What is it?

6 Fellow Nigerians, 2015 is around the corner. Elections are here again. Politicians will be up to their same old tricks, literally fighting for your votes. Who are these politicians? What do they want? What do they have to offer?The future belongs to the youth who range from age zero to 40 years old or is 50 or 60. It doesn't matter. What matters is that we have listened to the yearnings of the youth. They are tired of politicians. What they want is change, not just in their pocket but in government. Which is why we present to you the youth-friendly answer, the solution to Nigeria's problems, our very own revolutionary!(00.08-01.08, *Anything for the Vote)*

Chapter 4
Speaking in the Free Marketplace of Ideas:
The Stylistics of Humour in "Blogversations"

Bimbola Idowu-Faith
Bowen University, Nigeria

ABSTRACT

This chapter applies the mechanisms of conversational humour to interactional processes in blogs. With blogs giving room for uninhibited personal and interactional publishing which create virtual communities through written contributions that can best be regarded as conversations or "blogversations," blogs are veritable sites for the investigation of conversational humour. Drawing its data from Linda Ikeji's Blog, the chapter investigates how the blog author creates humorous keys to induce humorous turns from her readers and how the readers respond to and sustain the humour. The chapter also examines how readers undermine the seriousness of posts lacking keyed humour by generating humour against author's expectation. As humour occurs from both author's and readers' ends, it is established that conversational humour is a collaborative effort that strengthens social bonds and acts as a tool for sustaining entertainment and for motivating blog users to visit, to speak, to hear, and to be heard again.

INTRODUCTION

The weblog, that is "blog", is a participatory media genre within the broader field of computer-mediated communication (CMC) which emerged in 1997 and has ever since been growing as a virtual medium for the production of diary-like texts on diverse topics of interest. The growth of the blog is especially "driven by the twin motors of free, user-friendly blogging applications such as Bloggers and LiveJournal and the global media exposure of A-list bloggers" (Hookway, 2008, p. 94). Generally speaking, "blogs are web pages in which dated entries appear in reverse chronological order so that the reader views the most recently written entries first" (Page, 2014, p. 42). In terms of texture, blogs may be multimodal

DOI: 10.4018/978-1-5225-0338-5.ch004

Copyright © 2016, IGI Global. Copying or distributing in print or electronic forms without written permission of IGI Global is prohibited.

because different semiotic resources like writing, image, photograph, video, animation, and sound may be employed for textual composition. By this, blogs break down genre and media boundaries.

Though blogs are circulated in written forms, they are inherently speech as they are sometimes interpersonal, dialogues, loosely structured, concerned with the present, informal, narrative, event-oriented, contextualised, and concrete (Durant & Lambrou, 2009, p. 11). This thus explains why researchers continue to employ the tools of conversation and discourse analyses to the blogosphere and to other text-based virtual communities. The blog is not just a hybrid of both writing and speech; it exists within the democratic space in cyberspace. Wilson (2001) has significantly argued that cyberspace is a "liberatory" space which is both "equalising and non-discriminatory" in nature (par. 1). Thus, in cyberspace, "it does not matter whether you are a dog or a god in real life" (Oke, 2004, p. 16) because "the voice of the Other is not only accommodated, but it is also always aired and heard. [Such that]...the depressed, distressed, oppressed, repressed, and suppressed citizens of nations have no fear in 'walking' into the 'emancipatory' ambit of cyberspace for varied self-expressions … [which] give both Self and Other limitless and untrammelled opportunities for different forms of social experimentations" (Idowu-Faith, 2012, p. 4).

As a matter of fact, the democratic nature of cyberspace is greatly embedded in the invisibility of the persona in cyberspace. That users are invisible in cyberspace gives them the opportunity to express themselves without limits and to be creative in their use of language. Reasoning along this line of thought, Hookway (2008) says that "the anonymity of the online context … means bloggers may be relatively unselfconscious about what they write since they remain hidden from view" (p. 93). Following Carter's suggestion, North (2007) submits that "creativity is more likely to occur in familiar and informal contexts where there is less interpersonal risk, and for this reason, we might expect to find it in the informal written conversations that occur in online environments" (p. 538). Because the readers of Linda Ikeji's blog, the blog under investigation, are dispersed across different geographical locations within and outside Nigeria and rarely have course to meet face-to-face, it is not surprising that they exploit the blog as both a medium for publishing uninhibited personal and interpersonal texts and for producing conversational humours which are sometimes ingrained in conversational incivilities. Both readers' comments and readers' humour serve as the lifelines that sustain the existence of a blog. All these justify the blog medium as a veritable site for the investigation of spontaneous and naturally-occurring speech events.

BLOG AS CONVERSATION

Ever since the emergence of the Internet, scholars have been busy interpreting its implication from various theoretical and disciplinary perspectives. Silver (2000) however notes that most of such research has focused on the "'twin pillars of cybercultural studies': virtual communities and identities" (cited in Hookway, 2008, p. 91). As one significant cybercultural community, the blog has received remarkable attention from linguists who investigate the nature of language in computer-mediated discourses. For example, Jacobson (1996) investigated the pragmatics of naming in computer-mediated discourse; Herring (1994) examined intercultural aspects of politeness; Baym (1996) studied the management of disagreement; Herring (1999) considered interactional coherence; and O'Neill and Martin (2003) examined turn-taking.

One of the pertinent issues in the linguistic study of the blog medium is the extent to which discourse procedures in blogs as text-based interactions align with discourse procedures in speech or face-to-face interactions. Linguists are of the opinion that text-based interactions in blogs can best be described as conversations since the facilities for readers' comments in blogs is similar to second turns in face-to-face interactions. This is why Dynel (2011a) sees a conversation as "a verbal interaction, whether oral or written, between at least two interlocutors/conversationalists" (p. 218). Chovanec (2011) argues that though conversations characteristically relate to the spoken medium, text-based computer-mediated communication are conversational in that "textual contributions appear on screen in interlaced sequences that have a dialogic nature and can be analysed in terms of conversation analysis in a manner similar to speakers' turns" (p. 247). Emphasising the conversational nature of the blogosphere, Peters (2006) describes the current age of blogging as "the age of conversation" while Lovink (2008) avers that "through blogging, news is transformed from a lecture into a conversation. Blogs echo rumor and gossip, conversations in cafes and bars, on squares and corridors" (cited in Peterson 2011, p. 2). For Herring (2010), the fact that blog users regard their contributions as talks reveals that the users experience written conversations in almost the same way that they experience spoken conversation.

There is much prima facie implicit evidence that text-based CMC is conversation-like. In casual parlance, Internet users often refer to textual exchanges as conversations, using verbs such as 'talked,' 'said,' and 'heard' rather than 'typed,' 'wrote,' or 'read' to describe their CMC activities. Even published authors sometimes refer, unconsciously, it seems, to 'speakers' rather than online 'writers', 'talk' rather than 'typed exchanges', 'turns' rather than 'messages,' and so forth, when reporting on CMC. This linguistic usage attests to the fact that users experience CMC in fundamentally similar ways to spoken conversation, despite CMC being produced and received by written means (pp. 1-2)

In spite of the widely held view that text-based interactions are conversations, there are still objections to the equation of text-based interactions with natural face-to-face conversations. Natural conversation is not just spoken words; the speaker's emotion, which is largely conveyed via non-verbal means; the physical context; and background knowledge interplay with the spoken words to give the true sematic and pragmatic implications of the speech. However, all of these are lacking in text-based conversations. To compensate for this lack, blog users tend to employ informal language, acronyms, emoticons, intentional misspellings, vowel elongation, and other graphophonemic strategies. Peterson (2011) contends these strategies on the ground that the deployment of such performative conventions of conversation and non-standardized writing in blogs does not make blogs conversations neither does it make blogs more authentic or truthful (p. 15). On her part, Dynel (2011a) is of the view that the "text-based interactional markers" tend to be ambivalent because the use of a smiley, for instance "may mean that the speaker is not being serious or that he/she is smiling happily and subscribes to the propositional content conveyed" (p. 225). Whereas cases of ill-encoded and ill-decoded messages abound in face-to-face conversations, it does not imply that the speech interactions are not conversations. What speakers or hearers usually do is to cross-check whether the intended message is rightly decoded because "communication occurs when my expressions become your perception and your expressions become my perceptions simultaneously. This reversibility of consciousness and experience goes to the very heart of the recurring problem of communication in our lives" (Catt, 2010, cited in Peterson, 2011, p. 15).

Peterson (2011) also objects to the description of written interactions as conversation on the ground that conversations are normally directed at specific individuals from whom the speaker expects responses. Peterson argues that blog writers, in Scannell's terms, talk to absent audiences, and thereby write "for-anyone-as-someone" (p. 5) since blog posts have no specific addressor. He argues further that what blog writers do is to employ what Fairclough (1995) describes as "conversationalization" in order to attract and engage readers. In a blog like Linda Ikeji's Blog, for example, even though posts are not addressed to anyone in particular, the familial and communal feelings regular readers attach to the blog create a sense of duty in them such that they feel highly obliged to contribute their comments to posts any time they visit the blog.

The disruption of turn adjacency is another ground why some are against the parallel comparison of text-based computer-mediated conversations and spoken face-to-face conversations. Herring (1999) explains that disrupted turn adjacency in blogversations and other computer-mediated communication is caused by the fact that messages are posted in the order they are received rather than in regard of what the messages respond to. Herring (2011) however contends this argument by asserting that

From using conversational conventions of address, to chunking text to maintain a conversational pace, to 'quoting' to recreate conversational context, to modified turn-taking to optimize temporal resources, to use of private messaging as a 'back channel' in group discussion, to struggling to gain and maintain the conversational floor, and to expressing frustration when messages digress off-topic, there is much evidence to suggest that CMC users orient to conversational norms (p. 5).

In spite of the various objections that are raised in terms of whether written text of interactions in CMC can really be regarded as conversations, scholars continue to apply the tools of conversation and discourse analyses to such interactions on the ground that the written interactions manifest enough characteristics that qualify them as conversations, though in a context different from that of face-to-face speech interactions.

CONVERSATIONAL HUMOUR

Linguists have been paying significant attention to the subject of conversational humour as against (canned) and/or pre-packaged jokes in the recent time. Scholars have been concerned with the linguistic characteristics of conversational humour (Norrick 1993, 1994, 2003); the social functions of conversational humour in conversational interactions (Boxer & Cortés-Conde 1997, Hübler & Bell 2003, Dynel 2008, Chovanec 2011); and gender-related implications of conversational humour (Kotthoff, 2006), among other concerns.

Chovanec (2011) believes that conversational humour relates to "a range of devices that… aim to construct humorous effects in dialogic interaction, while being distinct from joke-telling" (p. 245). In her ground-breaking work where she classifies the different types of conversational humour that may occur in conversational interactions, Dynel (2009) defines conversational humour as "an umbrella for various verbal chunks created spontaneously or repeated verbatim for the sake of amusing the recipient, either directly contributing to the semantic content of the ongoing conversation or diverting its flow into a humorous mode/frame/key, in which speakers need not genuinely mean what their humorous verbalisations convey" (p. 1286). The crucial space that conversational humour occupies in verbal communication is revealed in a research conducted by Martin and Kuiper (1999), where 72% of situations eliciting laughter during social interactions arose from spontaneous conversational humours either in response to funny comments that people made or in response to amusing anecdotes they told about things that happened to them (Martin 2007, p. 12). With Dynel's (2011b) description of conversational humour as "humour relevantly interwoven into conversation" (p. 4), it becomes apparent that a central factor in any consideration of conversational humour is its spontaneous production in the course of the on-going verbal interaction which makes the humour to be "more context-dependent than joke-telling, and is therefore often not as funny when recounted afterwards ("You had to be there")" (Martin, 2007, p. 12). Holding the same position, Boxer and Cortés-Conde (1997) submit that "'being there' becomes a very important part of 'getting it'" (p. 277) in conversational humour. The implication is that conversational humour is tied to the situational context of the speech in which it occurs.

Conversational humour is equally considered to be important in maintaining collaboration and solidarity in a group. North (2007) argues that "conversational humour can be seen as a display of verbal dexterity in which the individual performance has to be choreographed to fit what others are doing in the group, thus helping to create and maintain group identity (p. 553). For Norrick (2003), conversational humour serves the complementary roles of aggression and rapport (p. 1342). Although humour in conversation may seem to be aggressive, such aggression is not face-threatening but is geared towards maintaining solidary among the members of the on-going conversational interaction (Dynel, 2008, p.241). Apart from maintaining group solidarity, conversational humour also "makes a person's presence in a conversation more strongly felt than other sorts of contributions" (Tannen 1984, cited in Norrick, 2003, p. 1342).

Conversational humour has been typified variously by scholars. While Norrick (2003) identifies the basic forms of conversational humour to be jokes, anecdotes, wordplay and irony, Chovanec (2011) classifies retorts, teases, banter, and putdowns as the types of conversational humour, whereas Dynel (2009) submits that the various types of conversational humour include lexemes, phrasemes, witticism, stylistic figures (e.g. similes, metaphors, hyperbole, paradox, and irony), puns, allusions incorporating distortions and quotations, register clash, retorts, teasing, banter, putdowns, self-denigrating humour, and anecdotes. These various classification nonetheless, Dynel (2011b) avers that teasing is the epitome of conversational humour (p. 4). Another point to be made about these classes of conversational humour is that they are not mutually exclusive as they sometimes overlap and sometimes combine for humorous effects in conversations.

BLOGVERSATIONAL HUMOUR AND HUMOROUS KEYING

Humorous keying relates to situations where speakers signal their humorous intentions "by using adequate nonverbal cues residing in body language, facial expressions or intonation, before, while or after producing a humorous unit, or by uttering introductory utterances, such as "Have you heard the one?", whereby he/she enters a humorous frame and signals that the hearer should follow" (Dynel, 2011a, p. 224). Kotthoff (2007) also notes that "conversational humor often works with contextualization procedures such as code switching, social stylistics, features of oral art, repetition, marked wording, prosody, interjections, laughter, mimicry, etc. that create a humorous keying" (p. 264). These contextualization procedures are however not available to interactants in the context of computer-mediated conversations such as blogversations. Just as speakers in CMC create different means to compensate for the lack non-verbal means that will cue the emotional aspect of their messages, they also employ different strategies that provide humorous keys for their humour. In lieu of non-verbal humorous keys, CMC speakers sometimes engage "the combination of emphasizing with capital letters, blurring words together without spaces, using exclamation points, and adding a canned textual laugh set the tone for the hypnotic humor" (Hübler & Bell, 2003, p. 280). Other means for keying humour in computer-mediated conversation include the engagement of abbreviations (such as lol, lmao, rotfl); written equivalents of linguistic cues (such haha, hehe, waoh); and other stylised writing (such as combining asterisk* and hash# with words).

LINDA IKEJI'S BLOG AND THE LIB COMMUNITY

The study draws its data from Linda Ikeji's Blog (henceforth LIB). Since the authority of a blog and its bloggers does not lie in how credible the blog contents are but in terms of the number of reader's comments (Page, 2014, p. 43), LIB is purposively selected as the data source for the study on the ground that it has a very large and active readership. LIB was started on Blogger by Linda Ikeji, an ex-beauty model, in December 2010. Linda's achievements since she started the blog have made her to be considered as one of the most successful internet entrepreneur in Nigeria and as the first billionaire blogger in Nigeria (see http://www.wealthresult.com/2015/01/linda-ikeji.html). These achievements point to the fact that her blog is widely visited and read. The topical issues the blog is concerned with, as indicated on the blog's homepage, are "News, Events, Entertainment, Lifestyle, Fashion, Beauty, Inspiration and yes…Gossip! *Wink*" (http://lindaikeji.blogspot.com). These topical issues indicate, in Rozie's term, the "serio-ludic" nature of the blog (cited in North, 2007, p. 539), which closely interweaves both work and play.

The peculiarity of the blog explains why many young Nigerian readers have made the blog a rendezvous for socializing, relaxing and sharing humour and celebrity gist, among other things. The popularity of the blog among Nigerian youth is attested to by Alexa.com's ranking of the blog in March 2015 as the 10th in Nigeria and the first in terms of content website. For this reason, LIB readers consider themselves members of a community where both the presence and absence of a member are always taken note of. This sense of communality greatly contributes to how they jointly create and participate in the playful attitudes that engender conversational humour in the blog. On her part, Linda makes effort to build and create the sense of belongingness in her readers as she takes time to celebrate them and to share their posts on the blog. Equally, she ensures the continued loyalty of her readers and attracts new commenters with her "LIB Monday Giveaway Programme" where readers who comment at a specific time on the last Monday of the month are awarded between ₦20,000 and ₦200,000 each. All these promote and build LIB as an in-group among the readers.

In a March 7, 2015 post titled "Wait, there are more people on LIB than Twitter Nigeria? Yay!" where she announced the Alexa.com rating of the blog, the communal spirit among LIB readers is evident in both the blogger's post and the readers' comments. Out of the 374 comments the post generated, five randomly selected comments are presented below.

Post: *Dancing shoki and Azonto! And of course,* ***I have only you lovely, dedicated LIB readers to thank.*** *I just checked my Alexa.com ranking today and I'm back to No.10, higher than Nigerian Twitter and still the highest ranking Nigerian content website. So proud! Thank You, LIB readers. Love you guys so much! #Basking! (my emphasis)*

1. **Olumide David:** *Issokay Linda... we like coming here too.*
2. **Anonymous:** *Don't mention Linda...we here to always exhaust our MB cos of u darling...do great n be great...*

3. **RareSpecie Z:** *Linda, what do u expect. I troll over 60 sites daily but only comment on urs which goes on to show how Species that are even Rare appreciate U. U r a hardworker GIRL!!!! Dude jst praying that ish won't affect ur Health. Luv u Bae.*
4. **ado ali:** *You deserve a higher position joor! Slowly but surely you will get 'there' babe. Your blog is so addictive. No day is complete without LIB. Even when on sedentary mode there's no boredom for me. And there is no shortage of laughter from the comments generated from your posts. A case in point was days back when paparazzi cornered NorthWest and she was sort of frowning at them. The comments that followed nearly killed me with laughter. Somebody was even asking who she help.* ***Your blog also makes me feel like I belong to an extended family - everybody is like a brother or sister.*** *By the way where is AbokiDaWarriBoy? Hope you did not kidnap him Linda. Congrats (my emphasis)*
5. **Baconyx Chris:** *Congratulations Linda! Without any gainsaying, you deserve it. This blog is indeed an awesome one. A stress reliever. Cheers!!!*

While announcing Alexa.com's rating of the blog to the community, she promoted readers' sense of belongingness as she took time to thank the readers for their loyalty to the blog which she believes was responsible for the rating. In response, Olumide David (1) spoke for the readers and indicated that they liked visiting the blog; an anonymous commenter (2) also replied using the plural pronoun "we" to suggest that s/he was speaking on behalf of other readers; RareSpecie Z (3) further projected the sense of belongingness s/he enjoyed on the blog by saying even though s/he usually visited about other 60 sites daily, s/he usually only contributed her/his comments to posts on the blog. RareSpecies Z further demonstrated the bonds s/he had with the blogger as s/he prayed that the blogger's health would not be affected by the hard work she was doing on the blog. Ado ali (4) expressed the essence of the blog in his life and indicated that his day would not be complete without visiting the blog. His comment further illustrated the familial essence he attached to the blog when he said "Your blog also makes me feel like I belong to an extended family – everybody is like a brother or sister." He even went further to ask about the whereabouts of AbokiDaWarriBoy, a consistent commenter, whose comments he, possibly, had not encountered for some time. Indeed, all the five commenters demonstrate that the blog is, for them, a space of socialization, conviviality, play and humour.

The familial and communal relationship exhibited by LIB users provides enough room for joint humour and any other form of play that is possible in interactional activities. Serfarty's (2004) submission that "the personal and candid nature of online diaries combined with their open-endedness… gives them their addictive and captivating quality" (cited in Hookway, 2008, 94) clearly explains the attachment of LIB readers to the blog. North (2007) argues that since "the hierarchy of everyday life is set aside as participants, identified only by nickname, create new interrelationships through a playful and often ribald discourse" (p. 539), CMC communities parallel Bakhtin's carnival which is "a pageant without footlights and without a division into performers and spectators … everyone is an active participant, everyone communes in the carnival act" to the extent that "Identities are masked, the social hierarchy is suspended, and speech norms are relaxed, leading to the playfully ambivalent use of profanity and abusive language" (p. 538). Thus, LIB is a carnivalesque which aptly provides the context for every form of conversational humour that can be generated among a group. Humour among the blog members is thus a tool for sustaining entertainment in the blog and a central factor that motivates the blog users to visit, to speak, to hear, and to be heard again.

As argued earlier, the anonymity of a blog reader largely contributes to the nature of the reader's linguistic creativity and unselfconscious expression. Thus, as LIB readers are invisible and fear no interpersonal risks in their conversations, they manifest obvious conversational incivilities that are interrelated with the different conversational humour observable in the blog. That is, conversational humour is bred in the blog, on many occasions, from the way users hide behind the freedom of speech, the invisibility of the persona in cyberspace, and the fear of no interpersonal risk to perpetuate hatred, malice, word wars, war words, name-callings and inappropriate address terms, ethnic and racial bias, political intolerance, rumour, taboo expressions, linguistic pornography, among others. Describing the way that the anonymity of the user in the blogosphere can be exploited, RoyA1, a reader of Permablog (cited in Durant & Lambrou, 2009, p. 134) submits thus:

It is like football fans who hurl vicious abuse at players during games, sometimes from a distance of a few yards, yet who would never behave like that if they met the player in the street. They feel protected by their anonymity as part of a crowd. In the same way, people commenting on blogs hide behind anonymity. They should behave as if they were talking face-to-face.

Although readers manifest interactional incivilities on the blog, such incivilities are by no means negative but are germane to the construction of conversational humour and the strengthening of social and interactional bonds in the blog in just the same way that banters are employed to show solidarity among members of the same social group in face-to-face interactions. Chovanec (2012), anchoring on Benwell's (2001) argument that "humour and language play are crucial in strengthening the bonds of identity within such groups" and on Norrick's (2003) conclusion that "aggression and rapport are two complementary functions of conversational humour" (p. 1342), concludes that "while humour may be based on mild forms of aggression, it simultaneously serves the purpose of bonding and enhancing group cohesion" (p. 141).

METHODOLOGY

Taking the blogosphere to be a space of naturally-occurring conversations, the objective of this study is to identify how the blogger creates humorous keys that cue humour in her posts and to examine how readers respond to such humours. These will equally necessitate the classification and description of the different types of conversational humour noticeable in the data, using Dynel's (2009) model. To fulfil its obligation, eight posts are purposively selected and subjected to a functional content analysis method which entails the description (identifying recurrent items), the explanation (adducing reasons for the use of the item), and the interpretation (deducing implications of the use of the items) (cf. Malmkjaer & Carter, 2002: 510) of the selected data.

The analysis of the selected data is carried out against the backdrop of the concept of context, that is, "the environment in which a text comes to life" (Halliday, 1978, p. 109). The rationale for this is the fact that the notion of context is highly crucial to the interpretation and analysis of conversational humour since Martin (2007) submits that "spontaneous conversational humor is more context-dependent than joke-telling, and is therefore often not as funny when recounted afterwards ("You had to be there")" (p. 12).

ANALYSIS

Establishing and Responding to Humorous Keys

Humorous keying refers to how speakers frame their speech to indicate that they are being "playful" rather than being "serious" (Chovanec, 2012, p. 143). Norrick (2003) argues that once a humorous frame has been introduced, all kinds of humour become acceptable (p. 1346). The idea of introducing humorous keying in a speech is therefore to identify that the speech is to be taken as an intended humour produced for the hearer's enjoyment and possible contribution. In LIB, the author employs questions, abbreviations, emoticons, and stylised writing, among others. The obligation in this subsection is to investigate the various strategies that the blog author employs in signalling humorous keys in the blog posts and the various ways that readers, as blogversational partners of the author, respond to the keyed humours.

Question as a Humorous Key

One significant way by which the author establishes humorous key is through the employment of question. In such situations, commenters, rather than take the questions as demanding answers from them, see such questions as humours which they appropriately respond to with laughter and various forms of humour. In datum 1 presented below, the author engages questions as humorous keys.

Datum 1

Title: *Guys, if she had the personality of an angel but with skin like this, would you still hit?*

Body: *Be sincere...she's got a great personality but some cheap cream messed up her skin, would you still take her home? Get naked with her? Let these hands touch you? Let these legs rob on you? Lol...*

Multimodal Co-Text: *Immediately after the post title is the picture of the hands and legs of a lady whose attempt at bleaching her skin from a dark one into a lighter one had gone awry.*

Note: The blog posts and comments analysed contain spelling mistakes and other unstandardized uses of language which are all preserved in the paper for the sake of authenticity.

In the post represented in datum 1, the author employs a question in the title of the post to establish a humorous frame. With the picture that comes immediately after the title, it becomes obvious that the pragmatic implication of the title of the post is not a question with the intention of eliciting a candid answer. Rather, the question is employed to pragmatically cue an intended humorous effect that will generate other forms of humour from readers. Subsequently, in the body of the post, the author engages four different questions to emphasise that she actually intends the post to be taken with a humorous effect. She complements the keyed humour in the questions with "lol" (laughing out loud) as a humour signalling lexeme.

Readers understand the intended humour of the author and therefore respond to the post in humorous ways. Six of the 341 different comments to the post are presented below.

1. **Tobiloba Akinyemi:** *Hey! Dapada*
2. **Richie:** *Blood of god!!! *runs with both hands and legs**

3. **Isaiah Ichoku:** *Hit what??? Drum??? If yes sef how are we not sure d drum surface will be the same...*
4. **Amaka eze:** *Jeez!!!!!! Linda!!!!! I di wicked to put this out to the guys..lolzzz*
5. **fatai temidayo:** *Cylinder, you are so funny. Would you yourself take this kind of demon in the making person home as a friend let alone a girlfriend not to talk of a wife*
6. **Anonymous:** *Hehehehe Hahahahah!!! Hello NoO!!! If she like mke she get personality like jesus!!*

Having appropriately bought into the intended humour of the author, commenter 1 exclaims and thereafter switches code from the usual English employed on the forum to Yoruba. It is necessary to note that "dapada" ("back to sender"), is a colloquial and humorous way of responding to negative conversational humour among Yoruba youth. Commenter 2, rather than employ the exclamatory phrase "Blood of Jesus," creates an equivalent humorous phraseme – "Blood of god" – together with three exclamatory marks to project the humorous disgust s/he feels. S/he (Where the need arises to use the singular pronoun in reference to a commenter, gender pointers from commenters' names have been guide in the selection of the particular pronoun used. For anonymous commenters and other commenters whose names are not gender specific, gender balance is engaged with the use of both female/male gender pronouns) thereafter employs asterisks with another humorous phraseme "*runs with both hands and legs*" to humorously imply that his/her legs only will not be fast enough to ensure a quick escape from the misfortune of the author's suggested humour. Commenter 3, like the author, employs questions, but emphasises the degree of the humour in his response with the use of three question marks. He extends the boundary of the author's humour by intentionally misconstruing the intended meaning of the word "hit" in the author's post. As a result, the commenter is able to humorously extend the idea of hitting a drum to that of a sexual activity. Commenter 4 reacts to the author's humour using exclamations, multiple exclamatory marks, and abbreviation with multiple letters to express her enjoyment of the author's humour. The commenter also jocularly teases the author by saying she was being wicked to have asked her male readers such questions. The reaction of commenter 5 to the author's humour results in a pun which he consciously uses in renaming the author as "Cylinder," bringing out a homophonous relationship between the author's name, "Linda" and the last two syllables of the word "cylinder." He goes further to disapprove of any relationship with the lady in the picture whether as a casual friend, an intimate girlfriend, or a wedded wife. Lastly, commenter 6 engages multiple textualised canned laughter and multiple exclamation marks to indicate her/his reaction to the author's humour. The reader also switches to Pidgin to convey her/his own humour that even if the lady in the picture possesses the personality of Jesus, it would still not be enough ground to consider her. In all the six comments, the commenters understand the intended humour of the author. As a result, instead of taking the questions as demanding answers, they take the questions as humour and respond to the humour appropriately.

Datum 2

Title: *What is wrong with this photo?*
Body: *Y'all see what I'm seeing? Lol. Who do we blame for this now?*
Multimodal Co-text: *The screenshot of a televised programme showing the Nigerian First Lady wrongly captioned as "President of Nigeria."*
Comments

1. **AbokiDaWartiBoy**: *President of Nigeria...rotfl*
2. **imade love**: *Lwkmd!!! President ko! Chairman of Nigeria ni*
3. **Anonymous**: *Lolllllllllllllllllll. Lindodo u no go kill me*
4. **Omoye Zenki Moye Brown**: *hahahahaaaahahahaaa.....President of Nigeria.......lolzzzz*

In datum 2, the author also employs questions to cue a humorous frame in the incongruity between the picture of the First Lady and the wrong caption used for her by the television station. As with datum 1, commenters take the questions in the post as keyed humour. Four of the 185 comments to the post presented below establish that the readers of this particular post take the post as humour which they respond to by (1) using abbreviations as lexemes which signal laughter (rotfl – rolling on the floor laughing; Lwkmd – laugh wan kill me die (Pidgin, indicating the intensity of the laughter the post generates); Lol – laughing out loud) (all commenters); (2) using ellipsis and multiple exclamation marks (commenters 1, 2, & 4); (3) using multiple letters (commenters 3 & 4); (4) textualising multiple canned laughter (commenter 4); and (5) mixing codes (commenter 2), switching code (commenter 3), and employing a jocular nickname for the author (commenter 4).

Establishing Humorous Key with Emoticon and Stylised Writing

LIB author also usually employs emoticons and stylised writing in keying humour in her posts. As the cases are with the posts in data 1 and 2, readers read the use of a smiley and stylised use of a hash as an invitation to participate in the humour cued by the author.

Datum 3

Title: *They say this is a job application letter from Ibadan...:-)*
Body: *It's not me that said it o. A LIB reader said it's a job application letter for fuel attendant position... that they received somewhere in Ibadan. #runsaway...*
Multimodal Co-text: *The picture of an almost illegible handwritten letter with several grammatical and spelling errors.*

This particular post is ingrained in the way people from certain tribes or regions of the nation are used as the butt of a humour. In view of the fact that Ibadan, in comparison with other Nigerian cities, is considered rustic and ancient, the city has consistently been the butt of humours especially in situations where low intelligence quotient and uncivilised behaviour/attitude form the subject of the humour. It is in view of the fact that the humour in the post pragmatically threatens the face of the average Ibadan indigene/inhabitant that the author denies being responsible for the post and that she attaches a hash tag to the post. As expected, many of the commenters enjoyed the humorous effect of the humour. Five of the comments to the post are presented below.

1. **Celine Oma**: *Hahaha! Linda keep running o. Cos if dem catch u, lol! Ibadan peeps so ain't smiling. Oya let d blasting begin*
2. **Eze Ify**: *Nooooo,come back...Hahahahhhaha!!! Yeye linda*

3. **omo ibadan**: *Linda mind ur self o, e be like sey one omo ibadan don break ur heart b4, no let me change am for u o.......*
4. **Linda Fashion Blog**: *Ibadan ppl go beat you one day Linda. LMAO*
5. **Adebola Adenola**: *Lwkm.....rotfl....wtf is dis bu hahahahahahaha.....ibadan kini so?*

Just as readers' reacted to the post presented in datum 2, commenters to the post in datum 3 also express their understanding of the humour in the post with laughter-signalling abbreviations; multiple punctuation marks, multiple letters, and Pidgin English. The commenters also extend the thread of the humour by creating humorous effects in their turns. Commenter 1, for example, replies to the author's hash tag by encouraging her to keep running away (from the possible grip of the Ibadan people) while commenter 2 asks her to come back. In anticipation of the abuses and putdowns that the face-threatening humour will generate from other commenters, commenter 1 jocularly declares the stage open for such abusive comments: "Oya let d blasting begin." Commenter 3 who describes her/himself as an Ibadan indigene/inhabitant humorously asks whether having been jilted by an Ibadan indigene at some point in the past is responsible for posting the face-threatening humour. "Linda Fashion Blog," that is, commenter 4, puts it to the author that she would one day be beaten up by the Ibadan people. Since the commenter views her/his comment as humour, s/he adds the abbreviation LMAO (laughing my a** out) with full capitalisation to emphasise that the comment should be interpreted as a play. In the fifth comment, the commenter engages the combination of three different laughter suggesting abbreviations and lexemes – Lwkm (laugh wan kill me); rotfl (rolling on the floor laughing); and wtf (what the f**k) together with reduplicated textualised canned laughter (hahahahahahaha) and a laughter intensifier (bu) to portray the extent to which s/he enjoyed the humour. In fact, the commenter will further extend the humour of the author by introducing humour into her/his turn with the teasing question – "Ibadan kini so" (how are you, Ibadan people?).

It is however significant to state that the face-threatening implication of the humour was not appreciated by all the readers as comments 6-12 show below. In this situation, readers resulted to putdowns and tease to react against the humour intended in the post. According to Dynel (2009), putdowns are "remarks which are truly abusive and disparaging, usually carrying no humour to be appreciated by the by the butt" (p. 1294). She explains further that putdowns are based on ridicule, mocking or sarcasm whose butt may be the addressee or another party regardless of whether they overhear the conversation or not (p. 1294). Whenever putdowns are employed, the genuine intention of the speaker is to denigrate the butt (Dynel, 2009, p. 1295).

6. **Bayo Olabiyi:** *Linda, stop insulting Ibadan people.Any body from anywhere can write this kind of letter.Ibadan people are amongst the most educated and enlightened in this country.*
7. **LIB FINEST MAN:** *It must be a job application by Abokidawarriboy*
8. **Anonymous:** *Linda, what's ur beef with Ibadan people?its annoying,as if ur people can write better than this..no news today abi? mtcheww.*
9. **Toronto Finest:** *Well said! In addition, he is far better than some hungry LIBERS that couldn't wait till the end of the month to get token from Linda.*
10. **Anonymous:** *I have to say my mind here Linda, you are encouraging tribalism on this forum. You keep dissing ibadan people or Edo people. Not nice at all. You have never seen anything wrong with your igbo people despite the lousy matter they conduct themselves around, an attribute you and Laura are exhibiting. Pls change. Post my comment*

11. **OGUNDIRAN OYINDAMOLA:** *Linda, I think u v issues wt ibadan pple or may b u lack undastd-ing abt d city, ibadan is nt as local n razz as u r painting it pls. Go visit d city mayb during easter n am so sure ur orientation abt d place wl change completely. Meanyl, ur igbotic pple worse pass*
12. **Anonymous:** *I don't understand why people find this funny. We should be ashamed at the qual-ity of education we getting from our government. At least this person is trying to get a job, unlike others who just decide to become criminals because the system gave them no choice.*

In his comments, commenter 6 directly addresses and instructs the blogger to stop insulting the sensibility of the Ibadan people on the ground that the ungrammatical letter should not be viewed as exclusive to the Ibadan people since the letter could have been written by anyone from any part of the nation. Against the assumption of the author that the majority of the Ibadan people are rustic, uncivilised and uneducated, he informs her that the Ibadan people are among the most educated and enlightened people in Nigeria. On her/his own part, also using a putdown, commenter 7, for no justifiable reason, identifies "Abokidawarriboy," a very popular reader and commenter in the blog, as the writer of the said application letter. Commenter 8 is equally annoyed with the post as s/he redirects the butt of the humour to the author's Igbo tribe while using a putdown to criticise the author for having nothing newsworthy to post. Commenter 9 defends the writer of the letter while directing a putdown at the readers of the blog who usually participate in the LIB Monday Giveaway Programme. Commenter 10 subtly employs a putdown to castigate the author by accusing the author of encouraging tribalism on the forum. S/he criticises the author further of having never seen anything wrong with people from her Igbo tribe who s/he says are lousy. S/he moves away from the tribal putdown to direct the putdown at both Linda and Laura (Linda's younger sister) as manifesting the said lousy nature of the Igbo people. Commenter 10 uses a putdown to criticise the author of lacking understanding about the Ibadan people while at the same time using a putdown against the Igbo people. Commenter 12 castigates everyone on the forum that finds the humour funny. S/he goes further to make both the Nigerian people and the Nigerian government as the butts of her/his putdown.

Keying with Stylistic Figures and Different Types of Conversational Humours

Dynel (2009) is of the opinion that stylistic figures such as simile, metaphor, irony, and sarcasm, amongst others can generate conversational humour (p. 1288). It is therefore not surprising that the blog author sometimes employs these stylistic figures and other conversational humours such as retorts and teasing to key humour into her posts.

Datum 4

Title: *Ronke Oshodi Oke thanks her fans for liking her pics on instagram*
Body: *All these prayer on top liking photos? Lol*
Multimodal Co-text: *The supposed Instagram picture of the actress as well as a screenshot of the text of the said long prayer.*

Datum 5

Title: *Calvin Klein now saying they never said Lupita's dress was worth $150k...lol*
Body: *When it hit town that Lupita's Oscars dress was worth a whooping $150k because of the handmade Akoya pearls on it, the dress designer, Calvin Klein didn't come out to debunk it o but now that one thief has removed the bra from their shoulders....hehe...they are now saying they never said the dress was worth that much or that the pearls were real. They are blaming Lupita's publicist for that misinformation...lol.*

In data 4 and 5, the author engages tease and sarcasm to key humour into the posts. Although the author uses both question and an abbreviation suggestive of laughter in datum 4, the consideration of the question which forms the body of the post vis-à-vis the actress' picture and the screenshot of her long prayer text imply that the major humorous key in the post is a tease. In datum 5, although the author uses some of the humorous keys analysed earlier, the author's most successful humorous key in the post is sarcasm. In his discussion of sarcasm, Partington (2006) relied on Webster's definition of the term as "ridicule or mockery...used harshly, often crudely and contemptuously, for destructive purposes" (p. 212). For Norrick (2003), sarcasm may range from "apparently harmless forms geared to mutual revelation to those forms clearly aggressive in attacking the personal characteristics and errors of others" (p. 1345). It is thus obvious that the objective of the author is to contemptuously ridicule and mock Calvin Klein, the designer of the controversial dress, who did not deny the claim that the dress was worth $150,000 because of supposed handmade Akiya pearls used in making the dress until the dress was stolen and thereafter returned by the thief who reveals that the dress was made of fake pearls. The bitter gibe and taunt (Partington 2003, P. 212) in the sarcastic humour about the designer's claim is facilitated by the fact that had the dress not be stolen and returned by the thief because of her/his disappointment with the fake pearls used in making the dress, the designer would have exploited the rave about the expensive worth of the dress in exploiting celebrities who may desire to acquire a similar dress but are ignorant of dress' true worth.

Humours in Serious Frames

As discussed in the previous subsection, commenters demonstrate that they understand and enjoy the humours the author keys into her posts. In some other situations, the author employs no humorous key in an effort to indicate that such a particular post is a serious one and with no humorous intention. In spite of such serious frames, LIB readers still find means of injecting humour into such serious frames. On many occasions, LIB readers employ tease and putdowns to play down the seriousness of the posts. Data 6 and 7 are examples of serious posts that readers inject humours into.

Datum 6

Title: *Laura Ikeji releases hot new photos as she turns a year older today*
Body: *My beautiful younger sister Laura Ikeji is a year older today March 15th and released these photos to celebrate her special day. Happy birthday baby sis. Love you forever!*

Multimodal Co-text: *Several pictures of Laura are attached to the post. In many of the pictures which she takes while walking around in a fenced apartment and on the street, she poses with mobile phones, luxurious cars, and travel packs.*

The author considers the post represented in datum 6 as a serious frame in that she informs the LIB community about her sister's birthday. Ordinarily, she expects that readers will appreciate her sister and wish her a happy birthday. While many of the commenters complemented Laura on her beauty and the pictures and wished her a happy birthday, some others see the post as an avenue to tease her and put her down. Some of the comments are illustrated below.

1. **wilheminna moses**: *Dia for be big problem ifto say laura manage fine.....aww hbd laura but ur sooo ugly! Just saying d truth, ur teeth na dracular. Choi!*
2. **Bonita Bislam**: *Haha enough pix to last for a century.Happy birthday to her. May her days be bright as always*
3. **MARGARET THATCHER**: *Pls. Lindodo. No spoiil ma ssundy wit dis ur miss ugly. SiSi guess ha teeth pass 32 oooooo, nawa ooooo*
4. **Anonymous**: *Would be surprised if there was no black gate in the background of any of the pics*

Both commenters 1 and 3 engage putdowns in making uncomplimentary references to Laura's physical appearance and teeth in spite of the fact that the author expects them to felicitate with the celebrant on her birthday. It may be argued that the invisibility of the commenters which put them at no interpersonal risk facilitates the humorous, though uncomplimentary, remarks made about the author's sister. The type of conversational humour observable in comments 2 and 4 is teasing. Teasing is a form of conversational humour with the element of criticism directed at a person with a view of effecting correction in the person (Partington, 2006, p. 144; Boxer & Cortés-Conde, 1997, p. 279).

Datum 7

Title: *ONYX Godwin releases new photos for the holidays*
Body: *LIB reader ONYX Godwin lovely in new photos released to celebrate the holidays*
Multimodal Co-text: *Seven pictures of ONYX Godwin.*

Datum 7 centres on one of the regular, popular and vocal readers of LIB. The author thus handles the post with a serious frame, while expecting only complements from other readers. However, the post generated 1327 comments, the majority of which are humorous reactions to the post. The central factors providing butts of humour for the readers are the feminine features and poses of the reader and his extremely slim figure. Ten comments are randomly selected for analysis.

1. **fikky babe:** *Thanks for comic relief. Had a laugh. Long boring day*
2. **okorie olekanma:** *Amma sit back and watch the comments roll in.*
3. **mel20:** *NAwa oo.linda uno get news again abi, who's this aboki ur boring us with.*
4. **Anonymous:** *My goodness! Is this guy anorexic? Looks kinda sick and starved. God help him*
5. **igwe Adaobi:** *Not hating but he looks like a broom. So thin.*

6. **Ozioma Nicole:** *Hiv patient. Always yabbing ppl. C how u look like okporoko.*
7. **Anonymous:** **holds laff* lemme just pretend like i didnt just see this...his got guts sha #GutsOverFear*
8. **Uduak Etim:** *What??? This girl is something else..and please don't tell me she's a boy!*
9. **tochukwu okoli:** *Ah! Linda! Ure very wicked. U know what ur doin. Lol... Lmao.... Lwkmd... Chai.... smh*
10. **Florence Anegbe:** *I'm sure Linda had a good laugh @ these pictures.*

Commenter 1 while humorously reading the post as the author's deliberate intention to steer laughter, thanks the author for providing a comic relief for her boredom. In view of the humorous putdowns anticipated as the responses from other readers, commenter 2 says s/he will sit back to watch the putdowns roll in while commenter 7 believes that Onyx must have had got guts to have sent his pictures to be posted since he knows that such pictures usually generate negative comments from other readers. Commenters 4, 5, and 6 make the slim figure of Onyx the butt of their humour. Commenter 4 humorously asked whether he is anorexic, sick and starved; commenter 5 compares him with a broom and justifies the comparison by remarking that he is so thin; and commenter 6 metaphorically refers to Onyx as an HIV patient and as "okporoko" (stockfish). Ozioma Nicole (commenter 6) rationalises her/his putdown with the fact that Onyx is equally fond of making abusive remarks to posts in the blog. Commenters 9 and 10 directly make the blog author the object of their teases because they both believe that the serious frame the author uses for the post is only feigned. Thus, commenter 9 teases the author as being wicked while commenter 10 teasingly accuses the author of having laughed at the pictures before posting them.

Datum 8

Title: *Toyin Lawani shows off her custom made Swarovski Stones Bikini*
Body: *Stylist and business woman Toyin Lawani took to instagram to share a pic of her 'custom made Swarovski stones bikini'.*
Multimodal Co-text: *A picture of the stone bikini*

In datum 8, the blogger's purpose is to celebrate the achievement of Toyin Lawani, a Nigerian celebrity, in acquiring a custom made Swarovski stones bikini. Rather than see the post from the author's perspective, many of the commenters criticised the post using tease and putdowns.

1. **Anonymous:** *Linda are u this jobless?*
2. **Adaora ibezim:** *K ooooh, ope dis 1 wn't end up lyk lupita's dress*
3. **Anonymous:** *If them steal am now Na hin we go hear say na fake jewels*
4. **E - Rella:** *Is that a fish net?. Lol.*
5. **Chi:** *Show off*
6. **obiora:** *Fake celebs,Fake stones,Fake lives.*
7. **keeping it real:** *after now Swarovski will come and deny its not custom made.Robbers should go and steal this one to reveal the real identity referred/tease/sarcasm*
8. **Akinwunmi Olalekan:** *Waiting for Etcetera before I comment*

Commenter 1 makes the author the butt of a putdown by implying in her/his remarks that the author must have been jobless for making news out of the post. Commenters 2, 3 and 7 make reference to the Lupita Nyong'o's Calvin Klein designed Oscars dress earlier discussed as datum 5. Apart from the allusion made to a previous funny post, the three comments engage tease and sarcasm to contest the veracity of the information presented in the post. As Norrick (2003) explains, "allusion to a text funny in itself has an obvious double humorous potential, first in its actual contribution to the current text, and second by recalling the original text for listeners in the know" (p. 1348). Commenter 4's question is a tease with an element of putdown. By asking whether the custom made bikini is a fish net, the commenter teases Toyin Lawani by denying the recognition of the bikini. In comments 5 and 6, the commenters use putdowns while commenter 8, having known what would be the reaction of Etcetera, a prominent Nigerian celebrities' critic, declares that he would wait for Etcetera before making any comment.

Data 6, 7, and 8 show that serious frames in the posts are undermined by the readers who creatively inject humour into their blogversations. With readers injecting humour into their blogversational reactions to posts with serious frames, the spontaneity of humour in conversations is again stressed.

CONCLUSION

The preoccupation of this study has been the analysis of the instances of conversational humour in the blog medium. Taking Linda Ikeji's Blog as the object of analysis, it is discovered that the blog author employs questions, abbreviations, emoticons, and stylised writing, amongst others, as the humorous keys that invite readers' participation in her posts. In their turns, readers appropriately respond to the humour by showing indications that they enjoy the intended humour and by extending the humour threads with their own humours. The readers variously employ devices such as humorous lexemes, humorous phrasemes, deliberate misinterpretation of author's meaning for humorous purposes, textualised canned laughter, multiple punctuation marks, tease, and sarcasm, among others in their humorous turns. These situations strengthen the argument that conversational humour is a joint and collaborative effort that helps in strengthening social and interactional bonds among members of an in-group. This is the understanding of Dynel (2011a) when she remarks that "humorous communication is a joint activity (Clark, 1996) collaboratively rendered by interlocutors (Coates, 2007), which entails not necessarily verbal contributions, let alone of equal length, produced by both interlocutors but the hearer's relevant reaction to the humorous utterance made by one speaker" (p. 225).

It is however important to note that conversational humour does not only occur in situations where humorous keys are existent in a post. Situations abound where the serious frames of posts are undermined by the readers who find occasions to humorously respond to posts. Such responses indicate the immediacy of conversational humour in the context of a speech. Whether conversational stems from humorous keys or from serious frames, the analysis so far indicates that conversational humour strengthens social and interactional bonds among the LIB blog users and acts as a tool for sustaining entertainment in the blog and as a motivating factor that is central to the blog users' needs to visit, to speak, to hear, and to be heard again.

REFERENCES

Boxer, D., & Cortés-Conde, F. (1997). From bonding to biting: Conversational joking and identity display. *Journal of Pragmatics*, *27*(3), 275–294. doi:10.1016/S0378-2166(96)00031-8

Chovanec, J. (2009). Simulation of spoken interaction in written online media texts. *Brno Studies in English*, *35*(2), 109–128.

Chovanec, J. (2011). Humour in quasi-conversations: Constructing fun in online sports journalism. In M. Dynel (Ed.), The Pragmatics of Humour Across Discourse Domains (pp. 243-264). Amsterdam: John Benjamins Publishing Company.

Chovanec, J. (2012). Conversational humour and joint fantasizing in online journalism. In J. Chovanec & I. Ermida (Eds.), Language and Humour in the Media (pp. 139-161). Newcastle upon Tyne, UK: Cambridge Scholars Publishing.

Durant, A., & Lambrou, M. (2009). *Language and media*. London: Routledge.

Dynel, M. (2009). Beyond a joke: Types of conversational humour. *Language and Linguistics Compass*, *3*(5), 1284–1299. doi:10.1111/j.1749-818X.2009.00152.x

Dynel, M. (2011a.) Joker in the pack: Towards determining the status of humorous framing in conversations. In M. Dynel (Ed.), The Pragmatics of Humour Across Discourse Domains (pp. 217-241). Amsterdam: John Benjamins Publishing Company

Dynel, M. (2011b). Pragmatics and Linguistic Research into Humour. In M. Dynel (Ed.), The Pragmatics of Humour Across Discourse Domains (pp. 1-15). Amsterdam: John Benjamins Publishing Company.

Halliday, M. A. K. (1978). *Language as social semiotic: the social interpretation of language and meaning*. London: Edward Arnold.

Herring, S. C. (1999). Interactional coherence in CMC. *Journal of Computer-Mediated Communication*, *4*(4). doi:10.1111/j.1083-6101.1999.tb00106.x

Herring, S. C. (2010). Computer-mediated conversation: Introduction and overview. *Language@Internet*, *7*. Retrieved from http://www.languageatinternet.org/articles/2010/2801

Hookway, N. (2008). 'Entering the blogosphere': Some strategies for using blogs in social research. *Qualitative Research*, *8*(1), 91–113. doi:10.1177/1468794107085298

Hübler, M. T., & Bell, D. C. (2003). Computer-mediated humor and ethos: Exploring threads of constitutive laughter in online communities. *Computers and Composition*, *20*(3), 277–294. doi:10.1016/S8755-4615(03)00036-7

Idowu-Faith, B. O. (2012). *Hyperfictional Language in Michael Joyce's afternoon, a story and Megan Heyward's of day, of night.* (Unpublished doctoral dissertation). University of Ibadan, Ibadan, Nigeria.

Kotthoff, H. (2007). Oral genres of humor: On the dialectic of genre knowledge and creative authoring. *Pragmatics*, *17*(2), 263–296. doi:10.1075/prag.17.2.04kot

Linda Ikeji's Blog. (2013, May 13). *More photos from Linda Ikeji's Mania magazine shoot* [Blog Post]. Retrieved from http://lindaikeji.blogspot.com/2013/05/more-photos-from-linda-ikejis-mania.html

Linda Ikeji's Blog. (2015a, February 12). *ONYX Godwin releases new photos for the holidays* [Blog Post]. Retrieved from http://lindaikeji.blogspot.com/2015/04/onyx-godwin-releases-new-photos-for.html

Linda Ikeji's Blog. (2015b, February 28). *Calvin Klein now saying they never said Lupita's dress was worth $150k...lol* [Blog Post]. Retrieved from http://lindaikeji.blogspot.com/2015/02/calvin-klein-now-saying-they-never-said.html

Linda Ikeji's Blog. (2015c, February 28). *They say this is a job application letter from Ibadan...:-)* [Blog-Post]. Retrieved from http://lindaikeji.blogspot.com/2015/02/they-say-this-is-job-application-letter.html

Linda Ikeji's Blog. (2015d, February 28). *Toyin Lawani shows off her custom made Swarovski Stones Bikini* [BlogPost]. Retrieved from http://lindaikeji.blogspot.com/2015/02/toyin-lawani-shows-off-her-cutosm-made.html

Linda Ikeji's Blog. (2015e, February 4). *What is wrong with this photo?* [Blog Post]. Retrieved from http://lindaikeji.blogspot.com/2015/02/what-is-wrong-with-this-photo.html

Linda Ikeji's Blog. (2015f, January 12). *Ronke Oshodi Oke thanks her fans for liking her pics on instagram* [Blog Post]. Retrieved from http://lindaikeji.blogspot.com/2015/01/ronke-oshodi-oke-thanks-her-fans-for.html

Linda Ikeji's Blog. (2015g, January 6). *Guys, if she had the personality of an angel but with skin like this, would you still hit?* [Blog Post]. Retrieved from http://lindaikeji.blogspot.com/2015/01/guys-if-she-had-personality-of-angel.html

Linda Ikeji's Blog. (2015h, March 15). *Laura Ikeji releases hot new photos as she turns a year older today* [Blog Post]. Retrieved from http://lindaikeji.blogspot.com/2015/03/laura-ikeji-releases-hot-new-photos-as.html

Linda Ikeji's Blog. (2015i, March 7). *Wait, there are more people on LIB than Twitter Nigeria? Yay!* [Blog Post]. Retrieved from http://lindaikeji.blogspot.com/2015/03/wait-there-are-more-people-on-lib-than.html

Martin, R. (2007). *The Psychology of Humor: An Integrative Approach*. Academic Press.

Montgomery, M., Durant, A., Fabb, N., Furniss, T., & Mills, S. (2000). *Ways of reading: advanced reading skills for students of English literature* (2nd ed.). London: Routledge.

North, S. (2007). 'The voices, the voices': Creativity in Online Conversation. *Applied Linguistics*, *28*(4), 538–555. doi:10.1093/applin/amm042

Oke, B. O. (2004). *Language and creative freedom in cyberspace*. (Unpublished Masters Thesis). University of Ibadan, Ibadan, Nigeria.

Page, R. (2014). Blogs. In M-L. Ryan, L. Emerson, & B. J. Robertson (Eds.), The Johns Hopkins Guide to Digital Media. Baltimore, MD: Johns Hopkins University Press.

Partington, A. (2006). *The Linguistics of Laughter: A corpus-assisted study of layghter-talk*. New York: Routledge.

Peterson, E. E. (2011). How conversational are weblogs? *Language@Internet*, *8*. Retrieved from http://www.languageatinternet.org/articles/2011/Peterson

Schmidt, J. (2007). Blogging practices: An analytical framework. *Journal of Computer-Mediated Communication*, *12*(4), 1409–1427. doi:10.1111/j.1083-6101.2007.00379.x

Wilson, M. (2001). Community without others. *Mots Pluriels*, *18*. Retrieved from http://www.arts.uwa.edu.au/MotsPluriels/MP1801mw.html

KEY TERMS AND DEFINITIONS

Blog: See Weblog.

Blogversation: The written interaction among blog users that simulate conversation and is thus considered as conversation.

Computer-Mediated Communication (CMC): Any form of communication that is mediated with the use of the computer.

Conversational Humour: Humour that spontaneously occurs in the course of speech interactions. Conversational humour contrasts with (canned) jokes that are believed to be pre-packaged.

Humorous Keys: The strategies speakers employ to cue humour in their conversation.

Humorous Keying: The signalling by speakers that their speech has humorous intention and should therefore not be taken serious.

Participatory Media: Computer-mediated communication platforms that allow users to exchange information and contribute to an on-going communication process.

Serious Frame: This contrasts with humorous keying. It is the signal that a speech should be taken serious as no form of humour is intended.

Weblog (Blog): A diary-like website with dated entries that appear in reverse chronological format that allows readers to view the most current entries first.

Chapter 5
Communicative Content of Selected Visual Construction of Humour on Facebook:
A Visual Social Semiotic Analysis

Ibrahim Esan Olaosun
Obafemi Awolowo University, Nigeria

ABSTRACT

This paper socio-critically analyses some visual constructions of humour on Facebook. Based on 17 visual data, gathered through the method of extensive Internet Ethnography, the paper indicates that members of the Facebook networking site are informal misogelasts, who through the methods of digital cloning, image cropping and digital impersonation, generate or appropriate visual materials and post such to generate social/communicational humour. Using insights from Visual Social Semiotics proposed by Hodge and Kress (1988) and Critical Social Semiotics espoused by Caldas-Couthard, Carmen Rosa and Van Leeuwen Theo (2003), analyses reveal that constructed visual humour incorporates and interrogates such social phenomena as religion, education, morals, love, health and politics. The paper concludes that Facebook is not just a site for meeting new faces and interacting with them but also a medium for obtaining information on these social phenomena and how they are represented in the minds of individuals.

The views and content expressed in this chapter are those of the author but not necessarily of the publisher and may contain some explicit ideas and concepts.

INTRODUCTION

One of the things that make human beings human and which reflect in their social lives is the use of language to provoke laughter and generate entertainment. Humour, an aspect of the aesthetic functions

DOI: 10.4018/978-1-5225-0338-5.ch005

Copyright © 2016, IGI Global. Copying or distributing in print or electronic forms without written permission of IGI Global is prohibited.

or uses of language, is a testimony to its (language) extensive nature. It is a discourse practice through which human beings soak up numerous absurdities of life. It can be regarded as a literary discourse because it uses language creatively and because it, like literature, performs entertainment, satirical and didactic functions.

Beyond its amusing content, a humorous discourse appeals to reason and understanding, sharpens the intellect and serves in constructing micro and macro ideologies. Because of its intellectual powers and other discourse significance, humour discourse has enjoyed tremendous attention of scholars in the fields of Literary Studies, Philosophy, Psychology, Anthropology and Linguistics. From the classical era of such scholars as Plato, Aristotle, Quintilian and Hobbes to the modern era witnessing such scholars as Critchley, Herbert Marcuse (a critical Philosopher) Erich Fromm (a psychologist), Daniel Wickberg, Michael Billig and Alison Ross, to mention but few, humour is a significant object of academic research. Several scholars (e.g. Morreall, 1983; Raskin, 1984; Mulkay, 1988; Provine, 2000) have published full length books on humour. Several journal articles (e.g. those of Suls, 1972, Storey, 2003; Tisljar & Berczkei, 2005) have also been written on the subject. These studies have generally dealt with the cognitive processes involved in the generation of humour and the social functions of the discourse.

Though rejectionists of humour have considered it as foul discourse, scholars, particularly from these fields have taken it as a serious discourse and have theorized superabundantly about it in respect of its nature, arts, origin, effects and functions. Several theories, the most popular of which include Superiority Theories, Incongruity Theories and Victorian Relief Theory (see (Michael Billig, 2005) have been developed to elucidate these ideas.

Changes in our social and cultural lives have brought about new forms of humour which relate to and illuminate contemporary social, economic and political matters as well as generate debates around these matters. Therefore, my concern in this paper is not to theorize humours but to contribute to debates on how humours are produced and made to function on the internet space. Essentially, this paper aims to connect visual humours on *Facebook* to the broad essence of humour, which according to Alison Ross (2005), include "surprise, innovation and rule-breaking".

This paper is expected to open up debates on characteristics and functions of 'computer mediated humour', especially as it relates to or differs from scripted, broadcast and spoken humour on radio, television and in the literary medium. It will also point up the creative ingenuities of *facebook* community members, some of who could be as fun provoking as many recognized comedian writers and performers in the Nigeria entertainment industry.

CONTEXTUALIZATION

In this modern day of digital technology, nothing seems impossible to do, particularly on the internet space. One of the amazing possibilities that accompany this technology and which manifests in *Facebook* discourse, is 'visual grafting' or 'personality cloning' ; the concept which I am using to describe the situation in which new persons or objects are created through the process of hybridization, similar to that used in plant or crop sciences. For instance, the head of an individual can be placed on the body of another individual, resulting in the phenomenon of 'digital impersonation'. An incidence of visual grafting that occurred in Nigeria recently involved a state governor who was framed as a porn artist engaging in an explicitly sexual action with a female porn actress. But for the efforts of individuals who traced the sources of the graft items, the publication would have marred the reputation of the governor.

Similarly, there is a digital form of cartooning which involves appropriating the photo actions of persons to result in the phenomenon of discourse manipulation and extension similar to that in lexical semantics. Also, there is the practice of photo importation, wherein photo actions are imported from one discourse domain to perform in another, usually different, discourse domain. Using these strategies, the online humour artists invent narratives, which, though may relate to their subjective impressions about persons and events, are of serious social values and concerns. Such narratives touch on such themes as politics, religion, education and metropolitan matters.

Discourses, emanating from the digital practices highlighted above, are objects of the present paper. These discourses, as will be demonstrated later in the paper, are a form of entertainment discourse because by trivializing important matters, they provoke laughter or generate the pleasure of the psyche. It will also be demonstrated that they are significant pieces of social revolutionary communication.

AIM AND OBJECTIVES OF THE PAPER

The aim of this paper is to shed light on humorous visual narratives on *Facebook* as discourses of social significance. Precisely, the objectives of the paper are to: (i) examine the socio- critical values embedded in humorous visual narratives on *Facebook* and (ii) describe how the narratives generate affective and attitudinal meanings. The paper pursues these concerns by describing the humorous components of the narratives; identifying recurrent themes of the visual humour and, inspired by the words of Mulkay (1988) that "humour cannot stand apart from the world of seriousness," relating them to the Nigerian social and political context.

METHODOLOGY

The data for this study consists of 17 visual humorous materials, obtained from *Facebook* through the method of internet ethnography. This method involves continuous visit to the site over a period of two months to obtain ample data that can be integrated for the sort of narrative analysis favoured in this paper. The data is analysed, using the principles of visual semiotics theory - the theory, which studies and explains how meaning is formed through visual signs with insights from Critical Social Semiotics as espoused by Caldas-Couthard, Carmen Rosa and Van Leeuwen Theo (2003). The theory is considered fit for this study because, among other analytical tools it offers, it emphasizes that texts, particularly multimodal texts like the one in this study, should be seen as playing an important role in the production, reproduction and transformation of social practices that constitute the society in which we live. Using this framework, I discuss the data for the study in terms of how they communicate social meanings and sentiments in addition to their pleasure-giving contents or comical values.

1. Analysis

Like in satirical literature, several serious social issues are trivialized through humorous visual construction on *Facebook*. One of such issues, depicted in the visual construction below, is the widespread issue of religious commodification in many African nations, particularly in Nigeria. This is depicted in Figure 1.

Figure 1.

The phenomenon of religious entrepreneurship which is prevalent in Nigeria today is captured in the above visual discourse that depicts church owners (pastors, deacons, etc.) as people living in affluence (see the comfy cars associated with them) and their victim-members as people living in penury (see the church member above wearing a pair of self-made nylon slippers). This is a true narration of a society that seeks spiritual panaceas for socio-economic problems and individuals who run to so-called religious ministers for solutions to the difficulties of their lives. It is a social lesson that the church industry is exploitative as the owners of that industry capitalize on the needs of their members for personal economic advancement. The narration is a visual affirmation of the view that religion is a stupefying thing. At the primary level of signification, the visual images above signify that the church owners actually own different types of car while the ordinary church members cannot afford any but rather depend on their feet for mobility. At a deeper level of analysis however, the images are mere representations of the opposite lives lived by the rich and the poor. The church signification itself is not just a representamen of how pastors bamboozle and exploit their flocks but also of the various means (economic, spiritual, psychological, physical, etc.) by which some people exploit other people.

For some people however, rather than allow religion (or any of other means of exploitation) to be used to hoodwink them, they will rather use it to further deceive those that have already been taken in by the institution (religious institution). For such people, religion is the best alibi for covering up all their dishonest practices as the visual communication below signifies.

It is amusing (at the same time, astonishing) that a woman- an old woman (as suggested by the totally wrinkled neck, patches on the forehead and flat chest - of the visual actor in the cartoon above) can be so immersed in beer consumption (particularly in a society where women are generally perceived as symbols of modesty and moral ideal) as to lie to her caller that she is in the church while, as the background of the visual indicates, she is in a beer parlour. The characteristic manner in which she slants her mouth and angles her wrinkled neck as she tells the lie, generates the humour aspect of the narrative. Capitalizing on the idiocy of the recipient of the phone call in the visual above, the old woman can take her time to gulp down -to the last drop- the content of those bottle of beer waiting around her like waitresses around eaters at restaurants. The success of this lie is suggestive of how people get by in the Nigerian society using the cover of religion and pretending to be ascetic and holy.

Figure 2.

Notwithstanding the strong headedness- or rather consciousness- of few individuals (like the woman in the above visual) who refuse to be cajoled, church or rather religious industry will continue to grow as long as the sort of religious idiocy reproduced below in Figure 3 persists in our society.

The strategy of humour used in the visual communication above is surprise: it is amazing- somewhat incredible- that a man could allow his head to be turned into a candle stand, bearing the heat of candle flame and the burning sensation of melting wax. The strategy is apt in reproducing the crazy dispositions of some people to matters of spirituality and their readiness to oblige whatever directives that come from their spiritual godfathers. If the church-man (in the visual above) could have absorbed his life difficulties as strongly as he bears the pains of the burning candle on his shaved head, solutions to the difficulties would have come naturally. Ironically some of the victims of these religious charlatans (who constantly impress on members of their fold the need to give to God a portion of what God gives to them) are also victims of the social system that pays them poor salaries and makes them pay taxes out of them, in spite of the high cost of essential commodities as depicted in the visual narrative of surprise below in Figure 4:

Figure 3.

Figure 4.

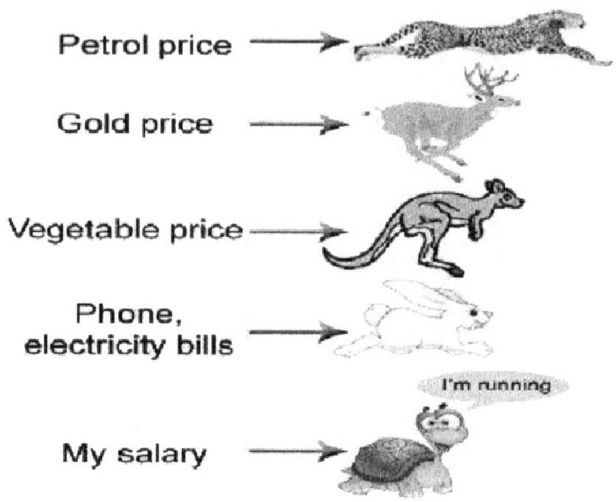

Through the contrastive signification of a very slow animal (the tortoise), running a race with fast speed animals (a cheetahs, an antelope, a kangaroo and a hare in a descending order), the narrative above, which is a terse explanation of the reason why the poor continue to remain poor in Nigeria, is also a ridicule of the salary of the average Nigerian worker and the polity that fails to regulate the cost of essential commodities in relation to low salary incomes of workers. By representing the workers' salaries using the tortoise symbolism, the producer of the above visual appropriates the Yoruba folkloric characterization of this animal as extremely shrewd.

The visual narrative is actually a transmutation of a Yoruba folktale titled "Race" or sometimes "The Great Race" that involves the tortoise and other animals. Invariably, Tortoise is always the winner. How does he do it? He plants his tribesmen or children at strategic spots on the way/route to be taken by the runners and before all other animals involved in the race, the last of the Tortoise's tribesmen strategically placed at the near-end of track, surfaces and is declared the winner of the race. This story relates to how Nigerian workers win the war of wages waged against them by the capitalist class (both the state and private corporations) by endurance, escapism into religion, child training/ education and plain denials. This symbolism is also a representamen of the shrewdness that most Nigerian workers apply to the management of their economic life in order to survive with meager salaries. The declarative sentence "I am running" by this tortoise is not just an informative utterance but also an ironic comment that borders on self-mockery, a loud lamentation which also calls attention to the sordidness of the situation of an average Nigerian civil servant and the injustice in distribution of the wealth of the land.

Given the situation depicted in the visual narrative above, the Nigerian workers, when pushed to the wall, (especially when in spite of their shrewd spending, life still remains shrinking) ask for increase in pay through strike actions. And whenever there are strike actions, the victims are no other persons than the poor masses (the part of which they are) of the country. The visual narrative in Figure 5 below captures the aftermath of one of the strike actions embarked upon by the Academic Staff Union of Universities (ASUU) in Nigeria.

In this visual discourse, activated through the strategy of distortion, students have abandoned their reading glasses, their books and school bags and dogs now take possession of them. This visual narrative

Figure 5.

plays up the agonies of Nigerian students during strikes. At such times, these students are free, abandon all academic work, live homes to their dogs (as suggested by the incredible actions- in the Nigerian context- of a dog sitting on a sofa, carrying a schoolbag and wearing a pair of glasses) and consequently become victims of untimely pregnancy, motor accident and public thuggery. The visual narrative is a reinvention of a fictional song of surprise, popular among school pupils (in Southwestern Nigeria) in the early 1980s, which gave an account of a dog in Agege, Lagos, that put on clothes, wore shoe on one foot and carried a bag with the other. The song, in the Yoruba language, is as follows:

Mo ré èmò lágége (I saw a surprise in Agege)
Ajá wo ẹ̀wù ó ró' so (A dog put o dresses and tie wrapper)
Ó fa báàgì lọ́wọ́ kan (It drew a bag in one hand)
Ó wọ bàtà sẹ́sẹ̀ kan (It wore shoe on one foot).
Gbamú̀ Gbamù, Jigí Jigì (suggestive of the drumming that accompanies the song)

If students abandon their reading glasses, books and schoolbags and dogs take possession of them, where then lies the so-called superiority of human intellect? The thought that inheres in the visual and induces satirical laughter is that tertiary education in Nigeria has gone to the dogs. It is also an indictment of government and other agencies in charge of the industry. Like this song of surprise, the above visual is indexical of distortions that characterize the society; it is a lamentation for a nation that flirts with its future by turning its education into mere bones that dogs fondle with.

As the youths, who represent this future, wander about aimlessly during strikes, they pay attention to somewhat unimportant things, but which pass significant messages as in Figure 6.

Figure 6, which shows a personal billboard advertisement of a laundry spelled as "Londri" and dry cleaner spelled as DRACLINAR, is suggestive of one of the aftermaths of strike actions by teachers- the breeding of semi-literate (halfhearted) class, pejoratively referred to as half-educated class in Nigeria. In the Nigerian context, this class (usually comprising artisans, commercial transport workers, motor cyclists and petty traders) is the most disapproving for they live within two complexes -superiority and inferiority. The class is the ever- ready instrument of political campaigns and local election malpractices.

Figure 6.

Reflecting the truism in the age-long adage- "an idle hand is the devil's workshop", the youth can afford to engage in such juvenile but humour-evoking and creative acts as the one in the visual below in Figure 7, which ridicules the female body (the image is constructed, using chicken laps, wings and orange peels and chaffs).

The humour in the visual above derives not only from the materials used in composing it but the foregrounding of the reproductive organs. The author compels viewers to see similarities between the human and the animal parts highlighted in the photos text and between the human (mammary glands) and the material (oranges). The idea that human beings are higher animals and possess greater intellectual capacities is indirectly interrogated by forcing us to concentrate on their physical parts (orange juice is sweeter than breast milk!).

Shifting attention away from the intellectual to the carnal always produces humour. That is why sex is a never-failing humorous subject. But for life denying prudes and hypocritical saints, the picture above would only provoke anger and rape! In fact, they would label it obscene. Why? They are enamoured of abstractions and impossible ideals.

Figure 7.

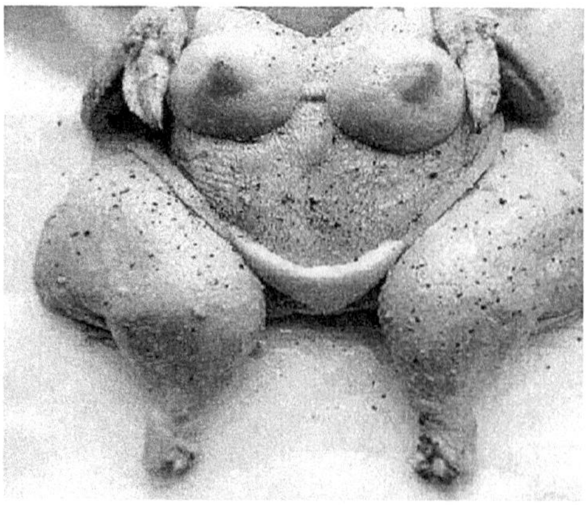

Also, at such strike periods, Nigerian students also have ample time to engage the social media and participate in public discourses. One of such social discourses is the discourse on the outbreak of Ebola fever in 2014 which generated serious concerns for the government of Nigeria and the country's health sector. At the time, restrictions were placed on certain social practices such as handshake, hugging, kissing and even, eating habits. As a result of these restrictions, life was very difficult for the people, who were used to a free and communal lifestyle. The situation is exaggerated in the visual below in Figure 8:

In the visual narration shown in Figure 8, a doctor is so much afraid of human contact and he turns an injection into a stone and a syringe into a catapult, which he uses to send the drug into the body of his patient as though it were a missile launcher. The humour engendered by this narration inheres in the instrument used by the doctor to administer the injection. Medicine is an art for healing. Using a catapult, an instrument for killing small birds and rats, for healing is incongruous. The paradox of healing and killing is signified. The great idea is that medical doctors hurt to heal. Though this narrative is incredible and exaggerated, it is indexical of the general pulse of the Nigerian society at that period of the Ebola epidemic in the country. This sort of exaggerated strategy of humour is also noticeable in the visual below which reproduces the sensitivity of even a baby to the Ebola crisis in Nigeria.

In the visual construction shown in Figure 9, many things are semiotically important. For instance, the breast is constructed as being milk-filled and completely ready to perform as suggested by its size and the direction of the nipple. The baby's gaze and the verbal exclamation- "Chai ooo!" suggest its desirousness (it is expected to look away if otherwise) to suck it. But the verbal affirmative of determination "I'M NOT HUNGRY" minimizes the semiotic ambiguity in the visual construction. The gaze and this verbal exclamation are incongruous. Whereas the gaze expresses desire to suck the breast, the exclamation signifies the fear of death by Ebola virus. The baby lives in self-denial by declaring I'M NOT HUNGRY". The contradiction between what Sigmund Freud would call the pleasure principle and the reality principle engenders laughter.

Figure 8.

Figure 9.

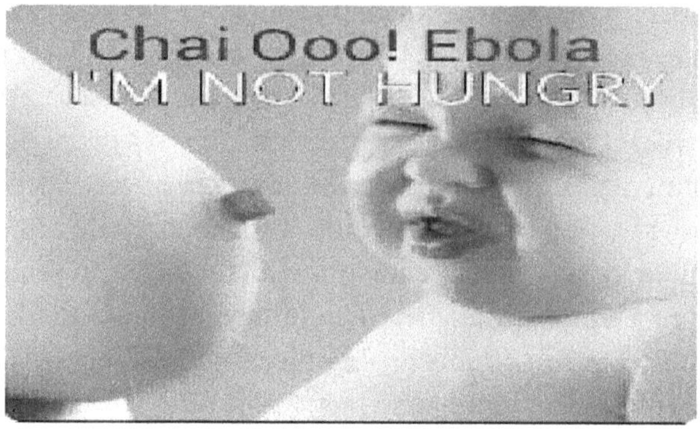

The message above, which came at the time when most Nigerians found it difficult to avoid, as suggested by medical experts, such practices as eating of certain bush animals, sex, kissing, handshake and hugging, is making a serious argument. There is surprise in this semiotic construction for the mother's breast milk is one of those things of life that are difficult to discount. The argument, activated through the semiotic transformation of the baby from its natural condition of innocence to that of experience, is that- if a baby, as in the visual above, can watch with disdain and reject her mother's waiting milk-filled breast for fear of Ebola, nothing should be difficult for an adult to avoid in preventing the spread of this disease. Though this is funny and hard to believe, its underlying message is that self-discipline is the best prevention of Ebola.

The visual above exemplifies some of the rare situations when the bond of love between mother and child can be broken. However, an ideal mother is always with her child. There are many semiotic acts in Yoruba culture which depict mother-child love. For instance, the irritating act of a mother putting her mouth on her baby's nostrils and drawing mucus from there is a semiotic act signifying passionate love. The visual below captures the sorts of mother's love for the child very explicitly

As could be observed from the visual in Figure 10, especially at the level of denotation, the physical pain of a child who is about to be injected is not as much as (see the fear in countenance of the mother above and compare with the innocent look of the child as the doctor draws out the injection needle) the psychological suffering of its mother. This visual illustrates incongruity in humour. As the Yoruba would ask in such a situation: Taa` la lu? Taa lo` n` ke`? (Who is beaten? Who is crying?). In order words, the mother's pain is fake, a put-on. Although her pain is vicarious, it is nevertheless real and serves as a gauge of her profound affection for her child. That is why the Yoruba people believe that *o`r`is`a bi iya osi (there is no love like mother).* Therefore, a child who appreciates the enormity of their mother's love will have no hesitation in picking 2 as the answer to the question ("which is the best love in the world?) in Figure 11.

Such a child will not act murderously like the child in Figure 12.

While the love in 2 is filial, nonsexual, gentle and has no limitations, the love in 1 is sexually driven, may be deceptive and as aggressive and conditional as the visuals in Figure 13 suggest.

The exaggerated size of the condom in Figure 13, the war-like posture of the man-image as well as the haste in which he tries to open it and the fearless or rather careless way the female-image lies on the bed, are all semiotic acts, signifying some of such paradoxes as the inseparability of pleasure and pain, the duality of energy and lovemaking as war of the sexes (gender war).

Figure 10.

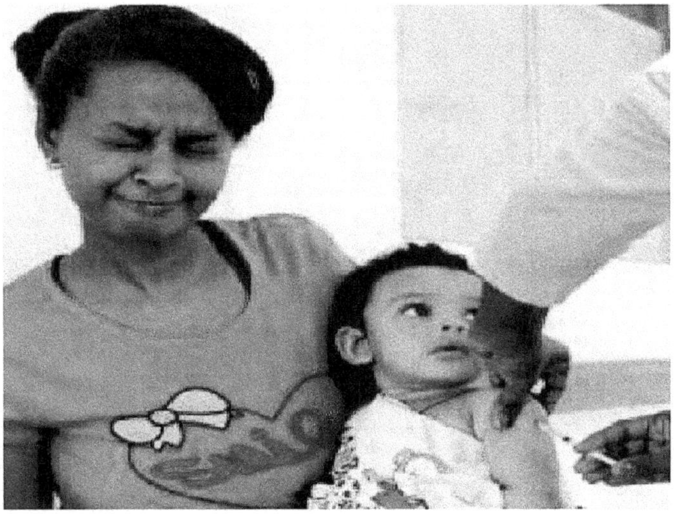

Figure 11.

Another instance of the use of exaggeration in *Facebook* humour is shown in Figure 14, which communicates or serves as a sign vehicle of the attitude (at the level of denotation) of the poster to reading.

The skeleton that reads is a good piece of graveyard humour. It makes a mockery of all knowledge. The mystery of death has been elusive to knowledge-seeking humanity. All human quests, strifes and thirsts end in the grave! Vanity upon vanity. Knowledge, especially scientific and technological, breeds pride. But death swallows all- knowledge, power, pride and their possessor. It is not for nothing therefore that the Yoruba people say: *Iku la ba maa bo, ka fi Orisa sile, nitoripe nigba tiku n pa ni, kini Orisa n wo, n'igba t'aisan n se ni, kini Orisa n wo?* (It is Death rather than Deities that we should worship because when Death kills us what do Deities do, when illness attacks us, what do Deities do?). The laughter produced by the visual is directed at the limitations of culture and the means of transmitting it – education.

Figure 12.

Figure 13.

Obviously, the poster of the visual above has a rejectionist attitude to reading, pointing to its (reading) emaciating effect. It can also be indexical of a society where reading has lost to viewing (the present age of internet technology) or where reading is treated with disdain. At another level of signification, the visual can be a harsh response to a society that does not reward reading and hence a warning to ardent readers in such a society that nothing is worth their reading efforts. The sort of rejectionist attitude, reflected in the visual humour above is contradicted by the one below, which draws some significant differences between education and ignorance

Figure 15, which reproduces the common expression in Nigeria – to have or not have books in the brain- is a reinvention of the aggressive manner in which uneducated people handle issues (see the mad

Figure 14.

Figure 15.

look and aggressive countenance of the image at the right) and the reasonable manner (see the gentle but the focused gaze of the image at the left) educated people handle them. Schooling, as this visual signifies, moderates behaviours and lack of it is frustrating.

The commonplace knowledge which the visual serves as the sign vehicle of is that the best answer to a fool is silence. Education is a tool of refining human character and overcoming bestiality and savagery. The laughter is derived from the feeling of superiority of the educated man. By keeping silent, and not answering the mad fool, he has shown that he is cultured, civilized and well-bred and has also distinguished himself from the raging and wild brute. Spectators are bound to notice the difference between urbanity and boorishness. If the educated man loses his calmness and replies in kind to the aggression of the boor, the spectator would take both of them as mad. Human civilization is engendered when the educated elite fails to live up to its billing and provide good leadership.

However, as beneficial as schooling is, so is it faced with many challenges, such as failing, even after reading for an examination. The visual communication in Figure 16 is a signifier of one of such challenges.

At denotative level of interpretation, Figure 16 captures the practice of selective reading (captured under the caption- expectation") which is common among most students and contrasts it with the realities of examination. It is not only a semiotic reconstruction of why students fail in examinations but also a depiction of the challenging nature of examination, and by extension, of schooling or pursuit of knowledge generally. It overtly states that selective readers often face disappointment during examinations.

At secondary level of semiotic analysis however, "summarizing before examination is analogous to the English proverb that warns against counting one's chickens before they are hatched. Candidates who make A's in examinations sometimes do selective reading. It is like playing the numbers game and hitting the jackpot. In contrast, candidates who cover the entire syllabus while preparing for an examination are not likely to hit the jackpot on account of overstretching themselves and thinning out their memory power. They may pass, but not as excellently well as those who have concentrated on likely questions and whose predictions have come true. The race is not to the swift. In order words, there is an element of chance and uncertainty in life. It takes hard work and some devilry to succeed in life. The visual is therefore a major commentary on human life: the contradiction between desire and actuality. Our desires are endless, but the means of realizing them are abysmally limited. Hence, there is abridgment of desires and expectations for the vast majority of people when their lives are examined and summed up. Yet, we all set out in life to succeed and be happy! Call no man happy, says the Theban Oracle, until he carries his happiness with him into his grave.

CONCLUSION

In this paper, I have brought together some visual signifiers posted on *Facebook* at different times (by different *Facebook* users) and utilized them (as a semiotic interpretant) to narrate some significant

Figure 16.

meanings deductable from them. From the foregoing analyses, it is evident that *Facebook* is not just a site for meeting new faces and interacting with them but also, borrowing the words of Harrison (2003), “a highly visual publishing environment” for obtaining information on such commonplace issues as education, politics, religion and moral matters and how these matters are represented in the minds of individuals. It is also a showroom of entertainment where people ease themselves off different forms of social repressions and exhibit their sense of humour through importation and creation of laughter -evoking visual materials.

REFERENCES

Billig, M. (2005). *Laughter and Ridicule. Towards a Social Critique of Humour*. London: SAGE Publications.

Clarke, A. (2009). *The Eight Patterns of Humour*. Cumbria, UK: Pyrrhic House.

Harrison, C. (2003, February). Visual Social Semiotics: Understanding How Still Images Make Meaning. *Technical Communication (Washington)*, *50*(1).

Martin, M. W. (1987). Humor and the Aesthetic Enjoyment of Incongruities. In J. Morreall (Ed.), *The Philosophy of Laughter and Humor* (pp. 172–186). Albany, NY: State University of New York Press.

Morreall, J. (1983). *Taking Laughter Seriously*. Albany, NY: State University of New York Press.

Morreall, J. (1987). *The Philosophy of Laughter and Humor*. Albany, NY: State University of New York Press.

Morreall, J. (1997). *Humor Works*. Amherst, MA: Human Resource Development Press.

Morreall, J. (2009). *Comic Relief: A Comprehensive Philosophy of Humor*. Malden, MA: Wiley Blackwell. doi:10.1002/9781444307795

Mulkay, M. (1988). *On Humour*. Cambridge, MA: Polity Press.

Provine, R. (2000). *Laughter: A Scientific Investigation*. Penguin.

Raskin, V. (1984). *Semantic Mechanisms of Humor*. Dordrecht: Reidel. doi:10.1007/978-94-009-6472-3

Ross, A. (2009). *The Language of Humour*. London: Routledge.

Shaw, J. (2010). Philosophy of Humor. *Philosophy Compass*, *5*(2), 112–126. doi:10.1111/j.1747-9991.2009.00281.x

Storey, R. (2003). Humor and Sexual Selection. *Human Nature (Hawthorne, N.Y.)*, *14*(4), 319–336. doi:10.1007/s12110-003-1009-x PMID:26190269

Suls, J. (1972). A Two-Stage Model for the Appreciation of Jokes and Cartoons: An Information-Processing Analysis. In J. Goldstein & P. McGhee (Eds.), *The Psychology of Humor* (pp. 81–99). New York: Academic Press. doi:10.1016/B978-0-12-288950-9.50010-9

Tisljar, R., & Bereczkei, T. (2005). An Evolutionary Interpretation of Humor and Laughter. *Journal of Cultural and Evolutionary Psychology*, *3*(3), 301–309. doi:10.1556/JCEP.3.2005.3-4.6

KEY TERMS AND DEFINITIONS

Counter-Intuitive Interpretation: Interpretation that is purely objective.

Digital Cartooning: Appropriation of the photo actions of persons.

Digital Impersonation: Making a human to act as another human.

Photo Importation: Importation of photos or pictures from one discourse domain to perform in another.

Pleasure of the Psyche: The laughter-inducing effect of visual humour.

Second Order Meaning: Connotative meaning of a text.

Visual Grafting: The situation in which new persons or objects are created through the process of hybridization, similar to that used in plant or crop sciences.

Chapter 6
A Rhetoric of Visual Humor on Facebook

Wincharles Coker
Michigan Technological University, USA

Stephen Kwame Dadugblor
Michigan Technological University, USA

ABSTRACT

A decade ago, Susan C. Herring (2004) urged scholars to study discoursal patterns of computer-mediated communications and not simply their microlinguistic features. This chapter contributes to the literature by examining the rhetoric of visual humor on Facebook. The purpose of the study is two-fold: (a) to develop a conceptual framework for understanding uses of humor on Facebook, and (b) to show that humorous texts on this social networking site are argumentative in focus. Using ideas from Aristotelian rhetoric, Barthian semiotics, and Saidian discourse analysis, the work contends that Facebook visual humor tends to perform four main functions. They can be gubernatorial, institutional, cultural, or grotesque, and often ridicule societal problems in either overt or covert ways. The findings are useful for developing a conceptual framework for studying the complexities of human culture in digital spaces.

INTRODUCTION

First launched in 2004 by Mark Zuckerberg and his colleagues as a social networking site for Harvard students (West, Lewis & Currie, 2009; Kofod-Petersen &Wegener, 2010), Facebook has undoubtedly wielded a tremendous impact on society. It enables users to satisfy a number of gratifications such as making new "friends," keeping in touch with old ones, constructing a sense of personal worth or social identity, earning cultural capital, and doing smart business. Among its many advantages, Facebook promotes simultaneous one-to-one, one-to-many, and many-to-many communications via texts and photographs (boyd & Ellinson, 2008). These affordances present users across cultures with unique opportunities to engage in a panoply of communicative acts that range from setting agendas, gauging public opinion, to raising critical questions about happenings in their immediate surrounds and on the international scene

DOI: 10.4018/978-1-5225-0338-5.ch006

Copyright © 2016, IGI Global. Copying or distributing in print or electronic forms without written permission of IGI Global is prohibited.

(Wyche et *al.*, 2013). Facebook has also been considered a very important social networking site for educational purposes (Mazer *et al.*, 2007; Munoz & Towner, 2009; Loving & Ochoa, 2011).

Studies have also explored how humor constitutes and maintains online communities such as Facebook. These include research in psychology, applied linguistics, and foreign language acquisition (Vandergriff, 2010). In an earlier work, Hübler and Bell (2003) showed that humor serves a critical function in online communities created by mailing lists. According to them, humor constitutes a virtual group ethos. Baym (2004) has also argued that the presence of humor in computer-mediated communication is critical to creating social meanings online. Using user surveys and five humorous messages from a Usenet newsgroup, Baym's study shows how the group's humor was influenced by close and distant relationships of participants in the soap opera. These relationships also distanced the participants from the opera's writers and producers. Baym concluded that group solidarity is a primary mechanism for establishing individuality despite shared ways of acting in a group.

Little work has, however, been done on the nature and role visual humor plays in the interactions and chats of Facebook users. Yet it is important to note that humorous visual texts on Facebook perform specific rhetorical functions. This chapter argues that far from being an evanescent appeal to an audience's emotions, Facebook visual humor makes a persuasive argument. The goal of this study, therefore, is to develop a conceptual framework for theorizing Facebook visual humor, and to show that this type of humor is not value-neutral. As social networking sites (SNSs) grow quantitatively and qualitatively, it is important that researchers study the many ways Facebook visual humorous posts tend to serve a deeper function than just their taken-for-granted assumptions. A look at the authors' personal Facebook pages, over the years, for example, shows that some humorous texts basically ridicule and satirize individuals, persons, and institutions, by capturing naturally occurring snapshots of social life in a way that performs special functions to users of the medium.

STUDY METHOD AND DATA

The methodology employed in this study was interpretive netnography. The authors' idea of interpretive research was informed by Denzin and Lincoln's (2011) four principles of interpretive work. According to them, interpretive research must, first and foremost, be a blueprint for cultural criticism since no cultural practices are hardly neutral. In this context, one may say that humorous visual texts on Facebook are often shaped by the worldviews, biases, and interests of its users. Second, the work should articulate cultural and political issues. This means that interpretive research does its work best when it is capable of bringing to light hidden ideologies. The third point, Denzin and Lincoln posit, is that interpretive analysis should inspire hope; it must critique how things are, and then go on to explore how they could be different. Finally, this type of research must be an emancipatory project for bringing about positive change.

Netnography was employed to extend carefully the methods and tools of traditional humanistic ethnography to online research (*cf.* Kozinets, 2010; Lopez-Rocha, 2010). As users of Facebook, the researchers themselves have been very active observers of, and participants in posting and reading online comments since the last seven years. However, for the present study data were gathered between January and March, 2015 from Facebook friends willing to share their posts with the researchers. Although the data were used anonymously, the study satisfied what Guillemin and Gillam (2004) call "ethically important moments." These are difficult and unusual situations that arise in the course of doing research. Ethically disturbing texts were also excluded from the analysis. For example, the 450-ish "corpus" excluded, *inter alia*, extremely salacious texts. In order to examine the texts, the researchers focused on the Ghanaian society, and dealt with issues considered relevant to Facebook users. This helped to contextualize the analysis. Data were coded, and examined by three other individuals to establish a fair level of coder-reliability.

ANALYSIZING FACEBOOK VISUAL HUMOR: A RHETOGRAPHICAL APPROACH

Data were analyzed using a *rhetographical approach* the authors developed using ideas from Aristotle's concept of rhetoric, Barthian semiotics, and Said's style of discourse analysis. Table 1 summarizes the major theoretical influences on the idea of rhetography.

A rhetographical analysis shows that online visual texts are rhetorical compositions whose messages are more complex than they appear. To unpack their meanings the contexts of the texts must first be identified to articulate their values. Essentially, a rhetographical analysis is a critical study of how iconographic and rhetorical choices shape the meanings embedded in online visual productions. Using this approach, the study identified four basic functions—called *rhetographs*—of visual humor on Facebook. These are (*a*) the gubernatorial, (*b*) the institutional, (*c*) the cultural, and (*d*) the grotesque. These rhetographs serve as a heuristic; the boundaries between them are simply discursive. Table 2 offers a bird's eye-view of the significance of each rhetograph.

Gubernatorial Rhetographs

Gubernatorial rhetographs are rhetographs that critique the ills of the state and its policies. Analysis of the data shows that gubernatorials are the most common type of rhetographs. They are mainly used by Facebook users to draw attention to the challenges society goes through as a result of perceived corrupt practices of the executive arm of government. An exigent example in Ghana is the persistent lack of electricity supply caused mainly by the Electricity Company of Ghana (ECG). Ghanaians have now come

Table 1. Major theoretical influences on the concept of rhetography

Theoretical Influence	Key Figures	Core Concepts
Classical rhetoric	Aristotle and the sophists	argumentation, pisteis (rhetorical proofs), kairos (exigencies of time and space)
Semiotics	Roland Barthes	visual text, studium, punctum
Discourse analysis	**Edward Said**	**wordliness of text, the taken-for granted, ideology**

Table 2. A taxonomy of rhetographs

Rhetograph	Target of Humor	Function
Gubernatorial	The state and its politicians	Exposes and critiques the ills of the state and its policies
Institutional	Social agencies and civil services	Critiques and ridicules their mandates
Cultural[1]	Everyday social constructions	Calls attention to the taken-for-granted doings of individuals in society
Grotesque	**Extremely not too pleasant risible acts**	**Derides deviant cultural norms**

to label it as "dumsor" or its Akan derivative "dum sɔ," to wit *turn off* and *switch on*, respectively. The term is used to describe frequent electric power outages in the country (Agbenyega, 2014). The crisis compelled the president, John Dramani Mahama, to indicate on a platform in Germany that he has even been nicknamed "Mr. Dumsor"—which is itself a sarcastic eponym (Obour & Gamor, 2015). In fact, it is important to note that *dumsor* has hugely affected worker productivity, businesses, and other sectors such as education and health care.

It is for this reason that to create humor out of this crisis should be seen as entailing more than laughter. The analysis shows it satirizes the government. The humor, as shall be demonstrated, criticizes government's inability to bring a lasting solution to the crisis.

Figure 1 uses two main visual strategies to make the argument. The perlocutionary force of the declarative "I TRUST ECG" and its graphical rendition express *distrust* of the government to deal with the energy crisis. To put it differently, the visual text is raising awareness of Facebook 'friends' not to be oblivious of the inability of the government to meet this need. This admonition is reinforced by the *punctum* of the rhetograph. If punctums, as Barthes (2003) rightly defines in "Camera Lucida," are visual elements that unusually intrigue observers in a way that draws a deeper connection between them and the elements, then, it can be said that the drying of the clothes on the electric lines by the man is extremely punctal. It speaks clearly: "Do not be scared to dry your clothes on electric lines because there will be no power till the clothes dry up." Will one laugh, and yet ignore the political message of the rhetograph? Only few may.

Figure 1. A gubernatorial rhetograph about persistent power crisis

Other gubernatorial rhetographs focused on hikes in fuel prices. In Figure 2 below, the audience's attention is drawn to this incident: it is unusual to see a locker on the fuel tank of a vehicle. This raises some questions. Do drivers often do this? Why would a driver lock up the fuel tank of his or her vehicle? While onlookers may choose to laugh about this, in Ghana, the high cost of fuel may compel individuals to understand reasons for this unorthodox practice. They may laugh, and yet will not fail to be "pierced" by the message of the locker. As a matter of fact, many Ghanaians may commiserate with the owner of the vehicle, and blame the government for the economic hardship in the country. In other words, this visual humor is politically loaded because it reminds onlookers and friends on Facebook that all is not well with the Ghanaian economy, and that in order to survive one needs to do the un-ordinary.

Institutional Rhetographs

Like gubernatorial rhetographs, institutional rhetographs also serve a political function. The main difference between the two, however, is that institutional rhetographs expose the rot in social agencies and civil services. The study reveals that despite the humor institutional rhetographs elicit, patrons of these visual texts usually use them to engage in a massive campaign against the civil service. It was observed that these rhetographs are efforts to bring to the attention of the Facebook community real problems facing employees and their welfare, and the fact that many state institutions are considered corrupt.

Figure 3 excoriates the high levels of unfairness caused by state institutions. The text introduces us to the two actors: the civil service and Ghana Black Stars, the senior national soccer team. The stark contrast between them is established by the binary line which, in fact, hits the viewer in no small way. The humorous text ridicules the essence of loyal service to the state and the ideal of patriotism. Questions the text raise include what is the sense in serving one's nation so ditufully and be remunerated with so little? Why should civil servants expend all of their adult life laboring for a nation that cares little about them? Why should footballers, and by extension government appointees, gain so much wealth so quickly, at the expense of hardworking civil servants?

Figure 2.

Figure 3.

The text may have been inspired by the scandal that rocked the Black Stars' participation at the football mondial in Brazil 2014. Various news outlets, local and international, reported the air lifting of US$ 3 million to address the team's protest not to play its final group G match against Portugal (BBC Sports, 2014). It was said that each player received US $ 100, 000 as appearance fee. On the contrary, a story carried by Ghana's Joy News Television, a private broadcaster, on a female nurse who has served for 41 years in the Ghana Health Service makes the above institutional rhetograph poignant. According to the bit, the retiree was given the equivalent of about US $ 1, 129.00 as lump sum. One may ask if this is the reward for a heptagenarian who has served her nation so diligently in almost all the ten regions of Ghana. This anecdote goes to suggest that humorous rhetographs are loaded messages than temporary comic reliefs posted online. Other rhetographs, on the other hand, focus on the everyday. They are socially constructed Facebook visual humorous texts that mainly call attention to the mundane acts of individuals in societies. An example is the cultural rhetograph.

Cultural Rhetographs

Cultural rhetographs directly deal with social relations among persons. These include culturals about marriage and gender parity in society. The analysis shows that what makes cultural rhetographs humorous is that they tend to be subversive. Below is an example.

Set in the Northern Region of Ghana, this visual text carries a number of meanings. At least, it performs three main rhetorical functions than simply making us laugh. First, it has a traditional value. Cultures in this region may not take kindly to what may be described as rebellion againt the androcentric order. Many cultures in Ghana tend to be patriachal, and so the payment of bride price is believed to be the responsibility of men. To fight and subdue a man, as can be seen in Figure 4, is deemed unwomanly. Second, the text performs a religious function by sustaining male power. Even though it cannot be claimed that

Figure 4.

religion is a tool for oppressing women, it, nonetheless, teaches them to be obedient to their husbands. Because many people in the Northern Region of Ghana are predominantly Muslims, it is interesting to observe how some women can call the bluff of men, and stand up for their rights in public spaces. This development may be due to the third reason: education. As more and more Ghanaian women become literate, they also are becoming economically independent. In other words, many Ghanaian women—Northerners included—frown upon being negatively discriminated against.

The text above thus appears to be a feminist argument. It is sending a clear message to all Ghanaian men that their female counterparts are becoming transcendental. This is to say that many Ghanaian women are no more in a state of immanence, where they exclusively relied on their men for survival. The text could be considered a social advocacy by and to women to fight for their rights. The caption in Figure 4 confirms this claim: "518 men report wives for beating them." The caption goes to support the view that the phenomenon is gaining roots in Ghana. Clearly, the text's content may be risible but its effect is persuasive: it is a call to reflect on the role of women in contemporary Ghanaian society. It raises questions such as how should acts such as those in Figure 4 be looked at in modern Ghanaian society? What do feminists say about such subversive actions? (See Butler, 1990 for a comprehensive discussion) Finally, like culturals, other rhetographs perform even more attention-grabbing functions on Facebook. These are grotesque rhetographs.

Grotesque Rhetographs

Grotesque rhetographs are usually perverse in nature. The analysis shows that grotesques tend to be salacious in content. The humor many grotesques elicit quickly vanish as a result of the reality of the content their messages communicate. Here is an example:

The text above points to a growing subculture in which many women fetishize huge posteriors. In Ghana, as in other cultures, some women seek ways to enlarge their buttocks. Already, such icons as Salma Hayek, Jennifer Lopez, and Frida Kahlo have done some "butt work." Lopez's posterior, for example, has been insured for a whopping US $ 1 billion (Guzmán & Valdiva, 2004). A recent study conducted by Oxford University researchers suggests that huge buttocks are rather resistant to chronic illnesses, and are less likely to develop cholesterol, heart diseases, and diabetes (Manopoulos, Karpe & Frayn, 2010). Some have also said that huge posteriors enhance sexual attractiveness and self-esteem. For example, Barrera (2002) has argued that "When aesthetic surgery is performed upon the buttocks, it is to enhance their attraction" (p. 408). This part of the body is today glamorized and has gained the status of acceptability in the media. Figure 5 is therefore a grotesque rhetograph that calls the attention of both men and women to the other side of beauty. It questions the rationale for faking one's own existence. Do women wear 'butt pads' because of cultural capital? While some may laugh at the scene of Figure 5, others may realize that the text is salacious. On this note, the admonition of a Facebook friend concerning sexual content is encouraging:

It may be helpful to note that one just does not see a salacious material on Facebook coated with humorous content, laugh about it, and go on unaffected: it may sow a seed. Restraint, however, needs to be exercised in discussing grotesque rhetographs. Some grotesques promote incandescent behaviors; others discourage them. What has been referenced in Figure 5 belongs to the latter. You need to be "CAREFUL WHAT U ALLOW UR EYES TO SEE." This is because after the humor 'evaporates,' the impact may still be felt. The problem with many grotesque rhetographs, therefore, is that they tend to be deviations from cultural norms.

CONCLUSION

The findings of this study are useful for understanding the complex nature of communication on Facebook. The analysis has shown that visual humor on this social networking site is not value-free. It has been argued that visual humorous texts on Facebook are rhetorical, multimodal compositions. The messages

Figure 5.

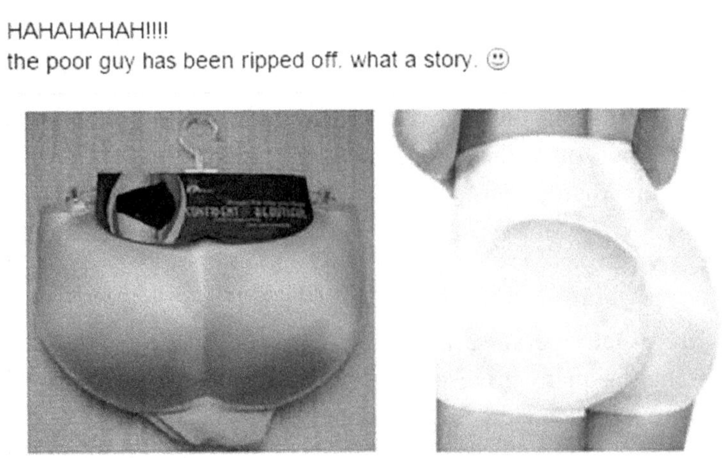

Figure 6.

others
August 23, 2012 ·

WARNING TO ALL SINGLES ON FACEBOOK!!!

There are some groups and pages that have been introduced on facebook which contain HIGHLY SEXUAL CONTENTS. These groups and pages say they teach sex positions and talk about sexual details and even go to the extent of showing pornographic photos to illustrate their point. BE CAREFUL WHAT U ALLOW UR EYES TO SEE. Many of u are falling prey to such immoral activities thinking that u want to learn but I have some news for u..... this will on... See More

they convey target specific individuals, political systems, cultures, and social structures. Often, they are mundane but sometimes subversive. As work in progress, the four basic rhetographs—gubernatorials, institutionals, culturals, and grotesques—are a heuristic. They are not sufficient in and of themselves. Further research is recommended to develop the typology.

This is because the study bears a number of limitations. First, there is the problem of cultural essentialism. Although empirical studies need to be situated in particular geographical locales, the results of the study may have been influenced by the authors' concentration on the Ghanaian context. Second, it is not too certain what role globalization played in the research. It was difficult to determine to what extent the visual images analyzed were putatively Ghanaian. This is because cultures influence one another, and so cultural productions are highly mobile. Some of the humorous texts may have originated from cultures other than Ghana.

As an interpretive study, it is hoped that the research create awareness of the subtle meanings rooted in the taken-for granted visual images in online communities such as Facebook. While gubernatorial, institutional, and cultural rhetographs perform a much more positive role, the place of the grotesque in ridiculing societal wrongs remains doubtful. Self-regulation needs to be encouraged to sanitize the ineluctable presence of visual texts such as grotesques online. Facebook visual humor, in a word, has two valences: it is pleasurable and yet argumentative.

REFERENCES

Agbenyega, E. (2014, April 10). *Ghana's power crisis: What about renewable energy?* Retrieved from graphic.com.gh

Barrera, M. (2002). Hottentot 2000: Jennifer Lopez and her butt. In B. K. M. Philips & B. Reay (Eds.), *Sexualities in history* (pp. 407–420). New York: Routledge.

Barthes, R. (2003). Camera lucida. In H. S. Karen (Ed.), *Ways of reading words and images.* Bedford, St. Martin.

Baym, N. K. (2004). The performance of humor in computer-mediated communication. *Journal of Computer-Mediated Communication, 1*(2).

Berger, P. L., & Luckmann, T. (1966). *The social construction of reality: A treatise in the sociology of knowledge*. Garden City, NY: Anchor Books.

boyd, D. M. & Ellinson, N. B. (2008). Social network sites: Definition, history, and scholarship. *Journal of Computer-Mediated Communication, 13,* 210-230.

Butler, J. (1990). *Gender trouble: Feminism and the subversion of identity*. New York: Routledge.

Denzin, N. K., & Lincoln, Y. S. (2011). The discipline and practice of qualitative research. In N. K. Denzin & Y. S. Lincoln (Eds.), *The Sage Handbook of Qualitative Research* (2nd ed., pp. 1–19). Urbana-Champaign, IL: Sage.

Guillemin, M., & Gillam, L. (2004). Ethics, reflexivity, and "ethically important moments" in research. *Qualitative Inquiry*, *10*(2), 261–280. doi:10.1177/1077800403262360

Guzmán, I. M., & Valdiva, A. N. (2004). Brain, brow, and booty: Latina iconicity in U.S. popular culture. *Communication Review*, *7*(2), 205–221. doi:10.1080/10714420490448723

Herring, S. C. (2004). Computer-mediated discourse analysis: An approach to researching online behavior. In S. A. Barab, R. Kling, & J. H. Gray (Eds.), *Designing for Virtual Communities in the Service of Learning* (pp. 338–376). New York: Cambridge University Press. doi:10.1017/CBO9780511805080.016

Hübler, M. T., & Bell, D. C. (2003). Computer-mediated humor and ethos: Exploring threads of constitutive laughter in online communities. *Computers and Composition*, *20*(3), 277–294. doi:10.1016/S8755-4615(03)00036-7

Kofod-Petersen, A., & Wegener, R. (2010). Like a poke on Facebook: Emergent semantics in location-aware social network services. In R. Taiwo (Ed.), *Handbook of Research on Discourse Behavior and Digital Communication: Language Structures and Social Interaction* (pp. 497–512). Hershey, PA: IGI Global. doi:10.4018/978-1-61520-773-2.ch032

Kozinets, R. V. (2010). *Netnography: Doing Ethnographic Research Online*. Thousand Oaks, CA: Sage.

Lopez-Rocha, S. (2010). Nethnography in context: Methodological and practical implications of virtual ethnography. *International Journal of Interdisciplinary Social Sciences*, *5*(4), 291–301.

Loving, M., & Ochoa, M. (2011). Facebook as a classroom management solution. *New Library World*, *112*(3/4), 121–130. doi:10.1108/03074801111117023

Manolopoulos, K. N., Karpe, F., & Frayn, K. N. (2010). Gluteofemoral body fat as a determinant of metabolic health. *International Journal of Obesity*, *34*(6), 949–959. doi:10.1038/ijo.2009.286 PMID:20065965

Mazer, J. P., Murphy, R. E., & Simonds, C. J. (2007). "I'll see you on Facebook": The Effects of Computer-mediated Teacher Self-disclosure on Student Motivation, Affective Learning, and Classroom Climate. *Communication Education*, *56*(1), 1–17. doi:10.1080/03634520601009710

Munoz, C., & Towner, T. (2009). Opening Facebook: How to use Facebook in the college classroom. In I. Gibson, R. Weber, K. McFerrin, R. Carlsen, & D. Willis (Eds.), *Proceedings of Society for Information Technology & Teacher Education International Conference 2009* (pp. 2623-2627). Chesapeake, VA: Association for the Advancement of Computing in Education (AACE).

Obour, S. K. & Gamor, E. (2015, January 21). *I've been named 'Mr Dumsor' in Ghana – Prez Mahama tells Ghanaians in Germany*. Retrieved from graphic.com.gh

Said, E. (1975). The text, the world, the critic. *The Bulletin of the Midwest Modern Language Association*, *8*(2), 1–23. doi:10.2307/1314778

Sports, B. B. C. (2014, June 25). *World Cup 2014: Ghana Sends $3m Cash To Players In Brazil*. Retrieved from http://www.bbc.com/sport/0/football/28021131

Vandergriff, I. (2010). Humor and play in CMC. In R. Taiwo (Ed.), *Handbook of Research on Discourse Behavior and Digital Communication: Language Structures and Social Interaction* (pp. 235–251). Hershey, PA: IGI Global. doi:10.4018/978-1-61520-773-2.ch015

West, A., Lewis, J., & Currie, P. (2009). Students' Facebook 'friends': Public and private spheres. *Journal of Youth Studies*, *12*(6), 615–627. doi:10.1080/13676260902960752

Wyche, S. P., Schoenebeck, S. Y. & Forte, A. (2013). Facebook is a Luxury: An Exploratory Study of Facebook Social Use in Rural Kenya. *CSCW, 13*.

ADDITIONAL READING

Apte, M. L. (1985). *Humor and laughter: An anthropological approach*. Ithaca, NY: Cornell University Press.

Arceneaux, N., & Schmitz Weiss, A. (2010). Seems stupid until you try it: Press coverage of Twitter, 2006-9. *New Media & Society*, *12*(8), 1262–1279. doi:10.1177/1461444809360773

Billig, M. (2005). *Laughter and ridicule: Towards a social critique of humour*. London: Sage.

Evans, J. E. (1987). *Comedy: An annotated bibliography of theory and criticism*. Metuchen, NJ: Scarecrow Press.

Gilbert, J. R. (2004). *Performing marginality: Humor, gender, and cultural critique*. Detroit, MI: Wayne State University Press.

Gournelos, T., & Greene, V. (Eds.). (2011). *A decade of dark humor: How Comedy, Irony, and Satire Shaped Post-9/11 America*. University Press of Mississippi. doi:10.14325/mississippi/9781617030062.001.0001

Jansen, B. J., Zhang, M., Sobel, K., & Chowdury, A. (2009). Twitter power: Tweets as electronic word of mouth. *Journal of the American Society for Information Science and Technology*, *60*(11), 2169–2188. doi:10.1002/asi.21149

Kline, M. (1999). Narrating the grotesque: The rhetoric of humor in John Kennedy Toole's aconfederacy of Dunces. *The Southern Quarterly*, *37*(3), 283.

Kotthoff, H. (2000). Gender and joking: On the complexities of women's image politics in humorous narratives. *Journal of Pragmatics*, *32*(1), 55–80. doi:10.1016/S0378-2166(99)00031-4

Kuipers, G. (2006). *Good Humour, Bad Taste: A Sociology of the Joke*. Berlin: Mouton de Gruyter. doi:10.1515/9783110898996

Kuipers, G. (2011). The politics of humour in the public sphere: Cartoons, power and modernity in the first transnational humour scandal. *European Journal of Cultural Studies*, *14*(1), 63–80. doi:10.1177/1367549410370072

Lockyer, S., & Pickering, M. (2008). *Beyond a joke: The limits of humour*. Basingstoke: Palgrave.

Lynch, O. H. (2002). Humorous communication: Finding a place for humor in communication research. *Communication Theory*, *12*(4), 423–445. doi:10.1111/j.1468-2885.2002.tb00277.x

Martin, R. A. (2001). Humor, laughter, and physical health: Methodological issues and research findings. *Psychological Bulletin*, *127*(4), 504–519. doi:10.1037/0033-2909.127.4.504 PMID:11439709

Meyer, J. C. (2000). Humor as a double-edged sword: Four functions of humor in communication. *Communication Theory*, *10*(3), 310–331. doi:10.1111/j.1468-2885.2000.tb00194.x

Morkes, J., Kernal, H. K., & Nass, C. (1999). Effects of humor in task-oriented human- computer interaction and computer-mediated communication: A direct test of SRCT theory. *Human-Computer Interaction*, *14*(4), 395–435. doi:10.1207/S15327051HCI1404_2

Nilsen, D. L. F. (2003). Introduction. In R. N. L. Ashley (Ed.), Art attack: Names in satire (pp. vii-x) New York, NY: 1st Books Library.

Palmer, J. (1994). *Taking humour seriously*. New York: Routledge. doi:10.4324/9780203380154

Raskin, V. (2008). *The Primer of Humor Research*. New York: Mouton de Gruyter. doi:10.1515/9783110198492

Ritchie, G. D. (2004). *The Linguistic Analysis of Jokes*. New York: Routledge.

Shifman, L., & Blondheim, M. (2010). The medium is the joke: Online humor about and by networked computers. *New Media & Society*, *12*(8), 1348–1367. doi:10.1177/1461444810365311

Smith, M. (2009). Humor, unlaughter, and boundary maintenance. *Journal of American Folklore*, *122*(2), 148–171. doi:10.1353/jaf.0.0080

Smith, S. A. (1993). Humor as rhetoric and cultural argument. *Journal of American Culture*, *16*(2), 51–64. doi:10.1111/j.1542-734X.1993.00051.x

Zandberg, E. (2006). Critical laughter: Humor, popular culture and Israeli Holocaust commemoration. *Media Culture & Society*, *28*(4), 561–579. doi:10.1177/0163443706065029

KEY TERMS AND DEFINITIONS

Facebook: Arguably the most popular social networking site that promotes both synchronous and asynchronous communication via texts, photographs, and videos.

Humor: A performative act that elicits laughter.

Netnography: The extension of ethnography to online communities and their cultures.

Punctum: The deeper level codification of a visual text.

Rhetography: The study of how visual texts in Facebook interactions perform specific communicative functions.

Rhetograph: A specific communicative function a visual text performs in Facebook interactions.

Studium: The denotation or surface level codification of a visual text.

ENDNOTE

1 The authors' understanding of "cultural" is mainly influenced by Berger and Luckmann's (1966) social construction of reality, for whom all human knowledge and action do not sit outside of their purview (p. 1). They contend that human agents have the capacity to control and determine what counts as knowledge, truth, and reality.

Chapter 7
A Linguistic Analysis of Klint Da Drunk's "Alcoholic" Talk Show

Faleye James Oladunjoye
Obafemi Awolowo University, Nigeria

ABSTRACT

Humour is culturally constructed depending on different experiences of a people. It thrives well in an atmosphere of freedom, which makes it possible for people to unleash their creative potential in cracking jokes on certain socio-economic and political realities. The Nigerian democratic space makes it possible for the emergence of 'stand-up comedians' who often entertain their enthusiastic audience via the English language or Nigerian Pidgin English. This creative venture reflects the innovative, entrepreneurial and imaginative usage of the English language in the entertainment industry. The 'Alcoholic Talk Show' (ATS) of Klint da Drunk typifies this linguistic discourse. Earlier studies on effects of alcohol on utterances have been limited to those produced by the intoxicated talker. This chapter examines the language performance of a stand-up comedian whose routines are based on drunkenness with a view to identifying the linguistic characteristics of simulated alcoholic utterances. Also, it discusses the exaggerated elements and the social issues in the alcoholic jokes. The data for the study was sourced from selected YouTube recordings of Klint da Drunk and it was subjected to perceptual analysis. The transcript of the video recordings was analysed to identify lingual distortions and social issues raised by the persona, using insights from Bergson's Theory of Comedy. The analysis revealed that ATS manifests lingual distortions and speech dysfluencies that are characteristics of utterances rendered in a state of stupor. The study concluded that thespians do not only dramatise actions but also mime speech styles.

INTRODUCTION

Humour and laughter are inseparable and they form vital aspects of human existence. They are universal in nature though they are culturally constructed. Humour refers to the way in which particular cognitive experiences provoke laughter and provide amusement. Sensitivity of human beings to things that can amuse them varies from one social context to another. The form of experience that amuses a Briton, for example, might not amuse a Nigerian, and vice versa.

DOI: 10.4018/978-1-5225-0338-5.ch007

Copyright © 2016, IGI Global. Copying or distributing in print or electronic forms without written permission of IGI Global is prohibited.

Homour manifests in an atmosphere of oppression as a therapy to escape from the pain of existence. However, it thrives well in contexts of freedom and liberty where speeches can be expressed with little or no inhibitions. The vistas of democratic freedom in Africa have opened up a new form of speech that has contributed greatly to humour production. The continent in the last decade has witnessed "a new wave of institutionalisation of democratic impulses" (Ninalowo, 1996: xix) which has greatly enhanced freedom of speech. Since 1999, Nigeria has witnessed uninterrupted democratic governance. This free democratic atmosphere, according to Ayakoroma (2013), has greatly contributed to the emergence of an artistic form christened the Nigerian Stand-up Comedy which involves humour production and commoditisation of laughter. Stand-up comic, according to *The Oxford English Dictionary* (2nd edition, Vol. XVI), refers to "a comedian whose act consists of standing before an audience and telling a succession of jokes". Schwarz (2010:17) succinctly describes stand-up comedians as

individuals who plant themselves in front of their listeners with their microphones and start telling a succession of funny stories, one-liners or short jokes, and anecdotes... in order to make their audience laugh.

This style of comedy involves three essential features which include: a performer who presents a humorous monologue; a live performance before an audience which elicits laughter, and a direct communication between the performer and the audience (Double, 2014). Due to its inherent creative distortion (Minttz, 1985), the performances "work and become a source of humour because they are so well done" (Adejunmobi, 2014:188).

The Setting in Nigerian Stand-up Comedy show provides practitioners atmosphere to freely crack jokes and make satirical comments on realities of the Nigerian state and her citizens. Like the 'fools' in Shakespearean plays, the stand-up comedians often analyse the threnodic nature of the Nigerian society as a strategy for entertaining their enthusiastic audience via mostly Nigerian Pidgin English and sometimes Standard English. All they do is make the people laugh in the face of misery, wanton neglect and colossal misrule.

While not underestimating the entrepreneurial skill of these thespians, this paper focuses on the innovative and imaginative use of the English language by one of them, Clinton Afamefuna Igwemba (a.k.a. Klint da Drunk), in the entertainment industry. Klint da Drunk is a celebrated humour merchant who specialises in Alcoholic Talk Shows (ATSs). ATS is a form of speech that simulates or dramatises expressions made under the influence of alcohol. Alcohol addiction has dire consequences on an individual and a society. Consequently, there is always a growing concern about its consumption. Concerns about the social behaviour of alcoholics evoke a sense of pity, anger or laughter in people.

In Nigeria, family members of alcoholics are usually bothered about their social behaviour, but other members of the public get amused at their behaviour especially by their speeches. Klint da Drunk as a stand-up comedian imitates a man called Scatter Mojo who was a real drunk in his village. The comedian admitted in one of his interviews that he found solace in recreating the drunk character, Scattaer Mojo, who was noted for his drunkenness in his village in comic performance (Klint, 2012).

It is indubitable that drunken speeches create some amusements for listeners. However, this paper is not investigating alcoholic utterances of a drunk. Rather, it examines the structural and lingual distortions on dramatised inebriated utterances of Klint da Drunk and analyses the strategies he uses in creating humour for his audience. Finally, it discusses the exaggerated elements and the social issues in the routines.

LITERATURE REVIEW AND THEORETICAL CONSIDERATION

For clarity, it is expedient to explain concepts such as alcoholism, dramatised alcoholic speech, comedy and humour. Alcoholism is a 'social disease' which is related to the use of alcohol (American Medical Association, 2008). It is an alcohol dependent syndrome or addictive. Polander and Shalin (2013) further describe it as poisoning by alcohol. An alcoholic is that individual who is addicted to the consumption of alcohol.

Polander and Shalin (2013) identify two types of alcoholism namely acute and chronic. Acute alcoholism, according to them, refers to the temporary effect of alcohol taken within a short period while the chronic alcoholism refers to the pathological condition due to habitual intake of alcohol. Alcohol addiction has dire consequences on an individual and a society. It causes changes or distortions in the patterns of speech behaviour of alcoholic individuals.

Dramatised drunken speeches are acted speeches. This type of speeches differs from the normal, uncontrolled speeches of an alcohol "since the actor controls the verbal expression in order to convey a certain effect to the listener..." (Erickson *et al*, 2006:2). They are utterances that are dramatised by comedians to mirror the speech behaviour of alcoholic personalities. Dramatised alcoholic speeches are treated in this paper as Alcholic Talk Show (ATS). ATS speech delivery style is a fast-paced succession of humorous stories, which constitute what is typically called a monologue. This style of delivery gives the actor, Klint da Drunk, ample opportunities to dramatise drunkenness and use some expressive gestures in order to maintain stage auditorium continuum. Some of the features noticeable in ATS are integral elements of oral performance (Rosenberg, 1970). The speech style comes with all the ingredients of melody of voice, loudness, vowel lengthening and gestures which Klint da Drunk often employs to make his comic messages vivid. Klint da Drunk is one of the Nigerian Stand-up comedians whose comic style mimics inebriated utterances. Scholars like Adetunji (2013), Ayakoroma (2013), Adejunmobi (2014), and Filani (2015) have carried out studies on Nigerian Stand-up Comedy. While Ayankoroma's (2013) traces and discuses the rise of Stand-up comedy genre in Nigeria from nothing to something in artistic entertainment, Adetunji's (2013) focuses on the interactional context of humour in this genre. Adejunmobi's (2014) study discusses Stand-up Comedy within the ethical orientations of popular performance in Nigeria while Filani (2015) describes Stand-up Comedy as an activity type in which the stand-up comedians try to negotiate all its parameters. All these studies situate Nigerian Stand-up comedy as an important genre of artistic entertainment that is making wave in Nigeria.

Comedy, according to Bergson (1928: 6), is an exclusively human activity, something mechanical in something living, purely cerebral and it has social functions. The elicitation of laughter is the goal of a good comedy. It should be stressed that through laughter, misrepresentations can be admonished and men/women and society can be called back to their true nature. But comedy is not all about laughter; high comedy appeals to the intellect and gives some therapy to the aching souls of the readers or audience. That is why humour which is one of the core components of comedy draws upon particular cognitive experiences to provoke laughter and provide amusement.

Several studies have been carried out on the analysis of speeches ranging from political, normal and deformed and alcoholic ones. Atoye (1991) has investigated word stress placement pattern in speech productions of Nigerian speakers of English through perceptual analysis. In the study, he identifies that the pattern of progressive stress-shift in Nigerian spoken English (NSE) is largely consistent. Sunday (2010) has worked on speech disorders in aphasia patients. Other scholars like Stain (1966), Trojan and Kryspin-Exner (1968), Sobell and Sobell (1972), Lester and Skousen (1974) and Beam *et al.* (1978) who ventured out of these conventional areas of speech investigations have explored the effects of alcohol on speech production. Scholars on the effects of alcohol on speech productions have identified some features associated with alcoholised utterances.

Studies like Trojan and Kryspin-Exner (1968), Lester and Skousen (1974) and Sobell *et al.* (1972) have investigated the perceptual and acoustic features of alcohol induced speeches. In the experiment carried out by Trojan and Kryspin-Exner (1968: 219) on the differences between the speech produced by 3 subjects on words before alcohol and at 2 levels of alcohol consumption, they identified that the speech of alcoholics is characterised by "general lingual dissolution", "phonetic disturbances" and "changes in verbal expressions". Also, Zaimov (1969) establishes that errors in speech increase as the amount of alcohol intake increases. He attributes these errors to the abnormalities of the patho-physiological nervous system which cause inhibition of regular paths and consequently the switching of the course of normal reactions. A further feature of alcoholic talk is established by Lester and Skousen's (1974: 233) view that "drunken speech appears to be drawn out". This is as a result of the lengthening in the vocal segments. These changes are attributable to changes in the central nervous system (CNS).

However, the present study differs from these earlier studies on alcoholic speeches in that it investigates dramatised alcoholic speeches of Klint da Drunk. In analyzing the data, the paper draws insights from Bergson's Theory of Comedy which describes aptly the core elements of what constitute comedy as something mechanical and cerebral which has social function(s). Comedy elicits laughter production. Further insight drawn from this theory is that laughter is thoughtful. People laugh because they have reasoned and identified errors made by somebody, the consequence of his or her stupidity. A drunk can neither behave nor think rationally. It is this momentary loss of the power of reason that people laugh at in an alcoholic. Alcohol robs a drunk of the ability to act and speak as an 'intelligent' soul and transforms the fellow into a fool. But comedy is not all about laughter; it appeals to the intellect and gives some therapy to the aching souls in the auditorium. The evocation of laughter comes with some social therapeutic functions. Klint da Drunk's ATS is presented in this paper as a comedy because his mimicry of a drunk's actions, expressions, dress styles and gestures often amuses his audience. A situation like this evokes laughter naturally from the audience. What are the structural and lingual features of dramatised alcoholic talks? How do the indentified features contribute to the creation of humour? What are the social issues raised in this ATS discourse? This study provides answers to these questions.

METHODOLOGY

In pursuing the aim and objectives as enumerated above, we obtained two *YouTube* recordings of Klint da Drunk's Alcoholic Talk Shows online. One was selected from his live show in Ghana (https://www.youtube.com/watch?v=elcxD1sw-dw) and the other one was from his Lagos show (www.9jacomedyvideos.com). They were purposely selected because of level of distortions in the utterances of the performer and the topic social issues treated in them. The recordings were transcribed into written script and subjected to perceptual analysis. The transcript of the *YouTube* video recordings was analysed to identify the linguistic signals of ATS in order to discuss the social issues raised in it, using insights from Bergson's theory of comedy.

ANALYSIS AND DISCUSSION OF DATA

A close perceptual and visual analysis of the data revealed that ATS shares some structural features of drunken speeches such as lingual distortions, phonetic disturbances and changes in vocal expressions. It also raises some social issues affecting the Nigerian society. The analysis that follows substantiates how these features manifest in the data.

Lingual Distortions

Under this category, we analyse some distortions in the linguistic utterances in the data. The data manifests the occurrence of some para-grammatical repetitions of words and phrases because alcohol has repressed freedom and power to use intellect and turns the speaker into a robot, an unthinking machine that performs the same function and cannot effect a change or reverse itself without the aid of an external agent. In contrast, a person who is not under the control of liquor is conscious of rules and able to self-reflect, correct a slip of the tongue, weigh words, employ the best synonym and generally control his articulation. For example, the following excerpt in example 1 aptly illustrates the repetitive patterns noticeable in ATS.

You're very stupid. You're an idiot. I'm telling you. You're.... you're very uncomfortable. What is wrong with you? You're... You're an idiot. You're very...

In contextualising this excerpt, Klint satirises the telephone etiquette of some Nigerians who in spite of using earpiece and Bluetooth in their mobile phones, still shout whenever they communicate using the phone. He dramatises this folly in his dialogue with the Master of ceremony (MC) of the stand-up comedy show in Ghana. He describes the anonymous phone user as 'a fool or a stupid person'. To underscore this foible, he employs repetitions at word and structural levels. In the excerpt above, the word 'stupid' and 'idiot' are repeated. Apart from the near synonymous nature of these two words, the actor deploys structural parallelism with SPC pattern in the indicative sentences.

Also, he explores and reiterates the display of folly at individual and collective levels in the data as demonstrated in example 2: *[...] the only person that was stupid. Honestly, I mean it. I know I am a very stupid person. I accept it. I am a very stupid, very idiotic, very useless [...].* He even extends the foolishness to everybody when he claims *I never knew that I had branches all over West Africa.* He logically extends this idea of universal foible with the metaphor of branches. The actor defamiliarises the audience's notion of 'branches' which collocates with 'trees or business' by extending it to foolishness. This semantic extension of 'branches' has a lot of cognitive appeal which tasks the intellectual capacity of the audience. Consequently, it elicits laughter from them. This underscores that humanity displays some foolish habitual behaviour. The laughter engendered by the word 'branches' could also be traced to the exaggerated claim of the comedian who puts all members of the audience in his school of buffoons and clowns, since he lacks the power of restraints, the virtue of modesty, a sense of proportion, and the

You	*'re*	*very stupid*	*You*	*'re*	*an idiot*	*I*	*'m telling*	*You*	*You*	*'re*	*an idiot*
S	P	C	S	P	C	S	P	C	S	P	C

discriminating force of the intellect. He imagines himself a business magnate, whereas in actuality, he is a clown who ironically, makes people pay for causing them to laugh. He turns the table against his audience. They are the fools paying for foolery. However, the audience could not but laugh when they realize that 'this idiotic person' is endowed to point out their follies and foibles.

Similarly, the phrase 'first lady' was repeated thrice in example 3: *I was appointed by the first lady as the interim security departmental officer of the first lady office of the first lady.* The import of this repetition of 'first lady' draws the audience attention to the prominence and the personality of the occupier of the office in the contemporary Nigerian polity. The First Lady is the hostess of the White House in the United States of America. The office is traditionally occupied by the wife of the President but in Nigeria, First Lady is the title of the wife of Nigerian President. The comedian appears to be referring to the Nigerian first lady Mrs Patience Ebele Jonathan, who has been described as one of the 'five presidents in the presidency' by Olusegun Obasanjo, shows that she has gone beyond the traditional roles of being a 'hostess' at Aso Rock to a dispenser of political patronage or someone who offers security appointments.

Moreover, the data displays some syntactic errors. These are errors that are associated with ungrammatical/ill-formed expressions in English. Solecisms are sources of laughter. We laugh at a person who commits such errors. What the audience are actually laughing at is his/her ignorance of grammatical laws. It is necessary, however, to point out that Klint da Drunk is deliberately violating the laws in order to provoke laughter. He knows the rules but pretends that he does not. The joke is on his audience. An instance of the occurrence of these syntactic errors is shown in example 4: *So at this point in time, I'm going to sang…say em…what?* In example 4 above, the 'to' cannot collocate with 'sang', the past tense of the verb 'sing'. This is because, the non-finite verb 'to + $X^{0'}$ (simple base verb proceeded by "to') as a rule does not mark tense, person and number. As shown in example 4, 'to sang' is a syntactic distortion. 'To' can only collocate with the present form of the verb 'sing' 'to sing'. The use of 'sang' therefore breaks the syntactic rule in English thereby rendering the utterance ungrammatical. Ditto, the structure of an English noun phrase in example 5: *I'm going to sing my own sing,* is made up of a modifier, headword and qualifier (mhq). As a rule, the 'headword' is usually a noun. However, it is observed that in the ATS, the verbal element, 'sing', occupies the headword position in the noun phrase 'my own sing' (mh) rather than selecting its noun form 'song'. This is an unacceptable grammatical structure in English. His question "who is fooling who here?" is crucial and pertinent. Comedy is serious business. Unfortunately, most people think it is frivolous. Some folks have the same perception of arts in general; they are useless and contribute nothing of significance to society.

Similarly, embolophrasia, a speech disorder in which meaningless words or sounds are interjected into sentences, manifests in the data. Klint da Drunk makes use of some of these meaningless words which he himself admits that he does not know their meanings as exemplified in example 6: *Do you imagine somebody dancing and tumbling. This is 'summertumbling'.* The word 'summertumbling' is an arbitrary coinage that is not part of the English vocabulary. What exists in English lexicon is 'summersault'. The latitude enjoyed by 'the drunk' gives him/her the freedom to unleash assault on the English language. One of the consequences of this novel creation is that it evokes laughter from the audience whose minds had been rigidly or mechanically constricted to the usage of 'summersault' to accepting 'summertumbling' as a replacement or a synonym. Also, Klint in example 7: *We are looking for 'the adjectival phrase of the metaphor so that the simile will become an adjectival phrase,* utters an expression that depicts the distortions in the mind of a drunk whereby words are uttered with no attention paid to effectively communicating the intended messages. The speed at which this utterance was uttered electrified the audience into frenzy and they clapped repeatedly without taking cognizance of the meaninglessness of the expression. The import of the above excerpt illustrates the fact that a fool is above the laws, be they grammatical or moral. Laws, as far as comedians are concerned are meant to be broken. There will always be imprecision and breakdown of communication because language itself is an imperfect tool. What is called 'meaningless expression' is the Drunk's meaning in the routine. Describing the reggae artists and the inspiration they associate with the smoking of 'weed' (hemp), he likens his performance of this type of music to *'the fiasco of electrical buggy buggy'.* What is the meaning? Hear him in example 8:

I'm in 'the fiasco of electrical buggy buggy'. Do you know the meaning? Do you know the meaning? (The audience says No and he answers). Neither do I.

Both the audience and the actor could not explain the meaning of the expression. His answer "neither do I" elicits a round of applause from the audience. The expression is also a play on 'boogie-woogie', a form of jazz, which is itself rhythmical nonsense, a series of improvisation that is not guided by rules.

Speech Dysfluencies

Under this category, we analyse some speech dysfluencies in the data. Speech dysfluencies are speeches that are not delivered fluently. They are characterised by a lot of distortions and irregularities that stall speech fluency such as fillers, false starts, omissions, etc. The data is replete with dysfluencies.

First, we observe that the actor makes use of fillers in achieving what he calls 'rhythmical madness' of the reggae music. Fillers are sounds or non-lexical vocables which contain no formal meanings. Klint da Drunk employs these non-vocables in musical renditions in his performance. In example 9: *Bass guitar man, […] I want you to play something like this for me man tu du du du du du.* He beckons to the 'bass guitar man' to play him a sound pattern with *tu du du du du du* prompts. The musical and rhythmical relevance of the *tu du du du du du* prompts contribute to creating aesthetics. Other non-lexical vocables in the data include *nwaka nwaka nwaka nwaka nwaka* which are used to imitate the sounds and musical rendition patterns of reggae music in example 10:

Another is the rhythmical madness does not just steady just like Nigeria NEPA. It goes like this: nwaka nwaka nwaka nwaka nwaka.

This rhythmical madness' is what we call life. The inability of human being to reflect on actions and thoughts and change is the genesis of madness. It makes a mad person a machine. Instability characterizes National Electric Power Authortity (NEPA). Uncertainty defines human life.

Second, Klint employs false starts in his performances. False starts are words and sentences that are cut off midway into the utterances. They are characterised by repeated syllables and phrases and omissions. Several instances of false starts occur in the dramatised drunken utterances. Example 11 below succinctly illustrates this feature.

I know I am very stupid person. I accept it. I'm very stupid, very idiotic. Very useless, (points to the audience). You are my friends. And they say show me your friends and tell you what you …. (beautiful), the expressions […]very useless, (points to the audience), you are my friends. And they say show me your friends and (sic) tell you what you …. (beautiful).

From the excerpt above, Klint deploys several declarative sentences to mirror his own stupidity. However, in the last sentence of the excerpt below, he employs incomplete utterances as a strategic tool for eliciting active audience participation. He devises this means as a strategy to break his monologue and facilitate feedback from the audience in order to gauge their level of involvement and enjoyment of his narrations. The performer deliberately fails to complete the expression "and tell you what you…". He allows the audience to fill in the gap with the verb 'are' since they, the audience, are familiar with the expression. His body language, pointing to the audience, reveals to them that he has successfully appropriated them as 'his friends'. The word 'friends' is ironically used. Irony, of course, is an unfailing source of laughter. It inverts all relationships and upsets all arrangements based on logic. Consequently, they then realise that they are equally 'stupid, and very useless'. This point of recognition elicits some laughter from the audience. A comedian, however, must be cautious not to insult or offend his/her patrons. Hence, the performer in this context enfeebles the power of the ironic word 'friends' with the epithet 'beautiful'. Of course the audience would be taken in and believe that they are truly beautiful.

Third, Klint da Drunk employs substitution which is replacement of sounds, words or phrases with something else. This replacement or substitution is done in such a way as to deviate from the normal pattern (mechanical behavioural disposition) of humans. For example, the actor, substitutes 'volume' with 'velocity'. These two words are not in the same semantic field, nor are they synonyms. The only similarity they share is the initial voiced labiodental fricative /v/ sound. 'Volume' in the context of the usage in the narration suggests the reduction in quantity of its loudness, while 'velocity' refers to pace or speed of an action. The words therefore are not synonymous. By deliberately selecting 'velocity' instead of 'volume', Klint succeeds in breaking the monolithic pattern in which human beings associate meanings with lexical items as if those meanings were not, in the first place, arbitrarily, assigned to words. Similarly, the performer substitutes 'Jah Rasta fried rice' for 'Jah rasta fari' which is a common greeting slogan of reggae artists. The last disyllabic word in the slogan 'fari' /faːrai/ is distorted and realised as 'fried rice' [fraid rais]. Since he brings in the idea of food, 'rice', he extends the distortion to 'Selassie eat it'. Klint plays on his knowledge of the central role assigned to Emperor Haile Selassie in the Rastafarian movement globally. Selassie is one of the names of Emperor Haile Selassie, the late President of Ethiopia. In the Rastafari movement, Haile Selassie is revered as a messianic figure who would lead a future golden age of eternal peace, righteousness, and prosperity (Barrett, 1988).

Other examples of substitution in the text which illustrate this incongruity include 'men to gen' for 'ladies and gentlemen' and 'Desmond idiot' for Desmond Eliot'. The members of the audience are used to hearing 'gentlemen'. The performer has consciously distorted this expression by inversing the orthographical representation of 'gentlemen to 'men to gen'. The syllabic consonant [tl] in 'tle' is transformed to [tu]. Also, 'Eliot' the surname of Desmond, a Nollywood star, is deliberately distorted as 'idiot'. Though this coinage rhymes with 'Eliot', it should be stressed that this 'creative distortion' (Filani, 2015: 77) brings in some incongruity which elicits hilarious feelings from the audience.

Lastly, sounds are deliberately distorted in the comedian's performance. In example 12, Klint pronounces 'past party people' [pæst paːti piːpl] instead of 'past participle' /pəst'paːtisipl/. The distortion in the utterance occurs at the penultimate syllable of 'participle' /paːtisipl/ where he realises [piː] instead of /si/ to produce 'people'. In his slurred speech, two sounds have been distorted which consequently affects the meaning of the utterance. Voiced bilabial plosive [p] and unrounded closed front vowel [iː] are used instead of voiceless alveolar fricative [s] and unrounded half closed front vowel [i]. Also, the distortion of the phrase, 'past participle', leads to the creation of a new phrase 'past party people'. The word 'participle' is distorted to form two words 'party people'. Additionally, in his bid to make jest of the bulging and protruding eyes of one of Nollywood stars in the audience, Segun Arinze, he creatively distorts the initial monophthong sound [a] in *Arinze* [arinze] and changes it to a closing diphthong /ai/ to make it sound like 'eye' [airinze]. His hyperbolic description of Arinze's eyes is captured succinctly in the example 13 below:

Segun, I don't know why they use 'eye' for your first name, Arinze, because of your eye. I told you dracular bite this man and turn to vegetarian. Dracular cannot eat blood again because of the fearfulness of his eyes...evil spirit came to his house and saw him and the evil spirit shouted, shouted, blood of Jesus...

Segun Arinze together with the audience laughed at the expression "the evil spirit shouted, shouted, blood of Jesus..." when it saw the bulging eyes of Arinze! Furthermore, 'Ghanaians' /gəneiənz/ was pronounced as 'Ghananians' [gananians] which is the typical rendition pattern of incipient bilingual Nigerians who have little or no formal education.

Social Issues in ATS

Like fools in most Shakespearean plays like *Twelfth Night, King Lear* and *Hamlet*, Klint da Drunk serves as the 'saner voice' in society. His simulated drunkenness gives him the limitless freedom of telling the truth to the powers that be and every segment of the society. In line with Nwana's (2013) position, Klint da Drunk is one of the young enterprising Nigerians who make jokes out of the many difficulties around them and by so doing entertaining the audience. This creative and humorous use of dramatised inebriated utterances is appreciated by audience who love to see him compere at conferences, workshops and parties and earn handsomely for his industriousness. Some of his jokes usually underscore some aspects of social behaviour that need to be remedied:

For example, the ill-effect of drug abuse (weed) is brought to the fore in his performance. Klint deconstructs the inspiration which reggae musicians associate with the intake of 'weed' before going on stage. He terms this 'back stage action'. According to him, the weed, rather than making them creative and inspirational, blocks 'their brain' and thereby makes them unnecessarily repetitive and monotonous as shown in example 14: *So, I decided, I decided..."* Tired of these repetitions, he asks rhetorically, *"decided to do what?* Even the wordings and the tunes of the music have been affected with this repetitive effect of 'weed' intake, as shown in the following text in example 15:

I say the hey, hey, hey, hey....
hew, hew, hew, hew
just the other day, just the other day
I say just the other day
hew, hew, hew
a wirry ooo ! ooooo!

Additionally, the incompleteness of the acronym MTEL as a brand name for the Nigerian Mobile Telephone is satirised. The actor simply interprets MTEL as 'my telephone'. This creative interpretation completely deviates from what the audience are used to. It takes the exchange between MTEL manager who sponsored the event and Klint to make the former realise the incompleteness of the acronym that fails to capture the 'Nigerian' component of the brand name MTEL (see example 16 below). It also takes the ingenuity of a drunk to ask the MTEL Manager, "where is N?" in 'Nigerian mobile telecommunication' which is the full meaning of MTEL.

Klint: *You work with MTEL? What is the full meaning of MTEL?*
MTEL Manager: *Nigerian mobile telecommunication*
Klint: *from MTEL, where is N? Let me tell you. I know the meaning. You work there; MTEL- my telephone.*

The performance also highlights how language can be deployed in manipulating the people in doing what they would not ordinarily do of their own volition. Verbal manipulation is a covert deployment of language to achieve certain goals/desires of the speakers without the listeners' awareness. This linguistic phenomenon often widens the illusionary subjective reality. Language manipulation is used in politics, religion, business and advertisements to make people do the biddings of political, business and religious leaders. Klint creates 'fear' which is one of the strategies used in language of religious manipulation. He deploys this strategy perfectly in making his audience to be on their feet in honour of the MTEL manager who bankrolled the expenditure for the concert. Example 17 vividly captures his manipulative tendencies. Hear him:

I want you all to … a standing ovation for these beautiful souls. If you don't stand, May all the things you are working for don't work for you in Jesus name (everybody stands).

From the excerpt above, Klint makes use of threat, *If you don't stand, may all the things you are working for don't work for you in Jesus name,* to cause the audience to give a standing ovation to MTEL manager. He explores believers' credulity and gullibility. They could have obeyed him probably because of their belief in the potency of the name Jesus. The effect of this threat couched in prayer with the evocation of "in Jesus' name", forces them to stand thereby doing his bidding of giving a standing ovation to the manager. Klint acknowledges the effectiveness of this strategy as shown in example 18 below

You can sit down now. I have converted all of them to church goers even Muslims, they are all standing. If I say stand for him, how many people will?

The rhetorical question "if I say stand for him, how many people will?" sets the audience into deep reflection and consciousness that Klint has successfully manipulated them. Realising how they have been fooled, they laugh.

CONCLUSION

This study has affirmed that thespians do not only dramatise actions but mime speech styles. Klint da Drunk as a thespian successfully mimes the speech style of alcoholic personality and his utterances exemplify lingual distortions and speech dysfluencies that are characteristics of drunken utterances. The performer deploys the miming of the lingual distortions and speech dysfluencies that are characteristics of drunken utterances as the tools for humour creation. The study has brought to the fore the relevance of stand-up comedy to society in general and in particular in that it draws attention to the social ills of drug abuse, social etiquettes of Mobile telephone usage, the language of religious manipulation strategy and the healing effect of laughter on the citizens. The genre is not just an avenue for laughter but an avenue for social reengineering of the mind, especially the virile youthful ones. Finally, language as a socio-cultural artifact reflects the innovative, entrepreneurial and imaginative usage of the English language in the entertainment industry.

REFERENCES

Adejunmobi, M. (2014). Standup Comedy and the Ethics of Popular Performance in Nigeria. In N. Stephanie & O. Onookome (Eds.), *Popular Culture in Africa: The Episteme of the Everyday* (pp. 175–194). New York: Routledge.

Adetunji, A. (2013). The Interactional Context of Hummour in Nigerian Stand-up Comedy. *Pragmatics*, *23*(1), 1–22. doi:10.1075/prag.23.1.01ade

American Mental Association. (2008). *AMA Reports of the Council on Science and Public Health: Substance Use and Substance Use Disorder*. AMA Annual Note.

Atoye, R. O. (1991). Word Stress in Nigerian English. *World Englishes, No.*, *10*(1), 1–6. doi:10.1111/j.1467-971X.1991.tb00132.x

Ayakoroma, B. F. (2013). The Rise of Stand-up Comedy Genre in Nigeria: From Nothing to Something in Artistic Entertainment. *The Rise of Stand-up Comedy Genre in Nigeria*. Retrieved from http://www.nico.gov.ng/features/1008-the-rise-of-stand-up-comedy-genre-in-nigeria.html

Barrett, L. E. (1988). *The Rastafarians*. Beacon Press.

Beam, S. L., Gant, R. W., & Mecham, M. J. (1978). Communication Deviations in Alcoholics: A Pilot Study. *Journal of Studies on Alcohol*, *39*(3), 548–551. doi:10.15288/jsa.1978.39.548 PMID:651363

Bergson, H. (1928). *Laughter: An Essay on the Meaning of the Comic*. New York: The Macmillan Co.

Double, O. (2014). *Getting the Joke: The Inner Workings of Stand-up Comedy*. London: Bloomsbury.

Erickson, D., Yoshida, K., & Meneze, C. (2006). Exploratory Study of Some Acoustic and Articulatory Characteristics of Sad Speech. *Phonetica*, *63*(1), 1–25. doi:10.1159/000091404 PMID:16514273

Filani, I. (2015). Stand-up Comedy as an Activity Type. *International Journal of Humour Research*, *4*(1), 73–97.

9. *ja Comedy Videos*. (n.d.). Retrieved from: https://www. 9jacomedyvideos.com

Kint da Drunk. (2015). Retrieved from: https://www.youtube.com/watch?v=elcxD1sw-dw

Klint da Drunk. (2012). *People don't Understand My Swag*. Retrieved from http://www.nigeriafilms.com/news/16623/13/people-dont-understand-my-swag-klint-da-drunk.html)

Lester, L., & Skousen, R. (1974). The Phonology of Drunkenness. In A. Bruck, R. Fox & M. W. LaGaly (Eds.), *Papers from the Para session On Natural Phonology*. Chicago Linguistics.

Mintz, L. (1985). Stand–up Comedy as Social and Cultural Mediation. *American Quarterly*, *37*(1), 71–80. doi:10.2307/2712763

Ninalowo, A. (1996). Contradictions of Military Governance and Industrial Democracy. In A. Ninalwo (Ed.), *The Quest for Democratization; Military Governance and Trade Union* (pp. 105–128). Yaba, Nigeria: Friedrich Elbert Foundation.

Nwana, E. (2013, August 13). The Business of Comedy in Nigeria. *Economic Financial Times*.

Panksepp, J. (2000). The Riddle of Laughter: Neural and Psycho Evolutionary Underpinning of Joy. *Current Directions in Psychological Science*, *9*(6), 183–186. doi:10.1111/1467-8721.00090

Polander, E., & Shallin, V. L. (2013). An analysis of Narrative and Figurative Language within Online Alcoholism Discussion Forum. *International Journal Mental Health Association*, *11*(4), 458–473. doi:10.1007/s11469-013-9431-8

Radcliffe-Brown, A. R. (1952). *Structure and Function in Primitive Society: Essays and Addresses*. New York, NY: Free Press.

Rosenberg, B. A. (1970). *The Art of the American Folk Preacher*. New York: Oxford, University Press.

Schwarz, J. (2010). *Linguistic Aspects of Verbal Humour in Stand-up Comedy*. (PhD Dissertation). Department of English, University of Saarland.

Sobell, L. C., & Sobell, M. B. (1972). Effects of Alcohol on the Speech of Alcoholics. *Journal of Speech and Hearing*, *15*(4), 861–868. doi:10.1044/jshr.1504.861 PMID:4652408

Stain, D. R. (1966). Linguistic Analysis of the Speech of a Selected Group of former alcoholics: A research note. *Quarterly Journal of Studies on Alcohol*, *27*, 106–109. PMID:5907517

Sunday, A. (2010). The Suprasegmental of Bilingual Nigerian Adult Aphasics. *SKASE Journal of Theoretical Linguistics*, *7*(2). Retrieved from http://www.skase.sk/volumes/JTL16/pdf_doc./03.pdf

Sypher, W. (Ed.). (1991). Comedy. The Johns Hopkins University Press.

Trojan, F., & Kryspin-Exner, K. (1968). The Decay of Articulation under the Influence of Alcohol and Paraldehyde. *Folia Phoniatrica*, *20*(4), 217–238. doi:10.1159/000263201 PMID:5671974

Vereen, L. G., Butler, S. K., Williams, F. C., Darg, J. A., & Downing, T. K. E. (2006). The Use of Humor when Counseling African American College Students. *Journal of Counseling and Development*, *84*(1), 10–15. doi:10.1002/j.1556-6678.2006.tb00375.x

Zaimov, K. (1969). Die Sprachtorungen als Kriterium der Bewußtseinstrubungen Psychiatrie. *Neurologie, und Medizinische Psychologie*, *21*, 218–225.

KEY TERMS AND DEFINITIONS

Alcoholic Talk: it refers to a form of speech that simulates or dramatises expressions made under the influence of alcohol.

Alcoholic Talk Show: It refers to utterances that are dramatised by comedians to mirror the speech behaviour of a drunk.

Embolophrasia: refers to a speech disorder in which meaningless words or sounds are interjected into sentences.

Lingual Distortion: This refers to some alterations in the linguistic utterances of speakers.

Speech Dysfluencies: this concept depicts speeches that are not delivered smoothly or fluently. Such speeches are characterised by a lot of distortions and irregularities such as fillers, false starts, omissions, etc.

Stand-up Comedians: It refers to comedians whose acts consist of standing before an audience and telling a series of jokes. They are humour merchants.

APPENDIX A

Klint da Drunk in Ghana (https://www.youtube.com/watch?v=elcxD1sw-dw)

Klint: *(Staggers to the stage, makes a phone call) you are very stupid. You're an idiot, I am telling you. You are, you are very uncomfortable. What is wrong with you? You are an idiot. You're very... In fact, I 'm not, I cannot speak with you at this moment... Honestly, 'excuse me.*

MC: *Then, I'm going to go.*

Klint: *sorry, I was on the phone!*

MC: *He got me there! (Laughs)*

Klint: *I'm trying to show you how stupid we people can be nowadays (gesticulates with hands) with earpiece especially with the Bluetooth when they are this one...and the other* ***way and they are shouting. You think you are the victim.***

MC: *(laughs) I'm glad. I'm done ladies and gentlemen (he leaves the stage).*

Klint: *(alone on stage, engages in a monologue) I never knew I had branches throughout West Africa. Honestly, I thought I was the only person that was stupid. Honestly, I mean it. I know I am a very stupid person. I accept it, very stupid. I am very idiotic, vey useless. You are my friends (points to the audience). And they say show me your friends and (sic) tell you what you... (He exclaims, beautiful!). I can't come to Ghana and go home free. I must context in this problem (programme) (points to the stage light). All of you must judge me today. If you don't judge me, honestly, I will look straight to you and judge you.. And you look cool and beautiful the way you have been looking since. You must judge me today. Because woe betides you if I judge you here, highest, you can't even arrest me because if you take me to court, I will tell you that I said it under the influence of alcohol (laughs, shakes head). So, at this point in time, I am going to sang... say emh... what is the part party people of sing? Past tense of sang is sing. That one is present continuous. We are for adjectival phrase of the metaphor so that the simile will become an adjectival phrase. I don't know, even understand what I'm saying and you people are clapping for me (audience laughs). I don't know who is fooling who here (staggers). Please I'm going on top of them but his people are trying. Do you imagine somebody dancing and tumbling? This one is summertumble. I am going to sang my own sing, and I say ... I 'm going to do my music personally. But you know, first of all put your hands together for all the Ghananaians. Put your hands together. I came all the way from Nigeria and know it has been a long time. I'm enjoying music. Am I lying? Desmond idiot (Eliot), am I lying. You confess Segun. I don't know why they use 'I' for your first name (Arinze) because of your 'eye'. I told you Dracula bite this man and turned to a vegetarian. Dracula cannot eat blood again because of the fearfulness of his face. Evil spirit came...and saw... you know all these things they do in all these Nigerian films. They do juju. Juju will come and attack you. Sometimes if you are not careful and acting that role they will come and attack you in real life. This man acted the role and he did not pray. Evil came to his house and saw him and the evil spirit shouted, blood of Jesus!(puts his hand up on his head). Put your hand together for him.*

I want to do my own music. Please without wasting time, why Nigerian music has not been going too far. ... all these Reggae musicians here. I'm glad you are wearing dark glass inside the house at night. What is wrong with you? Are you addicted to criminology? So the reason why Nigerian reggae music has not been making waves is because of this. Listen carefully. After preparing beautiful reggae music, they go back stage, smoke weed. It will block their brain. The lyrics of the songs will evaporate with the smoke of the weed. Then when they come on stage, they are confused. They look at the crowd, they are not seeing anybody. Then at that point, everybody's name will turn to man. Just like men here are called Charley Charley, charley. There are many Charlie here. I wonder why you people don't use Moses or Andrew! But see, every body's name will turn to man. That is why, when they come out and shout Hi man! If I say hi man, you answer yeh man! (He shouts hi man!) (Chorus) hey man! So, all of you smoke weed. (Laughs) at this point they now look at the bass guitar person and they call him bass guitar man!

I want you to play something like this for me man tu du du du du du (musical tune). The person with another form of rhythm –keyboard player, another is the rhythmical madness does not stay steady just like the Nigeria NEPA. It goes like this nwaka, nwaka, nwaka, nwaka, nwaks. You see. (Instructs the operator) rhythmically reduce the velocity (volume). You can hear the person playing the guitar has a madness that describe as multiple gralulu in random motion. Do not ask me the meaning. I don't even know the meaning.

I decided, I decided. Decided to do what? Hew, ew, ew, ew. The weed is still talking.Jah Rasta fried rice Selassie eat it.

I say the hey hey hey…
hew, hew, hew,
just the other day,
just the other day.
hew, hew, hew.
I wiry oh oh oh

APPENDIX B

Klint da Drunk live in Lagos (www.9jacomedyvideos.com)

(Staggers to the stage, dresses with his shirt flowing and one of his trousers pulled up) I want to ask a question. How many of you came to crack your ribs? How many people have their ribs cracked? Nobody? You know I did my show I was appointed by the First Lady as the Interim Security Departmental Officer of the First Lady Office of the first lady. So if you don't have your cracks, I meant your ribs cracked or crack ribs, I am going to crack it personally. And I am going to do it physically (points out a rod. is your rib crack? is it crack? why are you lying? open your teeth and crack your ribs now.

(Points to MTEL Manager) honestly, you work with MTEL. What is the full meaning of MTEL? (Sound effect) Shut up! Nigerian mobile telecommunication; from MTEl, where is N? Let me tell you, you. I know the meaning. You work there. MTEL, my telephone! (Laughs). Let me tell you the truth. for the organisation of this show, that for the whole thing that happen because some of you are outside…I want you to… a standing ovation for this beautiful soul. If you don't stand, May all the things you are working

for don't work for you in Jesus name (everybody stands). You can sit down now. I have converted all of them to church goers, even Muslims, they are all standing. If I say stand for him, how many people will? Please ladies and men to gen I want you to evaporate and condense. DJ, DJ, I want to dance. I am in the fiasco of electrical buggy buggy. Do you know the meaning? Do you know the meaning? Neither do I.

Excerpts

1. You're very stupid. You're an idiot. I'm telling you. You're.... you're very uncomfortable. What is wrong with you? You're... You're an idiot. You're very...
2. [...] the only person that was stupid. Honestly, I mean it. I know I am a very stupid person. I accept it. I am a very stupid, very idiotic, very useless [...].
3. I was appointed by the first lady as the interim security departmental officer of the first lady office of the first lady.
4. So at this point in time, I'm going to sang...say em...what?
5. I'm going to sing my own sing
6. Do you imagine somebody dancing and tumbling? This is 'summertumbling'.
7. We are looking for 'the adjectival phrase of the metaphor so that the simile will become an adjectival phrase,
8. I'm in 'the fiasco of electrical buggy buggy'. Do you know the meaning? Do you know the meaning?
9. Bass guitar man, [...] I want you to play something like this for me man tu du du du du du.
10. Another is the rhythmical madness does not just steady just like Nigeria NEPA. It goes like this: nwaka nwaka nwaka nwaka nwaka.
11. I know I am very stupid person. I accept it. I'm very stupid, very idiotic. Very useless, (points to the audience). You are my friends. And they say show me your friends and tell you what you .... (beautiful), the expressions [...]very useless, (points to the audience), you are my friends. And they say show me your friends and (sic) tell you what you .... (beautiful).
12. 'past party people'
13. Segun, I don't know why they use 'eye' for your first name, Arinze, because of your eye. I told you dracular bite this man and turn to vegetarian. Dracular cannot eat blood again because of the fearfulness of his eyes...evil spirit came to his house and saw him and the evil spirit shouted, shouted, blood of Jesus...
14. So, I decided, I decided..." Tired of these repetitions, he asks rhetorically, "decided to do what?
15. I say the hey, hey, hey, hey....
    hew, hew, hew, hew
    just the other day, just the other day
    I say just the other day
    hew, hew, hew
    a wirry ooo ! ooooo!
16. Klint: You work with MTEL? What is the full meaning of MTEL?
    MTEL Manager: Nigerian mobile telecommunication
    Klint: from MTEL, where is N? Let me tell you. I know the meaning. You work there; MTEL- my telephone.

17. I want you all to … a standing ovation for these beautiful souls. If you don't stand, May all the things you are working for don't work for you in Jesus name (everybody stands).
18. You can sit down now. I have converted all of them to church goers even Muslims, they are all standing. If I say stand for him, how many people will?

Chapter 8
Language and Humour in Cameroon Social Media

Camilla Arundie Tabe
Ecole Normale Supérieure, University of Maroua, Cameroon

ABSTRACT

This chapter explores language use that incites laughter in Cameroon e-mail, Facebook, Yahoo Messenger and mobile telephone SMS. The incongruity and the incongruity-resolution theory (Ritchie, 1999; Mulder & Nijholt, 2002) and Gricean maxims were useful in the analysis of 270 electronic chats and messages. Results indicate patterns of language that create humour like flouting of Gricean maxims, special repetition of punctuation marks, sound devices, emoticons and hyperbole. Cameroonians employ these humorous linguistic forms for pleasure, intimacy and to maintain cultural values. It was established that the Facebook platform was more hospitable to humour than the others because all the linguistic markers that were detected to generate humour were found in it with high rates of occurrences.

INTRODUCTION

Language that creates humour is significant in the linguistic field nowadays (Attardo, 1997; Attardo & Raskin 1991, 1994; Ruch, Attardo & Raskin 1993). This type of language use does not simply convey information, but produces a laughing effect. Some linguists (Attardo, 1993; Attardo & Raskin 1994) argue that such language most often defy the conventions of normal language but are socially unobjectionable. In order to communicate appropriately, online language users bring in linguistic resources such as spelling deviances, sound devices, special repetition of punctuation marks, emoticons and violation of Gricean maxims. Most of these involve the use of language in an absurd manner thus incongruity. In the process of producing these illogical linguistic forms, internet users are creating humour aimed at making their addressees to relax, enjoy the communication and "bond" with them. Humour is considered as pleasure in incongruity. And incongruity is based on the view of using language in an irreconcilable way (see Bai, 2011; Morreal, 2012; Raskin, 1985; Ritchie, 1999). It is therefore believed that when some CMC users write, they go against the cooperative principle and the rules of the language. They do this not only for friendliness with their addressee, but also to generate humour.

DOI: 10.4018/978-1-5225-0338-5.ch008

Copyright © 2016, IGI Global. Copying or distributing in print or electronic forms without written permission of IGI Global is prohibited.

Communication technologies like the Internet and mobile telephone are changing and engrossing more users steadily. Recent statistics from the Internet World Stats Newsletter (2015) puts the number of confirmed users for December 2014 at 3,075,047,787 with a 42.3% penetrate rate world-wide. There were 6.5 billion mobile subscribers in the world as of 2014. The number of mobile-only Internet has increased from about 14 million in 2010 to 788 million users in 2015. Cameroon is a component of this global Internet and mobile telephone community. 1.486.815 Cameroonians were on the Internet with 6.4% penetration in June 2014. Internet penetration in Cameroon saw an increase of 480.321 (1.4%) in two years from 1.006.494 (5.0%) in 2012 to 6.4% in 2014. This Information from the Internet World Stats Newsletter places Facebook (henceforth FBK) as the world leader social web with an increase in daily active users world-wide from 665 million in 2013 to 936 in 2015. This represents a 40.1% expansion rate. Cameroon had 562.480 (2.8%) FBK users as of December 2012. This remarkable increase in the use of communication technologies in Cameroon and the world is probably due to low Internet access cost, smartphones with better batteries and other mobile devices.

The fast development of these communication tools has eased contact between individuals in diverse parts of the world. This technological progress has led to the expansion of the social media with many friendly web designs such as FBK, Yahoo Messenger (here-in-after YM), electronic mail (hereafter e-mail), Whatssap and Tweeter. These platforms and their users have brought in some alterations in the way language is used. Some linguists (Baron, 2003, 2008; Crystal, 2006, 2008; Herring, 2001, 2012) have described the English used in these platforms as fractured, less complex and less standard. However, the Internet linguists think that it is a variety which is specific to the technological context, and it reflects the potency of creativeness in the language. As the linguistic media continues to grow, users bring in other forms of language and this gives linguists the opportunity to investigate them. This is the case of humour in Computer-mediated communication (CMC) contexts which is fascinating, yet has not been sufficiently explored.

The aim of this chapter is to carry out an analysis of language that creates humour in the context of Cameroon FBK chats, informal e-mails, YM chats and mobile telephone Short Message Service (SMS). It examines how the markers create additional meaning and help participants to "bond". The researcher probes into forms of humour that comprise new components in English and those that are unique to Cameroon. Participants' responses to humour are equally examined.

PREVIOUS STUDIES

The relation between language and humour in social media contexts has not been given attention by researchers in Cameroon. However, some studies out of Cameroon have investigated linguistic humour in CMC. Explorations into linguistic markers of humour in some online contexts are seen in works such as Adams (2012); Audrey (2012); Baym (1995) and Skovholt, Grønning and Kankaanranta (2014). Features like punctuation, ellipsis, emoticons, formatting and laughter were established to be humour patterns in CMC. Skovholt, Grønning and Kankaanranta (ibid) consider emoticons in workplace e-mails, among other things, as humorous irony markers. Bai (2011) examines humour from the dimension of relevance theory. Her discussion centres on garden-path, cognitive contrast and deduction of the implicature. Georgakopoulou (2011) affirms that some informal e-mail interactants in Greek and English bring in incongruous elements in their texts and this brings about various types of code-alterations.

A number of researchers (Edwards, Bresnahan & Edwards, 2008; Morkes, Kernal & Nass, 1999) have delved into humour in online learning environments. Most of the researchers hold that humour contributes to success in education; generates better affective learning and motivation in students and may improve likability of the instructor even when the latter is non-human. They support the use of humour in CMC interfaces. Huang and Szafir in "No joke: examining the use of humour in computer-mediated learning" are in support of this when they state that jokes play an important role in student-instructor relationship. Vandergriff and Fuchs (2009) compare language play in a synchronous text-only CMC and face-to-face contexts. Their findings show that learners engage in humorous play in both settings; language play is an essential part of L2 proficiency and this is similar to the results of Belz (2002); Belz and Reinhardt (2004).

Laughter as a component of humour is seen in Bennett (2012); Taylor (2009) and Vlahovic, Roberts and Dunbar (2012). The authors hold that laughter definitely forecasts happiness; it establishes the emotional nature of the communication. It is seen as a contextual cue in social media contexts. Taylor thinks that laughter can take the form of textual representation, emoticons and intensification. Ong'onda, Oketch and Ongorora (2013) report that students use laughter and emoticons among other prosodic features when communicating with their friends.

Shifman and Thelwall (2014) look at jokes from a translation perspective. They observed that internet-based diffusion of translated jokes is prevalent but differs greatly amid languages and among jokes. They suggest that CMC jokes serve as influential means of globalization. They equally offer many contributions to the understanding of the relationship between social media, language and humour. Baym (1995) evaluates humour in a usenet newsgroup and found that members create humour from the juxtaposition of close and distant reading of the soap opera. To her, humour builds solidarity among the participants and institutes individuality. Danet, Ruedenberg-Wright and Rosenbaum-Tamari (1997) found plays with identity, frames of interaction and typographic symbols in Internet Relay Chat (IRC). They concluded that the medium is very playful and helps users to express themselves more freely. The notion of failed humour, i. e. when humour changes to aggressivess in CMC context, is addressed in Laineste (2013).

The review of literature shows that a lot of research has been done on linguistic humour in CMC out of Cameroon. However, there is paucity of studies on language that creates humour in online contexts in Cameroon. The present investigation that relates language use in online contexts in Cameroon to humour will possibly serve as a milestone on how Cameroonians mark humour in CMC contexts.

THEORETICAL FUNDAMENTALS

Incongruity and the incongruity-resolution theory, and violation of Gricean maxims were identified to be applicable in the analysis of humour in Cameroonian e-mails, SMS, FBK and YM chats. The incongruity theory originated in the 18th century from remarks made by Aristotle in the *Rhetoric* (McKeon, 2001) who hinted that incongruity is the basis of at least some humour. The theory was adopted by Beattie (1778); Kant (1914) and Schopenhauer (1995 [1819]). This approach to humour has been refined and applied to the study of language by linguists such as Attardo (1997); Attardo and Raskin (1991, 1994); Raskin (1985) and Ritchie (1999) who have made significant contributions to the linguistic aspects of humour.

The proponents of the theory maintain that humour is contentment in incongruity. Many authors (e. g. Bai, 2011; Morreal, 2012; Raskin, 1985) have defined the term "incongruity" by alluding to Beattie

(1778). Ritchie (ibid) also repeats the words of Beattie in her scholarly meaning of incongruity when she writes:

Laughter arises from the view of two or more inconsistent, unsuitable, or incongruous parts or circumstances, considered as united in one complex object or assemblage, or as acquiring a sort of mutual relation from the peculiar manner in which the mind takes notice of them (Ritchie 1999, p. 78).

The definition above establishes that humour occurs when something is unusual or different from what is generally happening or expected. The incongruity theory is therefore, based on the awareness of something that contravenes our standard mental patterns and expectation. This is in consonant with Aristotle (cited by Morreal, 2012) who asserts that "one way for a speaker to get a laugh is to create an expectation in the audience and then violate it". He further notes that "jokes that depend on a change of spelling or word play can have the same effect".

The features of the incongruity-resolution theory put forth by its advocates for jokes are that, a funny story should have a *set-up* and a *punch line*. The set-up is the initial part of the joke; it produces the expectation. The punch line is the final component that defies the expectation; it brings in an element of surprise or an anomalous aspect. This makes the joke's ending to be incongruous with the beginning and our disappointed expectation therefore, incite laughter or smile in us. Suls (1972, 1983); Schultz (1976) and Ritchie (1999) have confirmed that the resolution of incongruity is what makes humour pleasurable. Schultz thinks that as we get a joke, we need to fit the inconsistent constituent into some abstract schema. There are different ways of resolving or interpreting the incongruity. Ritchie (1999, pp.79-80) presents the surprise disambiguation model by offering a characterization of the core elements which are stated below:

M_1: the first (more obvious) interpretation of the set-up
M_2: the second (hidden) interpretation of the set up.
M_3: the meaning of the punchline.

She equally gives the following important relations and constituents which are also stated in Mulder and Nijholt (2002, p.13):

- **Obviousness:** M_1 is more likely than M_2 to be noticed by the reader.
- **Conflict:** M_3 does not make sense with M_1
- **Compatibility:** M_3 does make sense with M_2
- **Comparison:** there is some contrastive relationship, even a clash, between M_1 and M_2.
- **Inappropriateness:** M_2 is inherently odd, eccentric or preposterous … These differ in terms of which norms are being flouted: those of everyday logic – leading to
- **Absurdity:** or those of socially acceptable discourse – leading to TABOO effects. According to Ritchie, texts could still be humorous without necessarily having all the properties listed above. Attardo (1994, p. 144) is in keeping with this when he underscores that "each humorous text includes an element of incongruity as well as an element of resolution. The resolution may be playful, it must not be complete, realistic and plausible". In addition, there should be a cognitive quality in what we find funny because jokes entertain us by evoking, shifting and dispelling our

thoughts. Some variables that mark humour include the social and cultural context of jokes, professional background and individual norms.

This incongruity-resolution theory may not be useful in all forms of humour, but is applicable in the context of social media because much humour in CMC is created through liberation of the rules of the language which is closely associated with incongruity. Most informal CMC discourse is non-bona-fide communication. We have non-respect of the cooperative principal. Grice's (1975) guidelines or general principles underlying the efficient co-operative use of language are stated below:

1. **The Maxim of Quality:** Say only what you believe is true or for which you have adequate evidence.
2. **The Maxim of Quantity:** Make your contribution as informative as is required, not more or less than is required for the current purpose of the exchange.
3. **The Maxim of Relevance (Relation):** Make your contribution relevant.
4. **The Maxim of Manner:** Be perspicuous or clear, brief, orderly and specifically, avoid obscurity and ambiguity.

The maxims specify what participants in a discourse have to do in order to speak or write in a maximally efficient, rational, co-operative way. Attardo (1993, p. 541) emphasizes that jokes often defy maxims of the cooperative principle. There is the bending of language rules which results to humorous discourse that is socially acceptable. Taylor (2009) strengthens this point when she refers to Mulkay (1998, p. 173) and Holcomb (1997, p. 5) who had this to say: "Highly structured situations restrict and confine humour, both in scope and quantity. Humour blossoms [however] when the course of social interaction is neither prescribed by convention nor regulated from above". This explains why most of the data in this study is drawn from informal social media contexts which are not synchronized with standard rules.

DATA AND METHOD

Table 1 presents the data that was used for this research, the participants and the corresponding year(s) of data collection. The table shows that the data for the study is composed of a random sample of 50 informal e-mail messages which are part of a larger corpus of Cameroon e-mails that the scholar has been collecting since 2005. (See Table 1)

Table 1. Corpus composition

Type of Data	Number	Participants	Year(s) of Collection
E-mail messages	50	Random sample of Cameroonians	2005-2014
FBK chats	70	Random sample of students of the Department of English of E. N. S. Maroua	2013-2015
SMS	100	Random sample of Cameroonians	2014-2015
YM chats	50	Random sample of students of the departments of Administrative Techniques and Accounting of ENSET Douala	2008-2010
Total	270		

Additionally, there are 70 FBK chats collected from 2013 - 2015, 100 SMS gathered between 2014 and 2015, and 50 YM chats got from 2008 – 2010. All the data came from Anglophone Cameroonians. The e-mail and SMS parts of the data were collected from randomly selected Cameroonians from all walks of life. The FBK fragment of the data is a random sample of hard copies of e-chats obtained from students of the Department of English in the Higher Teacher Training College (E. N. S.) of the University of Maroua in Cameroon. The students socialized on FBK and brought their chats to the researcher. The YM proportion of the data came from Anglophone students in the Departments of Administrative Techniques and Accounting in the Higher Teacher Training College for Technical Education (ENSET) of the University of Douala. Only one FBK chat was collected per participant, and not more than two of the other data types came from a single donor. Most of the participants are youths who were undergoing university education at the time the corpus was assembled. The participants knew those with whom they were interacting on the social media well, so the researcher was able to get information on the nationalities of their social media associates through them. The majority of the informants have a fair grasp of Standard English (SE), but a very good command of Cameroon English (CamE). Many of them also have a fair mastery of the social media used in communication. All the e-mails, SMS, FBK and YM chats are one-to-one. Most of the chats, SMS and informal e-mails dealt with trifling topics such as love and holidays.

The analysis of data is done both quantitatively and qualitatively. The analytic focus is on the various linguistic markers of humor found in the corpus and the functions of the humour indicators. The excerpts used as illustrations are presented the way they appeared on the chats, e-mails or SMS, so all short forms, typographical and language errors are not those of the researcher. For ease of reference to the examples used in this chapter, the data was coded. Those on e-mails range from E01 to E50, those on Facebook from FBK01 to FBK70, those on SMS from SMS01 to SMS100 and the ones on YM from YM01 to YM50. In addition, all real names on the e-mails, SMS and chats have been changed or replaced with letters for ethical considerations.

ANALYSIS

The illogical element in the incongruity theory that produces a surprise and elicits laughter or playful mood was found through a number of indicators in the Cameroon social media under study. Table 2 presents the humour markers and their general distribution in Cameroon social media.

Table 2 shows the kind of linguistic markers of humour that were found in the Cameroonian social media under study: flouting of Gricean maxims, spelling variations, sound devices, special repetition of punctuation marks, humorous anecdotes, laughter, play with identity, emoticons, hyperbole, metaphor and others. Statistics prove that the use of most of the humorous features is below average on the whole, but the most preferred way of marking humour is flouting of Gricean maxims with 252 (93.4%). This could probably be that most of the participants on the social media know each other and the interactions are informal, so they rely on their background knowledge to flout the maxims and create humour with the hope that their addressees will have no problem understanding them. In addition, other categories of humour fall short of these maxims and so combine to make it the most fashionable way of marking jokes. The other forms of humour that are least employed include metaphor and hyperbole with totals

Table 2. Types of humour markers and their general distribution in Cameroon social media

Type / Social Media	Flouting of Gricean Maxims	Spelling Deviances	Sound Devices	Special Repetition of Punctuation Marks	Humorous Anecdotes	Laughter	Play with Identity	Emoticons	Hyperbole	Metaphor	Others
SMS	82 (30.4%)	16 (16%)	11 (11%)	11 (11%)	35 (35%)	02 (2%)	02 (2%)	02 (2%)	-	-	23 (23%)
Facebook	70 (100%)	39 (55.8%)	46 (65.8%)	25 (35.8%)	06 (8.6%)	38 (54.3%)	17 (24.3%)	05 (7.2%)	04 (5.8%)	05 (7.2%)	04 (5.72%)
YM	50 (100%)	26 (52%)	19 (38%)	07 (14%)	-	04 (8%)	08 (16%)	03 (6%)	-	-	-
E-mail (informal)	50 (100%)	24 (48%)	06 (12%)	10 (20%)	03 (6%)	01 (1%)	08 (16%)	11 (22%)	11 (22%)	02 (4%)	03 (6%)
Total	252 (93.4%)	105 (38.9%)	82 (30.4%)	53 (19.7%)	44 (16.3%)	45 (16.7%)	35 (13%)	21 (7.8%)	15 (5.6%)	7 (2.6%)	30 (11.12%)

of 2.6% and 5.6% respectively. This could be accounted for by the fact that the context of communication is less hospitable for these types of humorous patterns. More on the type and trends of the humour mechanisms can be seen in the following discussion.

Flouting of Gricean Maxims

As earlier stated in the section on theory, humour in social media occurs through infractions of the cooperative principal (maxims of quality, quantity, relation, and manner) which is directly linked to incongruity. Data show that flouting of Gricean maxims records 100% in FBK, YM and informal e-mail. This makes it the humour feature with the most high frequency in the data. It is only in SMS that it registers 30.4%. Cutting (2008, pp. 35-39) develops the maxims of the cooperative principle further elucidating how they can be violated. Aaron (2011) also demonstrates how jokes could illuminate implicit understanding of such pragmatic conventions. Applying it to the data on Cameroon social media, one observes that there is a lot of infringement of the principle in the forms of humour patterns that were discernible from the data, and this brings about incongruity in the communication which is typical of humour as a whole. Consider the following instances where Gricean maxims are flouted.

(1) *Protect yourself and ur family from diabetes. A couple that have been married for 20 yrs were recently diagnosed with diabetes. Findings show that they both contracted de disease as a result of de names they called each other such as honey, sweety, sugar, sweet heart, and chocolate. start calling ur spouse names like yoyobitter, bitterkola, dogoyaro, bitterleaf etc. don't laugh alone share with friends. (SMS19)*

In the above SMS, the sender does not respect the maxim of quality because s/he is not saying the truth. S/he gives fictitious information by recounting that a couple contracted diabetes *as a result of the names they called each other*. At the end of the message s/he even writes "don't laugh alone share with friends". In such a case, the receiver will assume that the message should just be taken at face value; it is just for fun. The addresser does not also respect the maxim of quantity, since s/he does not give adequate information that is required for the addressee to value what s/he is saying. S/he does not cite the source of his /her findings so that the receiver can verify, and also writes "etc" after "bitterleaf" which implies that there are other things s/he has deliberately left out. The SMS is a non-bona-fide communication (non-serious) that is why the sender does not respect the principle of cooperation.

Considering the incongruous – resolution theory, the joke in the SMS contains a set up which is "Protect yourself and ur family from diabetes. A couple that have been married for 20 yrs were recently diagnosed with diabetes". Here, the M_1 means *diabetes is an illness*, and the M_2 denotes diabetes as *lovable names the couple calls each other*. The receiver detects M_1 first and may think that the sender wants to give him/her some recipes or advice on how to avoid the disease. This set up creates a relevant expectation. However, the punch line (the second part of the joke), *start calling ur spouse names like yoyobitter, bitterkola, dogoyaro, bitterleaf etc.*, deviates from this expectation and forms a contrast with the set up (M_1), thus generating a humorous effect. This indicates that the addresser intentionally implied a humorous function for the message aimed at pleasure and camaraderie with the receiver. However, if we have to allude to the hidden interpretation of the set up (M_2), then one can say that the punch line (M_3) is compatible with M_2. This is in keeping with Ritchie's (1999, p. 80) description of compatibility as "M_3 does make sense with M_2".

(2) *The FBI just announced dat u were caught with the following items: *1 billion bags of Blessings, *3 billion cartons of Peace, *5 billion boxes of Mercy, *7 billion packets of Favour, * 10 billion lorries of joy,. U may be sentenced to life in Prosperity and abundance of Grace in the court of Heaven but it depends on your answer to this question: "Are u guilty or not"? gd nite.. (SMS63)*

Here, the sender of the message is deliberately being insincere. What s/he says above does not represent what FBI announced thus s/he violates the maxim of quality. FBI cannot detain or condemn someone for being blessed or for an abundance of grace. In addition, the sender says 'it depends on your answer to this question: "Are u guilty or not"? gd nite.' This implies that s/he is saying what s/he thinks and not something declared by FBI. The maxim of quantity is also violated because the things the receiver was assumed to be caught with are too much: "*1 billion bags of Blessings, *3 billion cartons of Peace, *5 billion boxes of Mercy, *7 billion packets of Favour, * 10 billion lorries of joy". The maxim of manner is also not respected since the sender appears to be ambiguous. S/he avoids revealing his or her real thoughts to the receiver. For example, s/he says "U may be sentenced to life in Prosperity and abundance of Grace". So one does not know quite well what s/he wishes the receiver. The maxim of relation is equally not observed since FBI and court of heaven are not related. Heaven cannot also sentence someone for an abundance of grace.

Regarding the incongruous-resolution theory, the joke in (2) above has a set up thus: "The FBI just announced dat u were caught with the following items: *1 billion bags of Blessings, *3 billion cartons of Peace, *5 billion boxes of Mercy, *7 billion packets of Favour, * 10 billion lorries of joy". The M_1 means *blessings, peace, mercy, favour and joy are crimes*, and the M_2 specifies them as *good things that can bring about success or prosperity in life*. The receiver identifies M_1 first and could suppose that the sender wishes to give him/her some guidance on how to shun detention. This set up builds a pertinent expectation. Nevertheless, the punch line, *U may be sentenced to life in Prosperity and abundance of Grace...*, departs from this likelihood and creates a dissimilarity with the set up (M_1), hence producing a comic effect. This signifies that the addresser deliberately implied a funny function for the message meant at wishing the receiver well in life (M_3). Conversely, the concealed explanation of the set up (M_2) leads one to conclude that the punch line (M_3) matches with M_2.

(3) *Article 84 of Law N° 193/02/19 of 3rd Dec 1993 of d Frndship Code stipulates: Any one who abandons his/her friend for long without callx or textx him/her shall be punished with the payment of a fine of 1000 frs credit into d friends mobile phone account. After examining your case, d court has ruled and found u guilty. So send 1000 frs credit to dis number ..., good night. (SMS90)*

In this SMS, the addresser does not adhere to the maxim of quality since there is no friendship code in Cameoon, and the court ruling appears to have been invented. Nor is he following the maxim of manner, since he is not straightforward. The sender also violates the maxim of quantity because all the information needed to understand the supposed friendship code and court ruling are not given. The maxim of relation is flouted equally since the connection between failing to ring a friend and court judgment or ruling seems to be doubtful. The SMS looks like a court judgment; it is linguistically obscure and this creates a humour effect. The interpretation is that, it is a joke in which the sender is finding a nice way of letting his/her friend send him/her some airtime.

Other forms of non-respect of maxims associated with humour that were detected in the data include similes and hyperboles such as "Beautiful, like a soft warm sunshine, As a bead of water on the stem of a flower, Even more beautiful than the most beautiful rainbow it is you, my love that inflames my heart" (E 14). Taking it at face value, one may assume that it is an over- statement, but the interpretation could lead one to comprehend that the addresser admires and loves his partner very much. More on hyperbole and metaphor can be seen in sections 5. 9 and 5.10. Attardo (1993) highlights that jokes abundantly violate maxims. It is this violation of the maxims that engenders humour. Though the principle of cooperation is important for the effective use of language, some authors (Van Dijk, 1986; Yule, 1996; de Beaugrand & Dressler, 1990) still hold that natural language discourse is not completely plain. Relationship between sentences may exist without being uttered. Humorous discourse appears to be in keeping with this; it is ambiguous, but socially acceptable because the aim is to make people laugh.

Spelling Deviances

Texters, e-mailers and chatters manipulate spellings as a basis for fun both for themselves and their recipients. The way some words are spelt in internet and mobile telephone contexts violate the normal patterns and expectations and generates humour. This change of spelling brings in an element of surprise and this feeling of surprise conveys a lighthearted communication, thus incongruity-resolution. Statistics gleaned from table 2 show that the total frequency for spelling variations stands at 38.9%, and it is the second most preferred way of marking humour. Specific figures reveal FBK having the highest with 55.8%; followed by YM and informal e-mail with 52% and 48% respectively. The least in this category is SMS with just 16%. Spelling deviances are seen in the form of extended or repeated letters, number homophones and a hybrid of letters and numbers. More on these is given below.

Extended or Repeated Letters

Some social media interactants repeat some letters in words. This brings about incongruity in spelling, and produces humour. Some of the words appear new and appealing to participants. Examples of these elongated spellings can be seen in the excerpts below.

(4) **A:***are u still sickkk*
B:*bye*
A:*Ok tk cre, will call u. chaoooooooooooooooooooooooooooooooooo*
…
A:*whaooo, courage dear, realy wish to c u Emy*
B:*realy*
A:*yeahhhhh* Miss ur *smilessssssssssssss. Misssss u so much*
B:*realyyyyyyyyyyyyyyyyyyy.* so where r u (FBK 27)
(5) **B:** *friend has invited me to a party and I'm wondering if you might like to come with me.*
A:*Soooorrrry ooooooooh baby, I would have love to but I will be bizi*
…
B:*thanks. byeeeeeeeeeee*
A:*Byeeeeeeeeeeee* (FBK 25)
(6) *Ok ooooooo. waiting* (SMS 100)

The examples above show that some participants propel fun and friendship in social media contexts through repetition of letters. This spelling divergence is a form of linguistic play that Crystal (1996, p. 334) correctly articulates; "the enjoyment is a direct consequence of deviating from the normal use of language forms". This kind of humour pattern symbolizes strong friendly bond and is exclusive to social media milieu.

Number Homophones; Hybrid of Letters and Numbers

Another way through which participants played with spelling was by using numbers that have a similar pronunciation with some words to represent the words. In some other cases, the spelling of some words appears to be a mixture of numbers and letters. Through this, humour is stimulated. Examples of these are the italicized items below.

(7) We go *2* skool every day *4rm* mornx *2* evenx. (E 05)
(8) Gdmnx Dr, how is d family? hop *evry1* is fine… (SMS 100)

The cases above show a lot of inconsistency and freedom in the way words are spelt in social media situations which are directly linked to incongruity. Crystal (2008b) rightly thinks that social media participants intentionally use deviant spellings as a strategy for time reduction and beauty in their writing. This makes the messages humorous and pleasing to the participants.

Sound Devices

Sound devices deal "with the arrangement of words to produce desired sounds so that they give an impression when heard" (Tabe 2011, p. 153). They are used more often in poetry. Nevertheless, some (e.g. onomatopoeia, assonance) were observed in the data under study. They are one of the ingredients used by some Cameroonians to mark humour in this context. Generally, 82 (30.4%) sound devices occurred in the data with the highest rate (65.8%) coming from FBK and the least (11%) from SMS. It is the third most fashionable way of marking humour. The sound devices that were discernible from Cameroonian social media are discussed below.

Onomatopoeia

Onomatopoeia refers to words containing sounds similar to the noises they describe. It is a vocal presentation used by some participants for the enjoyment and humour of their messages by the addressees. Consider instances of this in the extracts below (the italicized items).

(9) *WAHO* THANKS 4 YOUR SMS.
2015 IS OPENING IN OUR FAMILY IN JESUS NAME.
MERRY X.MASS. LUCY (SMS 03)
(10) … *ehhhhhhhhhhh* why think as such. (E18)
(11) **A:***oh* i thought it stood for Cameroon
B:*oww* no (YM 35)

(12) **A:** i am just there
B:*Ok ohhhhhhhhhhhh*
...
A: I hv NT cook today
B:*chaiiiiiiiiiiiiii*
you *tooooooooooooo* (FBK 03)

The examples above are helpful as they contribute to the peculiar manner in which the mind takes notice of them. Other examples of onomatopoeia from the data include *click, Oh!, ooh!, oohh, Ah, Ah!!!, Hoo, woo!, Wahoo!, wah, ow, wow, aww, wehhh* and *wehhhhhhhhhhhhhh*

The strategy of onomatopoeia does not only make the messages interesting to the readers/recipients, but they equally build humour, the spirit of cooperation and friendliness among the participants.

Beginning and End Rhymes

Reading through some messages in the data, one may have the impression that they are stanzas in a poem. It was discovered that the words at the beginning and end of lines sound similar or identical. This gives some kind of regular rhyme pattern. The extract below demonstrates this.

(13) As u enter dis new year,
*X*pect
Xtra favor
Xtra blessxs
Xtra provisns
Xtra upliftments
Xtra protectns
Xtra conectns &
Xtra promotns
HAPPY NEW YEAR (SMS 46)

Here, there is repetition of "Xtra" at the beginning of lines (from the third to ninth line). There is also the repetition of "s" or "ns" which stands for *-sions/tions* at the end of most lines in the example above. The sounds from the repeated words are euphonies; they are pleasing. This adds a lyrical touch to the message; they help in memorising the message. In addition, the words are written in a way that deviates from the normal standard expectation. This variation brings about incongruity and creates humour. The writer does this not only for comedy, but also to confirm his/her profound warmth wishes for his/her addressee in the New Year. The lines in the poem-like SMS are also very short; made up of just one or two words. Crystal (2008a, 2008b) holds that such short lines have an individual force. Moreover, the space of SMS genre disallows intricate proper patterning; texters simply transfer and beautify what they had met in other contexts.

Assonance

Assonance has to do with the effect created when two words that are close together have the same vowel sound. This sound device was found in some of the data under study. Examples are shown in italics in the excerpts below.

(14) Hp u guys are all dox *greate* as in *gracious. (E17)*

Here, the /eɪ/ sound is repeated in the italicized words. It seems the writer is joking, and this credits the message with humour and a musical quality. It also emphasises the agreeable quality of things that the addresser wishes the addressees.

(15) **A:** mum she is still on holidays
i was intending on living with her …
B: great
that's right but if she doent have a place then give her a hand
cos we are *bless* to *bless* others … (FBK 36)

In the extract above, there is the repetition of *bless* hence the vowel sound /ɛ/ in the last line. This repetition adds a lyrical and playful touch to the chat.

(16) since you came back to maroua you've never bother to find out if am well no pb my life is definitely *a long night of nightmare.* (E22)

In this excerpt, the sound /aɪ/ has been repeated in *night* and *nightmare*. This emphasises the writer's terrible or difficult condition in life. However, the recurrence gives a playful, lyrical and humorous touch to the message.

Alliteration

Alliteration is one of the jokey ways through which Cameroonians use language in social media contexts. It is the use of the same consonant sound at the beginning of words that are close together as in the following example.

(17) **A:** so hw difficult is it
B: it is becoz am very far
A: remember *nno sweat no sweet* (FBK 53)

In the example above, the [n] and [s] sounds have been alliterated. The writer wants the receiver to understand that it is through hard work that one can live a pleasant or fascinating life. The use of these sound devices makes the messages appealing and hilarious. It is also a pointer that Cameroonians show skill in the construction of their messages. This is supported by Aarons (2011) who thinks that a successful joke relies on linguistic competence. Consequently, social media develops literacy. The sound devices add humour, pleasure or musicality to the messages.

Special Repetition of Punctuation Marks

The drive to be humorous in social media contexts has led to special repetition of punctuation marks as an approach to language play. Though deviant from normality, it is a sort of linguistic inventiveness aimed at adjusting language to fit the needs of context and humour. Information from table 2 reveals that special repetition of letters totals 53 (19.7%) with FBK and SMS containing the uppermost and lowest rates (35.8% and 11%) respectively. This kind of punctuation freedom is fun; and people are happy that social media has given them the opportunity to use language in such a free or unrestricted manner. The examples below illustrate this.

(18) hello aunty, hw @ u dox today*?????*jst checkx up on u.
Wen will u be return??? (SMS 85)
(19) CONGRATULATIONS*!!!!!!!!!!* (E28)
(20) **A:** Dear how do u do ? *!!!!!!!!*
long time …
B: Hahahahahahahaha … (FBK 12)
(21) **B:** May God be your strength ok*???*
So how is life in Maroua*????*
I hear it is really hot up there??? (FBK 10)
(22) **A:** What is that place the pple are they well coming
B: well they are trying but *?????????????????///* (FBK 16)
(23) **B:** … She went farming and a tree fell on her.
A: Oh my God*!!!!!!!!!!!!!!!!!!!!!!!!!!!!!!.* i can't believe that. (FBK 24)
(24) **A:** hello, am I dreaming*????*
B: y r u dreaming. so watz up …
A: glad to c u, so hw are u*??* where are u*??* …
A: Gud mrnx Dear. I'm glad he's now fellx fine. r u there*!!!!!!!!!!!* (FBK 27)

The instances above entail mostly multiple question and exclamation marks. They are playfully motivated and Crystal (2001) highlights that a natural way to learn language is to play with it. In example (20) above, B responds with laughter after the multiple exclamation marks. This indicates that the laughter is the consequence of humour created by the excessive exclamation marks. The creative punctuation marks are therefore entertaining, and they ensign the messages as humorous. This is one of the humour strategies that are peculiar to social media contexts.

Humorous Anecdotes

Humorous anecdotes are a subclass of humour that was identified in the data. Figures from Table 2 show that the total rate of humorous anecdotes is 16.3%. SMS contained the highest number (35, i.e. 35%) and YM records 0%. According to Ritchie (1999) and other proponents of the incongruous-resolution principle, a joke has a set up and a punch line. The inconsistency is seen between the set up (M_1) which is triggered first and the punch line (M_3). Consider the examples below.

(25) *Breaking News*

Paul Biya has been kidnapped and the kidnappers are asking for a sum of 100000 billion or they will use 50 lit of petrol to burn him so the Gov't is asking the pple to contribute for the release of Paul Biya. I have contributed 15 lit of petrol. So wat is your own contribution (SMS 26)

In this joke, the M_1*news is just arriving that Paul Biya has been abducted*; the people like and want him released is more accessible and creates a pertinent expectation. The M_2*it is not new that the citizens hate Paul Biya and desire him burnt or killed* contrasts with M_1. The punch line (M_3) "I have contributed 15 lit of petrol. So wat is your own contribution" deviates from our relevant expectation (M_1) and produces a humorous effect. However, by inference, M_3 matches or is compatible with M_2.

(26) Thieves entered a church and closd all d windows & doors. They told d congregation dat dey wld kill everybody & in alphabetical order. So dey wnt 2 d Pst &ask him wat his name was … **Father:***My name is Zzzakiariahzzebediah. Dy replied lucky u! Dey went 2 d pianist,* pianist: I am Zemanuel Zwilliam but de usher ova der is call Abigaiel Ann. **Usher:***U liar, bastard my name is Zzabigaiel Zzan. (E 21)*

The anecdote above has a set up with M_1 being that *the thieves want to kill everybody* and this generates a potent expectation that the robbers will slay everyone, even those whose names begin with Z. The M_2*they wish to know if the man of God and Christians are genuine or honest* is irreconcilable with M_1. The punch line (second part of the joke) violates the M_1; instead of killing the people, the supposed thieves were probing into sincerity. The punch line, therefore, seems relevant to M_2 and confirms Ritchie's (1999) relation of compatibility.

(27) A psychiatric had 3 mad pple and decided to ask them a question to know who to treat first. The Dr asked 3+3=? The 1st madman said 2500frs. The doctor said u r really mad. The Dr asked again 3+3=? The 2nd madman answered TUESDAY. The doctor replied u r close to ur grave. The Dr asked again 3+3=? The last madman answered 6. The doctor was encouraged and asked, hw di u get ur answer. The 3rd madman responded, I divided 2500frs by TUESDAY. The Dr replied u r a corps. (SMS 58)

Here, the M_1 is *the doctor is kind and willing to give medical treatment to the mad people.* The M_2*the doctor is indignant, hates the mad people and will not administer any treatment to them* contrasts with the M_1. Nonetheless, the subsequent expressions from the doctor (the punch line) digress from M_1 as he insults the first mad man "u r really mad"; the second "u r close to ur grave" and the third "u r a corps [sic]". This is humorous, but the punch line is compatible with M_2.

Some anecdotes found in the corpus are a mixture of English and Cameroon Pidgin English (CPE) or French. This renders them funnier from participants' perspective compared to the ones that appear only in English. In addition, they evoke some peculiarities of the context such as the multilingual nature of Cameroon and systems of belief of the people. These are exemplified below.

(28) *In skull d teacha said,class our topic 2day is "qustn tag".*

exampl1:*u have a bag, haven't u?*

ex2:*he can't come, can he?, nw class who can make a sentence usx a "questn tag".***Mary**

said: *"we go chop yam today, chopn't we?.teacha said: wat??? Dis is terrible.who in class can correct Mary? Nw little Jhony said:"anty no mind dat yam head!!!!!, and said: "we go chop yam today, yamn't we?, hahahahaha. Just tryx 2put out a smile on ur face. (SMS 29)*

In the illustration above, the humorous incongruity is created by the use of CPE in a classroom situation by "Mary" and "little Jhony". Using CPE in formal contexts in Cameroon such as lecture halls is forbidden; it deviates from the norm. The teacher begins the lesson in English, gives examples and hopes that the students will take it seriously and follow suit. However, the surprise comes in when the first student spoke in CPE. The teacher even expresses his astonishment and awful feeling by saying *wat???*. The next student (little Jhony) who was supposed to correct the first student worsened the situation by continuing not only in CPE, but turning the lesson into a playful act when he stated: *anty no mind dat yam head!!!!!*. The repeated exclamation marks make it further lighthearted. In addition, the sender uses laughter and meta-joke or comment at the end to announce that it was just for fun. All these contribute in making the humour successful. Nevertheless, a close reading of the joke unveils certain realities in the Cameroonian society. The hidden interpretation of the set up is that CPE is a lingua franca in the country. People are able to transfer it from informal contexts into official milieus, and this is evident even in administrative and school settings. As a result, the CPE expressions from the students (punch line) are compatible with this concealed meaning. The students seem to be so knowledgeable in CPE that they use it to give examples of question tags. The anecdote is humorous, but it relates to some of the linguistic specificities of Cameroon.

(29) Grandpa said to his grandson "see your teacher di come go hide because u nova go school for two days". Grandson replied "na u get 4 hide because i be take permission say u don die. (SMS 08)

In this joke, grandpa asks his grandson to hide from his (grandson's) teacher since he has not been to school for two days. The grandson produces a humorous incongruity by saying that the grandpa should instead be the one to hide from the teacher because he took permission that the grandpa was dead. The use of CPE makes the joke even more enjoyable. This joke reveals some aspects of Cameroonian life and culture namely, the departure from the old and appropriate behaviour by the youth, or a conflict between old and new ways of behaving. It demonstrates that in the grandpa's school days, pupils had much respect for their teachers and elders. They were very humble or submissive to them. They considered them as models, and some people deemed it a disgrace or a very bad thing to tell a lie to a teacher or parent. But the reverse appears to be true nowadays. The grandson is neither worried about the presence of his teacher nor his absence from school. He disobeys his grandpa, and is arrogant to him. He mocks or ridicules his grandfather's respect and/or anxiety about his (grandson's) teacher. The joke is therefore, a mockery of deviance. However, Mudler and Nijholt (2002, p. 7) refer to *frame theories* that could be used to explain the grandson's behaviour. The theories perceive joking as blithe compared to rigorous daily life. In keeping with frame theories, jokes originate from community and culture, but deviate from regular discourse. For humorous purposes, people can make comments and defy taboos without being offensive.

(30) *Toto décide d prendre les cours d'anglais. [Toto decides to take English lessons]*

Prof: *let's do some comparatives today. So I say small, smaller, smallest, okay?*

Toto: *okay!*

Prof:*big*
toto:*big bigger biggest*
Prof:*clean*
toto:*clean cleaner cleanest*
Prof:*(souriant [smiling]) very good!*
toto:*very good, very gooder very goodest*
Prof:*oh my god!*
toto:*oh my god, oh my goder, oh my godest*
Prof:*stop it now*
toto:*stop it now, stop it nower, stop it nowest*
Prof:*lol*
toto:*loll, loller, lollest.*
bn swr!!
Je sens k'avec l'allure si toto va nous dire bonjour, bonjourer, bonjourest …
[From the look of things, I think Toto will tell us good morning, good morninger, good morningest] (SMS 43)

Here, the teacher introduces the lesson (comparatives). S/he initiates and Toto response well at the beginning until the teacher is happy and with a smile says *very good!* Immediately after that, Toto starts generating amusing incongruities - *very gooder, very goodest, oh my goder, oh my godest, stop it nower, stop it nowest.* The teacher even employs *lol* to indicate the incongruities, but Toto still does not recognize them and continued with *loller and lollest*. The joke is a picture of what happens when a francophone who has no knowledge of English decides to start learning the language. It equally portrays that a rule is not totally generalized in English; there are irregular cases. The joke is also a critique of the English complicated grammatical system with a lot of exceptions or asymmetrical occurrences. These irregularities make it difficult for some learners to master the language. The French at the end of the joke emphasizes this; it is also evocative of the Cameroonian culture of bilingualism.

The instances of jokes discussed above show that the context of the participants influences humour. Their cultural background knowledge determines their linguistic behaviour both in face-to-face and social media contexts. The use of CPE and French in some anecdotes is a mode of 'Cameroonising' them. Herring (2001) and Baym (1995) are in support of this when they echo that users can transfer words and practices from offline cultures to online environments. Humour as a result, is able to offer insight into a culture and disclose aspects of the culture that would otherwise not be observed. Nonetheless, humour should engross some incongruity or ambiguous meaning. Goatly (2012) holds up this view by indicating that ambiguity plays a vital role in humour.

Laughter

Laughter is the act of smiling while making sounds with the voice that show something is humorous or you are happy. In the social media under study, it takes the form of typed texts that represent laughter sounds. Some authors (Attardo, 1994; Mudler & Nijholt, 2002, p. 7; Taylor, 2009) assume that laughter and humour are two dissimilar but related things. To them, even though laughter denotes humour, there are as well cases of laughter which entail no humour and patterns of humour with no laughter. Laughter was depicted in a total of 45 (16.7%) messages in the corpus, and FBK ranks first with 54.3% and e-mail the least with just 1%. Consider instances of humorous laughter below.

(31) **B:** You should be a big woman now
hahahahahahahahhahahahahahahah
A: whaooo that is great
B: Hope the heat has not changed your oyibo colour*???* [fairness in complexion]
hahahahaha (FBK 10)

The first laughter from B seems to endorse the friendly aim for his/her statement. The second laughter (*hahahahaha)* signifies the play mode and humorous purpose of B's question. The repeated question marks do not only tint the sentence as a question, but make it more jokey or comical. The example below shows joyous laughter.

(32) **B:** could we exchange pics?
A: for me there is no prob
because i understand the difference btn a pic and a kiss
B:*Hahahahahaha* (YM 21)

In the excerpt above, we have cheerful laughter to indicate B's happiness that A has succumbed to his request. Laughter is also used as a reply to humour. It is often the receiver of the funny message who appraises the joke and laughs to sanction it. In the following SMSs, for example, the first one is the opening move and the second the closing move. The two were exchanged on the 2015 edition of the International Women's Day.

(33) Amen n thx. Enjoy urself w the men around u (SMS 34)
(34) *HA! HA! HA!* U TOO! (SMS 38)

In the opening message, the sender desires the receiver to have pleasure with the men around him/her. This appears incongruous since it was women's day. The addressee perceives the contradiction and responds with laughter. The laughter here is recognition of humour. Participants in the interaction are an important variable that influence humour or laughter since they are those who make sense of what they read or hear. Laughter is thus, both humour marker and humour support. Mulder and Nijholt (2002, p. 8) refers to Muehlchen (2000) who rightly thinks that "laughter brings people together as a group, it signals 'bonding, affirmation, belonging, listening', it can be disarming and by means of laughter people can show more about themselves than what they are aware of."

Play with Identity

On social media platforms, participants play with identity in various forms. This includes the transfer of traditional spoken features of naming to online interaction, modification of real names so that they sound good and the use of funny nicknames. Data reveals that play with identity in its entirety stands at 35 (13%). FBK tops this category of humour pattern with 17 (24.3%), followed by YM and e-mail with 16% each. The least is SMS with 2%.

Some participants employ the lens of joke to depict cultural issues on naming in face-to-face communication in Cameroon. In Cameroon, senior citizens, especially men who belong to the same traditional background, do not address each other using their real names in face-to-face meetings. They employ the names given to them in the traditional camp. These names can signify certain animals, rivers, etc. The participants do not have any problems with this because they understand each other and the context very well. Some interactants have carried this over to social media. An instance of this is the italicized expression below that appeared at the end of an e-mail message.

Cheerio for now
D "*the Tortoise*" (E 38)

the Tortoise in the above extract diverges from the norm because human beings are not given animal names. It is therefore, incongruous and brings in a laughing effect or humour. However, it is reminiscent of cultural practices on naming in oral communication in Cameroon. Therefore, jokes are outlets for traditional values, and the context helps in understanding the real meaning of a joke.

Another way through which Cameroonians played with identity in online communication is the modification of real names so that they look new and pleasing. Consider the italicized items below. The full names are given in square brackets after the modified versions.

Helooooo Pr, Dr, Chief, Lekun *Timiskooooo*. (E 06) [Timisk]
nash (FBK 43) [Natasha, Nadege]
malexo (FBK 23) [Malcolm, Max]

The examples above point to playful identification mode slotted in by participants as a way of cooperating with their addressees, and this creates humour. The modified names are not the authentic names of the participants, hence they are incongruous. The first example is even more humorous and this is evident in the repeated letters and many titles given to the recipient.

Some other participants used abbreviations, acronyms or certain short forms to identify themselves in social media contexts. This is mostly common with youths who belong to the same social group. They do this not only to play with identity, but to strengthen their friendly relationships and construct humour. The following instances illustrate this.

k-4 (FBK 40)
BB (E 31),
DEBS (E 33)

The examples given above are not the genuine names of the participants, so they digress from reality and are humorous. The interactants do not face any difficulties identifying each other because they share some personal background knowledge.

The last humorous way employed by Cameroonians to identify themselves on social media is the use of funny nicknames. This was prevalent in YM and FBK. The examples given in Table 3 are pet names that were found in the data. They are incongruous since they are not the real names of the participants. The interactants know each other, but they employ nicknames as a way of playing and bonding among

Table 3.

cha chaaaa (E 11)	*ozmericler* (YM 35)	*STEVEN007* (YM 31),
sintas (YM 22)	*wafanka2000* (YM 13)	*Pupple Kizzi Zabra* (FBK 70)
Jacq Vision (FBK 01)	*chacha* (FBK 02)	*jars* is now online (FBK 12)
cajetan (FBK 19)	*boh/ booh* (FBK 31)	*oga, abi* (FBK 49)

themselves. This is contrary to the view of Danet, Ruedenberg-Wright and Rosenbaum-Tamari (1997) who hold that play with identity is common in IRC because the participants do not know each other. Humorous fun with personality or individuality hence reinforces relation within an in-group.

Emoticons

Many authors (e. g. Crystal, 2006, p. 39; Ong'gonda, Oketch & Ongarora, 2013, p. 170; Taylor, 2009) describe emoticons as pictograms intended to portray "emotional facial expressions" in CMC. They are employed to compensate for the lack of face-to-face cues or aural and visual information in social media contexts. Table 2 confirms that emoticons were found in some 21 (7.8%) messages in the corpus with the highest rate (22%) coming from informal e-mail. They are not prevalent in Cameroonian social media contexts probably because the participants are not acquainted with them. The majority of emoticons or smileys found in the data were used as visual representation for humour. Below are some examples.

(35) will always keep in touch
byeeeeeeeeeee (E 04)

Here, the smile emoticon employed at the end of the repeated letters is used to express happiness.

(36) *how are u girl & estel?...*
about eddy i think it's a good decision. ...
big kisssss.....see u very soon (E 46)

In this example, the first emoticon appears to communicate that the sender is wondering or confused about the state of the receivers. However, the following two emoticons express laughter or smile to denote the addresser's delight.

(37) **A:***xmas break is on the 20th of this month thanks for every thing bye!*
B:*catch you*
B: (YM 18)

In the case above, the emoticon (talk to the hand) is considered to emphasize leave taking thus contributes to friendliness, humour and play in CMC.

(38) **A:***Lets only hope so. I wish you good luck. Bye*
B:*thanks and see you soon*
B:*greet all*
B: (YM 19)

The emoticon above signifies *call me*. It indicates that the sender is signing off from YM, but invites further contact or communication with the receiver through the telephone. Emoticons therefore, add to features of humour. Some other participants prefer the use of asterisks to express their emotions as illustrated in the following extracts.

(39) **A:***u are blessed above a curse*
Takecare and bye
B:*thk*
Bye byeeeee•* (FBK 66)
(40) **A:***… hellllloooooooooo*
*oooooooooooooooooooooooooo** (FBK 35)

The dot and asterisk that follow the multiple letters express *kiss* and denote a playful style.

(41) *B *B *B (SMS 45)
…

Here, there is expression of *kiss and cool* through the use of **B*. The inclusion of smileys/emoticons in the messages portrays the successful use of English for visual humour, and also to enhance rapport between participants.

Hyperbole

Adams (2012, p. 3) defines hyperbole as "Non-literary meaning expressed by exaggerating or overstating the reality of a given situation or state". Some Cameroonian social media users employ exaggeration hence producing incongruity and funny outcomes. Information gleaned from Table 2 portrays that hyperbole is one of least humour markers employed in the corpus totaling 15 (5.6%). Personal e-mails have the highest frequency with 22%, while SMS and YM register 0% each. Consider the following examples.

(42) *…my luv 4 u is 4 times bigger dan de whole universe*. (E09)

Here, the addresser has exaggerated his/her love for the addressee and thus an incongruous declaration that creates laughter.

(43) **B:***how warm or cool is Maroua*
A:*it is boiling* (FBK 20)

In this example, the humour becomes obvious from the gross exaggeration that Maroua is *boiling*.

(44) **B:***what can i do??*
can u answer me please
...
A:*my heart is breaking in piecings* [sic] (FBK 61)

In the above instance, A says, *my heart is breaking in piecings [sic]*. This is not sincere; it is an overstatement. Hyperboles like the ones seen in this section are incongruous and add humour to the messages.

Metaphor

A metaphor is a playfully motivated language strategy employed in social media settings by some Cameroonians. It indirectly compares two things or people to show that they have the same traits. It is incongruous because the comparison is done in a way that is different from what is normally expected, and this renders the description powerful and humorous. Data show that metaphor is the least frequent humour pattern with just 7 (2.6%) on the whole. It is completely absent in the SMS and YM corpus, meanwhile FBK and private e-mails record 7.2% and 4% of metaphors respectively. Consider the examples below.

(45) **A:** hello B
hozw do u do
ur brother is a bundle of prob
he wants to bite me up online
B: hahhahahah
A: he is capable of doing any thing
that boy is hell ...
B: i know u luv him
A: tell ur brother to be careful with me
B: what makes u believe he will hurt an *angel like u?* (FBK 13)

ur brother is a bundle of prob, he wants to bite me up online and *that boy is hell* are all metaphors referring probably to the writer's lover. This is suggestive of the distress the boy is giving the lady. The hidden meaning could be that the boy is nice to the girl and they are in harmony. This is hinted by B who response with laughter *hahhahahah* to show that it is just a joke. Furthermore, B asks at the end *what makes u believe he will hurt an angel like u?* It is an extra clue that the girl is lovely to the boy thus they are in peace.

(46) yes *ma sugar*, happy happy. ha things coolin on ya side, hope u catching the feeling, ... (E 11)

ma sugar is a metaphor referring to the sender's lover. This pinpoints the writer's love and emotional feelings towards his/her lover. The metaphors appear ambiguous; compares things circuitously hence they are humorous.

Others

In this category, we have typographic and word play jokes. Statistics from Table 2 show that the general rate of occurrence in this class of humour marker is 30 (11.12%) with SMS having the highest (23%). They are discussed in greater detail below.

Typographic Play

Typography has to do with how messages in the social media under study are prepared or designed to appear before the reader. Data show that there is a lot of play with keyboard characters and this leads to humour and creativity in the way participants write. The play is not rule- governed, and so it is related to incongruity. Forms of typographic play in the data include songs and other witty creativities of some interactants. Illustrations of a song (example 47) and a humorous creativity (example 48) are given in Table 4. They show that some participants in social media contexts mark humour in the way they sing or type songs and other stylish inventiveness by means of keyboard characters. Typographic play is distinctive here because participants use words and other striking graphic symbols to create leisure or playful activities. Through this, a funny incongruity is created. They do this not only for amusement, but to impress the recipients with their talents and creativity.

Word Play Jokes

Some interactants use certain words not because they are meaningful, but as a playful or humorous tool. Consider the italicized items below.

Table 4. Examples 47 and 48

<table>
<tr><th>(47)</th><th>(48)</th></tr>
<tr><td>Jingle bell</td><td></td></tr>
<tr><td>////// ////</td><td></td></tr>
<tr><td>- - - -</td><td></td></tr>
<tr><td>· · ·jingle</td><td>Go mosquito go</td></tr>
<tr><td>bell</td><td></td></tr>
<tr><td>(í- - - (☼)- - - - -</td><td>/ / / / / / / /</td></tr>
<tr><td></td><td>(@@@))))>-</td></tr>
<tr><td><: : : : > jingle bell</td><td>go and bite those who slept without</td></tr>
<tr><td>| | |</td><td>wishing me gdnight (SMS 23)</td></tr>
<tr><td>- - - jingle</td><td></td></tr>
<tr><td>| | - -</td><td></td></tr>
<tr><td>· - -</td><td></td></tr>
<tr><td>bell</td><td></td></tr>
<tr><td>jingle all the … (SMS 50)</td><td></td></tr>
</table>

(49) **B:***seriously*
A:... *haha*
i am really feeling bad
its like u have a hidden secret (FBK 13)

The words *hidden* and *secret are* incongruous since they are similar in meaning. As a result, one does not expect the sender to use the two of them in the above context. But they are employed in close proximity for mere humour. The laughter (*haha)* at the beginning of A's written talk reinforces the playful nature of what s/he is saying.

Humour Support

Some humour in the data under study got responses while others did not. About 50% of the humour in the corpus did not attract any response. Some of the replies to humour in the corpus include the following:

a) Appreciation

Some participants send positive appraisal or comments as evidence that they understand the humour and have been amused by it. Instances of these literal statements are given below.

That's a good one. Have a wndfl day (SMS 31)
Thx for the funny sms (SMS 36)
Thank u for your last i enjoy it. (E 21)
It's interesting … (SMS 35)

The above excerpts are plain recognition of the receivers' appreciation or enjoyment of the humour.

b) Smile or Laughter

Smile or laughter is another response to humour employed by some Cameroonians. Examples of humour support consisting of smile or laughter can be seen below.

I'm *smiling* bc of the fun. Thx (SMS 59)
B: if ordinary facebook fit tire u den your bones them fit weak badly
A: foolish
B: *hahahaha*
A: *kkikikikikikiki*
B: *Lolololololololololo* … (FBK 01)

In this example, there is the use of CPE, and it renders B's statement very funny. Both participants laugh out as contribution to the humour.

c) Laughter and Positive Comment

Some other participants laugh and make positive comments as humour support. These are illustrated as follows.

Hahaha u r so funny (FBK 12)
B: *Hahahhahhahahaah*
funny woman
A: … u talk as if are not funny too (FBK 36)

The examples above are supplementary strategies for humour support.

d) Appreciation and Invitation of More Jokes

Another humour support strategy found in the data was approval of the humour and request for other humour as exemplified below.

Thx, have a nice eve; n keep sending the fun (SMS 54)

This section has presented the different strategies used by Cameroonians to support humour in social media contexts. They include appreciation, smile or laughter, laughter and positive comment and appreciation and invitation of more jokes. These mechanisms are similar to those in face-to-face humour support moves. In general, there were neither aggressive humour patterns nor uncompromising humour responses.

DISCUSSION

The analysis aimed at finding out features of language that create humour in the corpus of Cameroon social media. The study reveals that there are instances of language use that incite laughter in the Cameroon social media investigated. Twelve different forms of humour markers were identified in the data. They are: flouting of Gricean maxims, spelling defiance, sound devices, special repetition of letters, humorous anecdotes, laughter, play with identity, emoticons, hyperbole, metaphor, typographic and other word play. Cameroonians employ humour for pleasure, to reinforce intimacy/ solidarity, and also as a means of sustaining their cultural values. The humour marker with the highest rate of occurrence is flouting of Gricean maxims (93.4%); spelling deviances constitute the second preferred way of joking with 38.9% and metaphors constitute the least (2.6%). Apart from non-observant of Gricean maxims, all the other humour patterns in the data occur less frequently on the whole (below 40%). This could probably be due to participants' unfamiliarity with the social platforms, their frames of mind at the time of the interactions or antagonism of the software to humour. It was ascertain that incongruity is necessary for the success of humour. Some of the strategies used to respond to humour include appreciation of the joke, laughter/ smile and invitation of more jokes. However, the forms of jokes may vary from one society or class of people to another. Some variables that were considered to determine humour are the participants, personal background, age, social and cultural context of jokes.

It was established that humour indicators like some real-life anecdotes and certain nicknames were peculiar to Cameroon. This shows that Cameroonian traditional symbols are entwined in their jokes, and are being taken to a global level through the internet. Humour prototypes that were found to be outcomes of the social media under study include emoticons, special repetition of letters and some punctuation marks. They reflect linguistic novelties occasioned by the social media and the users. It was discovered that the humour markers were not evenly distributed in the four data. The researcher found that humorous anecdote was absent in the YM corpus; hyperbole and metaphor were not found in the SMS and YM data, and others (typographic and other word play) were also lacking in YM. All the humour markers were found in FBK and informal e-mails. However, FBK recorded the highest rates of occurrences in a majority of the humour patterns with some getting up to 100%. This depicts that the FBK social platform could be more hospitable to humour than the others. Besides, it is increasingly being adopted by many people as their favourite social platform.

Some of the humour indicators from Cameroonian social media such as emoticons and spelling deviances can be found in other social media settings elsewhere, but the degree of occurrence and the specific ways in which they are employed in those contexts may be different from those of Cameroonians. A few others (e.g. cultural anecdotes and names) are not universal, thus leading one to observe the autonomous nature of features that create humour in Cameroon e-mails, FBK, SMS and YM. It is hoped that as the communication revolution continues to advance, a lot of Cameroonians will become much more familiar with social media platforms and will develop new ways of marking humour hitherto undetected. This will instigate new insights into the relationship between jokes, local culture and globalization through new information and communication technologies.

CONCLUSION

This study is a basic stride into how language use can evoke laughter. It does not reveal how all Cameroonians mark humour. In addition, not all social media platforms used by Cameroonians were investigated for humour. Future research could look at a wider array of Cameroonians and other social platforms like tweeter, whatssap, and online learning settings in order to uncover more humorous mechanisms from Cameroonians. Furthermore, studies could examine gender differences in humour, i. e. how men and women mark humour in Cameroon CMC contexts. In addition, comparative analyses of humour in face-to-face conversation and online environments in Cameroon can also be carried out, or between Cameroonians and non-Cameroonians. It is only when such investigations are done, then explicit statements on the nature of linguistic humour in Cameroon social media could be made.

REFERENCES

Aarons, D. (2011). *Jokes and the linguistic mind.* London: Routledge.

Adams, A. C. (2012). *On the identification of humor markers in computer-mediated communication.* AAAI Technical Report FS-12-02. Artificial Intelligence of humor. Retrieved March 6, 2015, from https://www.aaai.org/ocs/index.php/FSS/FSS12/paper/viewFile/5554/5796

Aristotle. (1941/ 2001). The basic works of Aristotle. New York: Random House.

Attardo, S. (1993). Violation of conversational maxims and cooperation: The case of jokes. *Journal of Pragmatics*, *19*(6), 537–558. doi:10.1016/0378-2166(93)90111-2

Attardo, S. (1994). *Linguistic Theories of Humor*. Berlin: Mouton de Gruyter.

Attardo, S. (1997). The semantic foundations of cognitive theories of humor. *Humor: International Journal of Humor Research*, *10*(4), 395–420. doi:10.1515/humr.1997.10.4.395

Attardo, S., & Raskin, V. (1991). Script theory revis(it)ed: joke similarity and joke representation model. Humor: International Journal of Humor Research, 4(3), 293-348.

Attardo, S., & Raskin, V. (1994). Non-literalness and non-bona-fide in language: An approach to formal and computational treatments of humor. *Pragmatics & Cognition*, *2*(1), 31–69. doi:10.1075/pc.2.1.02ras

Audrey, A. (2012). *Humor markers in computer-mediated communication*. (M.A. thesis). Texas A & M University. ProQuest document, dissertations & theses - Gradworks. Retrieved January 2, 2014, from http://gradworks.umi.com/15/29/1529858.html

Bai, Y. (2011). Incongruity-resolution in English Humor. *Theory and Practice in Language Studies*, *1*(1), 83-86. Retrieved March 5, 2015, from http://ojs.academypublisher.com/index.php/tpls/article/viewFile/01018386/2468

Baron, N. S. (2003). Language of the Internet. In A. Farghali (Ed.), *The Stanford Handbook for Language Engineers* (pp. 59–127). Standford: CSLI Publications.

Baron, N. S. (2010). *Always on: Language in an online and mobile world*. Oxford, UK: Oxford University Press.

Baym, N. K. (1995). The performance of humor in computer-mediated communication. *Journal of Computer Mediated Communication*, *1*(2). Retrieved January 2, 2014 from www.ascusc,org/jcmc/vol1/issue2/baym.html

Beattie, J. (1778). *Essays*. Edinburgh, UK: William Creech.

Belz, J. A. (2002). Second language play as a representation of the multicompetent self in foreign language study. *Journal of Language, Identity, and Education*, *1*(1), 13–39. doi:10.1207/S15327701JLIE0101_3

Belz, J. A., & Reinhardt, J. (2004). Aspects of advanced foreign language proficiency: Internet-mediated German language play. *International Journal of Applied Linguistics*, *14*(3), 324–362. doi:10.1111/j.1473-4192.2004.00069.x

Bennett, G. A. (2012). Say what? (笑): The representation of laughter as a contextualization cue in online Japanese discourse. *Linguistica*, *52*, 187-199. Retrieved December 15, 2014, from www.dlib.si/stream/URN:NBN:SI:DOCMYWF5CHD/...0e5e.../PDF

Crystal, D. (1996). Language play and linguistic intervention. *Child Language Teaching and Therapy*, *12*(3), 328–344. doi:10.1177/026565909601200307

Crystal, D. (2001). *Language play*. Chicago: University of Chicago Press.

Crystal, D. (2006). *Language and the Internet* (2nd ed.). Cambridge, UK: Cambridge University Press. doi:10.1017/CBO9780511487002

Crystal, D. (2008a). *Txting: The gr8 db8*. Oxford, UK: Oxford University Press.

Crystal, D. (2008b). 2b or not 2b? *The Guardian*. Retrieved February 2, 2015, from http://www.theguardian.com/books/2008/jul/05/saturdayreviewsfeatres.guardianreview

Cutting, J. (2008). *Pragmatics and Discourse: A Resource Book for students* (2nd ed.). New York: Routledge.

Danet, B., Ruedenberg-Wright, L., & Rosenbaum-Tamari, Y. (1997). Hmmm... Where's that smoke coming from? Writing, play and performance on Internet Relay Chat. *Journal of Computer-Mediated Communication, 2*(4). Retrieved from http://onlinelibrary.wiley.com/doi/10.1111/j.1083-6101.1997.tb00195.x/full

de Beaugrande, R., & Dressler, W. (1990). *Introduction to Text Linguistics*. London: Longman.

Edwards, C., Bresnahan, K., & Edwards, A. (2008). The influence of humorous positive computer-mediated word-of-mouth communication on student motivation and affective learning. *Texas Speech Communication Journal, 33*(1), 1–8.

Georgakopoulou, A. (2011). "On for drinkies?": Email cues of participant alignments. *Language@Internet, 8*, article 4. Retrieved January 2, 2015, from www.languageatinternet.org.urn:nbn:de

Goatly, A. (2012). *Meaning and Humour*. Cambridge, UK: Cambridge University Press. doi:10.1017/CBO9780511791536

Grice, H. P. (1975). Logic and Conversation. In P. Cole & J. L. Morgan (Eds.), Syntax and Semantics:*Speech Acts* (vol. 3, pp. 41–58). New York: Academic Press.

Herring, S. (2001). Computer- mediated discourse. In D. Tannen, D. Schiffrin, & H. Hamilton (Eds.), *The Handbook of Discourse Analysis* (pp. 612–634). Oxford, UK: Blackwell.

Herring, S. (2012). Grammar and electronic communication. In C. Chapelle (Ed.), *Encyclopedia of Applied Linguistics*. Hoboken, NJ: Wiley-Blackwell. Retrieved June 16, 2012, from http://ella.slis.indiana.edu/~herring/e-grammar.2011.pdf

Huang, C. & Szafir, D. (n.d.). *No joke: Examining the use of humour in computer- mediated learning*. Retrieved January 15, 2015, from pages.cs.wisc.edu/~dszafir/documents/hci- final. pdf

Kant, I. (1914). *The Critique of judgment*. London: Macmillan. Retrieved February 5, 2015, from http://oll.libertyfund.org/titles/1217

Laineste, L. (2013). Funny or aggressive? Failed humour in Internet comments. *Folklore, 53*, 29–46. Retrieved from http://www.folklore.ee/folklore/vol53/laineste.pdf

Morkes, J., Kernal, H. K., & Nass, C. (1999). Effects of humor in task oriented human- computer interaction and computer-mediated communication: A direct test of SRCT theory. *Human-Computer Interaction, 14*(4), 395–435. doi:10.1207/S15327051HCI1404_2

Morreal, J. (2012). Philosophy of humor. *Stanford Encyclopedia of philosophy*. Retrieved March 5, 2015, from http://plato.stanford.edu/entries/humour/

Mudler, M. P., & Nijholt, A. (2002). *Humour research: state of the art*. Retrieved February 2, 2015, from wwwhome.ewi.utwente.nl/~anijholt/artikelen/ctit24_2002.pdf

Ong'onda, N. A., Oketch, O. & Ongarora, D. (2013). Prosodic features in facebook communication. *International Journal of Academic Research in Progressive Education and Development*, *2*(2), 166 – 180. Retrieved February 2, 2015, from http://www.hrmars.com/admin/pics/1884.pdf

Raskin, V. (1985). *Semantic mechanisms of humor*. Dordrecht: D. Reidel Publishing Company.

Ritchie, G. (1999). Developing the Incongruity-Resolution Theory. In *Proceedings of the AISB'99 Symposium on Creative language: Humor and Stories* (pp. 78-85). Retrieved March 5, 2015, from http:www.informatics.ed.ac.uk/

Ruch, W., Attardo, S., & Raskin, V. (1993). Toward an empirical verification of the General Theory of Verbal Humor. *Humor: International Journal of Humor Research*, *62*, 123–136.

Schopenhauer, A. (1995). *The world as Will and Idea*. London: Everyman.

Schultz, T. R. (1976). A cognitive-developmental analysis of humor. In A. J. Chapman & H. C. Foot (Eds.), *Humor and Laughter: Theory, Research and Applications* (pp. 11–36). London: Wiley & Sons.

Shifman, L., & Thelwall, M. (2014). Internet jokes: The secret agents of globalization. *Journal of Computer-Mediated Communication*, *19*(4), 727–743. doi:10.1111/jcc4.12082

Skovholt, K., Grønning, A., & Kankaanranta, A. (2014). The communicative functions of emoticons in workplace e-mails:-)*. *Journal of Computer-Mediated Communication*, *19*(4), 780–797. doi:10.1111/jcc4.12063

Suls, J. M. (1972). A two-stage model for the appreciation of jokes and cartoons: An information-processing analysis. In J. H. Goldstein & P. E. McGhee (Eds.), *The psychology of humor: Theoretical perspectives and empirical issues* (pp. 81–99). New York: Academic Press. doi:10.1016/B978-0-12-288950-9.50010-9

Suls, J. M. (1983). Cognitive processes in humour appreciation. In P. McGhee & J. Goldstein (Eds.), *Handbook of humor research: Basic issues* (pp. 39–58). New York: Springer-Verlag. doi:10.1007/978-1-4612-5572-7_3

Tabe, C. A. (2011). *A study of e-mail messages in Cameroon English*. (Unpublished doctoral thesis). University of Yaounde I, Cameroon.

Taylor, C. (2009). 'Laughter' in L2 Computer-Mediated Discourse. In M. Dynel (Ed.), *Advances in Discourse Approaches* (pp. 174 - 200). Cambridge, UK: Cambridge Scholars Publishing. Retrieved March 5, 2015, from http://www.academia.edu/426141/Laughter_in_L2_Computer_Mediated_Discourse

Vandergriff, I., & Fuchs, C. (2009). Does CMC promote language play? Exploring humor in two modalities. *CALICO Journal*, *27*(1), 26–47. doi:10.11139/cj.27.1.26-47

Van Dijk, T. A. (1986). *Text and Context: Explorations into the Semantics and Pragmatis of Discourse*. London: Longman.

Vlahovic, T. A., Roberts, S., & Dunbar, R. (2012). Effects of duration and laughter on subjective happiness within different modes of communication. *Journal of Computer-Mediated Communication*, *17*(4), 436–450. doi:10.1111/j.1083-6101.2012.01584.x

Yule, G. (1996). *The Study of Language* (2nd ed.). Cambridge, UK: Cambridge University Press.

ADDITIONAL READING

Apte, M. (1985). *Humor and laughter*. Ithaca, NY: Cornell University Press.

Attardo, S. (1998). The analysis of humorous narratives. *Humor: International Journal of Humor Research*, *11*(3), 231–260. doi:10.1515/humr.1998.11.3.231

Attardo, S. (2001). *Humorous texts: A semantic and pragmatic analysis*. Berlin, New York: Mouton de Gruyter. doi:10.1515/9783110887969

Attardo, S. (2014). *Encyclopedia of humor studies*. Thousand Oaks, CA: SAGE. doi:10.4135/9781483346175

Attardo, S. et al.. (1994). The linear organization of jokes: Analysis of two thousand texts. *Humor: International Journal of Humor Research*, *7*(1), 27–54.

Attardo, S., Hempelmann, C. F., & Di Maio, S. (2002). Script oppositions and logical mechanisms: Modeling incongruities and their resolutions. *Humor: International Journal of Humor Research*, *15*(1), 3–46. doi:10.1515/humr.2002.004

Bell, N. D. (2005). Exploring L2 language play as an aid to SLL: A case study of humour in NS-NNS interaction. *Applied Linguistics*, *26*(2), 192–218. doi:10.1093/applin/amh043

Billig, M. (2005). *Laughter and ridicule: Towards a social critique of humor*. London: SAGE.

Bonaiuto, M., Castellana, E., & Pierro, A. (2003). Arguing and laughing: The use of humor to negotiate in group discussions. *Humor: International Journal of Humor Research*, *16*(2), 183–223. doi:10.1515/humr.2003.010

Boxer, D., & Cortés-Conde, F. (1997). From bonding to biting: Conversational joking and identity display. *Journal of Pragmatics*, *27*(3), 275–294. doi:10.1016/S0378-2166(96)00031-8

Carrell, A. (1997). Joke competence and humor competence. *Humor: International Journal of Humor Research*, *10*(2), 173–185. doi:10.1515/humr.1997.10.2.173

Cekaite, A., & Aronsson, K. (2005). Language play, a collaborative resource in children's L2 learning. *Applied Linguistics*, *26*(2), 169–191. doi:10.1093/applin/amh042

Cheung, C., & Yue, X. D. (2013). Humor styles, optimism and their relationship with stress among undergraduates in three Chinese cities. *Humor: International Journal of Humor Research*, *26*(2). doi:10.1515/humor-2013-0015

Coates, J. (2007). Talk in a play frame: More on laughter and intimacy. *Journal of Pragmatics*, *39*(1), 29–49. doi:10.1016/j.pragma.2006.05.003

Cook, G. (2000). *Language play, language learning*. New York: Oxford University Press.

Daisley, M. (1994). The game of literacy: The meaning of play in computer-mediated communication. *Computers and Composition*, *2*(2), 107–119. doi:10.1016/S8755-4615(06)80003-4

Dubinsky, S., & Chris, H. (2011). *Understanding language through humor*. Cambridge: Cambridge University Press. doi:10.1017/CBO9780511977824

Glenn, P. (2003). *Laughter in Interaction*. Cambridge: Cambridge University Press. doi:10.1017/CBO9780511519888

Gray, J. A. & Ford, T. E. (2013). The role of social context in the interpretation of sexist humor. *Humor: International Journal of Humor Research,* 26 (2). Davies, C. (1998). *Jokes and their relations to society*. Berlin / New York: Mouton de Gruyter.

Herring, S. C., Stein, D., & Virtanen, T. (Eds.). (2013). *Handbook of the Pragmatics of computer-mediated communication*. Berlin, New York: Mouton de Gruyter. doi:10.1515/9783110214468

Holcomb, C. (1997). A class of clowns: Spontaneous joking in computer-assisted discussions. *Computers and Composition*, *14*(1), 3–18. doi:10.1016/S8755-4615(97)90035-9

Hubler, M. T., & Bell, D. C. (2003). Computer-mediated humour and ethos: Exploring threads of constitutive laughter in online communities. *Computers and Composition*, *20*(3), 277–294. doi:10.1016/S8755-4615(03)00036-7

Kazarian, S. S. (2013). Unveiling the humor mind of the "starving Armenians": Literary and internet humor. *Humor: International Journal of Humor Research*, *26*(2). doi:10.1515/humor-2013-0021

Kitazume, S. (2010). *How to do things with humor*. Tokyo: Eihōsha.

Kuczaj, S. (1983). *Crib speech and language play*. New York: Springer. doi:10.1007/978-1-4613-9502-7

Latta, R. L. (1999). *The basic humor process: A cognitive-shift theory and the case against incongruity*. Berlin, New York: Mouton de Gruyter. doi:10.1515/9783110806137

Martin, R. (2007). *The Psychology of humor: An integrative approach*. Burlington, MA: Elsevier Academic.

McGhee, P. E. (1979). *Humor: Its origin and Development*. San Francisco: W. H. Freeman and Company.

Morreall, J. (Ed.). (1987). *The Philosophy of Laughter and Humor*. New York: State University of New York Press.

Morreall, J. (2004). Verbal humor without switching scripts and without non-bonafide communication. *Humor: International Journal of Humor Research*, *17*(4), 393–400. doi:10.1515/humr.2004.17.4.393

Mulkay, M. (1998). *On humor: its nature and its place in modern society*. Oxford: Blackwell.

Norrick, N. R. (1993). *Conversational joking: humor in everyday talk*. Bloomington, Indianapolis: Indiana University Press.

Norrick, N. R. (2007). Interdiscourse humour: Contrast, merging, accommodation. *Humor: International Journal of Humor Research*, *20*(4), 389–413. doi:10.1515/HUMOR.2007.019

Norrick, N. R., & Klein, J. (2008). Class clowns: Talking out of turn with an orientation toward humor. *Lodz Papers in Pragmatics*, *4*(1), 83–107. doi:10.2478/v10016-008-0002-6

Palmer, J. (1994). *Talking humour seriously*. London: Routledge. doi:10.4324/9780203380154

Partington, A. (2006). *Linguistics of Laughter*. London: Routledge.

Pomerantz, A., & Bell, N. (2007). Learning to play, playing to learn: FL learners as multicompetent language users. *Applied Linguistics*, *28*(4), 556–578. doi:10.1093/applin/amm044

Raskin, V. (Ed.). (2008). *The primer of humor research*. Berlin: Mouton de Gruyter. doi:10.1515/9783110198492

Ritchie, G. (2003). *The linguistic Analysis of jokes*. London: Routledge.

Schurr, S., & Rowe, C. (2008). The 'dark side' of humour: An analysis of subversive humour in workplace emails. *Lodz Papers in Pragmatics*, *4*(1), 109–130.

Shifman, L. (2007). Humor in the age of digital reproduction: Continuity and change in internet-based comic texts. *International Journal of Communication*, *1*, 187–209.

Siegel, J. (1995). How to get a good laugh in Fijian: Code-switching and humor. *Language in Society*, *24*(01), 95–110. doi:10.1017/S004740450001842X

Smith, P. (1991). The joke of machine: Communicating traditional humour using computers. In G. Bennet (Ed.), *Spoken in Jest* (pp. 257–277). Sheffield: University of Sheffield Press.

Sudweeks, F., McLaughlin, M. L., & Rafaeli, S. (Eds.). (1998). *Network and Netplay: Virtual groups on the Internet*. Menlo Park, CA: AAAI/ MIT Press.

Sullivian, P. (2013). Humor styles as a predictor of satisfaction within sport teams. *Humor: International Journal of Humor Research*, *26*(2).

Triezenberg, K. (2004). Humor enhancers in the study of humorous literature. *Humor: International Journal of Humor Research*, *17*(4), 419–428. doi:10.1515/humr.2004.17.4.411

Veale, T. (2004). Incongruity in humor: Root cause or epiphenomenon? *Humor: International Journal of Humor Research*, *17*(4), 411–418. doi:10.1515/humr.2004.17.4.419

Walter, N. (1985). *The language of humour*. London: Longman.

Weeks, M. C. (2002). Laughter, desire and time. *Humor: International Journal of Humor Research*, *15*(4), 383–400. doi:10.1515/humr.15.4.383

KEY TERMS AND DEFINITIONS

E-mail: E-mail is used in this chapter to describe messages sent electronically from one computer to another via the Internet. The messages are sent to individual Cameroonians all over the world. This study makes use of only informal inline plain texts written by Cameroonians.

Facebook: The name of a social networking site (SNS) that connects people with friends and others who work, study and live around them. *Facebook chat*, i. e., a free service that enables Facebook users to conduct instant message-based conversations with Facebook friends, from Cameroonians were part of the data in this study.

Humour: A word used to describe pleasure in incongruity.

Humour Support: These are responses or reactions to humorous messages.

Mobile Telephone Short Message Service (SMS): It refers to short text messages transmitted to and from a mobile phone.

Social Media: A term used to describe a variety of Web-based or mobile telephone platforms, applications and technologies that enable people to socially interact with one another online.

Yahoo Messenger: It is Yahoo's instant message service. It has about 22 million users world-wide. Cameroonian chats from this service comprise part of the corpus used in this Chapter.

Chapter 9
"Can I Get in on the Joke, Too?": Analysing Racial Humor within the Public/Private Realm of the Internet

Frederick W. Gooding Jr.
Northern Arizona University, USA

ABSTRACT

This chapter explores the ramifications of having race-based "dirty laundry" aired through humor, without necessarily being dirty jokes. Not only is the United States of America reputed to be a "free country," but also there are few restrictions on Internet participation outside of obvious legal infractions. Thus, while repulsive in their worst form or in poor taste in their naive form, racist jokes are not regulated on the Internet. Nor is expressing or espousing racism online in and of itself illegal. Currently our legal system is designed to respond or react to manifestations of racist thought when acted out against another in the physical realm (e.g., denying another a job based upon their race or inflicting bodily harm when motivated by racial animus). While we presume that most would not want to entertain destructive thoughts, people are free to hold, share and emote racist ideas in cyberspace. Thus, with the ever-expanding role of the Internet in many of our lives, it is important to interrogate whether such publicly broadcast in-group humor will desensitize other members of other races outside of the joke. This chapter will tease out the implications of the continued sharing online of racial humor, with those both in and outside of the original joke.

INTRODUCTION

But It's Just a Joke, Right?

Ethnic Humor is a tricky breed. Every individual is an autonomous system of cells, moving blood particles and other live matter. At the same time, every individual is part of a larger system. We each claim various memberships to a myriad of social systems larger than us. Whether it be in the very large, eternally expanding sorority of motherhood, or the more specific grouping of your own college fraternity (complete with secret handshakes and door knocks), we belong to groups.

DOI: 10.4018/978-1-5225-0338-5.ch009

Copyright © 2016, IGI Global. Copying or distributing in print or electronic forms without written permission of IGI Global is prohibited.

Typically, every group membership has its perks and its pains. No matter how exclusive or well endowed, any group containing humans will find a way to exemplify humanity's tendency for imperfection. Meaning, no group is perfect and chances are if one remains a member long enough, they are likely to find other members of the group to be bothersome or frustrating at some point in time. At the same time, membership has it privileges. One privilege that most every group member does at some point in time is make fun of other members of the group. Why? Well, the membership grants the license based upon an implicit understanding of a shared experience. For example, a mother making fun of motherhood therefore is received by other mothers differently than jokes made by a male without children based upon his external observations of motherhood -- all the more especially if the male's jokes are of a critical or disparaging nature. The premise here is that the mother who "paid her dues" through childbirth, has literally and figuratively earned the right to participate in self-effacing humor. The presumption behind the premise is that as a member of the in-group, her intentions are not to disparage or demean but rather are to make light and delight within a larger collective experience since she knows intimately the "shared universe of shared experiences" (Jacquemet, 1992, p.736).

BACKGROUND

When it comes to ethnic humor, these rules are very similar, with profoundly different results, thanks to the Internet. Thus, online, more and more instances of in-group humor is being broadcast and shared with an international online audience. Even though an Mexican American through an online posting could in jest just be making fun of other Mexican Americans based upon a shared, common experience, now that it is published within a public forum, such humor is now fair game for all -- including those outside of the racial or ethnic group. A major risk in for example, a white person repeating a self-effacing joke made by a Mexican American person about other Mexican Americans is that historical and social narratives may attach different significance to the joke depending upon who is telling the joke.

In other words, the same racial "joke" when retold by a white person may no longer be funny. Moreover, if the same joke is shared exclusively by a white user with other whites, under the auspices that it was found out in the open Internet, a new undercurrent of racial disregard may manifest in the "real world." Now feelings are hurt, people are offended and are taking sides within the boundaries of their own social media platforms. This chapter will tease out the implications of the continued sharing of racial humor, with those both in and outside of the original joke.

Due to the wide, expansive and ever-expanding nature of the Internet, we shall employ three specific case studies to illustrate how racial humor is manifested and treated within online forums and platforms. The case studies are not dispositive, but are representative of larger themes surrounding acceptable versus inappropriate joke material and provide an entrée into further analysis.

MAIN FOCUS OF THE CHAPTER

Making Racial Noise

Humor of course, is in the eye of the beholder. Thus, that which is funny or humorous to the jokester may not be readily apparent to the outside audience. This was evident with the case of Alexandra Wallace.

In March of 2011, Wallace was a student at the University of California, Los Angeles and was rather perturbed by what she interpreted to be "too much" chatter amongst other students in the library and therefore took to the unfiltered and uncensored venue of the Internet to voice her displeasure.

In Wallace's case, not only did she express her discontent for students making too much noise in the library, but it just so happened all of the students with whom she had a problem were Asian American. In other words, Wallace launched a targeted attack wherein she blamed all Asian Americans for her inability to concentrate and study. Wallace took her private grievance public when she posted a video on YouTube first outlining her general complaint. As a hint of the video's malintentions, it was labeled "Asians in the Library." But then Wallace proceeded to "share" her impression/interpretation of what a typical Asian American "sounded like" while talking on cell phones in the library and became instantly infamous for punctuating her rant with indecipherable sounds such as "ching chong ting tong ling long."

Wallace's true thoughts and motivations are the subject of speculation since she subsequently withdrew from UCLA and has not provided many statements or interviews since. Yet, in watching the video, Wallace's "ching chong ling long" bit was an attempt at humor – albeit a failed one. Moreover, Wallace provided an apology for her video which went "viral" – or became very popular within a short span of time and became widely circulated to a large audience – as she publicly announced that she was withdrawing from UCLA while also pleading for privacy for her family. In the official apology, Wallace starts her letter with the following: "In an attempt to produce a *humorous* YouTube video, I have offended the UCLA community and the entire Asian culture" (Parkinson-Morgan, 2011) (emphasis added).

Based upon what we know, Wallace admits that humor is her defense. She believed that since she was "joking," she was somehow provided an additional layer of protection to truly express herself. To be clear, Wallace's offering was indeed racist and insensitive. Wallace tried to seize upon decades' old stereotypical narratives about the inability for white mainstream society to navigate language differences of ethnic groups. Apparently, Wallace was referring to her inability to understand Asian American students as they speak in their native tongues inside of the library. It is unclear what bothers Wallace more: whether she finds the high voice volumes distressing or whether she finds the volume of Asian American students as generally distressing, or that "too many" Asian Americans are now enrolled in an elite institution such as UCLA and have passed the "tipping point" (Takagi, 120). In other words, while many whites feel and act out on what they perceive to be physical threats by African Americans based upon dark pigmentation (Hall, 207) many whites are afflicted by psychological and intellectual fears of stereotype threats and underperform when juxtaposed against the "model minority" (Brest & Krieger, 330).

Wallace's move to voluntarily withdraw spared UCLA from having to act publicly and thus did not render any official punishment, as this scenario poses a free speech dilemma for such an institution. In this case, where UCLA failed or had yet to act, the court of public Internet opinion rendered its verdict. Wallace posted her video and the Internet universe posted their responses. More importantly, others used humor and satire as a tool to discredit Wallace's initial post. For instance, video blogger Jimmy Wong posted a musical response, rhetorically asking what did "ting tong" mean along with other sarcastic observations about Wallace's video, receiving over 1 million views. Wong also appeared on National Public Radio as a guest to discuss Wallace's rant and his parody video. Scores of other individuals posted their own humorous videos in response (e.g., "White Girls in the Library") and began circulating widely videos or commentaries that defended Asian culture generally while lampooning bigotry displayed by Wallace.

This case presents two fascinating developments: the first being that just as the Internet can be a place where people's identities can be attacked, the Internet also offers opportunity for targets or victims to launch effective counterattacks. Second, what cannot be overlooked is the mind state behind Wallace's original post, which emboldened her to make the original offensive offering under the guise of humor. Many an offensive statement has been uttered under the auspices of humor. Within the virtual space of the Internet, without direct social pressure to regulate initial submissions, it is likely Wallace is neither the first nor the last to promote such material.

Calculating the Harm of Racial Jokes

Wallace's case was unique in that the perpetrator of offensive racial content was confronted and dealt with both artistically on the Internet through countering YouTube videos and substantively with her subsequent apology to the targets of her racial ire (e.g., Asian American students at UCLA generally). Yet, the next case features an exclusive online posting, but without any response from the target or "victim." Here, the victim is a nameless young African American male who is the central figure of a "vine," or a 6 second-long looping video clip posted on the Internet. Similar to Twitter, which consists of typewritten messages limited to 140 characters per submission (sometimes accompanied by a video or other media), the shortened video vine format has elicited a wide array of creative ideas of expression given the constraints of time. Applications include the looping of spectacular sports highlights or video game exploits. Yet, many of the amateur vines created and posted comprise of videos that attempt to execute humorous ideas within a short time span.

This particular vine features a young boy, shirtless, standing in a poorly lit room. The boy can be no more than twelve years old, if not younger, and there is no other identifying information in the video for the participants or the filming location. There are two total parties to the video for an adult off camera first addresses the lad by asserting "You stupid." In defense, the kid quickly responds "No, I'm not!" which prompts the adult to test his stupidity hypothesis by asking the young lad to calculate a simple math equation. The adult then queries, "What's nine plus ten?" The little boy responds, "Twenty-one." The adult then responds to the incorrect answer in a gruff manner and berates the child again saying "You stupid!" before the vine concludes. While no slapstick, wordplay or contrived jokes were utilized, many who saw the original and shared it with others nonetheless viewed this vine as funny. The key question here is what was the fodder for the humor?

Firstly, this is not just any youth. It is an African American youth. Specifically, an African American male youth. More specifically, an African American male youth with his shirt off in a relatively darkened space. This imagery speaks strongly to age-old narratives of black impoverishment and being under resourced. For example, the vine does not take place outside in the park with greenery and sunlight surrounding him. Or at the pool, on a beach, at the mountains or on an expansive ranch. The video takes place within the context of black living conditions that appear limited and reflect poor living and poor social conditions; one where parenting is perhaps not taken seriously.

It is unclear what the relationship is of the adult with the child. But the harsh manner in which the adult aggressively asserts more than once to the child "You stupid" is enough to give anyone pause. Ideally, such material should not be the source of laughter as perhaps it should be the source of angst and furrowed brows, especially in light of national statistics that suggest a significant achievement gap is tangibly affecting the life chances and earning potential of black families (Orr, p.285) If this adult is the boy's father, then this video is a warning sign and a cry for possible intervention.

If the adult is not the boy's father, this video is nonetheless a warning sign and a cry for possible intervention as this private, intimate moment has been made public for millions to enjoy and delight in this young man's ridicule. How this child will be affected from a developmental standpoint when he grows old enough to learn that his one simple error has been the archetype for stupidity worldwide is a question that we may be unable to answer here. But in concert with the litany of African American images that stress or emphasize black incompetence in contrast to white intelligence, this shirtless little boy staring blankly into the camera does very little to deviate from this damaging narrative.

While many vines feature many people of different races in compromised positions or as the butt of jokes, including whites, very few feature young white children in this raw, half naked capacity where their miscalculations have become the source of merriment and laughter within a world wide Internet audience. So, this is not to say that no white children have been targeted as jokes, but the secondary question is why does this meme so fascinate and capture the imagination of the Internet? This meme was first posted in July 2014 and by December of that same year had nearly 9 million views total from two different sources. YouTube use "SwiftStar352" posted an audio song using sampled parts of this "21" vine, reaching 14.6 million views by December 2014 as well. It is unknown or unclear how the black male subject of this vine has responded to his Internet infamy.

Lastly, the ultimate irony with this vine posting is that it underscores that which it seeks to undermine since the vine – possibly from the filming adult's perspective – was a "humorous" referendum on intelligence. Yet, the adult voice off-camera belies a lack of education and training as well. In listening to the adult voice, he repeats the phrase "You stupid" twice – meaning, even in the process of communicating his disdain for the young African American male's miscalculation, the adult male expresses himself in a manner that lacks polish. While entirely possible the male voice belongs to an award-winning astrophysicist researcher with a PhD, such a possibility may be small indeed. The adult does not even have the decency to relay to the youth his low opinion of the child's intellectual capacity in a grammatically correct sentence (e.g., "You are stupid"), but instead offers intellectual shorthand by stating "You stupid."

But even a grammatically correct phrasing of the "stupid" sentiment is problematic. Any adult in this position would be wise to leverage their age and experience in a constructive manner on such a young and impressionable population. A simple "Not quite! Let's try again!" acknowledges the reality of the miscalculation, but assumes that ability to calculate correctly exists. The pronouncement of stupidity on a young child is dangerous and damaging – all the more especially for young black males who lack access to opportunities and resources for personal development based upon historical institutional and systemic barriers (Thompson, p.53). But in this case, "You stupid" is also the source of online humor for millions.

Singing the Praises of Racial Jokes

The first two case studies, while vastly different in their scope, share the similarity of being originally created or at the very least posted publicly on the Internet for humorous purposes. This next case study consists of a mini-trend based upon true, real life events that originally were not funny in the least. Within this last case study, there are at least three scenarios that featured newsworthy occurrences: an attempted rape, an apartment fire and a rescue from a decade-long kidnapping and torture saga. What all three scenarios have in common is that these real life scenarios were interpreted through the eyes and tongues of unpolished, impoverished African Americans on live news television, prompting for others (not the African Americans themselves) to seize upon the opportunity to frame these honest expressions and impressions humorously and also for profit.

At least the Gregory Brothers thought so. Three brothers originally from Radford, Virginia who since moved to New York, seized upon a pattern and created a niche for themselves. They had the idea of taking the original newscast footage and manipulating it so that it sounded like a song. Their series was originally entitled "Auto Tune the News" (now "Songify the News") but did not achieve true mainstream acclaim until they released their "Bed Intruder" song featuring Antoine Dodson.

Antoine Dodson

If you were to look up the name "Antoine Dodson" (online of course), you would discover that Dodson is an Internet celebrity of sorts who has more of an Internet presence than the average person. Just like Winston Churchill, Ghandi and Martin Luther King, Jr., Dodson has his own *Wikipedia* page, which is not something that all readers (or writers!) of this chapter can claim. Specifically, Dodson is described as "Internet Celebrity, singer and actor" currently, but it was not always this way for Dodson.

Antoine Dodson is from the Lincoln Park housing projects in Huntsville, Alabama. He became a newsworthy figure when he was interviewed on local NBC affiliate WAFF-48 News television to express his outrage. Dodson had a message for a burglar who broke into the house and attempted to rape his sister who was in bed at the time of the attack. Kelly was also interviewed, but Dodson's segment received considerably more time and exposure partly because it was so unique. Dodson looks square into the camera and addresses the burglar-rapist stating that "You are really dumb! You are so dumb! We gon' find you!" and then addresses the community stating: "Well, obviously we have a rapist in Lincoln Park. He's climbin' in yo windows, he's snatchin' yo people up, tryin' to rape 'em. So y'all need to hide yo kids, hide yo wife, and hide yo husband cause they rapin' everybody out here" (Gallagher, 2010). Dodson at the time of the interview wore a red bandana and a black tank top. He was rather expressive and fiery – understandable given the circumstances – but his on-camera presence was in stark contrast to the measured, controlled tones offered by the white newscasters.

The Gregory Brothers music band obtained the original footage and hatched the idea to turn this newscast interview into an entertaining song. They changed the pitch of Dodson's original voice tone with the help of auto-tune and manipulated the order of his phrasing to make appear that he was actually singing on beat. The Gregory Brothers hit the right note with their humorous rendition of Dodson's original telecast as evidenced by the 127 million views the "Bed Intruder" song received on YouTube. While they agreed to share proceeds with Dodson so that Dodson could move out of the projects, the "Bed Intruder" song sold over a quarter of a million copies on the online music store iTunes. The song and Dodson quickly became etched within mainstream culture, cracking into the Billboard Hot 100 list at #89 and won the 2010 award "Meme of the Year" by the Urlies. Dodson even made a cameo appearance in a Hollywood movie, "A Madea Christmas" where he repeated his signature line "Hide yo kids, hide yo wife."

Speaking of Christmas, Dodson teamed up with the Gregory Brothers again to create a "Holiday version" of the famous "Bed Intruder" song that had already "gone viral" the summer before by donning a "Santa's helper" costume and signing "He's climbing in yo chimneys…."). But others beside Dodson have joined in on the fun. After the Gregory Brothers posted the musical chords used to create the "Bed Intruder" song, more than 2,500 covers – or other artists recording themselves singing a song not original to their own creation – have been posted online. Another well-known Internet meme, the "Annoying Orange" added itself to the long list of satires, performing a "Kitchen Intruder" version as well.

Yet, one individual who has received little attention in juxtaposition to Antoine Dodson is Dodson's sister, Kelly Dodson. As the victim and target of a violent sexual attack, Kelly Dodson was undoubtedly upset that her privacy was violated and said so in the interview ("I was attacked, by some idiot in the projects…"). But even though Kelly Dodson was the whole reason why a newscast was recorded in the first place, she was not the focal point of the "Bed Intruder" song, nor was she targeted extensively during subsequent song remakes. In other words, very few may invoke the name of the actual victim who "suffered" an attempted rape in her own bed by a stranger. And here lies the danger of such online humor. Michael Gregory of The Gregory Brothers "told *Billboard* that he did question the appropriateness of taking a bad news story and making it into a musical parody but then came to the conclusion that "it's taking a terrible situation and making at least something positive out of it." The band is splitting the money they make from sales 50% with the Dodson family. (Peters, 2010).

But given the fact that the final video product is "funny" and contributes to a worthy cause (i.e., 50% of iTunes proceeds were split with the Dodson family), very few viewers may question the appropriateness of "Bed Intruder" song and similar to the "21" vine, actually interrogate what is actually humorous. For, upon further analysis, it is not difficult to build consensus around the concept that rape is a detestable crime. Rape represents a vile violation of human dignity that few fully recover from. Having a good laugh online is not illegal, but the question becomes what is our collective social responsibility if such laughter illegitimates another's traumatic experience.

Jason King, a songwriter and music journalist was quoted by National Public Radio (NPR) as describing the "Bed Intruder" song as "…catchy. It has a really good hook, but it's problematic, too. There's a way in which the aesthetics of black poverty—the way they talk and they speak and they look—sort of becomes this fodder for humor without any interest in the context of the conditions in which people actually live."(Chace, 2010).

African Americans, their culture and tragedies often are not nearly as respected as the dominant culture. Based upon historical, systemic and institutional traditions of devaluing blackness and black contributions, it is often harder for whites to not judge black imagery negatively and associate past "racist baggage" with such depictions in juxtaposition to the normal, dominant culture (Lane, p. 198). Thus, it is simply not "as big a deal" if a rape attempt occurs in the black community. If anything, Antoine Dodson's manner of expression is funny, and that can remain the excluive focus.

Sweet Brown

Following the success of their mainstream entrée, The Gregory Brothers inspired others to repeat their formula on Kimberly "Sweet Brown" Williams. Her Oklahoma City apartment caught on fire and upon NBC affiliate KFOR-TV interviewing her afterwards, she too, was unfiltered and expressive in communicating her perspective of a perilous situation that she narrowly escaped. This is where the humor comes in -- people are laughing at her expression, her predicament and more distressingly, people are laughing at her. Barefoot (because she ran out of the apartment without shoes on), and with her hair also wrapped up in a bandanna (similar to Antoine Dodson), she tells the interviewer how she reflected "Oh, Lord Jesus! Thar's a fire!" She delves further into her deductive reasoning stating that she thought somebody was barbecuing and when she realized the gravity of the situation, she took note of her own health condition and pragmatically reasoned that she would not be a good candidate to withstand smoke inhalation. She concludes the interview with a flourish by emphatically stating that since she had bronchitis, and because she saw smoke, she had to leave immediately because to stay in the apartment would be to endanger herself and worsen her condition and "ain't nobody got time for that!"

While not as popular as the "Bed Intruder" song, Sweet Brown's song registered 50 million views – 1 million within the first forty-eight hours – a phenomenal number when registering 100,000 views is considered extremely successful. Such overnight success also merited a bump in Sweet Brown's "celebrity" status and she too made a cameo in Tyler Perry's "A Madea Christmas" movie. Sweet Brown even was interviewed as a guest on ABC's "The View" and late night television host and comedian Jimmy Kimmel performed a parody of Sweet Brown that also resulted in 700,000 online hits apart from the Gregory Brothers' song punctuated by the famous phrase: "ain't nobody got time for that!"

It is subtle, but significant to note that this is not an upper middle class, blue-eyed, buxom, blonde woman standing in front of her four bedroom, three bathroom, single family dwelling. While the apartment fire may not appear as personally odious as being personally attacked by a would-be rapist and therefore may make it easier to laugh at since it is not "as serious," smoke inhalation from domestic fires is a real serious issue (Hall, 2011). The Sweet Brown video is very much racially coded, much like "21" vine and the "Bed Intruder" song. Viewers are laughing at Sweet Brown specifically as a proverbial, ignorant, overly-religious, unkempt, low income and loud black woman. For all we know, she does or does not embody any of these characteristics. However, historical narratives as Patricia Hill Collins explains already create these narratives within the minds of viewers (Collins, p.70). To underscore the point that Sweet Brown herself is the target of humorous derision, possibly in contrast to those who salve their conscience by claiming they were laughing at the way Antoine Dodson expressed his outrage, the accompanying video for "Ain't Nobody Got Time for That" is especially revealing.

It is foolhardy to assert that racial themes are not in play when analyzing the dance sequences spliced within the music video. The phrase "ain't nobody got time for that" is repeated several times, as if it were a chant, and visual images of people dancing to accompany the chant are included. Do note, that at roughly the 1:23 mark of the video, spliced in are a few seconds of chimpanzees also moving as if they were dancing. The literature that expounds upon the association between African Americans and primate symbology is well established (Mellinger, 1992, p.415). Further, "Bed Intruder" star Antoine Dodson makes a cameo as there is a still photograph of him and infamous African American fight promoter Don "Only in America" King barbecuing with their faces superimposed upon a drawing at roughly the 1:00 mark exactly. At the 1:40 mark, Sweet Brown is seen repeating the phrase "Oh Jesus it's a fire!" with subsequent clips of blacks "catching the spirit" at a religious revival (or "acting strangely" in juxtaposition to middle class norms) and concludes with images of a black (Harlem Boys) choir singing.

While viewers would like to comfort themselves in thinking that they are simply laughing at a "humorous video," in actuality, they are laughing at age-old narratives of undesirable and marginalized black culture.

Charles Ramsey

For our third and final scenario within our last case study, the principal subject Charles Ramsey was not the victim, but helped a victim escape from a traumatic scenario. He was blunt about the intersectionaliy of race and class when he said it was a "dead giveaway" that something was wrong when a "pretty little white girl jumped into a black man's arms." Specifically, in the spring of 2013, three women (Michelle Knight, Amanda Berry and Georgina DeJesus) held captive in Ariel Castro's home in Cleveland OH were finally able to escape with Ramsey's help. The three women were all kidnapped and abducted and held captive within walking distance of their own homes, with the longest period of time exceeding ten years. Castro created a house of horrors wherein the women were chained, beaten and brainwashed into believing that no escape was possible. One May day in 2013, Berry's six-year old daughter (fathered by Castro) who had "roaming" privileges in the house, informed her mother that Castro had left. After commanding her daughter to search every room to ensure it was not another "test of loyalty," Berry seized upon the opportunity to call for help. Ramsey arrived on scene and helped kick in the door to allow Berry to escape with her daughter and subsequently save the other two captive women with police help.

The Castro case is a haunting and chilling reminder of the depravity of humanity. Ramsey's popularity might in part be explained by his effusive and gregarious spirit as positioned as a positive alternative of what people can do for others, without any pre-existing relationship. Ramsey's popularity soared when his pragmatic and matter-of-fact delivery were on display in the initial 911 call (e.g., when asked whether Amanda Berry needed an ambulance, Ramsey blurted "You need an ambulance?! Or what? She need everything. She's – she in panic Bruh! I think she been kidnapped. So you know put yourself in her shoes.") (CBS/AP, 2013) and with his rather colorful interviews with the press after the story broke. For instance, he matter-of-factly explained "We used to eat ribs with this dude, but didn't have a clue [about his kidnapping of three women]." (Gross, 2013).

In a way, perhaps Ramsey is a hero in other respects. Based upon unwritten and unspoken rules or norms of middle class respectability, when in public, and especially when performing (e.g., on TV) the tendency is to behave conservatively and comport one's behavior with proper decorum to appear civil. Rare is the individual who has the chutzpah to willingly defy these norms and really express themselves effectively and not only tell the truth, but to do so in a truthful way. Even this chapter is "constrained" by numerous rules, some formal, many learned and understood as part of Academic culture. For instance, it would be "unprofessional" for the author to punctuate any sentence in this chapter with the phrase, "you know what I'm sayin'?" if the author still desires for same said chapter to be considered "scholarly" even though the substance of the information is the same, and arguably, may be more enjoyable and easier to digest. Hence, Charles' delivery was disarmingly honest. A colloquial expression that embodies Charles' delivery would be "keeping it real." So instead of stale platitudes about how unfortunate the scenario was and how happy he is that everyone is safe, Charles instead remarks: "This dude had big testicles 'cuz we seen this dude everyday!"

Middle class conventions would have likely prevented your local college professor (ahem) from expressing him or herself in a similar manner. Yet, all can appreciate the substance of what Ramsey is saying. For years, the sick and twisted mind of Castro allowed for him to hold women captive in his home while he kept up appearances that all was well and normal on the outside. Ramsey was incredulous and was not shy in saying so.

The Gregory Brothers proceeded to make a catchy tune entitled "Dead Giveaway" which obtained a modest 24 million views; and while more than the majority of YouTube postings, nonetheless was 100 million less than Dodson's "Bed Intruder" track. Unlike the "Ain't Nobody Got Time for That" video, the "Dead Giveaway" music video stuck to the script and used footage exclusively from television news broadcasts. Make no mistake, blackness once again is on display here. In contrast to the middle class, white dominated narrative of normalcy and authority (e.g., a white, shaven male with a suit and tie) Ramsey is an unshaven black male in a t-shirt clutching a napkin in one hand, while sporting a smile with a missing front tooth and a processed hair do. Ramsey also punctuated many of his sentences by naturally emphasizing his points through the full opening of his eyelids.

But Ramsey made a powerful point about "Dead Giveaway" indeed. While many have proceeded to freeze video frames of Ramsey with his eyes fully open (or making "bug eyes") and create memes and t-shirts (e.g., "Charles Ramsey for President: Saving the White Girl Since 2013"), his central point remains essentially unassailable. Ramsey appears to be a man who knows little about an upper class lifestyle through direct experience and fits the pattern established thus far by The Gregory Brothers' of selecting African Americans in what appears to be compromised financial and social conditions. As a result, Ramsey, presumably a man lacking in what middle class conventions would label as "polish," speaks to his life experience in a very real and direct way. Ramsey divined that something was amiss based upon the fact that Amanda Berry did not observe what the "Dead Giveaway" phrase implies are typical racial barriers for a man of his class status. Ramsey explained that "I knew something was wrong when a pretty little white girl jumped into a black man's arms." In other words, in a "perfect world" a pretty little white girl would likely not find herself in a situation where she would be jumping into Ramsey's arms for pleasure, friendship or business based upon typical norms of race and gender. Yet, the fact that Berry did jump in his arms in this case made Ramsey reflexively suspicious; and it turns out Ramsey was entirely correct that something was ghastly wrong and was far from a laughing matter.

CONCLUSION

But, Who Wants to Be the Butt of the Joke?

Presumably, we all like to laugh. Yet, with the auspices of free speech, who knows and who can regulate what people can laugh at? Humor is a very effective tool in having us think creatively about the small and large issues that we individually and collectively confront. After all, it has been said that behind every joke is some element of truth. But the truth of the matter is with much of the racial humor observed online, many jokes, vines, videos and memes elicit comments and responses that likely would not be uttered within a formal, public forum. Further, many of those who post online have the choice on whether to reveal their identity, and so the online format provides a layer of protection of anonymity between passive/aggressive behaviors or front stage/backstage behaviors (Picca & Feagin, 2007).

If we were allowed "backstage" to see the original intent and purpose of the Wallace "Ching Chong" video, or the "21" video or any of the three Gregory Brothers modifications of Antoine Dodson, Sweet Brown or Charles Ramsey, it is unlikely any of the creative forces behind any of the final products we now know circulated within the Internet were created with malicious, nefarious aims in mind to strike racial discord. However, good intentions do not wholly excuse negative impacts. For instance, the three auto-tuned news videos not only made the Gregory brothers rich, as in people have profited off of them, but they run the high risk of impoverishing the national dialogue further about the dignity and respect of black imagery. What are we laughing at again is the key question. Are we laughing at general scenarios that could apply to any person or any group of people? Or is there a specific unspoken association taking place?

In addition to the three case studies cited within this chapter, there are scores of other examples wherein people of color are indeed the butt of the joke. While The Gregory Brothers may counter that full exploitation is not at issue since it takes a creative component to splice and sift and figure out which natural patterns of speech rhyme and fit to a song. True, but these are real people with real problems without solutions that fit neatly within a three minute song, only to become the fodder for others to smirk, chortle and laugh as they innocently press "forward" on their screens to share the laugh with someone else.

Within the largely unregulated space of the Internet, these "jokes" represent a guilty pleasure where they jokes enjoyed by many members of the public within quiet and private circles of their friends whereas normally, there would be significant social costs associated with engaging in or promoting such imagery and symbology in public. Many viewers get to laugh at these videos without feeling any obligation to work towards alleviating the conditions that precipitated the joke in the first place.

We must continue to ponder the role of racial humor in our lives when distracted by the "deception of connection" that the Internet offers. In other words, people on the other side of the planet are only a few mouse clicks away, connecting us all. Yet, with the continued patronage of past problematic patterns premised upon racial prejudice – we run the risk of growing even further apart despite our virtual closeness.

And that's not funny…

REFERENCES

schmoyoho. (2010, Jul 31). *Bed Intruder Song!!! (now on iTunes)* [Video File]. Retrieved from https://www.youtube.com/watch?v=hMtZfW2z9dw.

Xuyah. (2011, Mar 13). *White Girls in the Library.* [Video File]. Retrieved from https://www.youtube.com/watch?v=zulEMWj3sVA.

PriceWaterhouseCoupe. (2011, Mar 15). *Asians in the Library (UCLA's Alexandra Wallace).* [Video File]. Retrieved from https://www.youtube.com/watch?v=yBxgtYfDgwM.

Jimmy Wong. (2011, Mar 15). *Ching Chong! Asians in the Library Song (Response to UCLA's Alexandra Wallace).*[Video File]. Retrieved from "White Girls in the Library" https://www.youtube.com/watch?v=PiEvmr3I-Ik.

theparodyfactory1. (2012, Apr 13). *Sweet Brown – Ain't nobody got time for that (autotune remix)* [Video File]. Retrieved from https://www.youtube.com/watch?v=bFEoMO0pc7k.

schmoyoho. (2013, May 7). *Dead giveaway!* [Video File]. Retrieved from https://www.youtube.com/watch?v=nZcRU0Op5P4.

Annoying Orange. (2013, Nov 23). *Annoying Orange – kitchen intruder (bed intruder spoof) with autotune remix!* [Video File]. Retrieved from https://www.youtube.com/watch?v=pezdRcVe04c.

Shadow Subscribe!. (2014, Jul 9). *9 + 10 Vine.* [Video File]. Retrieved from https://www.youtube.com/watch?v=BzVXbeASRiQ.

Brest, P., & Krieger, L. H. (2010). *Problem solving, decision making, and professional judgment: A guide for lawyers and policymakers.* New York, NY: Oxford University Press.

CBS News. (2013, May 9). *Cleveland neighbor Charles Ramsey's 911 call for missing girls.* Retrieved from http://www.cbsnews.com/news/cleveland-neighbor-charles- ramseys-911-call-for-missing-girls/ May 9, 2013.

Chace, Z. (2010, August 13). 'Bed Intruder Song' climbs the charts. *NPR.* Retrieved from http://www.npr.org/sections/therecord/2010/08/13/129178815/bed-intruder-song-climbs-the-charts

Collins, P. H. (2000). *Black feminist thought: knowledge, consciousness and the politics of empowerment.* New York, NY: Routledge.

Gallagher, P. (2010, August 14). Antoine Dodson: from local news item to internet sensation. *The Guardian*. Retrieved from http://www.theguardian.com/world/2010/aug/15/antoine-dodson-Internet-sensation

Gross, D. (2013, May 10). Why the web loves Cleveland hero Charles Ramsey. *CNN*. Retrieved from http://www.cnn.com/2013/05/08/tech/web/charles-ramsey-viral

Hall, R. E. (2007). Racism as Health Risk for African-American Males: Correlations Between Hypertension and Skin Color. *Journal of African American Studies*, *11*(3/4), 204-213.

Jacquemet, M. (1992, November). Imagining identities: Nation, culture, and the past. *American Ethnologist*, *19*(4), 733–748. doi:10.1525/ae.1992.19.4.02a00060

Mellinger, W. M. (1992). Postcards from the Edge of the Color Line: Images of African Americans in Popular Culture, 1893–1917. *Symbolic Interaction, 15*(4), 413-433.

National Fire Prevention Association. (2011, March). *Fatal Effects of Fire*. Retrieved from http://www.nfpa.org/research/reports-and-statistics/demographics-and-victim- patterns/fatal-effects-of-fire

Orr, A. J. (2003, October). Black-white differences in achievement: The importance of wealth. *Sociology of Education*, *76*(4), 281–304. doi:10.2307/1519867

Parkinson-Morgan, K. (2011, March 18). Alexandra Wallace apologizes, announces she will no longer attend UCLA. *Daily Bruin*. Retrieved from http://dailybruin.com/2011/03/18/alexandra_wallace_apologizes_announces_she_w ill_no_longer_attend_ucla/

Parkinson-Morgan, K. (2011, March 18). Alexandra Wallace apologizes, announces she will no longer attend UCLA. *Daily Bruin*. Retrieved from http://dailybruin.com/2011/03/18/alexandra_wallace_apologizes_announces_she_will_no_longer_attend_ucla/

Peters, M. (2010, August 19). Gregory Brothers take Antoine Dodson to Hot 100. *Billboard*. Retrieved from http://www.billboard.com/articles/news/956772/gregory-brothers-take-antoine-dodson-to-the-hot-100

Picca, L. H., & Feagin, J. R. (2007). *Two-faced racism: Whites in the backstage and frontstage*. New York, NY: Routledge.

Takagi, D. Y. (1993). Asian Americans and racial politics: A postmodern paradox. *Social Justice*, *20*(1-2), 115-128.

Thompson, E. G. (2010). Addressing institutional structural barriers to student achievement. *Race, Gender, & Class*, *17*(1/2), 51–57.

KEY TERMS AND DEFINITIONS

Apology: A symbolic gesture to indicate remorse for an action or statement deemed offensive by the recipient.

Black: The overarching racial category of those who inherit African legacies and/or are part of the African diaspora.

Humor: A shared understanding that ranges based upon the company present; is a loose philosophical understanding of deriving pleasure from a myriad of life scenarios.

Internet: Al Gore's invention! (This is a joke). In reality, it is a complex interface that sends electronic signals and information instantaneously, connecting all those who have access.

Joke: A short, humorous exchange based upon a shared reference point.

Offensive: An action or statement that goes against an individual or group's understanding of civility and dignity.

Privacy: A measure of dignity and respect allowing for a proper amount of space to be provided an individual whilst they attend to personal thoughts or affairs.

Chapter 10
Discursive Power Relations in *Naijabookofjokes.com*

Rotimi Taiwo
Obafemi Awolowo University, Nigeria

ABSTRACT

This chapter is premised on the fact that a close reading of humour can provide an insight into what is lurking in the social mind of the humorist. A critical discourse analysis of twenty-five jokes sourced from Naijabookofjoke.com, a website dedicated to jokes, mainly within the Nigerian socio-cultural setting observes the selected jokes are used to context social and symbolic order among the people, especially through the expression of power, Otherness and stereotyping. The study also reveals that jokes can either be offensive (sword) or defensive (shield) in nature. They employ literary conventions such as exaggeration, allusions, metaphors, wit, and satire to discursively express socio-cultural issues.

INTRODUCTION

One major pastime in modern society is making and listening to jokes. Jokes are part of the linguistic and interactional processes in every human society that help to break the routines of mundane life and allow listeners to relax. Jokes are generally believed to be expressions made with the intention to elicit laughter and amusement from the listener. They could vary in form: a short expression, a single word, a picture, a performance, a drama, a gesture, a story, and so forth. The space for sharing jokes also varies. They include, but are not limited to any social gathering (such as weddings, birthdays), workplace, classroom, church, newspaper, television, radio, and of recent the cyberspace. Before the advent of digital technology, making jokes was limited to face-to-face interactions. In the age of digital and multimodal discourse, we can talk about jokes in the newspaper, for instance, pictorial jokes in cartoons and caricatures. Pictorial jokes are believed to possess the same force of verbal jokes (Wekesa, 2012). Another kind of joke is a written joke, as we have in satirical writings (Simpson, 2003; Taiwo, 2007). However, there is advancement in technology and expansion in discourse patterning, the social space for jokes keeps expanding. The Internet was created as a space for serious communication, but became popular mostly due to its social and entertaining nature. Due to its social nature and exponential growth, the

DOI: 10.4018/978-1-5225-0338-5.ch010

Copyright © 2016, IGI Global. Copying or distributing in print or electronic forms without written permission of IGI Global is prohibited.

Internet became a space for experimenting and exhibiting playfulness and entertainment, particularly in chatrooms, blogs and discussion forums.

In recent times, making jokes has become a regular feature in live shows, especially in the electronic media. A popular kind of humour in the electronic media is situational comedy, also known as ''sitcom comedy''. Sitcom comedies are episode-based performances delivered through electronic media. They are very popular in America and Europe and gradually becoming popular in Nigeria.

Feigelson (1995) identifies the major types of humour as puns, goofing off, jokes (self ridicule, sexual, racial/ethnic), and teasing. Collison (1988) identifies three major functions of humour as to resist boredom, to conform and to control others. Pogrebin and Poole (1988) also identify a function they describe as 'coping strategy'. This is also supported by Obadare (2009). Humour sometimes helps to normalize crises and deal with circumstances beyond one's control. Ervin-Tripp and Lambert (1992) also identify four functions of humour, namely: equalizing, defending, sharing and coping. Listening to humour has become a favourite pastime in many urbanized areas. It is common for performers to entertain the audience in live performances. Their humorous performances are typically based on mutually shared background knowledge and value in the society. Brown and Levinson (1987: 124) confirmed this - that jokes may be used to stress the shared background or those shared values of the people in a society.

In Nigeria and many parts of the world being humorous has become a great asset and humour merchants have made a very lucrative business out of the art. For instance, some people gifted in making jokes like Julius Agwu, Basketmouth, Bovi, Gbenga Adeyinka, Teju Babyface, Ali Baba, Holy Mallam, to mention a few, have become very popular comedians in the entertainment industry. They have featured in difference performances across the country and outside. Such shows include: "A Night of a Thousand Laughs", "Crack ya ribs", "Holy Laughter", and so forth. Their kind of humour is popularly referred to as stand-up comedy. Stand-up comedy involves the use of verbal expressions as well as gestures, miming and movement to augment the humour of certain verbal expressions. Stand-up comedians are socio-cultural mediators and articulators who reveal the truth about a society. Their source books include newspapers, television reports and the information they generally gather from the society. Their themes are usually current, and their topical allusions have satirical understatement, (Tsang & Wong, 2004). The contents of the performances can vary greatly from one comedian to another. It could be satirical, vulgar indecent or just a mild joke.

Prior to the digital age, the print media and literary writing have become veritable platforms for media satirists. The emergence and popularisation of humour in the cyberspace among Nigerians is not unconnected with the post-military era when democratization began afresh in Nigeria. The cyberspace from the early 2000 has given freedom to people to freely express their minds about the leaders and the state of the nation. Humour is one major way people do this. Humourous postings have become very popular on the Internet and mobile phones in recent time, thus bringing out the social value of humour in these media (Taiwo, 2011). As Obadare (2009) observes, jokes serve as a tool for subordinate classes to deride the state (including its agents) and themselves. A number of Nigerian websites are dedicated to humour and jokes. *Naijabookofjokes* is one of such websites being studied in the work, is a classical example. Other websites that have humour sections include *Nairaland*, *Nigerian Village Square*.

For many Nigerians, humour is a means of dousing the harsh effects of the socio-economic realities of the nation caused for instance by unemployment/underemployment and poverty, among other. People who make jokes offline, especially in live shows, do so to make money. One major advantage of online jokes sharing is that it provides limitless access to jokes with very minimal cost. The subjects of jokes online may include politics, ethnicity, religion, as well as relationship, gender and so forth. In addition, making jokes jokes online gives people the freedom to talk about things that would ordinarily be seen as taboo offline.

Jokes are said to create humour in so many occasions. Nigerians are particularly known to make jokes at out of any issue of national concern. For instance, the *Boko Haram* insurgency in the country has become a subject of jokes online. It is also common to see people now create different pictures of the political class, portraying them in different lights to ridicule them. Other national issues people have turned to jokes include: the Dana Airline crash, the sack of medical doctors by the Governor of Lagos State, election campaigns, the First Lady of the country, Dame Patience Jonathan, and the re-naming of the University of Lagos after Late Chief M.K.O. Abiola, to mention a few.

In this study, we examine the discursive forms of humour by Nigerians in the cyberspace. The study did a critical discourse study of purposively selected verbal humours on a popular website specialized in the circulation of jokes on Nigeria and Nigerians - *Naijabookofokes.* The major goal of the study is to reveal the issues that lurk in the social minds of humorists and how these relate to the socio-cultural context of the country.

LINGUISTICS PERSPECTIVES ON HUMOUR

Humour and laughter are generally seen as therapeutic for relieving tension and anxiety. According to Abel (1998), humour appears to buffer an individual against the negative effects of stress. Other research reveals that a good sense of humour is related to muscle relaxation, control of pain and discomfort, positive mood states, and overall psychological health including a healthy self-concept (Deaner & Mc-Conatha 1993; Hudak *et al.* 1991). The primary goal of humour is to elicit amusement and laughter. Jokes, many times, are said to rid a listener of their tension. They aim at creating a concrete feeling of enjoyment for an audience, most commonly manifested in a physical display consisting of displays of pleasure including smiles and laughter (Beeman, 2000)

There has been a long tradition of humor research, which can be traced as far back as classical Greek philosophers (Jakoaho & Marjamäki, 2012). Humour research cut across different disciplines in the social as well as medical sciences. These include – psychology, anthropology, sociology, literature, philosophy, philology, education, semiotics, linguistics and medicine (Attardo, 1994:15).

Raskin (1985) identifies the major humour theories and classified them into three groups: incongruity, hostility and release theories. Incongruity theories argue that the notion of laughter is experienced through incongruous changes in jokes. Meyer (2000:314) remarks that incongruity plays a crucial role in humor as a social phenomenon, as most humor is based on violations of socially or culturally agreed norms. For hostility theorists, laughter is caused, for instance, by misfortune or ignorant actions of others, or feelings of malice or envy. Such laughter sends a clear message of superiority and hostility to others. A good number of ethnic jokes reinforce group membership by laughing at people outside the group who are subjected to ridicule. Release theorists believe that laughter is the cause of relief of tension and anxiety. According to Meyer (2000), humor springs from experiences of relief when tension is removed from an individual. Some jokes are made to defuse a potentially anxious situation. While one cannot claim that these theories can adequately account for every kind of humour, they can be said to fairly explain what characterises humour in different contexts. Holmes and Marra (2002b: 70–71), based on a critical discourse analytic approach (e.g., Fairclough 1995); distinguish between 'reinforcing' and 'subversive' humor. The former reinforces existing power or solidarity relationships, whereas the latter challenges existing power relationships.

A good number of humour researchers have focused mainly on the language forms and functions in humour. Rahman (2007) in an examination of African-American humour, explains how comedians exaggerate linguistic features that highlight characteristics they attribute to the African American community and people outside this community. The study focused on highly specific linguistic features such as vowel variation in narratives describing blacks and whites. Humorous television sketches are the focus of Balirano and Corduas (2006). In the study, the authors describe a British TV sketch show, and discuss some linguistic features of the text. Their interpretation of the message shows how a variety of statistical techniques can help describe the underlying humour and cultural significance of the British TV sketch show.

He (2008) carried out a linguistic study of a Chinese dialect film 'Crazy Stones', and discovers that the linguistic devices used for creating humorous effect in verbal interactions include phonetic, lexical and discourse devices. In addition, the author's findings reveal that language choice and language form as dialects which contrast with standard and connection with local culture in the socio-political context of modern China are used to create humor.

Archakis and Tsakona (2005) examine how humour is socially used for construction of solidarity and in-group identity in Greece. Their results show that a cohesive group of young Greek male interlocutors select targets either outside or inside their group. Their target of humor reinforces the already existing bonds among group members, while bringing the evaluative dimension of humor to the surface.

According to Ritchie's main practical contribution to joke research in his book (2004), there are two major joke categories: a propositional joke and a linguistic joke. A propositional joke has a delivery mechanism which indicates how the linguistic processing of the text can give rise to a pair of interpretations (loosely, pre- and post- punchline). It seems that such a joke must involve either a contrast between these two interpretations or some degree of inappropriateness in - or indirectly suggested by - exactly one of these interpretations. On the other hand, a linguistic joke is typically defined by a configuration of linguistic elements, which could involve notions such as phonetic similarity, segmentation into words, etc.

Jokes according to Fatt (1998), can be classified generally into: verbal, visual, and physical. Verbal jokes are jokes expressed through the use of the spoken form of language. Verbal jokes are further classified into ambiguity based jokes and non-ambiguity based jokes. Ambiguous jokes can be pun, lexical jokes, or syntactic jokes. Pun can be defined literally as a "play on words"; a humorous use of words that involves a word or phrase that has more than one possible meaning. According to Duchacek's taxonomy (1970), pun reveals the following features: homonymy and homophony. Homonymy can be described as words spelt and pronounced the same way but have different meaning (eg, *bow* – weapon for firing arrow and *bow* – the bend of head or body forward) paronymy describes words derived from the same root as other words; while homophony describes words that have the same pronunciation, but different meaning (eg, *bale* – a large bundle or package and *bail* – to be released under security temporarily)

Lexical jokes can be found among others in the headlines of a news story or a joke. An ambiguous headline is good example of a lexical joke. This could be as a result of different meaning that could be obtained from lexical items used in a linguistic context. Lexical ambiguity which leads to humour could be as a result of poor wordings, poor editing, inaccuracies, and so on.

Syntactic jokes can be portrayed through syntactic ambiguity. Syntactic ambiguity can be said to be an ambiguous use of word-class. Bucaria (2004) observes that the category of syntactic ambiguity, which can be further subdivided into class ambiguity and other types of ambiguity, considers the semantic shifts created by confusion between grammatical categories on the one hand, and, for example, phrasal attachment and elliptic phenomena on the other.

It should be noted that one of the factors common to all kinds of jokes is incongruity/inappropriateness. Binsted and Ritchie (2001:278) classified incongruity into two types: ambiguity and violated expectation. Humor does not occur accidentally in discourse aiming solely at the participants' amusement, but rather that it can be a very efficient means of the expression of identity, i.e. ''a person's sense of inclusion in (or exclusion from) a range of social roles and ways of being.''

Making jokes online is a contemporary issue, especially in Nigeria. Considering the nature of online communication, this study seeks to examine the discursive nature of making jokes online by Nigerians. A critical discourse study of the selected jokes will reveal the feelings of the people on the subjects of their jokes. Are the jokes just meant to relief the people from the tension all around them in the country or they are directed at the objects as their own ways of showing discontentment or revenge? These are some of the questions we hope to answer at the end of this study.

METHODOLOGY

Data for the study were elicited from a website dedicated to discussing jokes made by Nigerians: *Naijabookofjokes.* The website is dedicated to sharing all manner of jokes, mostly visual and verbal jokes. The data were purposively selected to represent five kinds of jokes identified by these researchers. They are: political, religious, ethnic, wit and intelligence and relationship jokes posted on these websites. All together, twenty-five jokes were selected, five from each of the above-mentioned categories of jokes. The jokes were subjected to critical discourse analysis to bring out how the social realities in the country are portrayed by humourists.

Critical Discourse Analysis (CDA) is chosen as the framework for analyzing the jokes because it is appropriate for interpreting the diverse social issues that are portrayed in verbal humour. Such issues include ideology, power, hierarchy, gender and ethnic relations. CDA always sees a relationship between a particular discursive event and the situation(s), institution(s) and social structure(s), which frame it. CDA is 'an interdisciplinary approach to language study with critical point of view for the purpose of studying language behaviour in natural speech situations of social relevance' (Wodak, 1989). Fairclough (2000) identifies three central tenets of CDA namely: social structure (class, status, age, ethnic identity and gender); culture (the generally accepted norms of behaviour in the society); and discourse (the words we use). The goal of CDA is to determine the relationship between these three central tenets. Our discourses reflect the societal norms and beliefs, *ie*, we say things in conformity with the way they should normally be said in our society, and there are certain things we do not say because the society has constrained us not to say them. Likewise, our identity in the social structure is shown in the way we think, act and speak. A text is a record of communication, which involves the presentation of facts, beliefs and the construction of identities of participants. It is produced by socially-situated speakers. It is therefore more than just words spoken or written on the pages of books, but how such words are used in particular social context (Huckin, 1997). McGregor (2003) identifies an aspect of CDA, which she calls the "discursive practices". These are rules, norms and mental models of socially acceptable behaviour in specific roles or relationships used to produce, receive, and interpret the message. Discursive practices then, are the processes involved in speaking, writing, hearing and reading texts. Since the selected jokes are products of the social process, this study will demonstrate how they reveal through their discursive nature the ideology, power, hierarchy and ethnic relations and biases in the Nigerian society.

FINDINGS AND DISCUSSIONS

The online jokes posted by Nigerian are closely linked with socio-economic and political issues in the country. These jokes are sometimes not merely meant to make people laugh. They are used to express people's concerns about the state of the nation. They are also intended to express power relations between the people, the state and the agents of the state. They contest the abuse of power by the leaders. For instance in Nigeria, there is a general belief among the politicians that the Nigerian electorate will sell their votes to the highest bidder (political party). However a joke emerged online to contest this general belief.

A man was asked by a politician how much his vote was worth and he replied with this breakdown, which he wrote on a piece of paper and handed over to the politician.

- ***Security:** N20,000/month × 12 = N960,000.*
- ***Generator:** N40,000/2 years × 2 = N80,000.*
- ***Fuel for Generator:** N1,000/day × 365 days × 4 years = N1.46 million.*
- ***Potable Water:** N500/day × 365 days × 4 years = N730,000.*
- ***Health:** N10,000/month × 12 months × 4 years = N480,000.*
- ***Education:** N5,000/month × 12 months × 4 years = N240,000.*
- ***Housing:** N500,000/year × 4years = N2 million.*
- ***Total:** N5.95 million.*

When the politician got the piece of paper, he went through it, squeezed it and threw it away saying that the man was being irrational. The man concluded that if the basic necessities of life appear irrational, what then is rational?

This joke, which came up while the nation was preparing for the 2011 elections, is clearly an expression of power relations in discourse between the electorate and the politicians. The primary goal of this joke is to sensitize the electorate to what the selling of their votes could possibly cost them – deprivation of all these basic necessities of life. The electorate employs this joke as a social force to discursively resist a general societal belief. This discursive resistance contests the power of the politicians to oppress the poor with their wealth. This is a dimension of the discursive value of political jokes. The employment of figures and mathematical symbols to give an estimation of the cost of the basic necessities of life (which are not provided by the government) shows Nigerians as well-informed people who can exercise power through the use of jokes to return the society to the practice of ethical political conduct.

Another angle of expression of power relation in jokes is seen in a joke on the sack of 788 medical doctors working for the Lagos State government in May, 2012 by the Governor after a protracted strike action. Many people saw the dismissal of the doctors as ridiculous and laughable. They considered it autocratic, unjust and unreasonable. The joke is reproduced below:

Breaking News - Due to the sacking of all medical doctors in all government hospitals by Governor (Emperor) Babatunde Fashola of Lagos state and the ban placed on all doctors from accepting job offers from Lagos state government by Nigeria Medical Association (NMA), in a quick reaction to this and the need to save lives, Lagos state government is currently employing all Traditional Herbal doctors, Witchcraft doctors, Sango/Ifa/Ogun priests, Babalawo, Boka, Okija priests, Magicians/Soothsayers, Pastors/Alfas (guaranteed that HEALING is their calling)..Please report to Ayinke House as recruitment has commenced fully. Save a life today. Best of luck...

This joke in agreement with the general belief, mocks at the exercise of power by the governor, who is described as an 'emperor' attempting to exercise absolute power over his subjects. The Governor's action was perceived as high-handed. He was also seen as insensitive to the health needs of the people of the state. The joke is a scathing criticism as well as a satire, which is presented as "breaking news". In reality, the government and the medical doctors' union were engaged in power tussle, which has created a crisis and stalemate in the health sector of the state. The proposed alternatives to the sacked doctors (herbal doctors, witch doctors, soothsayers, traditional/Christian/Islamic religion priests) are obviously not fit for the Western-oriented medical practices being employed in government hospitals in the country. While the joke exposes the absurdity in the government's action, it also demonstrates an allegiance to the sacked doctors by showing in a sarcastic way that government could not find easy replacements for them.

Jokes are sometimes used to portray group perceptions of other groups. Stereotyping is used in jokes to maintain social and symbolic order. Stereotyping is more evident in contexts of inequalities of power. For instance, in the typical patriarchal African society, women are more stereotyped in jokes than men, especially on what men perceive to be women's attitude to relationships and wealth. A joke titled "Prayer change", which was posted on *Naijabookofjokes* reads thus:

A lady was praying at church and she was like, "oh Lord I don't want to marry a short man, any short man that's coming my way, I bind him with the holy fire!"

Next to her was Mr. Bentum who was also praying for a wife, "Oh dear Lord I'm a billionaire but very short, please Lord I need a wife, a wife that will take me for who I am.

The lady then kept silent for a while and gave a new topic for her pray.

Now she prayed "...LORD I know your ways are not our ways, you know what's good and you give them to us, is that your voice I'm hearing? Father speak for your servant is listening, yes Father, who am I to say No, I know your blessings are in a disguise. I'll marry the CONTENT and not the CONTAINER.

This joke apparently mocks the religiosity of an average Nigerian. Beyond this, it portrays different angles of the perception of Nigerian women by men. The lady in the joke is portrayed as religious, pretentious, susceptible and directionless. She did not just change her prayer points when she got to know the content of the prayer of the "short billionaire man", she also justified her sudden change with allusions from the Bible. The climax of the joke is the last sentence, which engages the metaphors of CONTENT and CONTAINER. The joke also portrays the stereotyping of men by women as "necessary evils" (what you do not like, but must accept). The acceptance is conditioned by the wealth [CONTENT], while the appearance [CONTAINER], the hitherto rejected quality, has now been played down.

Another kind of stereotyping common in jokes is the stereotyping of ethnic groups. Nigeria has over 250 ethnic groups with three groups (Hausa, Igbo and Yoruba) considered as the major groups. Each of these major groups expresses some common stereotypes about the other. For instance the Yoruba are stereotyped as cowards and lovers of pleasure. Hausa people are portrayed as stupid and carefree and the Igbo are portrayed by the other two ethnic groups as greedy people who typically love and live for money. The joke reproduced below is a ethnic stereotype joke about the Igbo:

An Igbo multi-millionaire-Chief, to maintain a mistress in Lagos, bought a house in Lekki-Victoria Garden City (in his own name) for her to live in, plus a monthly allowance of N500,000. The house cost him about N75m in 2005. He sold the house last week for N225m, after they broke up. A quick calculation shows that after 5 years of a fling with the woman, he still had a net gain of N114m plus six years of free sex. When his wife found out, she was very mad at him and gave him a big mouthful. She yelled at him: BLOODY IDIOT!!! Why the hell didn't you keep two mistresses?"

Then butt of the joke is how the millionaire's wife's business sense made her blind to a five-year injustice done to her by her husband. Rather than being jealous and getting angry with her husband for cheating on her, she sanctioned his act and wished the husband had "kept two mistresses". This appears like an exaggeration of the extent an Igbo can go to make money, even at the expense of personal hurt. The witty business opportunities identified in a condemnable adulterous relationship is what produces the humour of derogatory stereotype of the Igbo by other ethnic groups in the country.

This ethnic joke, going by Rappoport (2005), can be considered offensive. Rappoport identifies in ethnic jokes sword and shield metaphor. The sword and shield metaphor holds that depending on the context, an ethnic joke can be seen as either offensive or defensive. For example, ridiculing a group based on a stereotype can be seen as offensive. This joke therefore is metaphorically a sword, an offensive instrument used against the Igbo. Despite that Rappoport's sword and shield metaphor were originally linked with ethnic jokes, it can be applied to any joke that stereotypes any group. For instance, the next joke's focus is Nigerian men, who are generally presented as promiscuous and unfaithful in relationships.

Wife drops him at the airport in Abuja to board Dana airline to Lagos, few minutes he pinged his wife claiming he is boarding and later switched of his phone.

He turned back to sleep in his mistress house there in Abuja and never actually boarded.

After the crash, the whole family were crying and thinking of going to Lagos for his corpse. He appeared and gave his confession. If you are his wife what will you do?

This joke was made shortly after Dana Air plane crashed in the country killing all the 153 passengers on board. After the crash, some Nigerians gave testimonies of how they narrowly missed the flight. The young man cheated on his wife and somehow, this saved him from being one of the victims of the plane crash. This joke typically depicts a defence – a shield and justification for the promiscuity of the man.

An act that is supposed to be negatively-perceived is presented as life-saving. The joke ends in a thought-provoking open-ended question “If you are his wife what will you do?” This joke reinforces the thought as expressed in Shakespeare’s *Hamlet* that “there is nothing either good or bad, but thinking makes it so”.

One of the discursive functions of jokes is to amuse people and make them relax even in tense situations. In this joke, there is a collision between two meaning relations that are somehow incompatible, and the humour lies in the ——oppositeness between these levels or layers (Raskin, 1985, p. 100), so that what is presented as funny contrasts with an otherwise serious or expected meaning.

Religious jokes are typically used to mock the profession or practices of the adherents of a particular religious group as in the joke presented below:

On Lagos-Ibadan express road, when a Pastor met a team of policemen who, quite naturally, wanted ‘something’ from him. Since he was not prepared to play their games, they asked for his papers and having combed through everything without any offence with which to nail the ‘stubborn’ pastor, they now asked him to open the bonnet of his car.

A careful scrutiny of the engine number against what was on paper revealed that letter ‘U’ was written in such a way that it could be mistaken for letter ‘V’. That was all the officer-in-charge needed to shout “stolen vehicle!” Sensing trouble, even when he knew he committed no offence, the pastor called the OC to say he was a priest to which the officer replied: “Please, leave that pastor thing...in any case, if you are indeed a pastor, then you must have a Bible in your car, bring it.”

The Pastor did as was commanded after which the officer now ordered: “Please read Matthew 5:25-26 to me”.

The incredulous Pastor opened to the recommended passage and read: “Settle matters quickly with your adversary who is taking you to court. Do it while you are still with him on the way, or he may hand you over to a judge, and the judge may hand you over to the officer, and you may be thrown into prison. I tell you the truth; you will not get out until you have paid the last penny.”

The man of God quietly made an “offering” of “just” N100 to his newly found “preacher”.

This joke is characterized by two different natures. Firstly, it is metaphorically a sword joke directed at Christians, in that it humorously justifies what the faith abhors. Secondly, it highlights the desperation of an average Nigerian police to extort money from any driver on the Nigerian road regardless of their conformity with the laws. The joke employs inversion, a device which turns human norms upside down in jokes in order to achieve humour. This is evident in the police officer’s perception of the pastor as “stubborn”, because he refused to give any form of gratification. The joke also used the content of the bible, a sacred book, to justify the criminal act of bribery. Despite that this joke focuses on two major actors – the pastor and the policeman, it is used essentially to highlight a major social ill in Nigeria, thereby ridiculing the nation for the endemic corrupt social system. It exposes two major issues in corruption – impunity on the part of the policeman and weak will on the part of the pastor. While the former ridicules bad policing, the latter ridicules hypocrisy in religion.

A macro-sociological analysis of social practice in this joke reveals that issues of power relations are clearly highlighted. The discourse channel in the joke is used to reinforce the illegal power engaged by the police over an ordinary citizen of the nation in the act of policing. Pastors are generally invested with religious power in the society. In addition, they have some form of social power which makes them to be well respected anywhere they go. Policemen are also empowered to enforce the law, but as seen in this joke, they could be dubious in exercising the power. The policeman was portrayed as engaging the discursive force of the content of the Bible to extort money from a priest.

Popular online jokes have adopted a character to project the intended humour. The character is referred to as Akpors, who is typically presented sometimes as an incredibly stupid character and sometimes as a clever person. Since jokes about Akpors started, many of them have gone viral on the Internet in several Nigerian blogs, discussion forums and jokes sharing websites. One typical Akpors joke is presented below.

Girlfriend: *Baby do you still love (event) me like before?*
Akpors: *Yes love! My love for you will never change.*
Girlfriend: *That's my baby!!! I want you to buy me something for val.*
Akpors: *Just name it sweetheart.*
Girlfriend: *It's just one BB Porsche shaa...*
Akpors: *No problem. Just find out the price and let me know.*
Girlfriend: *It's N450,000 naira.*
Akpors: *Is it manual or automatic? Is it still in a good shape, as in the engine. Have you checked the fuel consumption too?*
Girlfriend: *Honey, am not talking about a car oooh. It's a phone.*
Akpors: *Phone?! That means it will have a fridge, generator set, pure leather seat, plasma TV, a wardrobe and a portable toilet and bathroom, abi?*
Girlfriend: *Are you buying it or not? "After 5 mins"*
Girlfriend: *Helloooooo!*
Akpors: *Hiiiiiiii! Please am not oooh! I dey craze?*
Girlfriend: *Don't even border again. I'll call Alhaji to get it for me this evening.*
Akpors: *Better still, call Atiku he will be faster.*
Girlfriend: *Am going to delete you.*
Akpors: *Is your phone hanging? Cos I've deleted you since you mentioned porsche. Idiot! How much is bride price even in Igbo land sef?*

In this joke, which we classify as a wit and intelligent joke, a typical Nigerian girl in a relationship is portrayed as materialistic. The joke is conversational in nature, tagged as a *Facebook* chat between Akpors and his girlfriend. The joke presents the social reality of a typical relationship in Nigeria, in which women in a relationship demand expensive gifts, especially hand held devices, such as mobile phones and tablets from their lovers. The indices of a typical Nigerian chat context which are markers of the identity of the participants are seen in this chat. They include Nigerian English discourse markers (*shaa, oooh, abi*), the use of Nigeria Pidgin English, such as *I dey craze?* (Am I crazy?).

Akpors' pretense about what BB Porsche is triggers off the first phase of humour in the text. He pretended that he did not know that BB Porsche is a phone. Initially, the lady did not understand that Akpors was pulling her legs until he asked some more ridiculous questions. The second phase of humour came with the threat by the lady to delete Akpor's contact from her phone and Akpors' response. The allusion to "bride price… in Igbo land" may be hinting at the fact that the Akpors' girlfriend is an Igbo. An average Igbo family is said to charge their daughter's suitors very high prices. Comparing the price of a phone to bride price is the punchline in the joke.

VALUES OF ONLINE JOKES IN THE NIGERIAN DEMOCRATIC SETTING

Humour has a common phenomenon in face-to-face discourse and it could occur in different settings, ranging from casual conversation to even formal exchanges. The coming of the Internet creates a great opportunity for people to do most of the things they have been doing in face-to-face interactions in virtual contexts, and these include chatting, gossiping, debating, dating, counseling, bullying, voting, teaching, learning, paper presentations at conferences, to mention a few. The nature of online communication allows creativity and this could be motivated by social factors, such as the need to reinforce intimacy between group members or exclude non-group members. These, we were able to make clear in the online jokes analysed.

Since online jokes are written, they lack all the cues that face-to-face jokes have. The Internet is an open space for people to share their feelings on anything and it is easier for people who would not ordinarily make jokes in face-to-face interactions to do so online where there is a high degree of anonymity. The rate at which Nigerian users circulate discursive materials in form of jokes online is increasing in recent times and this can be directly linked to the democratizing force of the Internet. Now, because of the Internet, low-resource individuals are able to disseminate their feelings through blogs and other user-generated content platforms. The coming together of people online to form interest groups that share jokes which spotlight individuals and groups in the country has the tendency to exert power on political decision makers and other visible social actors.

CONCLUSION

The present study has revealed that these jokes are not just meant to make people laugh. Underlying them are issues of power relations among the people and between Nigerian and the political actors. Jokes are used to foster solidarity among the people against the rulers. In addition, jokes are used to contest social and symbolic order among the people, especially through stereotyping of the other group. The study also identified that jokes can be employed metaphorically by a group as either an offensive weapon - a sword, or a defending weapon – a shield. A new and interesting development in joke making in Nigeria is the fictionalising of jokes with a major character – Akpors, who is adapted to play different roles from a little schoolboy to an adult, as the comedian. This new practice makes this character the butt of jokes. However, the deep social implications of such jokes are still evident. The study concludes that the use of jokes online by Nigerians has implications for democratic and social practices in the country, as these jokes have the tendency to impact on citizenship and leadership accountability in the country. Recently in the country, the President and other political actors have been the butt of online jokes and the recent moves by the country's national assembly to regulate the social media is an indication that these jokes have implications for democracy in the country.

REFERENCES

Abel, M. H. (1998). Interaction of humor and gender in moderating relationships between stress and outcomes. *The Journal of Psychology*, *132*(3), 267–276. doi:10.1080/00223989809599166 PMID:9540225

Adetunji, A. (2013). The interactional context of humor in Nigerian stand-up comedy. *Pragmatics*, *23*(1), 1–22.

Archakis, A., & Tsakona, V. (2005). Analyzing conversational data in GTVH terms: A new approach to the issue of identity construction via humor. *Humor: International Journal of Humor Research*, *18*(1), 41–68. doi:10.1515/humr.2005.18.1.41

Attardo, S. (1994). Humor Research: Vol. 1. *Linguistic Theories of Humor*. Berlin: Walter de Gruyter.

Balirano, G., & Corduas, M. (2006). Statistical methods for the linguistic analysis of a humorous TV sketch show. *Quaderni di Statistica*, *8*, 1–24.

Beeman. (2000). Humor. *Journal of Linguistic Anthropology, 9*(2).

Collinson, D. L. (1988). Engineering humour: Masculinity, joking and conflict in shop floor relations. *Organization Studies*, *1*(3), 58–76.

Deaner, S. L., & McConatha, J. T. (1993). The relation of humor to depression and personality. *Psychological Reports*, *72*(3), 755–763. doi:10.2466/pr0.1993.72.3.755 PMID:8332677

Ervin-Tripp, S. M., & Lampert, M. D. (1992). Gender differences in the construction of humorous talk. In Hall, K., Buchholtz, E. & Moonwoman, B. (Eds.), *Locating power:Proceedings of the Second Berkeley Women and Language Conference* (pp. 108-117). Berkeley, CA: Berkeley Women and Language Group, Linguistics Department, University of California.

Feigelson, S. (1989). Mixing Mirth and Management. *Super Vision*, *50*(11), 6–8.

He, Y. (2008).Humor in Discourse: A Linguistic Study of the Chinese Dialect Film, *Crazy Stone*, *in* Marjorie K.M. Chan and Hana Kang (Eds.) *Proceedings of the 20th North American Conference on Chinese Linguistics* (NACCL-20), Columbus, OH: The Ohio State University.

Hudak, D. A., Dale, J. A., Hudak, M. A., & Degood, D. (1991). Effects of humorous stimuli and sense of humor on discomfort. *Psychological Reports*, *69*(3), 779–786. doi:10.2466/pr0.1991.69.3.779 PMID:1784666

Jakoaho, V., & Marjamäki, S. (2012). *"OH MY GOD, THAT NIGGER SAID GUN!": Use of Ethnic Humor in Modern Stand-Up Comedy*. (Masters Thesis). University of Jyväskylä, Finland.

Meyer, J. C. (2000). Humor as a Double-Edged Sword: Four Functions of Humor in Communication. *Communication Theory*, *10*(3), 310–331. doi:10.1111/j.1468-2885.2000.tb00194.x

Obadare, E. (2009). The Use of Ridicule: Humour, 'Infrapolitics' and Civil Society in Nigeria. *African Affairs*, *108*(431), 241–261. doi:10.1093/afraf/adn086

Pogrebin, M. R., & Poole, E. D. (1988). Humor in the briefing room: A study of strategic uses of humor among police. *Journal of Contemporary Ethnography*, *17*(2), 183–210. doi:10.1177/089124188017002003

Rahman, J. (2007). An Ay For an Ah: Language of Survival in African American Narrative Comedy. *American Speech*, *82*(1), 65–96. doi:10.1215/00031283-2007-003

Rappoport, L. (2005). *Punchlines: the case for racial, ethnic, and gender humor*. Westport, CT: Praeger Publishers.

Raskin, V. (1985). *Semantic mechanisms of humor*. Dordrecht: Reidel.

Raskin, V. (1985). *Semantic mechanism of humor*. Dordrecht: Reidel.

Simpson, P. (2003). *On the Discourse of Satire: Towards a Stylistic Model of Satirical Humour*. Amsterdam: John Benjamins. doi:10.1075/lal.2

Taiwo, R. (2007). Satirizing Politicians and Public Officers in Nigerian Newspapers. *The International Journal of Language Society and Culture*, (22), 19 – 28.

Taiwo, R. (2011). Emerging Trends in English Language in the New Media: A Case Study of Satire in Nigerian Text Messages, *Journal of Nigeria English Studies Association Journal*, *16*, 58-73.

Tsang, W. K., & Wong, M. (2004). Constructing a shared 'Hong Kong Identity' in Comic Discourses. *Discourse & Society*, *15*(6), 767–785. doi:10.1177/0957926504046504

KEY TERMS AND DEFINITIONS

Critical Discourse Analysis: Interdisciplinary/multidisciplinary critical approcahes to the study of discourse that probes the discursive sources of social practices, such ideology, power, identity, and so forth.

Cyberspace: The imaginary, intangible, virtual space in which interactions of texts, images and sounds occur between different computers.

Discussion Forum: An online forum, also known as message board where people post messages on any subject of interest to them and expect to find responses to such messages.

Ethnic Joke: A humorous remark or narrative that made for an audience to ridicule or stereotype an ethnic group.

Naijabookofjokes: A Facebook page where different kinds of jokes mainly about Nigeria and Nigerians are shared.

Power Relations: A term used in critical discourse study and sociology to describe how individuals and groups exercise power in discourse within the social structure through means such as, manipulation, domination, suppression.

Punchline: The aspect in jokes that elicits provides humor, thereby eliciting laughter from listeners.

Stand-Up Comedy: A show performed by a person who makes jokes in front of a live audience.

Chapter 11
Pragmatics of Humour in a Nigerian University's Departmental Chat Rooms

Onwu Inya
Federal University of Technology Akure, Nigeria

ABSTRACT

This chapter develops an elaborated Pragmatic Act Model (ePAM) and applies it to humorous interactions in students' text chats in a Nigerian university. The model draws insights from Giora's Graded Salience Hypothesis (GSH), Mey's Pragmatic Act theory and incorporates current issues in pragmatic theorising such as the dialectics between a priori and co-constructed, emergent intention. The data for the study is got from three departmental chat room interactions in Federal University of Technology, Akure. Four humour types are analysed: canned jokes, punning/wordplay, question and answer jokes, and hyperbole/overstatement. Similarly, five pragmatic acts are performed in the identified humour types, namely, satirising, eliciting laughter, electioneering, teasing and overstating. In each of the humour types, the pragmatic mechanism drawn upon to comprehend the joke and to perform the pragmatic acts is indicated. Overall, the chapter argues that the effective appreciation of any humour act would require a pragmatically and culturally enriched context.

INTRODUCTION

This chapter is on the pragmatics of humour in students' interaction in a Nigerian University to the extent that it seeks to 'describe chosen types, functions and mechanisms of humour as a communicative phenomenon' (Dynel, 2011, p. 2). The basic pragmatics of humour is the claim that it is a violation of Grice's (1975) Cooperative Principle (Attardo, 1993, 1994). Attardo (2001) argues that humour is an actual violation of the CP and not a mere flout, as the CP is violated 'without an intention to let H [hearer] arrive at an implicature' (Attardo, 2001, p. 168). In other words, CP violation in humour is unlike other violations, for instance in lying, because the goal of humour is a socially accepted phenomenon (Attardo, 2001). However, Gricean pragmatics has been critiqued for being too individualistic and its

DOI: 10.4018/978-1-5225-0338-5.ch011

Copyright © 2016, IGI Global. Copying or distributing in print or electronic forms without written permission of IGI Global is prohibited.

focus on intention as the *a priori* mental state of the speaker and on communication as recipient design and intention recognition by the hearer has come under fire (see Kecskes, 2014 for details). The critique against this approach could have implications for its application to humour analysis. An alternative perspective is the context-based, socio-cultural-interactional line, which construes intention as 'a *post factum* construct that is jointly achieved through the dynamic emergence of meaning in conversation' (Kecskes, 2014, p. 6). Since intention is co-constructed, this perspective underscores the importance of societal factors in the communication process, albeit to an almost hyperbolic degree. As Kecskes (2014) notes in his Socio-cognitive approach (SCA), a balanced perspective is that which brings the individual and the social in a dialectical relationship. This is because 'the ideal individual lives in a social world with opportunities and limitations that have bearings on their intention' (Inya, 2012, p. 2017). Therefore, the pragmatic model for analysing humour, as pursued in this chapter, toes the middle ground between the strictly cognitive and the strictly social perspectives to pragmatics.

Secondly, pragmatic considerations of humour have largely focused on the manifestation of the phenomenon in native English-speaking context (e.g. Attardo, 2001, 2003; Norrick, 2003; Dynel, 2009; 2011 etc). The only known works that have examined humour in the Nigerian context are Orhiunu (2007) and Adetunji (2013), the former a sociolinguistic study and the latter an endeavour in pragmatics, and this makes the latter of particular interest to the current study. Adetunji (2013) explores the pragmatic strategies that Nigerian Stand-up comedians and their audience employ to co-produce and co-consume humour. He itemises six pragmatic strategies namely: linguistic coding; stereotyping; formulas; call-and-response; self-depreciation and shared experience that are germane to the performance of humour in Nigerian Stand-up comedy. The current study differs from Adetunji's (2013) in two ways: 1) theoretically, the current study is based on a different pragmatic orientation: the socio-cultural perspective represented by Mey's (2001) Pragmatic Act, which we expanded by integrating into it, Giora's (2003) Graded Salience Hypothesis and pertinent issues in current pragmatic theorising. 2) While Adetunji's (2013) data is sourced from Nigerian Stand-up comedy, the current effort focuses on the doing of humour in students' interactions in departmental chat rooms, which is an aspect of computer-mediated communication. Chat rooms are electronically-mediated, synchronous environments where interlocutors converse in real-time through the aid of a computer, or a smart phone and the Internet. Jepson (2005) indicates that because of its real-time characteristics, text chat has been acclaimed as akin to face-to-face interaction as such it 'may carry many of the same language development benefits such as negotiation for meaning and repair moves' (Jepson, 2005, p. 81; cf. Herrinng 1999). The particular chat rooms investigated here were created by students of three departments in the Federal University of Technology, Akure for quick dissemination of information. The chat rooms are hosted on WhatsApp, which is a cross-platform instant messaging app for smart phones. Although these chat rooms are primarily used to convey information, they are platforms for doing humour either in terms of canned jokes posted about politics, society, expression of emotions, etc or conversational humour that arise in the interaction of the interlocutors.

Overall, the goal of this chapter is to examine the types of humour recurrent in students' text chats, the pragmatic mechanism for comprehending these humour types and the pragmatic acts performed therein. To account for this overall goal, we have proposed an elaborated Pragmatic Act Model (ePAM), which is a coalition of Giora's (2003) Graded Salience Hypothesis (henceforth, GSH), with respect to the initial activation phase of her interpretation heuristics and pragmatic act theory reinforced with ideas from Kecskes (2014). To indicate the internal workings of the humour types identified, insights from humour theories are incorporated into the analytic framework.

THEORETICAL FOUNDATIONS

The theoretical foundation of this chapter is based on three broad theories: Giora's (2003) GSH, Pragmatic act theory, and humour theories.

1. Graded Salience Hypothesis (GSH)

GSH is credited to Giora (2003, 1997b etc), the basic thrust of which is that the degree of the salience of a lexical item plays an active role at the initial stage of discourse interpretation. Salient meaning equals lexical or lexicalised meaning of an expression, which is stored and is retrievable from the mental lexicon. Salience is motivated by four criteria: frequency, familiarity, conventionality and prototypicality. Thus, a salient meaning of a lexical item is that which has been more frequently used, more familiar to the user or community of users, more conventional or prototypical, such meaning would be quicker and easier to access and retrieved during interpretation. Giora (2003) argues that salience admits degrees so that lexical meanings could be salient, less salient and non-salient. While the first two are the lexicalised aspects of meaning, the latter is pragmatically derived (Borjesson, 2007).

Giora (2003) opines that discourse interpretation occurs in two phases, namely, initial activation process and the integration phase of retention or suppression of initially activated meaning. The organising principle for the initial phase is GSH such that upon encounter of the lexical stimuli, the recipient evokes its salient meaning irrespective of contextual compatibility or otherwise (Giora, 2003, p. 37). In other words, the initial phase of interpretation involves the activation of salient meanings of the lexical stimuli, which is usually independent of contextual information. For instance, the fact that the lexical stimulus *erect* is used in a non-sexual context does not prevent the activation of its sexual connotations. After the initial activation phase, two main things happen namely, if the salient meaning available is consistent with contextual expectations, it is retained and integrated into the interpretation of the discourse. If, on the other hand, it is not consistent; the following course of action is pursued:

1. The default action is to abandon the salient, but contextually inappropriate meaning for a less salient, yet contextually appropriate meaning.
2. A contextually inappropriate meaning may be retained, if and only if:
    a. It is key to the construction of the intended meaning;
    b. It does not disrupt the interpretative process;
    c. Its salience is high and hence difficult to suppress (Giora, 2003, p. 38)

What we have done in this chapter is reinterpret Giora's (2003) heuristics in pragmatic parlance. While we retain her initial activation phase, we construe the second phase in terms of a pragmatic context into which utterances are embedded for effective interpretation (Capone, 2005).

2. Pragmatic Act Theory

Pragmatic Act theory, a socio-cultural interactional view on pragmatics was proposed by Mey (2001). The theory is based on the premise that the speech act theory lacks an action theory, which means that the seeming action in speech act stems from the individual's intentions and the strategies s/he employs in achieving them. As such, pragmatic act theory promotes 'the priority of socio-cultural and societal factors in meaning construction and comprehension' (Kecskes, 2010, p. 1) and focuses heavily 'on the interactional situation in which both speakers and hearers realize their aims' (Mey, 2009, p. 751). The thrust of the theory is simply that utterance or speech act is only one factor which must work hand in hand with other situational/contextual factors for meaning realisation or for the performance of a pragmatic act. Thus, Mey (2001) argues that 'there are no speech acts but only situated speech acts or instantiated pragmatic acts" (p. 218); therefore, the emphasis is on characterising a general situation prototype, which is called a pragmeme, and can be realised through individual pragmatic acts (Mey 2001, p. 221).

According to Capone (2005), '[a] pragmeme is a situated speech act in which the rules of language and of society synergize in determining meaning, intended as a socially recognized object sensitive to social expectations about the situation in which the utterance to be interpreted is embedded' (Capone, 2005, p. 1357). He further indicates that a pragmeme requires three types of embedding:

- The embedding of an utterance in a context of use, with an aim to determine the referential anchors that complete the propositional form of the utterance;
- The embedding in rules that systematically transform whatever gets said in a context into whatever is meant there, in conformity with the social constraints and rules bearing on the utterance in question;
- The embedding in the co-text, whose features are transferred onto the utterance by eliminating semantic or otherwise interpretative ambiguities and enriching further its (range of) interpretations, by making them more specific (Capone 2005, p. 1357).

This requisite embedding of an utterance in the co-text and context is largely an interpretative process that enriches the propositional form of such utterance, and assigns a particular contextual configuration that will make the meaning of the utterance more specific, thereby discarding other alternative interpretations that may not be inferable from such a situational configuration. It is a norm of utterance interpretation that relies on the societal context of the utterance and other co-textual elements. In the words of Capone (2005), 'the norms for the interpretation of pragmemes come from a societal perspective on language' (p. 1358).

Capone (2005) and Mey (2001) construe pragmemes as transformations utterances go through when acted upon by the forces of context, transformations that 'reshape the original illocutionary value of a speech act by adding contextual layers of meaning, or even may change the illocutionary value of the speech act' (Capone, 2005, p. 1360). Such transformations according to Capone (2005) 'are based on the knowledge of a number of principled and conventional interactions between utterance meaning and certain contextual and situational configurations' (p. 1360).

Kecskes (2014) is of the view that Mey's (2001) privileging of the situational factor over and above the individual and the linguistic factors is a little quite overemphasised. He opines that equal considerations should be accorded both the situational and the individual factors in meaning construction and comprehension. The justification for this position is that interlocutors bring their prior context (which could be encoded in the linguistic elements) and experience with them into the communicative process and it is the interplay 'between prior experience and actual situational experience, which produces the dynamism of meaning construction' (Kecskes, 2014, p. 40). Furthermore, the focus of Mey's (2001) perspective on the environment trivialises intention as the *a priori* mental state of the speaker and rather promotes intention as *post factum.*Kecskes (2014) harmonises these disparate perspectives and argues that intention can both be *a priori* and co-constructed as the interaction progresses. It is on the basis of this that we argue that the intention to elicit laughter and simultaneously perform certain pragmatic acts should be understood both as the *a priori* mental state of the interlocutors and a *post factum,* co-constructed, emergent property of the interaction. This means, for instance, that the 'funniness' of certain humour act, especially aggressive jokes, is usually up for negotiation among interlocutors; especially if the interlocutors have different socio-political perspective to the target of the joke.

3. Humour Theories

Humour theorising has focused on the structure of the humour discourse and the motivation for laughter at humorous contents as against laughter in other contexts (Schwarz, 2010). Generally, humour theories have been classed into three broad categories: incongruity theories, hostility theories and release theories (Raskin, 1985, pp. 31-40; Attardo, 1994). According to Attardo (2007) the incongruity theories are basically characterised by these three elements: contrast between frames of the joke, which will lead to incongruity in the expectations created by the frames of the joke and the resolution of which results in laughter. Norrick (2003) has observed that this class of theories 'describe the humorous object in terms of clashing frames of reference or sets of expectations, they do not focus on the humorous text' (p. 1334). The hostility theories focus on the social dimensions of humour taking into account 'the interpersonal, and often adversarial nature of the humour game' (Bro^ne, 2008, p. 2029). The theories construe the target of humorous interaction as the less privileged persons in the society and that laughter at their misfortune is a show of superiority by the more powerful, privileged people (cf. Schwarz, 2010, pp. 47-51). The third set of theories provides a psychoanalytic outlook to the humour phenomenon. The main advocate of this view is Sigmund Freud, who avers that 'humour is used to release tensions or to make one feel liberated when talking about taboo topics such as sex' (Schwarz, 2010, p, 51). Generally, the release theories consider laughter as that pleasurable, sudden release of pent-up psychic energy. Norrick (2003) credits Freud as the first person to work on actual joke texts and his 1960 work as the initial linguistic analysis of humorous text where he identified joke techniques relating to the use: 'sounds, syllable, repetition and variation' (Norrick, 2003, p. 1334).

A more elaborate and explicit linguistic treatment of humour is Raskin's (1985) Semantic Script-based Theory of Humor (henceforth, SSTH), which was later revised to the General Theory of Verbal Humor (GTVH) (Attardo & Raskin, 1991). The basic thrust of SSTH is that joke has to do with two scripts that are opposed to each other in a special way. The joke text reads fairly well until the punch line is encountered, which triggers a frame shift from the initial script to the intended, albeit, surprising script and this results in humour (see Raskin, 1985; Attardo, 1994). According to SSTH, script opposition manifests at three levels of abstraction: the highest being the opposition between real and unreal, the lower is between actual and non-actual, normal and abnormal and the lowest level of script opposition could be between good and bad, sex and non-sex etc. Attardo (1994:197) argues that the main thesis of SSTH is as follows:

A text can be characterized as a single-joke-carrying-text if both of the [following] conditions are satisfied:

i) *The text is compatible, fully or in part, with two different scripts*
ii) *The two scripts with which the text is compatible are opposite (...).*

The two scripts with which some text is compatible are said to be fully or in part in this text (Raskin, 1985, p. 99).

The conditions simply imply that for a text to be called a joke, there should be the possibility of two opposite interpretations. The first initial interpretation comes across to the recipient as the natural one. However, the punch line of the joke surprisingly forces a frame shift from the initial meaning to the new humorous interpretation, which is intended by the interlocutors.

METHODOLOGY AND DESIGN

The data for the study is got from students' interactions in three departmental chat rooms in Federal University of Technology, Akure, Nigeria. Threads of discussions that are adjudged humorous were extracted and analysed. To retain the anonymity of the students and their contacts only initials of their names or the first three digits of their phone numbers appear in the extracts below. The analytical framework, dubbed elaborated Pragmatic Act Model (ePAM), retains the initial activation phase of Giora's (2003) interpretation heuristics, and construe the second phase in terms of a pragmatic context into which utterances are embedded for effective interpretation (Capone, 2005). The model also addresses itself to the current issue of the double-sided nature of intentions in pragmatic theorising (Kecskes, 2014). Lastly, insights are drawn from humour theories to account for the humour effects of the data analysed. The chapter pursues a strictly qualitative analysis, as such no attempt is made at quantifying the instances of humour types. This research design is consistent with our objectives of analysing humour types in the chosen interaction and demonstrating the interpretative possibility of the elaborated Pragmatic Acts Model (ePAM) espoused in the chapter.

ANALYSIS AND FINDINGS

Four humour types are identified, namely, (canned) jokes, punning/wordplay, question and answers and hyperbole/overstatement. In each of the humour types, the pragmatic mechanisms drawn upon by the interlocutors to comprehend the humour and to perform the pragmatic acts are indicated.

1. Canned Jokes

Popescu (2011) construes canned joke as the most common humour type. This humour type could be a narrative or a dialogue that has a punch line usually at the end of the joke, which serves to resolve the incongruity and reveals the humour effect. Hockett (1960) indicates that the internal structure of a joke comprises three components, namely, the build-up, the pivot and the punch line. The build-up introduces the joke and indicates the complicating situation or the incongruity in the joke. The pivot on the other hand is the linguistic element around which the ambiguity is created, while the punch line concludes the joke and most often presents a surprising counter-perspective to the preceding thought flow. Schwarz (2010) further observes that the build-up section of the internal structure of a joke could be optional, while the pivot and punch line have to be present for the joke to be successful. Extract 1 below is an illustration of this humour type.

Extract 1

1. *10:16PM, Oct 12, 2014 - N: A Journalist went to*
2. *interview a Doctor of a mental hospital & the following*
3. *conversation ensued:*
4. *Journalist: How do you determine whether to admit a patient*
5. *or not ?*
6. *Doctor AKPOS: Well, we first fill a bathtub with water till the*
7. *top. We then give a teaspoon, a glass cup and a bucket to the*
8. *patient and ask him/her to empty the bathtub.*
9. *Journalist: Obviously a normal person would use the Bucket*
10. *because it's bigger.*
11. *Doctor AKPOS: No, you're stupid! A normal person would*
12. *pull the DRAIN PLUG!*
13. *Nurse, admit this idiot in Ward 7.*

Lines 1-3 present the build-up of the joke as it tells us about a journalist who goes to interview a doctor in a mental hospital. Lines 4-10 is the pivot of the joke. It is within this section that the complicating action in the joke occurs, the journalist wants to know what diagnostic yardstick the doctor uses to admit his patients and the doctor tells him that the patients are presented with a simple intelligence test (6-8), the behavioural response to which will determine the sanity or otherwise of the patient. The journalist indicates that the normal way of emptying a bathtub filled with water is to use a bucket, because it is bigger than a teaspoon or glass cup. The punch line, which concludes the joke and introduces the element of surprise, has the doctor telling the journalist that what he assumes to be the sane thing to do is in fact the stupid option because the sane option is to 'pull the DRAIN PLUG' (12). And on the basis of the journalist's failure to identify the right course of action, he is going to be confined to ward 7! (13)

The humour triggers in this joke are quite many. First, there is a script opposition between the title 'doctor' and the name 'Akpos', the doctor script presents a medical personnel, who has been trained to diagnose and treat sick people. Usually, doctors are expected to be intelligent and thorough. Within the Nigerian context, the Akpos script epitomises stupidity and naughtiness, so that, for anyone familiar with Nigerian jokes, the mere encounter of the phrase 'Doctor Akpos' is a sufficient reason for a good laugh and an ample evidence to expect a humorous outcome at the end of the narrative/dialogue. The second humour trigger in the joke is the seeming simplicity of the diagnostic test Doctor Akpos gives his prospective patients. The task looks obviously simple and the option of using the bucket, instead of the teaspoon or the glass cup, to empty the bathtub, seems intelligent because the means will save time and energy. The journalist is surprised, as we are, that the actual intelligent course of action is to pull the drain plug. It is significant to note that the pull-the-drain-plug option was not indicated initially, which makes its sudden mention even more punchy and surprising. This surprise effect, which triggers amusement and laughter, is thc unique characteristic of the punch line in any joke (Schwarz, 2010).

Furthermore, the absurdity of Doctor Akpos' method for determining a mentally challenged patient is another source of laughter. The fact that an individual thinks that the best way to 'empty' a bathtub filled with water is by using a bucket amongst other options is not sufficient to confirm that he/she is mentally ill. It could just be that such a person did not remember that pulling the drain plug could be an alternative. It could also mean that the individual's salient interpretation (Giora, 2003) of the task, the props and the lexical item *empty*, which is usually thought of as *empty out,* may have informed his choice. At any rate, confining the journalist to ward 7 because of his answer was an insane thing to do. In the end, it is the sanity of Doctor Akpos and the absurdity of his diagnostic method, and (sometimes) by extension, that of medical practices in the country that are at issue here and not that of the journalist and possibly other patients in ward 7. One could look at it from another point of view, what if; indeed, it is the intelligence of the journalist that is being called to question. It is expected that the practice of journalism- information gathering and dissemination- should afford its practitioners access to various array of knowledge both sophisticated and mundane. It is therefore disappointing to see that the journalist failed a simple intelligence test. The joke can be read as *satirising* the institutions of medicine and journalism in the country

The pragmatic route for appreciating/comprehending the humour triggers indicated in the preceding paragraph viz, the script opposition in the phrase 'Doctor Akpos', the surprise effect at the end of the punch line and the absurdity of the diagnostic procedure runs through Giora's (2003) GSH in our elaborated Pragmatic act model. For instance, the salient meaning of doctor and diagnostic procedures is associated with rigorous training, professionalism and thoroughness. This interpretation is further warranted by the contextual information provided in the build-up section of the joke, especially because journalists often interview people whose points of view are considered authoritative and newsworthy (Reuter Handbook of Journalism, 2008). The need for revising the initial salient interpretation begins to emerge at the pivot section of the joke, when it is discovered that the doctor in question is Akpos, a referent whose name activates a humorous frame (on the activation of humorous frame see Norrick, 1993, 2003; Dynel, 2011 etc) in the Nigerian socio-cultural setting. Once the absurdity of the diagnostic procedure is discovered and the punch line delivered, the initial salient interpretation is abandoned for a non-salient, humorous one. It can be argued that the pragmatic acts of this joke are *satirising* key (medical and journalistic) institutions in the country and *eliciting laughter.* With regards to the second act, Attardo (2003) argues that 'a humorous text is a text whose perlocutionary goal is to amuse its hearer' (p. 1288). Of course, this is not to imply that laughter is the exclusive response to humour nor is it the exclusive preserve of humour as other responses to a humour are possible (cf. Drew, 1987) and other stimuli besides humour have the capacity to trigger laughter (cf. Attardo, 2003).

The next extract is a one-liner joke (see Chiora, 1992: 65ff; Nash, 1985:38ff). As the name implies, one-liners have a single line.

Extract 2

11:58, Mar 28 - +234 810 xxxxxx: Weather forecast has shown that there'd be heavy down pour in southern nigeria, so get ur umbrellas guys n drop the broom

At first glance, this joke does not seem to have any humorous effect. It reads like a normal weather report. Thus, initial interpretation activates the salient meanings of *Weather forecast, heavy down pour, umbrellas* and *broom* and presents a literal reading that borders on the speech act of advising/warning people to take precautionary measures so as not to be beaten by the rain. However, when this initial salient interpretation is integrated into the pragmatic context, its inappropriateness begins to manifest, as does the humorous effect and the actual pragmatic import of the joke. First, the date of the post, March 28, is pragmatically significant, as it is the day the Nigerian 2015 General Election for the presidency was held, which was more prominently contested by the two leading political parties in Nigeria: the Peoples Democratic Party (PDP) and the All Progressive Congress (APC). The activated socio-political knowledge implies that the post is not about the weather; rather it is about elections and the politics of electioneering. The understanding provided by this new script would mean that the salient meanings of *Weather forecast, heavy down pour, umbrellas* and *broom* are to be revised and the initial literal interpretation of the post is to be revisited.

Following from the lexical items, *Weather forecast* metaphorically stands for political information; *heavy down pour* can be interpreted as the political clout or might of the erstwhile ruling party, while the *umbrellas* and *the broom* are the party symbols of PDP and APC respectively. The non-salient meanings of the lexical items force the recipient of the joke to abandon the more salient, literal interpretation of the post for a less salient, metaphoric and hence humorous interpretation of the joke (Giora, 2003). The humorous effect of the text is motivated by the opposition between the weather report script and the electioneering script, as well as the incongruity introduced in the last half of the sentence, which forces a reinterpretation. Furthermore, given the socio-cultural knowledge, the pragmatic force of the utterance is also compelled to change from the speech act of advice to the situated pragmatic act of *electioneering*. This is an instance of the transformations utterances go through when acted upon by the forces of context (Capone, 2005; Mey, 2001). Capone (2005) specifically observes that such transformations 'reshape the original illocutionary value of a speech act by adding contextual layers of meaning, or even may change the illocutionary value of the speech act' (p.1360).

2. Punning/Wordplay

Punning is an ambiguity based humorous phenomenon (Attardo, 1994). In other words, 'the element which sets puns apart from other forms of humour is linguistic ambiguity present in the surface structure' (Seewoester, 2011, p. 72), which could manifest as either phonological, lexical or syntactic ambiguity. These manifestations of linguistic ambiguity are not always clear-cut, but it is beyond the scope of this paper to go into the nitty-gritty of the debates (for a review, see Seewoester, 2011) but suffice it to say that the three manifestations of ambiguity intersect at one point or the other. Extract 3 below presents an instance of phonological/sound based ambiguity, which Seewoester (2011:74) defines as involving 'manipulations of words at the sound level'.

Extract 3

1. *22:53, Mar 10 - +234 703 xxxxxx: Csc tutorial 7:30am*
2. *tomoro...148*
3. *22:54, Mar 10 - +234 806 xxxxxx: Impossicant...149*
4. *22:54, Mar 10 - +234 703 xxxxxx: Deyy dere 150*
5. *22:54, Mar 10 - +234 703 xxxxxx: Paul, we dey hlp u count o..151*
6. *22:55, Mar 10 - +234 818 xxxxxx: Lol*
7. *22:55, Mar 10 - +234 818 xxxxxx: Seriously e no make sense at all*
8. *Oh*
9. *22:56, Mar 10 - +234 808 xxxxxx: Am nt comin 153*
10. *22:56, Mar 10 - +234 703 xxxxxx: Jst jokin oOoooOo 154*
11. *22:57, Mar 10 - +234 818 xxxxxx: Beta oh 155*
12. *22:57, Mar 10 - +234 806 xxxxxx: U dont av to CUM early 156*
13. *23:00, Mar 10 - +234 701 xxxxxx: lol 157*

The opening turn for this extract is a piece of information about a coming tutorial (1-2). In subsequent turns the interlocutors variously express their disapproval for the tutorial, then in (9), someone says 'Am nt comin', which serves as the basis for the punning observed in (12) 'U dont av to CUM early 156'. The words at variance here are 'comin' and 'CUM'. While 'comin' is the present continuous tense of *come*, the second word 'cum' (which can also be spelt as *come*) carries a sexual sense, which means to reach orgasm. The humour in the example derives from the manipulation of the homophonic relations between the two words as well as the ambiguity motivated by the polysemous meaning of 'come'. A humorous effect is also triggered by the ostensive misinterpretation of the statement in (9) by the speaker of (12), who imposes a sexual interpretation on an otherwise, literal non-sexual activity. From Giora's (2003) perspective, this is an exercise in accessing salient meaning regardless of a contrary contextual wind. The context of the interaction does not warrant a sexual interpretation of 'Am nt comin', nonetheless, the salient meaning, i.e. the foremost meaning on the mind of this interlocutor is activated. In this case, the activated salient meaning is intended to be humorous and this is not lost on the last interlocutor, whose 'lol' signals an appreciation of the humorous effect of the wordplay.

In commenting on the pragmatics of pun-making, Seewoester (2011) observes that 'it is the intertwining of co-text (and general context), linguistic form, and meaning that enables the phenomenon of punning' (p. 71). In the same vein, we argue here that the pragmatics of punning, and that of humorous interaction in general, is the result of the interaction between the co-text, context, the linguistic form and the initially activated salient meaning that brings about the pragmatic import of the interaction. For instance, in the example being considered, the success of the pun is predicated on the incongruity of the utterance in (12), on the context of the preceding turns and the ability of the forces of context to transform this seeming piece of advice to the pragmatic act of *teasing*.

3. Question-Answer (Q&A) Jokes

The next humour type to be considered is the question and answer (Q&A) jokes. Schwarz (2010, p. 77) indicates that many of this joke type begin with 'How many' and end with an answer that triggers laughter. However, this humour type in the data demonstrates a unique structure of its own. The Q&A jokes in our data act more like retorts (Norrick, 1984, 1986, 1993). Dynel (2009) defines retort as 'a quick and witty response to a preceding turn with which it forms an *adjacency pair*' (p. 1291; cf. Norrick, 1993; Sacks, 1974; Schegloff, 1986). Instances of the Q&A joke type are extracts 4 and 5 below.

Extract 4

1. *7:55AM, Sep 19, 2014 - S: Go na..d 1 wey dey ground sef still dey hot*
2. *7:56AM, Sep 19, 2014 - +234 816 xxxxxx: Ok*
3. *7:56AM, Sep 19, 2014 – Y L: Abi oooo*
4. *8:27AM, Sep 19, 2014 - O D: Wetin dey ground*
5. *8:27AM, Sep 19, 2014 - Y L: Sand and soil*
6. *8:28AM, Sep 19, 2014 - O D: Clown*
7. *8:28AM, Sep 19, 2014 - O D: Lmao*
8. *8:28AM, Sep 19, 2014 - D: Just dey joke ooo*

Extract 5

1. *22:32, Feb 25 - +234 816 xxxxx: Abeg Wetin Arsenal dey play*
2. *22:34, Feb 25 - +234 806 xxxxx: Football sir*
3. *22:35, Feb 25 - +234 816 xxxxx: Lol*
4. *22:35, Feb 25 - +234 816 xxxxx: I mean scores*
5. *22:36, Feb 25 - Student: 2-0*

The amusement in Extract 4 is triggered by one of the interlocutor's humorous misunderstanding of the meaning of the speaker's question 'Wetin dey ground' (4). While the meaning of *ground* in the question is metaphorical, the listener activates the literal meaning of the lexical item, which forms his response of 'Sand and soil' (5). The incongruity that motivates the joke is the opposition between the metaphorical and the literal meaning of *ground* and in Giora's (2003) GSH parlance, the answer draws on the salient meaning of the lexical item *ground*, which of course, is not the intended meaning of the speaker and is not consistent with the context of the interaction. The extract further demonstrates the dialectics between *a priori* intention of the speaker and the co-constructed, emergent intention that is negotiated in the course of an interaction (Kesckes, 2014; cf. Dynel, 2011). The *a priori* intention of the speaker was to seek for a specific kind of information, namely, the details of a previous situation of conflict referred to by one of the interlocutors. The listener, in his response, provides a different kind of information, which nonetheless, is one possible answer to the question, albeit a contextually inappropriate one, and which surprisingly defeats the speaker's intention. The response pragmatically modifies the initial intention of this segment of the interaction and thus changes the course of the conversation from a serious discourse to a humorous one, from one seeking a factual answer to one that provides a light-hearted inappropriate answer. The surprising shift in the interaction is motivated by a modified, emergent intention, and an evidence that the speaker has abandoned his earlier intention, is further signalled by his response to the answer: 'clown, lmao (laughing my ass off)'. The last interlocutor brings the conversation back to the non-humorous frame by meta-linguistically commenting on the inappropriateness of a joke in such a serious discourse frame (8). This is a fine illustration on how frame shifting between humorous mode and the non-humorous mode occur (Dynel, 2011).

In Extract 5, a similar humour mechanism plays out as well. Here, as in Extract 4, the speaker's question (1) receives a quick witty retort (2) that generates humour. As indicated above, the response (2) exploits the salient meanings of certain lexical items in the question, viz *Arsenal* and *play*. The former is a professional football club that participates in the English Premier League, while the latter denotes participating in games or sports, and following from this therefore, the seeming appropriate response is (2). However, when this initial salient interpretation (2) gets integrated into the pragmatic context of the interaction, the humorous intent behind its production becomes manifest, and this is acknowledged by the laughter-response (3) produced by the speaker of (1). It can be argued that at this point the *a priori* intention of the speaker to elicit certain information is momentarily suspended and an emergent intention is currently being negotiated. However, unlike the interaction in Extract 4, where the speaker's intention was completely abandoned for the emergent intention, the speaker, of (1) in this example, reinforces his initial intention by rewording his question in unambiguous terms (4) to which an appropriate answer is provided (5) by another interlocutor. The forces of the pragmatic context acting on the responses in the examples being considered transform them into the pragmatic act of playful *teasing*. The pract is so called because outside the humorous frame the responses will be taken as genuine misunderstanding of the speaker's intention and when the speaker's intent is then properly conveyed, the misunderstanding is resolved. However, in the cases being examined, it is the other interlocutor's intention to joke and this is achieved indirectly.

4. Hyperbole/Overstatement

Hyperboles are overstatements that exaggerate some object, situation or personality. Norrick (as cited in Schwarz, 2010:134) asserts that overstatements should be semantically interpreted as claims that are higher (or lower) on some scale than warranted. The potential of hyperbole as a humour type is steeped in the incongruity it sets up between the overstated phenomenon and the reality to which it is compared (Schwarz, 2010). Norrick (2004) observes that hyperbole can be construed as 'the simultaneous perception of an object within two contrasting frames of reference or the compatibility with opposed 'semantic scripts'' (Norrick, 2004). In the examples analysed below, these features of hyperbole and much more are unravelled.

The interaction in the example below revolves around the Faculty programme organised for students and one feature of such programmes is the presentation of awards to various deserving students/participants. One of the interlocutors, OJ, has won an award and this situation is exaggerated to produce humour. In the first turn, we are told that OJ has a place on the high table, a pre-eminent position, which of course is exaggerated by the speaker of (1) and then OJ playing along says 'Thank yhu boiz' (thank you boys). It should be noted that OJ and the other interlocutors are colleagues; and in a serious, non-humorous frame, he should not address them as *boys*. However, the humorous frame activated warrants this form of address and is also justified giving OJ's exaggerated position on the high table.

Extract 6

8:19PM, Oct 2, 2014 - YL: O boii con see where julious sit for sems programme today na for high table the guy sit
8:19PM, Oct 2, 2014 - DY: Juli na u oh
8:35PM, Oct 2, 2014 - ÕJ: Thank yhu boiz
8:36PM, Oct 2, 2014 - ÕJ: U c d award wey dem gv me
8:20PM, Oct 2, 2014 - DY: Lol...mumu
8:36PM, Oct 2, 2014 - ÕJ: Ur Vc self dey jealous me
8:37PM, Oct 2, 2014 - ÕJ: David dnt worry very soon yhu will get dia, like 10yrs time
8:21PM, Oct 2, 2014 - Y L: Yes na... Yu were given 17 Awards
8:22PM, Oct 2, 2014 - D Y: Juliet u no serious
8:39PM, Oct 2, 2014 - ÕJ: Nope... It was 28 but I shared d remaining jawe, I dnt like been proud
8:24PM, Oct 2, 2014 - DY: Lol
8:24PM, Oct 2, 2014 - YL: Yes I can recollect
8:25PM, Oct 2, 2014 - YL: It was now later yu were begging for egg bounce and table water

In (5), OJ wonders if his colleagues saw the awards he was given and this turn triggers a series of hyperbolic contributions from the interlocutors. In acknowledgment of the humorous frame initiated by (5) DY laughs and insults OJ (6), who is not deterred from pursuing the fantastic story of how he received so many awards that the Vice Chancellor of the University envied him (7), which is another instance of overstatement; because it is absurd for the Vice Chancellor of the university to be jealous of a first year student who is being awarded. The absurdity of the overstatement is the source of amusement for the interlocutors. Of the three interlocutors, DY is the most reluctant to key into the humorous form and therefore is teased by OJ in the next turn. Dynel (2009) argues that teasing is construed as 'a higher-order concept embracing jocular utterances performing a variety of pragmatic functions' (p. 1293 cf. Drew 1987; Norrick, 1993; Martin, 2007 etc). The pragmatic function of the utterance in (8-9) is to *mock* DY. YL brings the interaction back to the fantasy frame when he says that OJ received 17 awards. However, OJ is quick to correct him and state that he received 28 awards and gave some out because he does not like to be proud (12-13). The statement in (13), about OJ not wanting to appear proud, provides a punch line for the humorous interaction because it supplies a piece of information that is incongruous to the ones indicated in the preceding turns. Furthermore, while DY laughs, a sign that he enjoys the humour, LY corroborates OJ's story, only to deliver the punch line that sees the exalted OJ begging for snacks (16-18), a rather belittling thing to do. According to Norrick (1989), besides concluding the joke, the punch line frequently introduces 'a conflicting point of view or a new scene entirely' (p. 188). The punch line in (13) has this characteristic as does the one in (17-18) as they both present an alternative perspective to the high and mighty OJ.

The mechanism drawn upon to effectively execute the humorous performance in the example above is called joint fantasising (Hay, 1995; Kotthoff, 2007), which is 'a fantasy/imaginary scenario created by interlocutors' (Dynel, 2009, p. 1294). Though Dynel (2009) discusses this concept in relation to banter, we find it very useful for analysing the example above. The interlocutors maximally collaborated in the performance of the joke as they created an exaggerated scenario of the awards that OJ received at a faculty programme. As indicated above, the humour in hyperbole/overstatement is motivated by the incongruity, and sometimes absurdity that the overstated phenomenon or experience evokes when compared with reality. For instance, it is absurd to think that the Vice Chancellor of a University would envy a first year student for receiving so many awards (7).

CONCLUSION

In this chapter, we have analysed four humour types from the text chats of students from three departments in the Federal University of Technology, Akure, namely, (canned) jokes, punning/wordplay, question and answer joke and hyperbole/overstatement. In each humour type identified, the pragmatic mechanism for appreciating/comprehending the humour and the pragmatic acts performed were indicated. The pragmatic mechanism that underlie the interpretation of the humour, is here, construed as an elaborated Pragmatic Act Model (ePAM), which incorporates Giora's (2003) GSH and Mey's (2001) pragmatic act theory and insights from Kecskes (2014). According to this model, interpretation occurs in two stages: initially activating the salient meanings of the expression, which is then embedded in the pragmatic context to determine the appropriateness or otherwise of this initial interpretation. There exists in the literature the debate as to whether interpretation of humorous phenomena goes through a single-stage or multiple stage processing (see Norrick, 2003; Gibbs 1994). In this chapter, we subscribe to the multiple-stage processing model, as is demonstrated in our analysis.

Our model also accounts for the pragmatic functions or acts performed in the four humour types identified. Overall, five pragmatic acts were identified: *satirising*, *eliciting laughter*, *electioneering*, *teasing* and *overstating* and there are the instantiations of the pragmeme of doing humour. In the analysis, we showed how contextual information acting on utterance can transform it from a speech act to a pragmatic act. The model proposed in the chapter also comfortably handled the question of intention and aligns with Kecskes' (2014) take that intention should be both *a priori* and negotiated in the course of interaction. Lastly, as Dynel (2009) indicates, each of the humour types offers ample research opportunities from various linguistic perspectives.

REFERENCES

Adetunji, A. (2013). The interactional context of humor in Nigerian stand-up comedy. *Pragmatics*, *23*(1), 1–22. doi:10.1075/prag.23.1.01ade

Attardo, S. (1993). Violation of conversational maxims and cooperation: The case of jokes. *Journal of Pragmatics*, *19*(6), 537–558. doi:10.1016/0378-2166(93)90111-2

Attardo, S. (1994). *Linguistic theories of humor*. Berlin: Mouton de Gruyter.

Attardo, S. (2001). *Humorous texts: A semantic and pragmatic analysis*. Berlin: Mouton de Gruyter. doi:10.1515/9783110887969

Attardo, S. (2007). A Primer for the Linguistics of Humor. Academic Press.

Attardo, S. et al. (1994). The linear organization of jokes: analysis of two thousand texts. *Humor*, *7*(1), 27-54.

Attardo, S., & Raskin, V. (1991). Script theory revis(it)ed: joke similarity and joke representation model. Humor, 4(3/4), 293-347.

Bateson, G. (1953). The position of humor in human communication. In H. von Foerster (Ed.), *Cybernetics* (pp. 1–47). New York: Josiah Macy, Jr Foundation.

Bateson, G. (1972). A Theory of Play and Fantasy. In G. Bateson (Ed.), *Steps to an Ecology of Mind* (pp. 177–193). Chandler.

Bro^ne, G. (2008). Hyper-and misunderstanding in interactional humour. *Journal of Pragmatics*, *40*(12), 2027–2061. doi:10.1016/j.pragma.2008.04.011

Capone, A. (2001). *Modal Adverbs and Discourse*. Pisa: ETS.

Capone, A. (2005). Pragmemes: A study with reference to English and Italian. *Journal of Pragmatics*, *37*(9), 1355–1371. doi:10.1016/j.pragma.2005.01.013

Chiaro, D. (1992). *The language of jokes: analyzing verbal play*. London: Routledge. doi:10.4324/9780203327562

Drew, P. (1987). Po-faced receipts of teases. *Linguistics*, *25*(1), 219–253. doi:10.1515/ling.1987.25.1.219

Dynel, M. (2009a). Beyond a joke: Types of conversational humour. *Language and Linguistics Compass*, *3*(5), 1284–1299. doi:10.1111/j.1749-818X.2009.00152.x

Dynel, M. (2011). *The pragmatics of humour across discourse domain*. Amsterdam: John Benjamins Co. doi:10.1075/pbns.210

Freud, S. (1960). Jokes and their relation to the unconscious. New York: Norton.

Gibbs, R. W. Jr. (1994). *The Poetics of Mind*. Cambridge, UK: Cambridge University Press.

Giora, R. (1991). On the cognitive aspects of the joke. *Journal of Pragmatics*, *16*(5), 465–485. doi:10.1016/0378-2166(91)90137-M

Giora, R. (1997). Understanding figurative and literal language: The graded salience hypothesis. *Cognitive Linguistics*, *8*(3), 183–206. doi:10.1515/cogl.1997.8.3.183

Giora, R. (1997a). Discourse coherence and theory of relevance: Stumbling blocks in search of a unified theory. *Journal of Pragmatics*, *27*(1), 17–34. doi:10.1016/0378-2166(95)00065-8

Giora, R. (2002a). Literal vs. figurative language: Different or equal? *Journal of Pragmatics*, *34*(4), 487–506. doi:10.1016/S0378-2166(01)00045-5

Giora, R. (2003). *On Our Mind: Salience, Context, and Figurative Language*. New York: Oxford University Press. doi:10.1093/acprof:oso/9780195136166.001.0001

Grice, H. P. (1975). Logic and conversation. In Speech Acts. Syntax and Semantics (pp. 41–58). New York: Academic Press.

Gruner, C. R. (1978). *Understanding laughter*. Chicago: Nelson-Hall.

Gruner, C. R. (1997). *The game of humor: a comprehensive theory of why we laugh*. New Brunswick, NJ: Transaction Publishers.

Hay, J. (1995). *Gender and humour: Beyond a joke*. (Unpublished Master's thesis). Victoria University of Wellington, Wellington, New Zealand.

Herring, S. (1999). Interactional coherence in CMC. *Journal of Computer-Mediated Communication*, *4*(4). Retrieved from http://jcmc.indiana.edu/vol4/issue4/herring.html

Hockett, C. F. (1977). Jokes. In C. F. Hockett (Ed.), The view from language (pp. 257-289). Athens, GA: University of Georgia Press.

Inya, O. (2012). Defending a Thesis: Pragmatic Acts in Contemporary Christian Apologetics. *Theory and Practice in Language Studies, 2*(10), 2016-2023.

Jepson, K. (2005). Conversations and negotiated interaction in text and voice chat rooms. *Language Learning & Technology*, *9*(3), 79–98.

Kecskes, I. (2010). Situation-bound utterances as pragmatic acts. *Journal of Pragmatics*, *42*(1), 2889–2897. doi:10.1016/j.pragma.2010.06.008

Kecskes, I. (2014). *Intercultural Pragmatics*. Oxford, UK: Oxford University Press.

Koestler, A. (1969). *The Act of Creation*. London: Hutchinson & Co.

Kotthoff, H. (2007). Oral genres of humor. On the dialectic of genre knowledge and creative authoring. *Pragmatics*, *12*(2), 263–296. doi:10.1075/prag.17.2.04kot

Martin, R. (2007). *The Psychology of Humor. An Integrative Approach*. Burlington, MA: Elsevier.

Mey, J. (2001). *Pragmatics: An Introduction* (2nd ed.). Oxford, UK: Blackwell.

Mey, J. (2009). Pragmatic Act. In Concise Encyclopedia of Pragmatics. Elsevier.

Nash, W. (1985). *The Language of Humour*. London: Longman.

Norrick, N. (1984). Stock conversational witticisms. *Journal of Pragmatics*, *8*(2), 195–209. doi:10.1016/0378-2166(84)90049-3

Norrick, N. (1986). A frame-theoretical analysis of verbal humor: Bisociation as schema conflict. *Semiotica*, *60*(3-4), 225–245. doi:10.1515/semi.1986.60.3-4.225

Norrick, N. R. (1982). In K. Detering, J. Schmidt-Radefeldt, & W. Sucharowski (Eds.), *On the semantics of overstatement. Sprache erkennen und verstehen* (pp. 168–176). Tübingen: Niemeyer.

Norrick, N. R. (1989). Intertextuality in humor. *Humor: International Journal of Humor Research*, *2*(2), 117–139. doi:10.1515/humr.1989.2.2.117

Norrick, N. R. (1993). *Conversational Joking*. Bloomington, IN: Indiana University Press.

Norrick, N. R. (1993a). Repetition in canned jokes and spontaneous conversational joking. *Humor: International Journal of Humor Research*, *6*(4), 385–402. doi:10.1515/humr.1993.6.4.385

Norrick, N. R. (2000). *Conversational narrative*. Philadelphia: Benjamins. doi:10.1075/cilt.203

Norrick, N. R. (2001). On the conversational performance of narrative jokes: Toward an account of timing. *Humor*, *14*(3), 255-274.

Norrick, N. R. (2003). Issues in conversational joking. *Journal of Pragmatics*, *35*(9), 1333–1359. doi:10.1016/S0378-2166(02)00180-7

Norrick, N. R. (2004). Non-verbal humor and joke performance. *Humor*, *17*(4), 401-409.

Norrick, N. R. (2005). *Saarbrücken Corpus of Spoken English (SCoSE): Jokes*. Retrieved from http://www.uni-saarland.de/fak4/norrick/index2.htm

Orhiunu, W. (2007). *Tribal stereotypes in Nigerian comedy: The Calabar example*. Retrieved on August 2, 2009 from http://www.nigeriansinamerica.com/articles/1951/1/Tribal-Stereotypes-in-Nigerian-Comedy-TheCalabar-Example/html

Popescu, C. (2003). Understanding ethnic humour in Romanian jokes. In M. Dynel (Ed.), *The pragmatics of humour across discourse domain* (pp. 173–190). Amsterdam: John Benjamins Co.

Raskin, V. (1985). *Semantic mechanisms of humor*. Dordrecht: Reidel.

Sack, H. (1974). An analysis of the course of a joke's telling. In R. Bauman & J. Sherzer (Eds.), *Explorations in the ethnography of speaking* (pp. 337–353). Cambridge, UK: Cambridge University Press.

Schegloff, E. (1986). The routine as achievement. *Human Studies, 9*, 111–51.

Schwarz, J. (2010). *Linguistic Aspects of Verbal Humor in Stand-up Comedy*. (Unpublished PhD Dissertation). Universität des Saarlandes.

Seewoester, S. (2011). The role of syllables and morphemes as mechanisms in humorous pun formation. In M. Dynel (Ed.), *The pragmatics of humour across discourse domain* (pp. 71–104). Amsterdam: John Benjamins Co. doi:10.1075/pbns.210.07see

ADDITIONAL READING

Dynel, M. (2009). *Humorous Garden-Paths: A Pragmatic-Cognitive Study*. Newcastle: Cambridge Scholars Publishing.

Hay, J. (2000). Functions of humor in the conversations of men and women. *Journal of Pragmatics, 32*(6), 709–742. doi:10.1016/S0378-2166(99)00069-7

Hay, J. (2001). The pragmatics of humor support. *Humor: International Journal of Humor Research, 14*(1), 55–82.

Leech, G. (1983). *Principles of pragmatics*. London: Longman.

Partington, A. (2006). *The linguistics of laughter. A corpus-assisted study of laughter-talk*. Oxon: Routledge Studies in Linguistics.

Ritchie, G. (2004). *The linguistic analysis of jokes*. London, UK: Routledge.

KEY TERMS AND DEFINITIONS

Chat Room: An electronically-mediated, synchronous environment where interlocutors converse in real-time through the aid of a computer, or a smart phone and the Internet.

Humour: An utterance, object or depiction that is intended to elicit laughter.

Pragmatics: A branch in linguistics that studies language use in social contexts.

Pragmeme: A generalised situational type that is particularised by specific instances of pragmatic acts.

Punch Line: Usually occurs at the end of a joke. It concludes the joke and most of the time introduces a surprising counter-perspective to that which is present in the build-up of the joke.

Salience: A property of lexical items that makes them prominent in the mental lexicon of language users and easily activated in the course of interpretation.

Script: The structure of knowledge of an object, a phenomenon or a situation that is activated in the course of interpretation.

Chapter 12
Stand-Up Comedy and Addressivity:
The Example of Joan Rivers

Akin Adetunji
Emmanuel Alayande College of Education, Nigeria

ABSTRACT

This chapter highlights the linguistic value of addressivity in two Youtube downloads of Joan Rivers' stand-up comic performance, Live at the Apollo. Despite the devotion of the six articles of Comedy Studies 2(2) to analyses of the data, very little was said about the linguistic content and identity of the performance. Despite the givenness of a performer's deployment of linguistic resources in any kind of stage performance, the salience of some of the stand-up comedy-specific linguistic forms—repetition, disfluencies, formulaicity, paralanguage, timing, parenthetical expressions, figurative language, direct audience address—is foregrounded in Rivers' performance. These forms are located within and interpreted with Bakhtin's notion of 'addressivity'. It is argued that her elaborate audience interaction and thematic preoccupation with social, biographical and autobiographical issues are one macro act of addressivity, foregrounding the complex intersection of speaker (comedian), listener (present audience) and third person/superaddressee (non-present audience/previous discourses).

INTRODUCTION

Although stand-up comedy has been subjected to a limited amount of academic research, especially when compared with other performance oral genres, its linguistics has been worse off. Coming from a linguistic pragmatic perspective, this study is focused on Joan Rivers' significant deployment of linguistic features in her stand-up comic performance, with the intention of revealing how these engender and foreground comedian-audience interaction in the co-production of humour. It is argued that Rivers' act belongs in Bakhtin's notion of 'addressivity' (an utterance is always addressed to someone and anticipates a response), a framing which confirms her comic style as dialogic and conversational (see Blackburn, 2013).

DOI: 10.4018/978-1-5225-0338-5.ch012

Copyright © 2016, IGI Global. Copying or distributing in print or electronic forms without written permission of IGI Global is prohibited.

Stand-up comedy is conventionally conceptualised as an encounter between a single performer who stands in front of an audience and behaves comically and/or talks to them intentionally to amuse them or make them laugh (Double, 2014: 19; Mintz 1985: 71). But, more recently, attention has shifted to its major features. These, as outlined by Double (2014: pp. 19-20), include funniness, personality (at least a person in front of an audience), direct communication (between performer and audience) and present tense (live performance). Traditionally, stand-up comedy is realised as routines of canned jokes, which the comedian prefaces (or explicitly announces), rehearses (hears or creates before telling), and decontextualises (detaches from the context of the joke telling) (Attardo, 2001: 62). However, modern enactments have shown this type of comedy to be less structurally predictable, more dialogic, creative, contextual, spontaneous and dwelling on improvised material (Furukawa 2011; Gilbert 2004; Limon, 2000; Schwarz, 2010). As a type of performance, stand-up comedy subsists on certain conventions and presuppositions. These include, but are not limited to, solo performance, comic content, direct address, spontaneity in comedian-audience interaction, comedian's proximity to audience, audience's expectation of to be amused and shocked, and audience's constant feedback (smile, nod, laughter, heckling, silence, clap) (Double, 2014; Furukawa, 2011; Gilbert, 2004; Peacock, 2011; Rutter, 1997; Yus, 2002).

Of these, comic content and audience feedback are probably the most salient. Linking both features as the major determinants of the success of a stand-up comic performance, Limon (2000) posits three theorems (which deictically locate 'you' as a second-person plural, the audience) as generic constituents of stand-up comedy: '[1] If you think something is funny, it is. [2] A joke is funny if and only if you laugh at it. [3] Your laughter is the single end of stand up' (pp. 11-12). Expatiating on Limon's postulations, the first theorem claims that the funniness of a joke is determined not by individual assessments but through the reaction of the majority of the audience, the second theorem holds that a joke can only be regarded as funny when and if the audience reacts to it with laughter, and the third theorem, that audience's laughter minimally marks the end of a joke. Apart from foregrounding the value of the audience in stand-up comedy, two of the theorems specify the salience of laughter. And as noted by Rutter (1997), laughter is quintessential to comedian-audience interaction, not as a response to a humorous stimulus, but rather as interactive and ordered. The audience (and its reaction) as such, crucially defines stand-up comedy, since it has to 'cooperate' with the comedian to make a joke funny. So, following Limon (2000), comedians and their audiences are hardly distinguishable, since it is the audience that makes a joke one. In sum, stand-up comedy greatly affords both comedian and audience the opportunity to respond to and engage each other in the mood and energy of performance in real time. One of the stand-up comedians who has (or had) a global reputation for deep-seated audience engagement is Joan Rivers.

Joan Rivers (real name, Joan Alexandra Molinsky) (1933-2014) was a famous American stand-up comedian, actress, writer, producer, and television host whose popularity and comedic persona are often traced to her 1965 guest role in the American talk show, *The Tonight Show*. Although she earned global recognition for her identity as an outstanding stand-up comedian during a career which spanned about fifty years, it was her book, *Diary of a Mad Diva* (2014) that earned her a posthumous Grammy Award in 2015. Rivers' comedy has been interpreted, variously, as being too personal, too gossipy, biographical (Blackburn, 2013) and autobiographical (Gray, 1994). As well she has been read as sometimes blurring the boundaries between the serious and the not-serious, for instance by making serious historical incidents, such as the Holocaust and the Gaza conflict, part of her comic material (Khan, 2014). Being a female comedian in an (originally) androcentric comic world, she bridged the gap between self deprecatory jokesters and the liberated women comics (Zoglin 2008), displaying a bit of the traits of both types of comedians, such that she was classified both as a 'whiner' and a 'bitch' (Gilbert 2004). Rivers' comedy is essentially a juxtaposition of images: immigrant (Jewish) and American identities (Horowitz, 1997); self deprecation and aggression (Gray, 1994); reinforcement and resistance of Western culture, especially concerning the female body; commoner and elitist identities (Mock, 2011). And as she (Rivers) confirmed, this ambivalence is deliberate and functional, a style meant to achieve continuous relevance and visibility: '[my] whole humor is actually based on the loneliness and hurt of being left out, of being thrown over— which I always fear and dread' (Rivers, 1992:126). However, as regards Rivers' deployment of linguistic resources, the opinions are less divided. Whether when directed at others or herself, her language is considered acerbic or caustic, expressing a deep-seated anger (Gilbert, 2004: 132) characteristic of female performers, especially those who started performing at the time she did (when most comedians were male) and pushing the boundaries of propriety and comic licence in lexical choices and usage (Blackburn, 2013).

This article is divided into five sections; apart from the introductory section 1, section 2 dwells on theoretical framework, section 3 contains a review of literature, section 4 describes the methodology employed, section 5 is focused on analysis, while section 6 is devoted to the discussion of findings and conclusion.

ADDRESSIVITY

The term 'addressivity' (*addressivnost/obrashchennost*) is traceable to the Russian scholar Mikhail Bakhtin (1895-1975), who coined the term in reaction to the monologic (one-way) concept of meaning identified with structuralist linguistics. While structuralist linguistics had dwelt on the simple dichotomy of langue (language rules) and parole (language use), Bakhtin (as espoused in his 1981 publication) thought of an alternative model that would capture the social and pragmatic aspects of language, especially the creativity in any dialogue between real people. Distinguishing utterance (unrepeatable context-dependent speech act) from sentence (repeatable, non-occasion-specific language unit), Bakhtin holds that an utterance requires more than a sentence to be meaningful and that addressivity is that feature of the utterance that the sentence lacks (Morson, 2009: 14). Thus, an utterance is viewed as part of, and as naturally signaling, dialogue, in itself, a property of discourse. Morris (1994: 35) expatiates:

... each of the distinguishable significant elements of an utterance and the entire utterance as a whole entity are translated in our minds into another, active and responsive context. **Any true understanding is dialogic in nature.** *Understanding is to utterance as one line of a dialogue is to the next. Understanding strives to match the speaker's word with* **a counter word**. *(emphasis in original)*

So, when one understands an utterance, one is actively engaged in translating the meaning which a speaker intends the utterance to communicate. As such, a listener's response indicates both an understanding of an utterance as well as a dialogic relationship with the speaker.

Addressivity, essentially, connects three elements, speaker, listener, and 'third person'. Communication is conventionally assumed to include a speaker, who in every utterance, encodes information through a particular medium, and a listener, who decodes the speaker's information. For addressivity, in addition, an utterance is co-owned by both speaker and listener inasmuch as the utterance is made with a particular audience in mind. So, a listener does not just passively decode, he or she actively understands; such understanding becomes 'personal, processual, and active' (Morson, 2009:15). A listener, then, has a major part to play in making an utterance meaningful, since, according to Mey (2000:238), '[b]eing addressed implies taking the responsibility for the common production of the utterance and assuming one's part of the duties that are incumbent upon the interlocutors, as co-owners of the utterance'. The listener's response is active both during and after an utterance is made; he or she comes to terms with 'how the utterance is meant to affect him or her, how it responds to past and potential utterances, and how third parties might respond' (Morson 2009: 14). 'Third parties', in the foregoing quotation, is the plural form of 'third person'. The 'third person' has been understood to mean two things. One, it could mean previous speakers or previous utterances on a given topic. As Morson (2009: 15) rightly submits, "[e]very topic has been 'already spoken about' and the words referring to this topic implicitly 'remember' the earlier things said about it and the contexts in which they were said". Thus, each utterance is a historical unit: no speaker makes an utterance on any topic *in vacuo* and each utterance engages previous ones made by other speakers in dialogue.

Secondly, a third party may be a 'superaddressee'. This refers to the 'ideal listener' (Morson 2009: 15) or 'external authority' (Mey 2000: 283) who is usually invisible but implicitly projected as a sanctioning authority for the speaker's utterance. The superaddressee could be the imagined audience whom the actor/actress addresses in a video film, with the question, 'Please, I ask, am I not doing the right thing?' It could also be personified as God or 'the voice of history' (Morson 2009: 15).

In sum, addressivity is 'the act of addressing or being addressed' (Mey 2000: 134), an act in which the addresser and addressee(s) are all actively, even if implicitly, involved. Although originally meant to capture inner speech and conceptualised to be applied to literary dialogue, Bakhtin's addressivity has been found useful to linguistics, especially as it concerns the sharing of social meanings in the 'dialogue of inner and outer speech.' (Morson 2009: 15). Addressivity is, thus, the quality of being addressive, of engaging in communication based on the active cooperation of, or for the sake of, one's interlocutor.

REVIEW OF RELEVANT LITERATURE

Research has identified a wide range of linguistic and discursive features which are identifiable with stand-up comedy. These features include repetition, disfluency, pause, parenthetical expression, reincorporation, figurative language, false start, direct address to audience, discourse markers, marked lexical choices, and paralinguistic forms, such as gesture and intonation (Rutter, 1997; Schwarz, 2010). To the extent that these forms characterise all aspects of stand-up comedy, only some of them have been appropriated as its generic linguistic features (see Schwarz, 2010). As may be expected, the linguistic features abound to a greater or less extent in a given performance. The most prominent linguistic features in Rivers' performance will be analysed in this study.

In its linguistic literature, the interactional tenor or comedian-audience co-construction of stand-up comedy has been approached from various perspectives, done in different contexts, and yielded different results. Discourse-analytic studies have shown the prominent use of paralinguistic features to ensure audience's co-construction of humour (e.g. Li 2014) and a demarcation of context of the joke and context in the joke (Filani, 2015). Sociolinguistic studies have revealed the prominence of the audience in comedians' performances for the purposes of identity construction (e.g. Furukawa, 2007; Tsang and Wong, 2004), language planning and maintenance (e.g. Moriarty, 2011), and cross-cultural comparison (e.g. Katayama, 2008). Conversation analytical studies have underscored the value of specific conversational devices to achieve audience participation (e.g. McIlvenny, Mettovaara, & Tapio, 1992).

Linguistic-pragmatic studies have projected the significance of cultural representations (Yus, 2002), linguistic coding (Adetunji, 2013) and activity type (Filani, 2015).

Specific to Joan Rivers' comedy, generally speaking, research has shown her style to be conversational and biographical (Blackburn, 2013). As a fact, the data being studied, were the subject of the six articles of a journal, *Comedy Studies* (Volume 2, Number 2). In its rich, inter-disciplinary content, the (year) 2011 publication reveals the amenability of the data to various methodological inquiries. Lockyer did a sociocultural interrogation of gender identity and sexuality and revealed a complex style which could be classified as traditionally feminine and traditionally masculine, all at once. Matte and McFayden's pragmatic study framed the data as theatrical performance and scrutinized them using essentially Brown and Levinson's politeness principles. They concluded that just like with theatre practice, Rivers' act treaded the thin line between off-record (non-serious) and on-record (serious) face threats. In the process of subjecting the data to the three major theories of humour (superiority, incongruity, relief), Mills noted Rivers' performance as socially valuable, because it revealed a pleasurable co-construction of humour between the comedian and audience who shared a similar repertoire of knowledge. For Mock, the data existed within performance and cultural studies as they authenticated and echoed Rivers' identity as a Jew. Peacock did a semiotic analysis, as theatrically modelled by Tadeusz Kowzan and Patrice Pavis and submitted that, given the synchronic, diachronic, and polysemic nature of stand-up comedy, a wholly independent semiotic study was limiting. In Waisanen's systematic analysis of the data as political-rhetoric, he found a clustering of the themes of optimism, uncertainty, egocentrism, and realism, all of which added up to underscore the ambivalence of Rivers' performance as a form of public communication.

A thread that runs through the articles in *Comedy Studies 2(2)* is the interpretation of the data either as theatrical performance or as social communication. Thus, despite the pragmatic orientation of Matte and McFayden's article and the semiotic study of Peacock, none of the studies interpreted Rivers' performance as purely linguistic data or using the linguistic features identified with stand-up comedy. As such, this study fills some of the gap left in the 2011 publication, essentially by presenting a more holistic picture of the linguistic resources with which Rivers speaks to and speaks with her audience. Moreover, this study is a novel attempt at interpreting the linguistic aspects of stand-up comedy via the lens of addressivity.

METHODOLOGY

This is a descriptive study. It is focused on Joan Rivers' *Live at the Apollo*; her stand-up comedic performance at the Apollo nightclub in London, broadcast on December 10, 2007. The data, gathered from the Internet via two *Youtube* clips, are contained in a two-part transcript of about 16 minutes of Rivers' performance before a live audience; Part 1 covers 9 minutes and 56 seconds, Part 2 spans 6 minutes and 11 seconds. The two parts are thematically and structurally linked, such that Part 2 is an extension or continuation of Part 1. Again, while Part 1 contains purely Rivers' performance of rehearsed and improvised material, Part 2 additionally positions her answering previously written audience questions (as promised at the start of Part 1). Rivers opens and closes the show. The transcript is subjected to thorough visual and descriptive analyses, the latter according to the interpretive ability of the researcher. For ease of verification, each excerpt (from the data) used for the analysis is identified, first according to the Part in which it is located and its duration (in seconds). Excerpts are selected from the data based on their appropriateness or relevance to the analyses. The data are presented via some peculiar transcription forms (see Appendix), for ease of analysis.

The data are analysed for their linguistic and paralinguistic content and interpreted within addressivity. As such, addressivity, as seated in linguistic pragmatics, is the theoretical basis for this study. This choice is informed by the form and content of the data, a stage performance involving a comedian working with an audience. It is thought that addressivity will be invaluable for teasing out the peculiarities of the dialogue or conversation constitutive of Joan Rivers' stand-up comedy. Stand-up comedy is a verbal art form which subsists on performance (action accomplished in the presence of an audience) of utterances and so will be amenable to addressivity, 'everything that takes the resources of speech and turns them into an utterance' (Morson, 2009: 15). And the audience is crucial to stand-up comedy: the audience's response to the comedian's jokes and the two agents' (audience's and comedian's) co-ownership of the performance contextualise the interactive tenor of stand-up comedy. Thus, addressivity, as related to stand-up comedy, would concern the co-authorship of utterances made by comedian and audience, the interactional contextualisation of the performance of a comedian not just before and with a live audience but also the audience at large. As such, the most significant linguistic features which project addressivity are identified and analysed within the context of Rivers' performance.

ANALYSIS

Repetition

Comedians use repetition for emphasis and rhythm. Norrick (1992) has distinguished mechanical repetition (reproduction of exact words) from creative repetition (creation of new words from the foregoing). Rivers uses both forms to great effect. In the initial part of her Christmas tree routine, the mechanical repetition of 'up' and 'gorgeous' are meant to co-create with the audience a mental picture of a Christmas tree, as regards supposed acceptable height and aesthetics:

(I) *I got a two-storey high Christmas tree [... gesturing upwards] up up up up up up- gorgeous gorgeous gorgeous.* (Part 1, 7:45-8:31)

More comprehensively, in the following excerpt in which she rounds off her performance (in Part 2), Rivers creatively deploys repetition in a restatement of three expressions— 'look at the person', 'C'mon', 'I'm so glad'— in the process of physically and linguistically yielding some ground to the audience in the scripting of the joke.

(II) *I want you to all* <u>*stop*</u> *and* ***look at the person*** *you're with and I want you to say* ***I'm so glad.*** *We never do this. We, we're always complaining. Look at whoever you're with. Oh see. Exactly****I'm so glad. C'mon, look at the person. C'mon****don't look at me.****Look at the person****This is not* <u>*fucking hard.*</u>***Look at the person.****We're gonna say it three times. This is what life is all about One,****I'm so glad. C'mon****guys.****I'm so glad****(…)****I'm glad****(…)****I'm so glad****(…) I'm not you.* (Part 2, 5:29-6:11)

The expression, 'C'mon' (abbreviated form of 'Come on') said three times, reveals a transition from admonition (in the first two occurrences) to frantic urging (in the last occurrence), to reveal Rivers' intention to convince her audience to cooperate with her. This intention is furthered by the mild directive, 'Look at the person', with which Rivers requests members of the audience to perform a specific action, looking at another. The directive contains a creative repetition in 'Look at whoever you're with', which rephrases the preceding, 'Look at the person you're with'. Most importantly, the joke's content lies essentially in the repetition of 'I'm so glad'. This emphatic utterance, said six times in the joke's setup, is used initially to suggest or anticipate affiliation, only to surprise the audience as disaffiliation, when taken with the punchline ('I'm not you').

Moreover, the excerpt (II), reveals Rivers' repetitive use of deixis for anchoring her relationship with the live audience. This is especially obvious in her deployment of three major types of person deixis— 'I', 'me', 'you'. The first person singular pronoun 'I' has two distinct referents, Rivers and her audience (as a collectivity or as individual): the former sense is instantiated twice (the first two mentions), the latter, seven times (all the other mentions). Also, in the five instances of 'you', the first four refer to the audience as a unit while the last signals any member of the audience sitting beside the speaker or deictic centre. And there are four instances of 'we', all inclusive-we forms. As such, the shift in deictic centre, from comedian to audience, and the deployment of inclusive-we forms underscore addressivity in the joke.

Disfluency

Disfluency occurs when a comedian, in the process of telling a joke or reacting to comments made by the audience, makes a slip and tries to recover as quickly as possible. This is enacted in false starts, incomplete utterances, and repetition of words. Disfluency has been found to encourage the audience's attention and participation as well as the comedian's timing (Schwarz 2010: 143). In excerpt (III)—a preface to Rivers' joke about the longevity of men's sexual life in contrast to women's— Rivers' first utterance is incomplete, her second utterance which should have completed the first is more incomplete, and the third is a reordered utterance correcting the false start in the second utterance.

(III) *Men don't know... Men. Nothing bothers men.* (Part 2, 1:20-1:26)

In a longer excerpt (IV), the three markers of disfluency, identified above, are obvious.

(IV) *(1)Because you know what (2)because age (3)because you all (4)It's a young audience (5)You know it's like age (6)And it will happen to all of you (7)Ha ha ha (8)As the body drops (9)My breast (10) I can have a mammogram and a pedicure at the same time.* (Part 2, 0:08-0:35)

Apart from utterances (4), (6), and (7), all the others could be read as false starts or incomplete utterances, since the propositions they are supposed to convey are incomplete. Yet, the audience fills in the gaps to recover the meanings of the said utterances, most probably because of Rivers' previous and frequent engagement with the issues of age and self-image.

Timing

Although in the wide sense, timing encapsulates the overall structure and tempo of conversational humour (Norrick, 2001), it is operationalised here in a narrow sense to mean a deliberate use of pause and rhythm to control comic performance (Double, 2014). As noted by Double (2014: 373) Joan Rivers considers the pause the major index of timing in comic performance. And so it is no surprise that the data present a marked deployment of pauses.

In stand-up comedy, the pause is a rhetorical strategy of timing which affords the comedian the opportunity to think about want to say next, to give the audience time to predict or imagine what the comedian will say next, to heighten the effect of a switch in direction between what the comedian will say and what the audience expected, to increase the intensity of laughter, and to strengthen the punchline (when it precedes the punchline) (Double, 2014; Schwarz, 2010). Rivers puts the pause to these uses, to a greater or less extent.

At the very beginning of the performance, she pokes fun at celebrities, present and non-present in her audience. She does this through a strategic deployment of pause to achieve humour, most prominently, by surprising her audience about what she says about the celebrities. While in (V) she 'combines a joke about [Angelina] Jolie's adoption of African orphans with a joke about anorexia' (Matte and McFadyen, 2011: 165), in (VI) she ridicules Katie Holmes (the referent of 'she' is contextually retrieved from previous discourse).

(V) *You want a thin starving black child? [...] How about Nicole Ritchie?* (Part 1, 4.40-4.47)

(VI) *She is so unhappy. She never talks [...] but watch her eyes. She blinks [...] SOS, SOS, SOS.* (Part 1, 5.25-5.32)

As such, in (V), the pause conveys the element of surprise, as the audience's expectation is defeated as regards an example of an underfed child. However, in (VI), the audience's expectation is heightened about why a non-dumb person will never talk (first pause) and what such a person blinks about (second pause). A slightly different situation of pause meaning is presented in (VII), where the pause indicates an allowance for the audience to predict what the comedian will say about the Irish, despite the stereotypical categorisation of these people (Irish).

(VII) *To James Nebbitt, Irish actor. A lot of Irish people (…) Are the bars closed?* (Part1, 1.50-1.55)

Even if the group 'Irish' is a recurrent butt of jokes in the United Kingdom, the comedian could select from so many stereotypical scripts about this group (e.g. dirtiness, stupidity, Catholicism) (Davies 1990), rather than the 'love for alcohol' or 'drunkenness' inferred. (Moreover, it is the activation of the 'communal lexicon' or 'set of word conventions in individual communities' (Clark 1997: 107), shared between comedian and audience, that would predict the audience's interpretation of 'bars' as 'places for drinking alcohol' rather than its numerous other senses).

Again, in the next excerpt, Rivers uses the pause to join the audience in sharing the humour of a preceding joke. Here, Rivers significantly pauses twice, in quick succession, while laughing about her immediately preceding joke about Heather McCartney's poor attempt at tap dance.

(VIII) *And [comedian's laughter] (…) By the way [comedian's laughter] (…) You are the audience over there.* (Part 1, 2.30:2.35)

The pauses, on either side of the utterance, 'by the way' have been strategically timed to allow for audience input in the creation of the joke. And with excerpt (IX), Rivers switches the direction of the audience's expectations by modifying their understanding of the lexeme, 'celebrity'.

(IX) *Hello, hello, hello. And there are lots of celebrities, theoretically (…) in the audience.* (Part 1, 1:00-1:05)

Here, after a modification of 'celebrities' with the adverbial, 'theoretically', she pauses significantly to make sure that the audience has understood her intention. This is not only intended to surprise the audience but also to activate an awareness of the possible relexification or redefinition of the lexeme, 'celebrity'.

Formulaicity

According to Schwarz (2010: 140), formulaic discourse markers are 'relatively fixed units of words which are often repeated during a performance' and which are capable of supporting both the speaker's and listener's processing simultaneously. Rivers' major formulaic utterance, 'It was just' or 'It's just', which come post-punchline, is used as an independent rhetorical form, twenty times, in the data.

Additionally, modified forms of this formula, are used to start a post-punchline utterance, whose completion comes after the predicted audience laughter, on three occasions: first, when she mocks the sincerity of Angelina Jolie's desire to make people happy when she (Angelina) is dating Jennifer Aniston's husband (X); second, when she emphasises how much her parents hated her (XI); and, lastly, in her (edited) attempt to introduce another comedian (Patrick Kielty, a guest comedian, according to Lockyer, [2011: 116]) (XII):

(X) *It's just [audience laughter] makes sense to me.* (Part 1, 4:10)
(XI) *They just [audience laughter] hated me.* (Part 1, 6:23)
(XII) *He's just [audience laughter] adorable.*

This high incidence of Rivers' formula (used twenty-times in just sixteen minutes of performance) affords the audience the opportunity to predict, and thus co-produce, its regular occurrence and almost automatic, post-punchline placement.

Paralanguage

Paralinguistics concerns how a speaker communicates his/her intentions with non-verbal device, which could include any or all of voice dynamics, facial expressions, gestures, movements. Since stand-up comedy situates the comedian before a live audience, comedians necessarily compliment their utterances with paralinguistic content. Research has shown that comedians need to alternate their voice so as to invest specific utterances with special meanings or emphases (e.g. Schwarz 2010).

Right from the onset of her performance, Rivers deploys intonation to meaningful effect, using both the falling and rising tunes to achieve emphases. For example, she starts her performance with excerpt (IXa), a repeated form of (IX) but with different emphasis.

(IXa) *Hello, hello, hello. And there are lots of celebrities,* ↓***theoretically****(…) in the audience.* (Part 1, 1:00-1:05)

Here, she switches her voice to a different tone, a falling tune, to emphasise the word 'theoretically'. She, thus, uses intonation to invite the audience to give special attention to the denotation conveyed by the modification of 'there are lots of celebrities' with 'theoretically'. On the other hand, she sometimes switches to rising intonation for achieving the same effect as in (IXa.). This is evident in (XIII), an excerpt which prefaces her routine about the importance of looks, where she deploys rising intonation to make the audience see where her discourse focus lies:

(XIII) ↑***Looks count****. Education puh.* ↑***Looks count.****This is my message Great Britain.* (Part 1, 9.05-9.07)

The superiority of good looks to education is thus offered, both linguistically and paralinguistically, to the audience, which is more shocked than amused, since it replies more with noise than laughter.

One major way in which Rivers deploys intonation is via voice adoption. Rutter (1997: 234-236) has demarcated two types of (comedian's) voices in stand-up comedy: 'voice as costume' (the comedian uses a different voice for the whole performance) and 'voice as prop' (the comedian changes to a different voice for a short period of time). In the data, Rivers uses only the latter. In the two instances, highlighted in excerpt (XIV), she tries to mimic the manner in which a referent could have made an utterance, all in an attempt to make her audience accept the reality of her message. In the joke, she relates how much her parents hated her.

(XIV) *My parents hated me, ok? (…) We're all gonna hear the story around here [in a babyish voice] (1)* ***'My parents hated me too'*** *My parent, all I ever heard all I ever heard growing up was [in a stern voice, gesturing like an adult talking down to a kid] (2)'* ***Why can't you be like your cousin Sheila*** *?* ↑***why can't you be like your cousin Sheila****?'Sheila had died at birth. They just hated me.* (Part 1, 6:10-6:20)

Here, she adopts two different voices, labelled (1) and (2), respectively. In (1) she uses a babyish voice to rubbish anybody else's claim of having had equally unfriendly parents, while in (2), she deploys a harsh, uncompromising voice to enact her parents' rejection of her. The contrast in the voicing of (1) and (2), on the one hand, and that between the pitches of the repeated utterances of (2), on the other, are meant to ensure the audience's uptake of the value of her voice adoption.

Also, Rivers uses gestures and movements as paralinguistic devices either to the audience's shared knowledge or to significantly compliment the linguistics of her jokes. Related to the first situation, she makes a marked use gestures and movements to identify the nightmarish situation of a woman having to endure five hours of sex in her joke about the longevity of men's sex life (Part 2, 1:20-3:12). As such, she and the audience share the burden of giving meaning to her performance. Regarding the second observation, Peacock's (2011) analysis of Rivers' joke about being the only Jewish kid in a Catholic neighbourhood (Part 1, 6:44-8:33) is succinct. Applying Kowzan's semiotic model to the joke, Peacock (2011:131) identifies Rivers' use of word, tone, mime, gesture, and movement in the realisation of the joke, and reiterates the fact that 'the auditive and visual signs combine to convey optimum meaning in the funniest way'. Yet, the value of paralinguistics in Rivers' performance can only be acknowledged and responded to by an audience which understands it and whose understanding is anticipated by the comedian.

In the introduction of one of her long jokes, the one about Angelina Jolie (Part 1, 3:35-4.51) she tries to describe her (Angelina Jolie), by identifying what she believes is one of her prominent features:

(XV) *Also, Angelina Jolie … Is she here? Look for a woman with big phh [gestures to her lips] Men love that [holds her lips together with her right hand]. Like pelican lips.* (Part 1, 3:37- 3: 42)

As such, Rivers not only emphasises the large size of Angelina's lips by comparing them with those of the pelican (bird), she also makes sure that her (Rivers') lips and hands accentuate the description.

Parenthetical Expression

Rivers hedges her utterances intermittently with parenthetical expressions intended for making her expressions more explicit and contextually enriched. For instance, in the short excerpt that follows, from her joke about being sexually attractive, her parenthetical utterance indicates her reason for keeping sanitary pads in her purse.

(XVI) *I'm telling you till this day I carry* ***because no man will look at you if they think you're over*** *I'm telling you I still carry Tampon in my purse.* (Part 1, 9:36-9.52)

And in the long joke about her childhood, the parenthetical expressions, numbered and highlighted, are intended for wooing the audience into having an interest in, and endorsing the veracity of her story.

(XVII) *I had a very bad childhood and that's because (1)* ***and I'm sure none of you give a damn*** *I was the only Jewish kid (2)* ***this is the absolute truth*** *growing up in an all-Catholic neighbourhood. (3)* ***You know what's that*** *? Only Jewish kid in a Catholic neighbourhood. (4)* ***You know what that's like?*** (Part 1, 6:44-6.58)

Here, she puts four utterances to parethentical use: (1) and (2) functioning as hedges, (3) and (4), as rhetorical questions. As such, her rhetorical emphasis on Jewishness surrounded by Catholicism and her efforts at enriching the knowledge of her audience about this asymmetry, foreground her positioning of her audience as a "not-Jewish" entity (Mock, 2011: 103). And since Rivers is known for projecting in her previous comedy acts a Jewish autobiographical persona (Horowitz, 1997; Mock, 2011), her comedy can be said to be historical addressive.

Figurative Language

Generally speaking, figurative language encompasses any utterance or statement which intentionally deviates from literalness or common usage made with the intention of emphasising, clarifying, or embellishing meaning. Rivers' abundant use of figurative language makes her message more pungent and her act more memorable. Specifically, we find instances of sarcasm, irony, allusion, pun and hyperbole. In excerpt (XVIII), she sarcastically presents love as infidelity, using a member of her audience as an example.

(XVIII) E*amon Holmes, where are you? Oh my joy, he is here. Where is the wife? I want you to know your husband loves you very … very much. Whenever, he's making out with other women when he climaxes he says your name.* (Part 1, 0:35-0:43)

It is conventional to think that a loving husband would stick to his partner and will not engage in extra-marital affairs. However, Rivers' humorously twists this common knowledge to imply that a husband could still be regarded as loving yet unfaithful, as long as his wife's name is always in his mouth. The emphatic stress on the adverb of degree 'very' to qualify the quality of a socially-acceptable behaviour (love), in the joke's set up, is set against the plain rendition of the joke's punchline. Notably though, the joke is co-constructed by Joan Rivers and the Holmes, in an interplay of comedian-audience linguistic and paralinguistic exchange. As the camera reveals, Holmes wife giggles and holds the arm of her husband lovingly, when Rivers makes the utterance that serves as the joke's set up (I want you … much). However, rather than frown or display any form of disaffection as a reaction to the punchline, Mrs. Holmes goes a step further in overtly showing affection to her husband by kissing him on the cheek. This supplementary paralinguistic act signifies Mrs. Holmes's uptake (that she understands the sarcasm intended, implies that she is willing and able to respond to and complete the joke) and thus, foregrounds the addressive identity and pragmatic force (or effect) of the joke.

Again, in this short joke, in her reaction to a text-message sent to her cell-phone from a fan wanting to know how she had maintained her slim figure despite her old age, she sarcastically depicts fat women as societal rejects who are loved only by the people who keep in business.

(XIX) *Because these big fat ladies sit and cry. And they go like 'Nobody loves me'. But that's not true. The butcher loves them and the baker loves them.* (Part 2, 6.12-6.18)

Here, Rivers ridicules obese and overweight women by claiming that they are loved only by the same people (butcher and baker) whose activities (producing beef, bread, and confectionaries, all containing fatty and high cholesterol foods which induce obesity) make them unloved by the rest of the society. She thus, by the way, uses humour to reinforce the Western cultural preference for slim women.

In another joke, Rivers combines irony, sarcasm and allusion in satirising Angelina Jolie, an American actress:

(XX) *Also Angelina Jolie is a very good friend of mine who is very charitable and lovely … All she wants to do is do good for people And she's been saying to me If I can just make one person happy Joan, I'll die satisfied. And I say, easy, just give Jennifer Aniston back her husband. It's just.*

Here, she alludes to Angelina Jolie's romantic relationship with Jennifer Aniston's husband (at that time), Brad Pitt. Attardo (2001: 114) posits that irony is inferentially processed and suggests 'relevance' and 'antiphrastic/antonymous assumption' as determinants of the its value:

In other words, after having recognized a part of a text as ironical, the hearer assumes that the maxim of relevance holds and that the relevance of the irony lies in the direction of an antiphrastic meaning (i.e. in the direction of the opposite of what the speaker is saying) with a special emphasis on S's [Speaker's] value judgements.

As such, since the words 'charitable and lovely' and 'All she wants is to do good for people' would be inappropriate for qualifying a woman dating somebody else's husband, the audience would process these (isolated) utterances as ironical, based both on the utterances' meaning as well as a mutual, shared understanding of socially-sanctioned propriety.

Also, Rivers' instantiates both forms of the third party in this joke. First, her claim 'remembers' or recalls the rumours and previous media claims about the Brad-Angelina romance. Second, her words appeal to the sanction of the audience, here functioning as the superaddressee, for the veracity of her allegation (of Brad Pitt's infidelity). And since the audience only responds with laughter, and not with any expression of disagreement (for example, heckling), the dialogic exchange is established as co-constructed.

Rivers makes a profuse use of hyperbole in her jokes. Her extravagant exaggerations can be found all over the data, most especially in her engagement with the (sub)topics of looks, age, and men's sexual lives. Decontextualised examples include Mother Teresa's ugliness ('Even lepers were throwing their fingers at her' [Part 1, 9.00] and '36-hour erection for a 90-year-old man' [Part 2, 1.56]. More explicitly, in the jokes to follow, Rivers enacts her essentially negative comic persona (Mintz 1987) both as a 'whiner' (a female comic persona who exploits self-deprecatory humour to make the audience feel safe or superior) and as a 'bitch' (an angry female comic persona who uses humour subversively) (Gilbert 2004).

In excerpt (XXI), Rivers exaggerates her lack of sex appeal by claiming that the sight of her (impliedly naked) body not only disgusts peepers, but also that her gynaecologist (someone she pays for doing their job) cannot bear the sight of her.

(XXI) *Looks count. I've had no sex appeal and it has screwed me up for life. Peeping Toms look at my window and pull down the shade. You have no idea My gynaecologist examines me by telephone.* (Part 1, 9:05-9:22)

In the first joke, she claims that her breasts have fallen so much that they reached her ankles and might be needing an x-ray, in anticipation of a probable surgery:

(XXII) *I can have a mammogram and a pedicure at the same time.* (Part 2, 0:10)

In the next joke, she jokes about her ageing private part.

(XXIII) *If my mother had said to me, 'Joan, when you get old your vagina is gonna drop', it's a good thing, because you can have sex in the bedroom and still be watching TV in the living room.* (Part 2, 0:40-1.18)

The humorously unimaginable act, of having sex in a place and watching TV in another, seats deeply extravagant exaggeration.

And in excerpt (XXIV), the exaggerated feeling of abjection is pragmatically instantiated. Here, she implies that she no longer experiences her monthly period, based on the mutually accessible medical knowledge that being over seventy years old, she must have reached her menopause.

(XXIV)*Do you know when it changes for a woman? When you no longer have a period. I'm telling you**till this day**I carry because no man will look at you if they think you're over. I'm telling you I**still**carry Tampon in my purse. When no one's looking at me I open my purse and a Tampon drops out. And I oops ... I can just, die.**It's been so long**if I ever got a Tampon I won't know which end to put it. It is just.* (Part 1, 9:36-9:56 and Part 2, 0:01-0:08)

She claims that she still carries sanitary pad (Tampon) with her wherever she goes, so as to look sexually attractive to and available for men. With 'till this day', 'still', and 'it's been so long', she not only triggers the knowledge she shares with her audience about her old age she also expects the audience to conjecture that at her age she might no longer be sexually attractive and would thus need to make conscious efforts to attract men. And to remind the audience of the jocular context of her utterance, Rivers' punchline contradicts her setup: although she is old she wants to hoodwink men to think she is young and available by carrying sanitary pad around, yet believes she won't know how to use the pad (because she's too old to have any use for it).

Moreover, Rivers deploys puns to great effect, based on an assumption that her audience can recover the meaning successfully. Norrick (2003) refers to punning as a type of word play which may function either to amuse or to verbally attack. Rivers uses her puns to amuse. Her unique neologisms, 'gocksuckers' (Part 1,1:10), 'overeaters anonymous' (Part 2, 4:35), 'viagra plus' (Part 2, 1:35), convey different types of lexical creativity. For example, gock in "gocksuckers" homophonically and homographically instantiates Gok (the person with whom Rivers was to do the business of producing lollipops) just as the whole word ("gocksuckers") plays on "cocksuckers", a coinage whose sexual connotation will predictably amuse the audience. The compound expression, 'overeaters anonymous' is ironical, since Rivers uses it to refer to self, while trying to answer a question asked about how she is still lanky despite her (old) age. Given that overeaters are supposed to be fat (and she is not), I guess the audience's response of laughter to the expression will be more of bewilderment or surprise rather than an expression of uptake, since the conventional sense of 'overeaters' has been invalidated. However, with 'viagra plus', the surprise element is less curious. Although Rivers' mention of the expression is greeted with silence at first, the explanation she gives to it (as a drug that enhances sex or erection for more hours than ever thought of) validates the literal meanings of 'viagra; and 'plus', which makes the punning easier to identify.

Direct Address to Audience

This is an unmistakable linguistic technique through which Rivers integrates the audience into her performance. The technique is enacted both minimally and maximally. At the minimal level, this addressivity index is initiated by Rivers and lexically realised both as a rhetorical question, 'Am I wrong?' (Part 1, 8:26, Part 2, 1:23), and as a polite request, 'Let's talk to each other here' (Part 2, 8:53). However, it is in the several instances of Rivers' conversation with the audience that this linguistic feature becomes most prominent.

Immediately she comes on stage, Rivers begins the show by telling the audience the cost and economic importance of her furcoat:

(XXV) *A hundred and sixty-fifty pounds. I have to show it to you or it doesn't go off my income tax.* (Part 1: 0.01-0.04)

She then proceeds to single out celebrities in the audience and engages them in some conversation. The celebrities are Eammon Holmes (and wife), Gok Wan, Andrea Corr, James Nesbitt, and Craig Revel Horwood, arranged in the order in which they are recognised. She cracks jokes which indicate her knowledge of the professions or vocations of the celebrities who respond either minimally (gesturally) or maximally (by responding with relevant utterances). Corr and Nesbitt each respond with smiles, after raising their hands. Holmes and wife have the camera specially focused on them as they react to Rivers' comments in (XXVI) (This excerpt is repeated here since it illustrates a different feature).

(XXVI) *Eamonn Holmes, where are you? Oh my joy, he is here. Where is the wife? I want you to know your husband loves you very, very much. Whenever, he's making out with other women when he climaxes he says your name.* (Part 1, 0:35-0:43)

As shown in the video clip, Holmes and wife nod their heads in agreement after the utterance "very, very much" but giggle, laugh and kiss, at the end of the excerpt.

However, Wan and Horwood provide verbal responses: let's illustrate with Wan's.

(XXVII) **Rivers:** *Where is Gok? Gok, Gok Wan, where are you?*

(Gok raises his hand)
Rivers: *How are you?*
Wan: *Fabulous. Men you look gorgeous*
Rivers: *I look gorgeous. (Holding her coat) well it's yours*
(Wan's and audience's laughter)
...
Rivers: *But it's lovely to see you.*
Wan: *Lovely to see you too. (Part 1, 0:48-1:20)*

In this conversation, Rivers addresses Wan directly, and by humorously that he owns the coat she wears, she triggers the larger audience's background knowledge of Gok Wan's identity as a fashion icon.

Since Rivers' pseudo-conversations with the audience (as a whole) and some of its members constitute part of the scripts and routines which attract laughter and other forms of audience feedback, the co-construction of the jokes by comedian and audience becomes unmistakable.

DISCUSSION AND CONCLUSION

The analysis of (this twin instance) Joan Rivers' comedy has revealed her engagement with the audience in the production of humour on basically social issues and specifically, issues of age, sex, relationship, parenthood, and self-image. To accomplish this, she not only deploys the specific linguistic and paralinguistic resources (discussed in the sub-sections above) but also involves the audience in the co-construction of her comedy.

Specifically, she begins her performance by 'working the room' (Mintz 1987: 78; Double, 2014), albeit minimally, making utterances about six specifically-mentioned members of the audience, thereby setting the tone for the dialogic humour to follow. With repetitions and disfluencies, Rivers reiterates and reorders the content of her jokes to enhance better audience understanding. For example, her incomplete utterances are used to invite the audience to fill in "the blank spaces", based both on comedian-audience shared knowledge of the world and their awareness of her comedic style and stage persona. Her use of the formula, 'It's just', is a deliberate verbal style with she became a signature practice. Rivers' use of pause has foregrounded the value of this rhetorical strategy for heightening the effect of the joke or refocusing the direction of the audience's thought. Notably, she hasn't used the pause as a discourse-filler, to allow her some time to plan her next utterance, as the literature has often suggested. This underscores Rivers' use of pause as another signature practice.

Moreover, Rivers has deployed parenthetical expressions to make her audience active listeners, who would be expected to react in certain ways, willy-nilly to the utterances which the expressions hedge. Her deployment of exaggeration dwells greatly on incongruity, which she expects the audience to identify effortlessly. Notably, her exaggeration of negative female stereotypes (through which she self-disparages) are meant not just to reduce the sociocultural distance between herself and her audience, that she is very much one of her signature practices (Lockyer, 2011) but also to engage the audience in conversation, by reinforcing or interrogating its extant beliefs. And Rivers' utilisation of paralanguage has been for supplementary and complementary functions. This informs Peacock's (2011) holistic view of the nature of her performance (in the data) as a significant combination of the auditive and the visual

It has been shown that the Rivers' performance has successfully and efficiently connected speaker (comedian), listener (audience) and third person/superaddressee (non-present audience or previous discourses or voice of authority) in a meaningful nexus. Rivers is almost always the speaker except occasionally when she yields the conversational floor to members of the audience. The listener is either a member of the audience as selected by Rivers (the celebrities she ridicules or engages in conversation) or the audience as a unit. The third party/parties are either members of the audience at large, that is, the non-present butts of Rivers' jokes or the previous discourses on the topics of her jokes or the voice of authority (of ethnic stereotypes, of Western culture, of gender stereotypes). This latter part of the superaddressse explains the dialogic understanding with which Rivers expects her audience to activate the meanings embedded in the ethnic and gender stereotypes, concerning the Irish, the body image of women and fidelity in marriage, respectively. Moreover, Rivers has a way of repeating her jokes (like all comedians), especially those that relate to her body image, much in the self-deprecatory tradition. As such, her words implicitly remember earlier discourses about this topic, in the tradition of the historicity of addressivity.

Significantly, Rivers also addresses third persons, in both senses identified by Morson (2009). Third persons or superaddressees are enacted as the audience, the media, and/or as an invisible God-like authority. And because she shifts the focus of her humor quite randomly, her third persons change rapidly. When she jokes about herself or about others not in the audience, members of the live audience are the most significant third persons. When she focuses on women (their body images and especially on how they depreciate with age), men, the Western culture and a personified God are projected as superaddressees. Most tellingly, Rivers' utterances, concerning the actions and identities of Hollywood stars (Angelina Jolie, Brad Pitt, Jennifer Aniston, Nicole Richie, Britney Spears, Katie Holmes), engage not only members of the audience but also the rumours and stories in the popular media in dialogue. Also, Rivers' direct address to her audience, minimally and maximally, instantiate an involvement of her audience, as co-owners of her scripts and as active addressees. As a macro speech act, Rivers' engagement with topics like age, sex, relationships, parenthood and self-image, especially as life stories and biographical anecdotes (Blackburn, 2013) has been well documented and has carved for her a stage persona. Since such an engagement has become recurrent, the utterances with which she verbalises such topics can be said to remember earlier discourses about such topics, and so trigger the historical identities of such utterances. Rivers' performance thus dwells on Bakhtin's concept of addressivity, in all its ramifications.

In sum, Rivers makes an abundant use of linguistic and paralinguistic forms, which instantiate Bakhtin's notion of 'addressivity' and indicate its amenability to stand-up comedy. And even at the death of its performer, Rivers' comedy still affords ample space for research into contemporary stand-up comedy.

REFERENCES

Attardo, S. (2001). *Humorous texts: A semantic and pragmatic analysis.* Berlin: Mouton de Gruyter. doi:10.1515/9783110887969

Bakhtin, M. M. (1981). *The dialogic imagination: Four essays* (C. Emerson & M. Holquist, Trans.). Austin, TX: University of Texas Press.

Blackburn, R. E. (2013). *Fem and funny: Three women who changed the face of stand-up comedy.* (Unpublished MFA thesis). Virginia Commonwealth University, Richmond, VA.

Clark, H. H. (1996). *Using language.* Cambridge, UK: Cambridge University Press. doi:10.1017/CBO9780511620539

Davies, C. (1990). *Ethnic humor around the world: A comparative analysis.* Bloomington, IN: Indiana University Press.

Double, O. (2014). *Getting the joke: The inner workings of stand-up comedy* (2nd ed.). London: Bloomsbury.

Filani, I. (2015). Stand up comedy as activity type. *International Journal of Humor Research, 4*(1), 73–97.

Filani, I. (2015). Discourse types in stand-up comedy performances: An example of Nigerian stand-up comedy. *The European Journal of Humour Research, 3*(1), 41–60.

Furukawa, T. (2011). *Humor-ing the Local: Multivocal Performance in Stand-up Comedy in Hawai'i.* (Unpublished PhD dissertation). University of Hawai'i.

Gilbert, J. (2004). *Performing marginality: Humor, gender, and cultural critique.* Detroit, MI: Wayne University Press.

Gray, F. (1994). *Women and laughter.* Charlottesville, VA: University Press of Virginia. doi:10.1007/978-1-349-23275-8

Horowitz, S. (1997). *Queens of comedy: Lucille Ball, Phyllis Diller, Carol Burnett, Joan Rivers, and the new generation of funny women.* Amsterdam: Gordon and Breach.

Katayama, H. (2008). Humor in Manzai stand-up comedy: A historical and comparative analysis. *The International Journal of the Humanities, 6*(1), 213–223.

Khan, M. (2014). *Reflecting On Joan Rivers Rant On Israel Gaza Conflict: Palestinians 'Deserve To Be Dead'.* Retrieved on November 27, 2015 from www.ibtimes.co.uk

Li, C. (2014). Two immigrant humor styles of stand-up comedy: A linguistic perspective. In *Proceedings of International Conference on Education, Language, Art and Intercultural Communication (ICELAIC-14)* (pp. 276-279). Atlantis Press. doi:10.2991/icelaic-14.2014.70

Limon, J. (2000). *Stand-up comedy in theory, or, abjection in America*. Durham, NC: Duke University Press. doi:10.1215/9780822380504

Lockyer, S. (2011). From toothpick legs to dropping vaginas: Gender and sexuality in Joan Rivers' stand-up comedy performance. *Comedy Studies*, *2*(2), 113–123. doi:10.1386/cost.2.2.113_1

Mcllvenny, P., Mettovaara, S., & Tapio, R. (1992). I really wanna make you laugh: Stand-up comedy and audience response. In M.K. Suijanen & A. Kulkki- Nieminen (Eds.), *Folia, Fennistica and Linguistica:Proceedings of the Annual Finnish Symposium*.

Mey, J. (2000). *When voices clash: A study in literary pragmatics*. Berlin: Mouton de Gruyter.

Mills, B. (2011). "A pleasure working with you": Humour theory and Joan Rivers. *Comedy Studies*, *2*(2), 151–160. doi:10.1386/cost.2.2.151_1

Mintz, L. E. (1985). Standup comedy as social and cultural mediation. *American Quarterly, 37*(1), 71-80.

Mock, R. (2011). Really Jewish? Joan Rivers Live at the Apollo. *Comedy Studies*, *2*(2), 101–111. doi:10.1386/cost.2.2.101_1

Moriarty, M. (2011). Minority languages and performative genres: The case of Irish language stand-up comedy. *Journal of Multilingual and Multicultural Development*, *32*(6), 547–559. doi:10.1080/01434632.2011.604420

Morris, P. (1994). *The Bakhtin reader: Selected writings of Bakhtin, Medvedev, Voloshinov*. New York: Oxford University Press.

Morson, G. S. (2009). Addressivity. In J. Mey (Ed.), *Concise Encyclopedia of Pragmatics* (2nd ed.; pp. 13–16). Oxford, UK: Elsevier.

Norrick, N. (2000). *Conversational narratives*. John Benjamins. doi:10.1075/cilt.203

Norrick, N. (2001). On the conversational performance of narrative jokes: Towards an account of timing. *Humor: International Journal of Humor Research*, *14*(3), 255–274. doi:10.1515/humr.2001.003

Norrick, N. R. (1992). Repetition in canned jokes and spontaneous conversational joking. *Humor: International Journal of Humor Research*, *6*, 285–302.

Peacock, L. (2011). Joan Rivers—reading the meaning. *Comedy Studies*, *2*(2), 125–137. doi:10.1386/cost.2.2.125_1

Rivers, J. (1992). *Still talking*. New York: Avon Books.

Rutter, J. (1997). *Stand-up as interaction: Performance and audience in comedy venues*. (Unpublished doctoral dissertation). University of Salford.

Schwarz, J. (2010). *Linguistic aspects of verbal humor in stand-up comedy*. (Unpublished doctoral dissertation). University of Saarland.

Tsang, W. K., & Wong, M. (2004). Constructing a shared Hong Kong identity in comic discourse. *Discourse & Society*, *15*(6), 767–785. doi:10.1177/0957926504046504

Waisanen, D. (2011). Jokes inviting more than laughter… Joan Rivers' political-rhetorical world view. *Comedy Studies*, *2*(2), 139–150. doi:10.1386/cost.2.2.139_1

Yus, F. (2002). Stand-up comedy and cultural spread: The case of sex roles. *Babel AFIAL*, *10*, 245–292.

Zoglin, R. (2008). *Comedy at the edge: How stand-up in the 1970s changed America*. New York, NY: Bloomsbury.

ADDITIONAL READING

Brodie, I. (2008). Stand-up comedy as a genre of intimacy. *Ethnologies*, *30*(2), 153–180. doi:10.7202/019950ar

Dean, G. (2000). *Step by step to standup comedy*. Portshmouth, NH: Heinemann.

DeCamp, E. (2015). Humoring the audience: Performance strategies and persuasion in Midwestern American stand-up comedy. *Humor: International Journal of Humor Research*, *28*(3), 449–467. doi:10.1515/humor-2015-0067

Fang, Z. (2011). An adaptation-relevance model analysis on verbal humor in Zhou Li-bo'Shanghai-style stand-up comedy.

Glick, D. J. (2007). Some performative techniques of stand-up comedy: An exercise in the textuality of temporalization. *Language & Communication*, *27*(3), 291–306. doi:10.1016/j.langcom.2007.01.003

Greenbaum, A. (1999). Stand-up comedy as rhetorical argument: An investigation of comic culture. *Humor: International Journal of Humor Research*, *12*(1), 33–46. doi:10.1515/humr.1999.12.1.33

Miles, T. (2014). No greater foe? Rethinking emotion and humour, with particular attention to the relationship between audience members and stand-up comedians. *Comedy Studies*, *5*(1), 12–19.

Myers, L. (2011). 'It's about expecting the unexpected': Live stand-up comedy from the audiences' perspective. Retrieved on December 2, 2015 from dspace.brunel.ac.uk

Nilsen, A. P., & Nilsen, D. L. F. (2000). *Encyclopedia of 20th century humor*. Phoenix: Oryx Press.

Quirk, S. (2011). Containing the Audience: The 'Room'in Stand-Up Comedy. *Participations: Journal of Audience & Reception Studies*, *8*, 220–238.

Scarpetta, F., & Spagnolli, A. (2009). The interactional context of humor in stand-up comedy. *Research on Language and Social Interaction*, *42*(3), 210–230. doi:10.1080/08351810903089159

Wells, P., & Bull, P. (2007). From politics to comedy: A comparative analysis of affiliative audience responses. *Journal of Language and Social Psychology*, *26*(4), 321–343. doi:10.1177/0261927X07306978

Wilson, N. (2011). Divisive Comedy: A Critical Examination of Audience Power. *Participations: Journal of Audience & Reception Studies*, *8*, 276–291.

Yus, F. (2004). Pragmatics of humorous strategies in El dub de la comedia. *Current trends in the pragmatics of Spanish, 123*, 319.

Yus, F. (2005). Dave Allen's stand-up monologues: An epidemiological approach. Thistles. A Homage to Brian Hughes. Essays In Memoriam", ISBN, 84-609. Alicante: University of Alicante, Department of English Studies.

KEY TERMS AND DEFINITIONS

Addressivity: The discourse characteristic of an utterance to respond to a previous utterance or anticipate an utterance in the future.

Audience: The consumer(s) of stand-up comedy, whether present or non-present at the venue of the performance.

Mikhail Bakhtin: A 20th century Russian thinker usually identified as the originator of the term, "addressivity".

Joan Rivers: (1933-2014) Popular Jewish-American stand-up comedian.

Linguistic-Pragmatics: The study of natural language (as demarcated from fictional/literary language) as used in context.

Punchline: The final or climactic part of a joke, where the audience's expectation is usually subverted.

Stand-up Comedy: An encounter enacted by a standing performer behaving comically and/or saying funny things directly to an audience, often through a microphone.

APPENDIX: TRANSCRIPTION PECULIARITIES

Bold typeface: Utterance in focus.
Underlining: Emphasised utterance.
…: Irrelevant (for the discussion) part of the utterance(s).
(…): Marked pause.
?: Question intonation.
[ ]: Non-verbal or paralinguistic act by comedian.
'': Quoted speech or adopted voice.
(): Non-verbal or paralinguistic act by audience.
↓: Falling intonation.
↑: Rising intonation.

Chapter 13
Humour in Visual-Verbal Code-Pairing in Selected Comments on the Facebook Forum

M. T. Lamidi
University of Ibadan, Nigeria

ABSTRACT

Visual verbal texts can be interpreted from the perspective of multimodality and intertextuality. This chapter investigates the manner in which visual-verbal code-pairing in texts becomes humorous within specific contexts and the role of incongruity as a major ingredient of humour. Adopting a combination of visual semiotics theory, incongruity theory and superiority theory, the author analyzed 50 purposively sampled humorous texts on Facebook for the meaning and humour inherent in them. The author demonstrates that the two parts to the visual-verbal humour may constitute a composite whole, forming the unexpected portion, while the background to the joke serves as the expected.

The views and content expressed in this chapter are those of the author but not necessarily of the publisher and may contain some explicit ideas and concepts.

1. INTRODUCTION

A code is a mode of communication used in conveying a specific idea to people with whom one shares the same culture, background or knowledge. It is a 'social convention that links signs with meanings' (Potts 1996: 21); and 'consists of both signs and the rules and negotiations determining the context and the style of those signs as well as the possible combinations in order to build up more sophisticated messages' (Parsa & Parsa, 2002: 36). A code can be verbal, visual, gestural or symbolic. It is verbal when it is spoken or written, visual when it is an image or a picture that conveys meaning (e.g. a cartoon), gestural when body movements are used (as in sign language) and symbolic when signs and symbols are used as icons representing specific ideas.

DOI: 10.4018/978-1-5225-0338-5.ch013

Copyright © 2016, IGI Global. Copying or distributing in print or electronic forms without written permission of IGI Global is prohibited.

In multilingual societies, more than one language occurs among many codes used for communicating different messages. The codes may be spoken/written language, sign language, drum language, etc. However, there may be overlapping of languages and codes, such that both can be said to operate as language or code, since both are means of communication. For instance, verbal communication is a language code.

Codes are used in face-to-face communication as well as in online interaction. In virtual communities, the means (or codes) of communication, as should be expected, are also many and varied. The major means of communication on the Internet are written words, photographs/images, smilies/ emoticons, video/audio clips, etc. Sometimes, however, any of these may fall short of a poster's needs at a particular point; hence, forcing a recourse to the use of multiple or supplementary codes to convey intended messages. More importantly, posters on the web often use their creativity to conjure up images/pictures that approximate the ideas they want to express and for them to be understood by other readers. For instance, an image can take different forms: it can be an authentic photograph of an individual, a caricature of a person or just a cartoon. Sometimes, photographs may be edited, such that the head, nose, ear or mouth is bigger or smaller that the body; a photograph can be twisted to any form, using computer simulation (photoshop), just to communicate different and specific ideas or information.

Part of this creativity is what can be described as *visual-verbal code-pairing*. Visual-verbal code-pairing is a phenomenon where images and written words are creatively merged to give composite meaning in discourse (The concept is further explained in Section 3). In this sense, an image that represents an idea (visual) is used and supplemented with written words (verbal). In other words, neither the image nor the expression can be sufficient in the context in which both can be used; hence the collaboration.

The aspect of visual-verbal code-pairing in communication had, until now, escaped much rigorous scholarly scrutiny; and this study is a probe in this direction. Hence, this study deals with two codes co-occurring in a text, one paring with the other and completing/balancing its sense. In other words this study deals with the combination of an image (in form of photographs, cartoons, caricature, etc) and written expressions (largely in the English language) which are used to communicate specific ideas. In addition, one of the different functions of visual-verbal code-pairing is its use for humour. In this paper, we shall be dealing with how visual-verbal texts become humorous within specific contexts and the role of incongruity as a major ingredient of humour. Hence, the focus of this paper is to see how visual-verbal code-pairing is deployed to achieve humour on the Facebook Forum.

2. THE FACEBOOK FORUM

The Facebook Forum is a virtual community established by Mark Zuckerberg in 2004 (Delise, 2012). It is one of the very prominent social networks on the Internet (others are Twitter, Instagram, Nigeria Village Square, 2Go, Badoo and Nairaland) with over 800 million active users by 2011 estimates (Delise, 2012). The forum requires would-be members to register with their names and photographs. Members of the Facebook forum do a lot of things on the forum. These include posting information, thinking aloud about things that affect them, advertising, announcing events such as convocation, burial, wedding and naming ceremonies, connecting with friends and chatting with them openly or in private (through messages), passing comments on social events, etc. A topic can start with just a story, a picture or a video clip. Facebook members can access it from their various homes and pass comments on it. Such responses or comments can also be in different forms, usually through written words or pictures. The pictures can be monomodal or bimodal. Our interest in these comments is in the bimodal (visual-verbal) texts that evoke humour to readers. But first, what is humour?

3. HUMOUR

Several definitions of humour have been offered in the literature. According to Sen (2012), humour consists of jokes which elicit laughter or generate mirth. Crawford (1994: 57) defines humour as communication that brings positive cognitive response/emotions from listeners that are individuals or organisations. Jensen (2009) has also described humour as a social thing. It is considered a highly individual concept which is based on personal tastes and preferences as 'sense of humour may differ from person to person, and within the same person' (p2). This means that humour is not constant. It changes according to the context of situation. From the foregoing, Sen (2012) concludes that there is no single universally all-encompassing definition of humour. Hence, we shall take as our working definition the simple description of humour as communication which elicits amusement as a result of its incongruity with known facts.

Humour is also described as positive, negative or general. Cahill and Densham (2014) describe positive humour as 'affiliative and self-enhancing' and negative humour as 'self-defeating and aggressive'. In positive humour, individuals tell jokes and present funny anecdotes to play harmless practical jokes on colleagues and peers. Negative humour on the other hand is used to put down an individual or self. One may deprecate self to attract attention when delivering a lecture and use satire to tease a friend. Salal *et al.* (2002) identifies the third type, general humour, as neither negative nor positive. This type is plain humour, based on the general incongruity in the humour/text. These humour types occur in the data analysed in this study.

There are different forms of humour. These include jokes, satire, comedy, parody, caricature and sarcasm. *Ridicule* is a means of putting down another person. It can be in the form of taunt, derision, and mockery. *Satire* is used to poke fun at powerful people that are considered superior to the speaker. In a subtle manner, it presents them with a picture of themselves as seen by other people. *Sarcasm* is a form of ridicule in which people say the exact opposite of what they mean. It aims at humiliating the target. The focus of this study is on the nature of visual-verbal humour; how visual-verbal texts evoke humour.

Regardless of its form, humour in whatever form can be used for a variety of functions. One of these is that it is often expected to evoke laughter. However, it can either achieve this or fail woefully. This depends on the listener's (1) understanding of the text, (2) sense of humour and (3) disposition to the subject of the text. In the first case, if a person does not understand the text, laughter will not be elicited. Hence the joke will fall flat. In the second case, what someone considers to be humorous may not be humorous to another (Malone, 1980). In the third case, a joke may fail if the listener is the object of a joke, especially satire. Even when such jokes are funny to other people, s/he may not find it humorous at all.

Context is very important in understanding humour texts. Context can be defined as the environment where expressions become meaningful. Humour is located in a particular context. Hence, the listener to a humour text needs to be aware of the background to the humour, the participants involved and more importantly the incongruity in the whole scenario. It comes out of the ordinary, such as making strange faces, dressing awkwardly, making funny gestures, etc. Humour can be facilitated through verbal and non-verbal means. However, in virtual communities such as the Facebook Forum, both verbal and non-verbal forms often cooperate to provide humour.

3.1 The Humour Text

The humour text is the totality of humour that constitutes the joke. Scholars have different opinions about the structure of a humour text. First, Schiwarz (2010) has described it as having three components:

1. Build-up
2. Pivot
3. Punchline

In this structure, the build-up serves as the body of the joke and lays a foundation for the pivot. The pivot is the turning point in the joke; the point of divergence from the expected conclusion to the joke. Finally, the punchline concludes the joke and often presents the conflict or contrast. It therefore serves as the surprise element and accounts for the 'amusement and appreciation, normally expressed in general laughter.'(p65)

Berk (2005-06) has also described humour text as either a trifecta or a bifecta. 'Humour trifecta' are presented orally and contain three elements:

1. **Expected:** Serious set-up with commonly understood situation or context.
2. **Expected:** Build-up of tension.
3. Unexpected twist.

However, script humour has no build-up of tension, no element (b). It is a bifesta: the expected is followed directly by the unexpected. 'The punchline is the point of collision between two conflicting trains of thought: serious sentence meets unexpected ending. The shock is our recognition of incongruity' (Berk, 2005-06). Raskin's (1985) view seems to support 'humour bifesta'. Raskin says a humour text is 'a single joke carrying text' if the following conditions are met:

1. The text is compatible, fully or in part, with two different scripts.
2. The two scripts with which the text is compatible are opposite [...] (p. 99).

These two conditions match the description of humour bifesta above; since the two texts are opposites and are combined to form a meaningful text. However, Berk's 'expected' (a&b) in the trifesta can be easily merged into one; and Schwarts' 'pivot' is the 'build up' in Berk's. His 'punchline' also contrasts with Berk's punchline. Punchline in the former is the unexpected in the latter. Hence, one can suggest that the humour text contains only two parts but scholars have given them different names. In addition, the 'pivot' or 'punchline', referring to the point at which a twist occurs is not marked by any new expression and hence need not be named.

The visual-verbal humour text also aligns with Berk's bifesta and Raskin's description of humour text. Either part of the visual-verbal text can be the expected while the unexpected second part serves as the punchline. The meeting point is where the incongruity is set off for the punchline, but it is just a twist in expectation (not physically represented by words or phrases). Notice that the pattern is not the same for all pictures. In one case the punchline/incongruity might be the verbal text; in another, it might be the visual image. Everything depends on the creativity of the author of the text.

A further development of this structure is found in Jensen (2009) who credited Alison Rose with the development of three general features of incongruity-based humorous expressions

- Conflict between what is expected and what occurs in jokes.
- The conflict is caused by some ambiguity at some level of language.
- The punchline is surprising because it activates meaning which is not expected, since it is not compatible or coherent with the rest of the joke, or discourse.

This further development does not seem to apply to visual-verbal texts simply because there is no ambiguity in the text. As long as the picture is clear, the unexpected text from the two codes will serve as the punchline, which will then make the humour text amusing.

Nevertheless, Fearman (2014) has downplayed the role of incongruity in humour. He argues that in the processing of jokes, new theories no longer view surprise as such a necessary factor for a joke to be funny, 'it is the searching for an alternative schema that can generate funningness' (p10). The listener to a joke is said to be actively looking for the incongruity and possible other schemas, rather than waiting for the incongruity to present itself. Incongruity is therefore not surprising, but is expected (p10). Fearman's view here may be appropriate in a situation where the listener already knows that the speaker is telling a joke. In cases where the joke is spontaneous, coming out of the blue, the surprise element cannot be avoided. The major uniting form is the background and context. According to Critchley (2002: 67),'humour is local and a sense of humour is usually highly context-specific'. The background knowledge makes it possible to interpret it accurately.

4. VISUAL-VERBAL CODE-PAIRING, MULTIMODALITY AND INTERTEXTUALITY

The visual-verbal text can be interpreted from the perspective of multimodality and intertextuality. The visual code gives a particular meaning. One can see a photograph, interpret it and make deductions as to the import of the image. The verbal code (whether spoken or written) also gives a specific meaning. In communication, there are recognised sounds and orthography for specific languages. Once the orthography conforms to acceptable linguistic forms, the verbal expressions can be interpreted. As separate codes, they are monomodal and each has separate interpretations. However, the two codes can be combined to produce another meaning, different from the individual meanings the visual and verbal expressions had before the merger. When two or more codes are employed in conveying the same message, multimodality is involved. Multimodality is defined as the use and combination of different semiotic elements, including design, layout, images, photographs, film, color and scent (Zebrowska, 2014: 9). According to Kress and van Leeuwen (2001) multimodal texts are a product of the deployment of signs from more than one semiotic mode and they are subsequently integrated. Hence, the phenomenon of code-pairing becomes relevant. Since there is a transition from one code to another within the same text, multimodality may include code-pairing.

The phenomenon of code-pairing brings to mind the concept of code-switching. Code-switching has been defined as the switching from one language to another in the course of a sentence. It is also possible between a sign language and a spoken language (Hein, 2006). Beyond code-switching, however, code-pairing is being suggested for the phenomenon where two codes are used to convey meaning. Code-pairing entails the coming together of two different codes, say visual and verbal, in which case a code pairs up with another of a different type to balance or complete the meaning or sense of the first code. In this manner, the combined verbal and visual codes produce meanings in a compositional manner, with one part complementing the other; and each part conveying only part of the intended meaning. This means that there is complementarity between verbal and visual codes.

Code-pairing is different from code-switching/mixing in the sense that code-switching may be verbal, and still be contained in a code within the pair that is used for communication, usually the verbal part of code-pairing. In addition, code-pairing accommodates two structurally different codes (e.g. visual and verbal codes), but code-switching is restricted largely to verbal language codes (with the exception of verbal-sign language switching). Communication in code-pairing is a once-and-for-all thing in the sense that communication starts and ends with one episode of communication (i.e. a complete text). Conversely, code-switching may contain many episodes of communication, and more importantly, switches frequently occur. In code-pairing, only a twist-switch occurs between a visual code and a verbal code. However, one or more switches may occur within the verbal part of the code-paired message, but in a pictorial text, only a twist can occur. The word *twist* is adopted because it is not restricted to only the visual-verbal discord but also extends to visual-visual expected-unexpected pair.

There is also intertextuality between visual-verbal text and the context of its creation. The text derives its meaning from the background which is shared by the creator of the text. A text cannot be divorced from its context without affecting the meaning of the expression. According to Halliday and Hasan (1989: 47), ‘part of the environment for any text is a set of previous texts, texts that are taken for granted as shared among those taking part’. This is intertextuality. According to Lester, (2000: x) ‘[T]he most powerful and meaningful messages are combined with words and pictures equally.’ In the context of this paper, the visual-verbal texts rely very much on shared background knowledge about the subject in the image. Without such background, the meaning may not be realised and the text may not have humour. This is partly what (Jenson, 2009) means when he says humour is local. If a joke is told in a strange locality, the listeners who have no background to it may not notice the incongruity and may therefore not find it funny. Thus, intertextuality includes the contexts of occurrence, of situation, of co-text and of culture. All these play roles in proper understanding of the meaning of the visual-verbal text.

5. THEORETICAL ORIENTATION

This study has adopted an eclectic approach in the theoretical framework. It uses a combination of visual semiotics theory, incongruity theory and superiority theory. Semiotics is the study of signs. According to Eco (1976: 7) “A sign is everything which can be taken as significantly substituting for something else”. Thus, a sign is a word, a sound or a visual image that means something. Saussure divides sign into signifier and signified. The signifier is the sound, word or image and the signified is the concept or meaning. However, the relationship between the signified and the signifier is arbitrary, being arrived at only through convention. Visual semiotics is a new branch of semiotics that deals with ‘visual’ signs. It deals with how cartoons, photographs and other similar images convey meaning.

According to (Sharp, 2011), Peirce presented a sign as a triadic system: a sign is a *representamen,* something which stands for another; the sign creates the *interpretant,* an impression on the decoder of what the sign is; and the decoder perceives the *object*, the meaning of the sign in relation to the context of interaction.

Box 1. Peirce's Triadic Model (Sharp, 2011, p. 2)

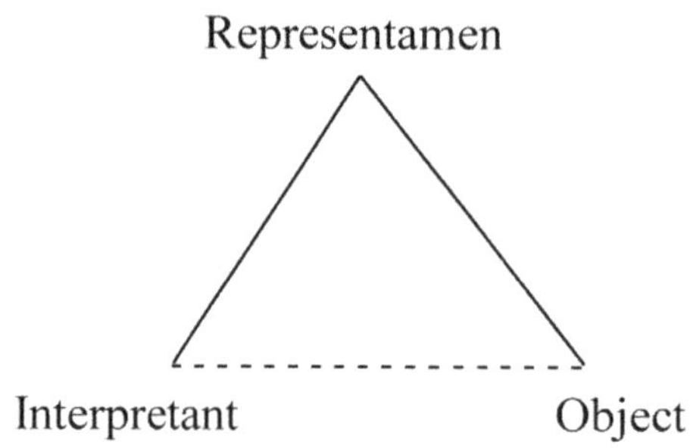

The pattern of meaning in signs has also been categorised as iconic, indexical and symbolic. These same features occur in visual semiotics. A sign is iconic if the signifier represents the signified and both are alike, as in photographs, caricature/cartoons and other visual texts. It is indexical if there is an inherent relationship between the signifier and the signified, such as a smoke signifying fire; and it is symbolic if the relationship between the signifier and the signified is arbitrary. Hence, visual semiotics analysis is multi-layered, dealing with the interpretation of each of these levels. Semiotics relates the present to the past; i.e. it relies on our background knowledge for correct interpretation of the present sign.

Incongruity theory entails the presence of a conflict or incongruity between what a listener expects from a joke and what actually occurs (Veale, 2004; Jensen, 2009: 3). Jensen observes that the levels of language with potential for incongruity include phonology, graphology, morphology, lexis and syntax. In this study, the focus is on visual-verbal texts.

Weaver (2011: 258) has criticised incongruity in the following words: 'The problem of incongruity can be described as the observation that although all jokes are constructed with the use of incongruity, not all jokes are funny in all situations and not all incongruities are humorous'. This is true in most cases as the interpretation of funningness depends on individuals' dispositions and background knowledge.

Another theory is the superiority theory. In this theory, humour is generated when the joker feels superior to others by putting them down in a joke (Sen, 2012). This is done by mocking others, making them suffer some verbal indignity (Jensen, 2009) which leads to humour. Sometimes, however, a speaker may use self-deprecating humour to distract attention from the gaffe that they had made (Sen, 2012: 2). In this paper both incongruity and superiority theories are applicable as there are instances of these in the data. Hence, visual semiotics is used in the interpretation of icons, indexical and symbols; incongruity explains the humour in incongruous texts and superiority theory accounts for the relationship of figures within texts.

6. METHODOLOGY

This study employed a two-stage sampling of data. Several topics were presented and commented on on the Facebook Forum. Popular and recent themes such as those on politics, celebrities, and sports were first searched out through convenient sampling: only the ones available were selected. These included topics on the political future of Retired General Muhammadu Buhari in the then impending 2015 general elections; popular Nollywood characters allegedly having illicit affairs; a camera that caught an angel that was flying; a Nollywood actress allegedly sharing a picture of herself in which she was making love to her man; the photograph of two students, male and female, kissing in a deserted classroom; the issue of an 11-year old girl that got pregnant; President Jonathan's frequent visits to churches for prayers; and a student that posted nude pictures of his girlfriend because she cheated on him. The comments on these were many and varied. Some were verbal, some were pictorial, using images, cartoons, caricatures, real and computer simulated photographs, etc. while some were visual-verbal. The visual-verbal texts were purposively sampled for the study. Out of a total of 107 visual-verbal data selected, 50 were purposively sampled for use in the study. They are analysed for the meaning and humour inherent in them.

7. PREVIOUS STUDIES

There have been studies on different aspects of monomodal and bimodal visual and verbal texts. In this section, some of these studies are explored and their relevance or otherwise to the current paper brought out. One of these is Taiwo (2013), who discusses satirical humour in text messages among Nigerians. He uses the content of the messages to reveal creativity and innovation in the critique of the social and political institutions in the country. The paper is on a similar turf with the current paper as they are both within the precincts of the New Media: while it is on short messages sourced from phone users, the current paper works on data sourced from the Facebook Forum, a social media. They differ, however, in the sense that while it is on verbal communication, the current work is on visual-verbal communication; and while it concentrates on satire, the current work is on humour in general.

Another study that has also examined humour on the Internet is Laineste (nd). The author explores the relation between online humour and aggression in the analyses of comment sequences in the Delfi news portal (www.delfi.ce) from 2000-2009. The paper draws boundaries between humour and verbal aggressiveness, and addresses the notion of failed humour in online communication. This paper is principally on verbal aggressiveness and verbal humour which is different from humour in visual-verbal texts under consideration. The only similarity is that they both deal with online comments. But while Laineste used verbal data, the current study used visual-verbal texts; and while the former is based on Delfi, the latter is based on Facebook. While the former explains why humour fails, the latter identifies and explains how humour is created in visual-verbal texts.

Ademilokun (2012) discusses non-verbal discourse of student soccer fans of Obafemi Awolowo University. He attempts to reveal the communicative imports of visual images used as data. He finds out that subjects use jerseys, head wrappers, belts and hand bands as indexical and symbolic signs to construct presentational, orientational and organisational semiotic meanings. These resources were used to construct identities in the discourse, show commitment and loyalty to their favourite football clubs and make fashion and financial statements in the discourse environment. The current study is similar to Ademilokun's in the use of visual images as data; but it differs in two ways; (1) it examines the pairing of visual and verbal codes which form a unique meaning; and (2) the data are studied for the humour they elicit.

Another study, Chik *et al.* (2005), attempts to measure humour in pictures. Using selected Cantonese speaking Chinese primary school students, they presented 30 pictures of celebrities who are portrayed either veridically (congruously) or incongruously. They conclude that the children's responses clearly indicated that incongruous pictures were rated as significantly funnier than congruous pictures. This study is similar to the current one, which, however, looks at incongruity from two perspectives - the incongruity within the picture itself and the incongruity between the picture and the verbal message on it. In addition, while they used only pictures, this study uses visual and verbal data.

Like the current paper, Baran (nd) also discusses visual humour on the Internet. The author discusses how imagery is blended with pictures in online web pages and blogs. She suggests that the creative context of the Internet has given a new life to figurative expressions and people now provide interpretations in virtual communities which are different from traditional ones. Baran's study is very similar to this paper in the sense that they both used visual-verbal texts as data in humour discussion. However, they differ in some respects. First, Baran's data are purely from Estonian website while the current ones are from Facebook. Baran discusses the link between images and figurative expressions, but the current one is not restricted to figurative expressions. Baran's study is, however, a good stepping stone for the current study which looks at how visual-verbal texts elicit humour.

Ngamsa (2013) has discussed intersemiotic cohesion in between visual and linguistic texts in films. In his study of three films, he finds out the linguistic items that refer to objects in the film. He then concludes that there are patterns of visual verbal synchrony where exophoric reference items function as discourse pointers and connectors for meaning-making to readers, viewers and listeners. Place and person deixises are also said to improve and develop patterns of intersemiotic cohesion for referential explicitness which provides a direct connection between implicit lexical items and their corresponding explicit visual composition. This paper is also relevant to our paper as it discusses bimodality and visual verbal text. However, it differs in the sense that it focuses on film while ours look at visual-verbal images. In addition, it identifies linguistic items that serve as cohesive element while the current paper takes a holistic view of the visual verbal image.

Finally, coming from a background of the unsolved 'problem of incongruity' in the philosophy of humour, Weaver (2011) investigates the styles of fan and journalistic commentary and blogs on the comedians Russell Peters and Chris Rock. The study discusses how fans construct descriptions of funnyness, and acceptable, unacceptable or offensive joking. Although this deals with blogs and commentary, it differs from the current study which uses code-paired visual-verbal comments. Both papers, however, have a meeting point in the concept of incongruity, which this study considers fundamental to humour. In what follows, the visual-verbal text is analysed for its humour.

8. DATA ANALYSIS

Verbal texts/written words can be funny without necessarily having photographs/images at the background. In the same vein, some photographs communicate funnily without any accompanying expressions. These constitute individual texts. Code-paired visual-verbal texts also constitute a text and it can be as funny as individual texts. These are explored in this section.

In Figure 1, we see a picture, a similitude of a former Nigerian President and his Vice. Both are presented as typical hawkers on streets. They wear faded Jeans' trousers and T-shirts, typical of roadside hawkers/sellers in Nigeria. We are able to identify them through their faces and their respective trademark caps: the President with a hat and the VP with a Hausa cap. These serve as indexes for interpreting the pictures. While the President sells some liquid in the bottle, his Vice sells Hausa–made wallets and pirated musical or movie Compact Discs. It is assumed that the President is selling local brew that the people in the southern Nigeria are known for while the VP sells those items the northerners normally sell. The association of the president and his vice with menial jobs being done by the common people

Figure 1. Photoshop of a president and his Vice

in the society is funny. That is the incongruity in the picture: it is incongruous that the president and his vice will be dressed in rags and be hawking goods by the roadside. The picture is a deliberate attempt to ridicule the duo. This is the underlying message.

By the same token, there is also the strange advertorial in Figure 2, where 'quality sperms' are advertised by an 'ejaculating company' to women who want to 'get pregnant without complications'. In the first place, it is gross to advertise sperm since it belongs to the field of taboo terms. Second, it is also gross to imagine the existence of an 'ejaculating company', and finally, the wording of the message is humorous because of different levels of incongruity: sperms are not known to prevent complications in pregnancies; the 'ejaculating company', if it exists, is the first of its kind in Nigeria or in the world!; and its 'door to door delivery' service is also unheard of until now. All these put together make the post hilarious. Underlying the post however, is the indictment of the Nigerian person, who can go to any length to make money, especially from other people's predicament. This is a satire on such people. Figures 1 and 2 are therefore negative humour since they tend to put down some targets.

Figure 2. Advertisement

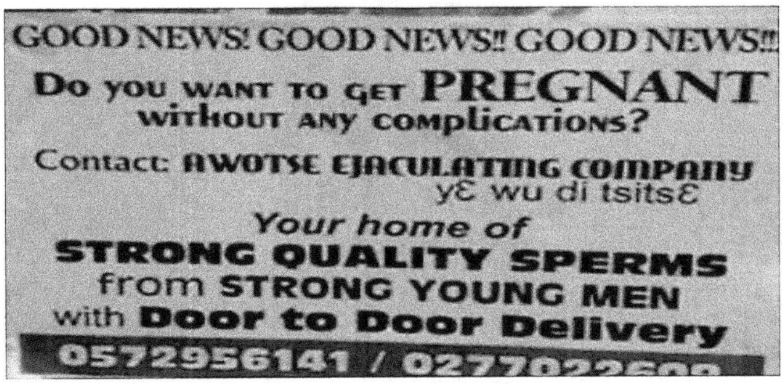

The foregoing are monomodal humour texts with visual and verbal texts separately presented. However, with a combination of an image and some expressions, the reader/viewer has opportunities to appreciate and understand varieties of a visual-verbal humour. This is where code-pairing is relevant. Two codes of visual and verbal texts are intertwined to bring a different meaning. These are discussed in the rest of this section.

Figure 3 is a picture of the late Osama bin Laden, known for his campaigns against the US; and he reportedly bombed quite a number of places, including US embassies, before he was, allegedly, finally killed by the Americans. It is ludicrous to 'learn' that the major reason why he had bombed people were because of similar supposedly stupid posts like the one being referred to here that they had made. This is incongruous and humorous. Figure 4 is a computer simulated image of an individual whose ear is pulled taut. The individual is assumed to be the initial poster whose thread is being responded to; and he/she is undergoing that 'punishment' because a superior poster considers what s/he posted to be rubbish. The incongruity is in the pulling of the ear to make it as long as that of a hare and for no offence other than 'posting rubbish'! The first Figure (3) is a real photograph of individual/celebrity in the society while the second is a photoshopped picture. The essence of all is to evoke laughter/humour. The two texts can be classified as general humour, because they are just to make people laugh.

Next, consider the following examples, which are politically motivated. The two most prominent parties in Nigeria are the All Progressive Congress (APC) and People's Democratic Party (PDP). These parties are always at logger heads, with one criticizing the other's activities or inactions. The following photoshopped images were posted during the 2015 general elections in Nigeria when each party was trying to win voters to its side. The supporters of each party went online to support their party or candidates and lampoon the opponents. The code-paired picture came in handy for their purpose because it says a lot in little time and space.

In Figure 5, there are two female boxers, one representing APC, and the other PDP. As the picture shows, the APC boxer seems to have pummeled PDP such that she had two black eyes and she could no longer fight. The picture is hilarious, but the poster is just trying to draw an analogy of APC defeating

Figure 3. Late Osama Bin Laden

Figure 4. Photoshop of an unknown ordinary man

Figure 5. Women boxers

PDP at the polls. In Figure 6, however, we see two babies, one representing PDP and the other, APC. Here, the PDP child seems to be pinching the APC child on the ear and the latter is crying. The PDP child goes ahead to tell his opponent 'I no be ur mate oh' (I'm not your mate). The abbreviations APC and PDP are indexical of the identities of the two women in the ring and the two children on the bed: both represent the two leading parties in Nigeria. Hence, the two photos show the rivalry between the two parties. The import of the two photographs is captured in the superiority theory. Each party tried to demonstrate its superiority over the opponent through the use of the pictures. Each also tried to push the other down through the messages. It is incongruous that the political contest was presented in the pictures as a test of physical energy. And what's more, the contest had been won even before the elections held!

In Figure 7, Boko Haram leader, Abubakar Shekau is seen 'pleading' with Nigerians: 'VOTE PDP, DON'T SPOIL MY BUSINESS'.The question is: what business does he have? Boko Haram is known for the current raging insurgency in Nigeria and the neighbouring countries of Chad, Niger and Cameroon. Former President Jonathan had fought unsuccesfully to curb the excessess of the terrorists, least of all

Figure 6. Baby pinching mate's ear

Figure 7. Abubakar Shekau's photograph

eradicating them. The Nigerian government, on this account had been labelled inept and weak. Its solders either deserted or were accussed of running away from the front or aiding and abetting the enemy. An Australian, Davies had alleged that Retired General Ihejirika, Nigeria's immediate past Chief of Army Staff at that time and Alhaji Alli Modu Sherriff, former Governor of Borno State, were sponsors of the Boko Haram insurgents. However, the president did not arrest either of them. Instead, he was reportedly hobnobbing with Alhaji Alli Modu Sheriff. This probably forced some people to conclude that president Jonathan instigated or supported Shekau's insurgency.

The photo, taken from one of the video clips Boko Haram had released, is based on this premise. Shekau's men bombed many places, raided many places in the north, stole money, explosives, animals and foodstuff; kidnapped school children and women; and conscripted people into its fighting force. On the contrary, supporters of APC claimed that General Mohammadu Buhari (GMB) would put an end to terrorism if voted into power. It was on this premise that, Shekau, 'knowing' fully that GMB could crush his organisation and would do as he promised, 'begged' Nigerians to vote Goodluck Ebele Jonathan's (GEJ) party so that he (Shekau) could continue to plunder the country. The idea was that he would continue to thrive under GEJ's government, in the business of spilling Nigerians' blood, but not under GMB's. This is hillarious as we see the fearful Shekau in his trademark war dress with his rifle, 'pleading' for Nigerians' votes for GEJ. Really, this is incongruous, as it is abnormal for a terrorist to beg when he has not been captured; and there is also sarcasm in the text. The idea is to lampoon the president for being ineffective in dealing with the insurgency; and the message is that if Nigerians should vote GEJ in again, Shekau would continue to wreak havoc in Nigeria. The picture also has the symbol of the PDP on the top left hand side. This means that the Shekau in the picture is a PDP member.

Furthermore, many times, first posters of topics also get lampooned. It is either the reader does not believe the first poster or one of the commentators on the post.

In the first picture (Figure 8), the author shows unbelief by saying he wants to ask Ifa. Ifa is the oracle being used in Africa, especially among the Yoruba, to divine things and find out the true situation of things. The poster uses it to show that he does not believe the story in the topic. It is, however, incongruous that one has to consult the oracle for a story on the Internet. This is the punchline of the humour. The second one (Figure 9) is that of a silhouette that doffed his cap to the poster, saying: 'I respect ur lies'. The fact is that the author of the visual text considered the post a craftily worded lie that only the discerning person would find out the truth about. Hence, the image in the photo bows in respect, removing its cap in the process. It is also incongruous that one would respect lies. People respect intelligence, integrity and other positive values; not lies! The bottom line is that the poster does not believe the story; it is considered to be a lie. This is sarcasm.

Following this is a picture of a seemingly intelligent young man who sits watching (Figure 10). He encourages the poster to go on with the story, since he already knows that the poster is lying. The next example (Figure 11) is a photo of a young boy who seems knowledgeable. He sits calmly, looks up from the newspaper he is reading and says 'thunder that would fire you is doing press-up'. This is a curse on the first poster. In Yoruba and Igbo communities in Nigeria, thunder is a deity that people fear. The deity fights with lightning and fire. The person in the photo invokes this thunder on the poster and matches it with the military practice of doing press-up before they start a task. In essence, thunder is warming

Figure 8. A diviner

Figure 9. A bowing silhouette

Figure 10. An intelligent boy

Figure 11. Another intelligent boy

up to strike the poster! These are general humour with superiority intent: the comments show that the reader/poster is superior to the first poster and can therefore discern that he or she was lying. There are also elements of incongruity in them as the author wants to be funny.

Sometimes, the commentator may deliberately want to create fun. In such situations, he or she brings photographs with wordings that may not be in tandem with the situation.

The first photo (12) shows a man in a flowing *agbada*. He is going, as it were, to tell the Igwe (Igbo king) about the content of the story. In traditional Igbo society, there is always an Igwe to whom subjects report incidents that affect the society. This photo is just to serve as a kind of comic relief to readers and commentators on the forum. The man in the picture wears a flowing gown (known with the Yoruba of Nigeria) without a cap, and walks without trousers. It is incongruous as the story (in this case of President Jonathan visiting churches) does not relate to that which can be reported to Igwe. It follows that the visual-verbal text may be used arbitrarily without considering the topic. Second, it is not clear whether he wants to report to Igwe through the Internet. The total picture of the man and what he sets out to do is hilarious. This is a general humour.

The other photos (Figures 13-15) are not subtle. They invoked their anger on the poster's mother (uwaka), father (ur father) or s/he herself/himself (fuck you) because they did not enjoy the news item

Figure 12. A photoshop of busybody

Figure 13. Local culture insult

Figure 14. Local culture insult

Figure 15. Foreign culture insult

or details of the story. The first two gestures are traditional ways of insulting a person's mother. They are symbols of insults to people in whose culture they are used. But the posters rub this in by writing the words: your mother and your father, possibly to let strangers to the tradition known what is meant. The fact is that such expressions are used when the speaker feels hurt and has no means of retaliating immediately. The third one (15) is a modern saying when we want to tell a person to *go to hell*. The accompanying gesture is a creation of the poster. Translated literally, it also has some sexual connotation which was not in the original meaning of 'fuck you'. And as we can see, the image for this is a white hand, depicting the source, (white culture); while the other ones are caricatures of black hands, representing African or Nigerian origin. Many of the stories are on politics and if a poster or a commentator says what another poster does not like, he may get this treatment. Again, these serve as comic relief.

Notice that these three examples are incongruous since they are not the expected answers or comments to the first post. In this sense, the original post by the first author is expected and the response here is a punchline. They are also negative humour.

The next example (Figure 16) rests on a general perception among people, especially Nigerians that women are better cooks than men. The photo here is out to prove the contrary; that men are better cooks. Hence, a man who wants to cook chicken soup merely puts his pot on fire and a live chicken inside the pot. In the picture, we see him tasting the soup, possibly for salt or other condiments he may have put. Perhaps, he liked the taste as he said: '…and they say men can't cook'. This is funny as everyone knows that this is not the way to prepare delicious chicken. If the fowl is not tied on the legs it would flip its wings and fly out of the boiling pot. If it is tied and it dies in there, the man will not be able to eat the desired chicken. The man in the photo is generic, referring to the stereotypes of men that cannot cook. He is an indexical for all men. The superiority theory is also at play here, and one should suspect that the photo was created by women liberation apologists or feminists. Whichever way one looks at it, both the acts in the photo and the accompanying statement on it are incongruous.

Similarly, the next picture (Figure 17) is that of a man who wants to eat up a bowl of rice, cartons of bottled water and other drinks. He seems prepared for the great task as he wears only boxers. This is the mode of dressing when men want to do difficult jobs like splitting wood, digging a well or street gutter, etc.: they have to remove other dresses that can get in the way. Hence we see a greedy man trying to do the impossible. This is subtle satire, criticising the greed of some men. Even if he is starving, he cannot eat up that mound of food! Figures 16 & 17 belong to the category of general humour.

The next example (Figure 18) is the cartoon of a man and a woman at table. The impression one gets is that they are on a date and they are introducing each other. The bespectacled bald-headed old man claims to be a 32-year old politician who is honest while the woman claims to be a 29-year old prostitute who is a virgin. The author seems to be drawing comparisons between the two: trying to find out the smarter or better/greater liar between a politician and a prostitute. The first thing we note about the man is that he lied about his age because he is obviously older than 32 years and this makes him dishonest.

Figure 16. A male cook

Figure 17. A greedy man

Figure 18. A caricature of a couple on a date

Generically, politicians are assumed to be liars. For the lady, we tend to believe that she is a prostitute because she wears a see-through dress which makes her breasts visible and she exposes her thighs too. It is also possible that she is 29, given the hazards of her trade or her genetic make-up that can make her bigger/fatter and older than her age. However, there is no way a prostitute can be a virgin. In essence, the poster is trying to present readers with grades of liars in our society. This is also a satire on politicians. The poster seems to be saying that politicians tell barefaced lies like a prostitute that claims to be a virgin. The incongruity lies in the false statements made by the two characters. This is a general humour.

Figure 19 is the photograph of a man eating a tough piece of meat. He does not see any importance in the original/initial Facebook post since it has nothing to do with him. Hence, he says *wetin concern me?* 'What concern of mine is that?' But he seems determined to eat the tough meat, which is his immediate concern here. The humour here lies in how he dissipates all his energy to subdue a piece of meat. From experience too, one can say he is a poor man; because rich people can afford more tender

Figure 19. A photoshop of a man eating tough meat

pieces of meat. And if they come across such tough meat, they either use a piece of cutlery to cut it into sizeable pieces for consumption or abandon it entirely. But a poor man that struggled to buy a miserable piece of meat will ensure that he eats his money's worth out of it. If he fails at this, he may swallow it! The incongruity in this is that, rather than comment on the post, the man expends a lot of energy in the struggle to eat a tough piece of meat. This is general humour.

The other side of the divide is that there are visual-verbal humour texts that also fall flat. Although they are meant to be humorous, they do not evoke humour.

For example, it is not clear what humour some authors of these texts intended by using animals' images in their texts. There is a photo (Figure 20) where a she-goat peeps behind a shed and the statement on it is 'I just dey look U.' (I'm just looking at you). This joke fell flat because one can hardly relate to it. Another is the photo of a monkey (Figure 21) in a traditional African dress. The monkey laughed and said: 'hahahahahhahha, funny post. That's why I spread Ebola.' But it does not communicate intelligently. Yet another (Figure 22) is the picture the late Osama bin Laden who raised his hand and said 'I rate it 9/11'. Now one cannot relate the incident of 9/11 to the topic under discussion; neither do we see him as a mathematician or a teacher in class. Again there is a caricature (Figure 23) which resembles no one but still makes comments that is intended as a joke. The picture indicates the target of the joke, but it often happens that the post immediately before it and to which it points is not the intended butt.

Figure 20. A goat

Figure 21. A monkey

Figure 22. Late Bin Laden

Figure 23. A caricature

It is worse if this unintended butt has written something grand. The visual-verbal text stands out of place! It doesn't seem hilarious to the researcher. The final example (Figure 24) is that of an astronaut who is relaxing with a bottle of beer, possibly in the moon. He says 'that's why I left the earth'. Again, the researcher can hardly relate to it. What these texts lack is incongruity and contextual foundation for the interpretation of the texts. However, these are personal opinions of the researcher; maybe there are readers that can relate to them and laugh after reading the texts. After all, it has been noted that not all jokes can be funny to everyone.

9. CONCLUSION

From the foregoing, we can say the structure of the visual-verbal humour text has two parts. The first part is the image and the second part is the verbal text, either of which constitutes the punchline. The visual part may be the expected/known while the verbal part is the unexpected. Conversely, the verbal part may be the expected while the visual part is the unexpected (as in the Figure 16). Again, both the visual and the verbal parts may form a composite whole, forming the unexpected portion, while the background to the joke serves as the expected (as in Figure 8). Finally, the statement by the first poster may constitute the expected while the visual-verbal text constitutes the unexpected (as in the Figures 12-14)

Further, the humour may involve incongruity as observed in several examples above. From the foregoing analyses, we find out that incongruity occurs in many photographs and these account for the humour in them. In addition, incongruity may come in many forms: within an image, between an image and a verbal comment and between the background story and the image in the humour text. In some cases, however, the verbal expression is the cause of humour. It serves as an incongruous response to the initial story being responded to.

The humour text can also be classified as positive, negative or general humour. However, there are more negative and general categories of humour. This is possibly because humour thrives on negatives and general statements rather than on positive ones. Visual-verbal texts are also often used arbitrarily. Once created and posted online, other participants often copy and use them anywhere they so please

Figure 24. An astronaut

without considering the context. Thus, while some may be humorous, some may not, probably because they are not used in appropriate contexts.

Finally, Visual-verbal texts are also described in this paper as code-paring text. This is distinguished from code-switching. However, both concepts belong to the field of contact linguistics. Code-paring may have to be further explored to establish its features with other paired codes. Notice too that not all code-paring texts are humorous and not all humorous texts are code-paired. Code-paired texts can also occur with ordinary meanings devoid of humour.

REFERENCES

Ademilokun, M. (2012). Communicative Imports of Visual Images in the Discourse of Some Nigerian Student Soccer Fans. *IBADAN Journal of English Studies*, *8*, 75–94.

Baran, A. (n.d.). *Visual Humour on the Internet*. Retrieved from http://www.folklore.ee/pubte/eraamat/eestipoola/baran.pdf

Berk, R. A. (2005). LAUGHTERPIECE THEATRE: Humour as a Systematic Teaching Tool. *Essays on Teaching Excellence toward the Best in the Academy*, *17*(2), 1-8.

Cahill, S., & Densham, R. (2014). *Women, Humour and Power...in the workplace: A Review of the current literature for funny Women*. Accessed in February 10, 2015 from http://www.funnywomen.com

Chik, M. D. Y., Leung, C. S., Benjamin, M., & Geoffrey, N. (2005). Develoment of a Measure of Humour Appreciation. *Australian Journal of Educational and Developmental Psychology*, *5*, 26–31.

Crawford, C. B. (1994). Theory and Implications regarding the utilization of strategic Humour by Leaders. *The Journal of Leadership Studies*, *1*(4), 53–67. doi:10.1177/107179199400100406

Critchley, S. (2002). *On Humour*. London: Routledge.

Delise, N. N. (2012). Me, Myself, & Identity Online: Identity Salience on Facebook vs Non-Virtual Identity. *University of New Orleans Theses and Dissertations*. Paper 1431.

Eco, U. (1976). *A Theory of Semiotics*. Bloomington, IN: Indiana University Press. doi:10.1007/978-1-349-15849-2

Fearman, R. J. (2014). *Punchline Predictability Comprehension Speed, and Joke Funningness: Investigating Incongruity theories of humour*. (Honours Psychology Thesis). Department of Psychology, University of West Ontario, London, Ontario, Canada. Retrieved from http://ir.lib.uwo.ca/psychd_uht

Halliday M. A. K., & Hasan, R. (1989). *Language, Context, and Text: Aspects of Language in a Social-Semiotic Perspective*. Oxford, UK: Oxford University Press.

Hein, K. (2006). Switching between Estonian Sign Language and Spoken Estonian in a School Environment. *EESTI RAKENDUSLINGVISTIKA UHINGU AASTRAAMAT*, *10*, 91–106.

Jensen, K. E. (2009, Fall). Humour. Modern World.

Kress, G., & van Leeuwen, T. (2001). *Multimodal Discourse: The Modes and Media of Contemporary Communication*. London: Arnold.

Laineste, L. (n.d.). Funny or Aggressive? Failed Humour in Internet Comments. *Folklore, 53*. Retrieved on February 10, 2015 from http://www.folklore.ee/folklore/vol53/laineste.pdf

Lester, P. M. (2000). Visual Communication: Images with Messages (2nd ed.). Wadsworth.

Malone, P. (1980). Humor: A Double-edged tool for today's managers?. *Academy of Management Review*, *5*(3), 357–360. doi:10.5465/AMR.1980.4288842

Ngamsa, J. (2013). Patterns of Intersemiotic Cohesion in the Moving Image Text. *New Media and Mass Communication*, *9*, 11–17.

Parsa, S., & Parsa, A. F. (2002). *GöstergebilimÇözümlemeleri*. İzmir: Ege Üniversitesi Basımevi.

Potts, A. (1996). Sign. In R. S. Nelson & R. Shiff (Eds.), Critical Terms for Art History. London: University of Chicago Press.

Raskin, V. (1985). *Semantic Mechanisms of Humour*. Dordrecht: Reidel.

Salal, F., Krupat, E., & Roter, D. (2002). 'Satisfaction and the Use of Humour by Physicians and Patients'. *Psychology & Health*, *17*(3), 269–280. doi:10.1080/08870440290029520

Schwarz, J. (2010). *Linguistic Aspect of Verbal Humour in Stand-up Comedy*. Dissertation.

Sen, A. (2012). Humour Analysis and Qualitative Research. *Social Research Update*, *63*, 1-4. Accessed from http://sru.soc.surrey.ac.uk/

Sharp, H. J. (2011). *Semiotics as a Theoretical Foundation of Information Design' Conference for Information Systems Applied Research 2011 CONISAR Proceedings*. Wilmington, NC: Academic Press.

Taiwo, R. (2013). Emerging Trends in English Language in the New Media: A Case Study of Satire in Nigerian Text Messages. *Journal of the Nigeria English Studies Association*, *16*(1), 58–73.

Veale, T. (2004). Incongruity in Humour: Root Cause or Epiphenomenon?. *Humor: International Journal of Humor Research*, *17*(4), 419–428.

Weaver, S. (2011). Definitions of the Humorous in Chris Rock and Russell Peters Fan Blogs: A discussion of the Problem of Incongruity. *Participations Journal of Audience and Reception Studies*, *8*(2), 257–275.

Zebrowska, E. (2014). Multimodal Messages. *Journal of Multimodal Communication Studies*, *1*, 8–15.

Chapter 14
Socio-Semiotics of Humour in Ebola Awareness Discourse on Facebook

Lily Chimuanya
Covenant University, Nigeria

Esther Ajiboye
Covenant University, Nigeria

ABSTRACT

Humour has often functioned as a tool for the relief of depression, anxiety and stress. People have continually turned to humour, in serious life threatening situations in order to find relief. Facebook users eagerly expressed their thoughts and opinions on the Ebola epidemic that raged across some parts of West Africa in 2014 through humorous graphics, texts and memes posted online. An awareness of the peculiar patterns and use of such humour creating strategies is crucial to the understanding and interpretation of socio-semiotic realities of such online interactions. This study identifies and analyses specific semiotic patterns in Ebola-related graphic posts in Nigerian online social discourse, particularly on Facebook, and argues, that such posts are not merely a bunch of humour. Instead, they are informal awareness campaigns that are even more apt than explicit verbal or written messages. The study applies Kress and Leeuween's approach to multimodal discourse analysis.

The views and content expressed in this chapter are those of the author but not necessarily of the publisher and may contain some explicit ideas and concepts.

INTRODUCTION

The digital world is a vibrant society with various discursive practices and discourse on the Internet is usually reflective of the human society; however, because of the anonymity that the Internet offers, it has become a platform for unrestricted self-expression. The speed at which the Internet transmits messages

DOI: 10.4018/978-1-5225-0338-5.ch014

Copyright © 2016, IGI Global. Copying or distributing in print or electronic forms without written permission of IGI Global is prohibited.

has also made it a very viable platform for different types of communication. For instance, internet memes among others have become a regular feature of the cyberworld. Memes refer to jokes, images, videos, etc. that are dispersed from person-to-person via the Internet (Shifman, 2014). Ding (2015) notes that Internet users consciously look out for internet memes daily, for varying doses of humour. He argues that these memes, however, sometimes frame individuals or groups of people as discursive practices that are capable of reflecting socio-cultural realities. The present study argues that Internet memes are not merely a bunch of humour; rather they integrate, through a range of semiotic signs, some underlying discursive messages that serve as publicity or awareness campaigns. This study is an investigation of the socio-semiotics of humour in the discourse of Ebola awareness among Nigerians online.

BACKGROUND TO STUDY: THE EBOLA EPIDEMIC

Ebola is a chronic and highly infectious disease caused by Ebola virus, spread through direct contact with body fluids like blood, saliva, urine, sperm, or sweat of an infected person and by contact with contaminated objects, equipment or clothing. It is highly fatal with a death rate of up to 90%. However, the Ebola virus may be easily eliminated with heat, alcohol-based products, and sodium hypoctilorite (bleach) or calcium hypochlorite (bleaching powder) at appropriate concentrations (Akharumere, 2014).

Ebola Virus Disease (EVD) was first discovered in 1976 in Sudan and in the Democratic Republic of Congo. Subsequent multiple outbreaks have occurred in Central Africa, mainly near tropical rainforests, especially in remote villages. However, the Democratic Republic of Congo, Uganda, South Sudan and Gabon have consistently been the worst hit regions since the first outbreak in 1976. About 2,200 cases of EVD outbreaks have been reported with well over 1,500 deaths since 1976 (Kaye, 2014).

The Ebolavirus, which is responsible for EVD is transmitted by members of the filoviruses family which comprises five distinct species: Bundibugyo Ebolavirus, Tai Forest Ebolavirus, Reston Ebolavirus, Sudan Ebolavirus and Zaire Ebolavirus. All except Reston are restricted to Africa and found in primates. The Zaire species is most lethal, with a fatality rate of up to 90%, and it was found to be the cause of the February, 2014 Guinea outbreak (Akharumere, 2014; Kaye, 2014).

In August 2014, 'Doctors without Borders' reported an Ebola virus outbreak in Monrovia, Liberia's capital. A number of quarantined patients escaped which resulted in further spread of the disease to other regions including Sierra Leone, Guinea, Mali, Senegal, and Nigeria. While Guinea, Liberia and Sierra Leone are the three most affected countries with many deaths, only seven people died in Nigeria (Oketola, 2014). It was reported that EVD was introduced to Nigeria on July 20, 2014 by Patrick Sawyer, a Liberian-born American diplomat who travelled from Lome, in transit to a conference in Calabar the Cross River State capital (Denkey, 2015).

The former Nigerian President, Goodluck Jonathan, declared a state of emergency on the 8th of August, 2014, on the outbreak of EVD in Nigeria. Interestingly, as the Nigerian government searched for ways to curtail the spread of the deadly EVD, many social media users utilised *Facebook* to make jokes about the disease, humorously suggesting ways to treat and avoid the virus. Comical conversations and pictures of "the Ebola hug," "the Ebola kiss," "the Ebola handshake," the use of protective gloves and clothing appeared on *Facebook* walls of many Nigerian users.

Oketola (2014) asserts that the social media helped Nigerians to contain EVD. This suggests that humorous *Facebook* posts, and or memes may be perceived beyond mere jokes. Hence this work seeks to identify the different strategies employed by Nigerians to create Internet memes; to highlight the embedded messages in each of the selected posts and to measure the extent to which sampled memes fulfilled intentional and unintentional messages.

SOCIAL MEDIA USE IN NIGERIA

Social media are offshoot of global advancement in technology, modernisation and globalisation. They include the various online technological tools that enable people to communicate easily and to share information through the Internet (Greendhow, 2009). People employ them to express and publish their thoughts online; while socialising, they share information and pictures that may generate threads of contributions and participations from friends and online community members.

Facebook is one of the most popular and subscribed variant of the social media; most attractive to both the young and elderly Nigerian. *CPAAfrica.com* in their May 2015 report submits that Nigerians have overtaken South Africa as the largest users of *Facebook* in Sub Saharan Africa with over 11 million users (www.cp-africa.com). In their characteristic innovative nature, Nigerians have bent the *Facebook* platform to enable them express virtually every form of communicable thought, action, information, resource, picture and image.

One of such uses to which Nigerians have employed *Facebook* is in posting and sharing of textually and graphically constructed humour. Practically every socio-cultural and political event generates Internet memes in Nigeria; one of which includes the Ebola virus epidemic in the nation in the middle of 2014. This resulted in the hosting of a *Facebook* community referred to as 'Ebola Jokes', comprising one hundred and fifty-six (156) active members and 2,110 followers (https://www.facebook.com/pages/Ebola-jokes/). This is one of many online communities that focussed on EVD jokes. However, the 'Ebola Jokes' community on *Facebook* is the community with quite a number of humorous graphic texts and memes on the EVD. Some of the humorous pictures constitute genres of intentionally absurd textual and graphic structures and patterns which are forms of completely liberated speech/text patterns that ignore all norms, even those of elementary logic (Thompson, 1982). While it may be possible that Nigerians used such jokes to diffuse the seriousness and fear that engulfed the nation at that time, there are possibilities that underlying messages were missed while appreciating the humour in the posts.

HUMOUR IN LANGUAGE USE

Humour is perceived as a product of a comic, well-meaning and tolerant mind. However, following the Anglo-American tradition, humour is seen as a broad term that encompasses everything that elicits laughter: wit, non-sense, sarcasm, satire, irony and comedy. The implication of this stance on humour is that humour is made to assume all positive and negative meanings; from aggressive humour to joke (Ermida, 2008).

The diversity of the language of humour makes the concept difficult to define. Norrick (1993; 2003) observes how extremely complex in both form and functions, humorous communication can be and submits that there is no one straight way of defining the language of humour. This is coupled with the reality that humour spans diverse areas of inquiry such as linguistics, psychology, sociology, philosophy, etc. Evrard (1996) identifies the remarkable 'semantic flexibility' of humour and its 'enigmatic character' and states that 'its range of degrees, procedures, themes, its subtle and diffused character make it a difficult phenomenon to spot or define' (p.4).

Humour can be either verbal or non-verbal; it can be a subjective experience or serve communicative purposes; it can express everyday reality or consist of fiction and imagination; it can charm or attack, be created spontaneously or be used as a well-prepared technique of personal and professional interaction; it can be a simple joke told among friends or amount to the kind of sophistication found in literary texts (Ermida, 2008). Everything can be humour as long as it elicits an element of laughter. Humour can be intentional or unintentional. Intentional humour is deliberate and planned to the least detail, while unintentional humour may occur as a slip caused by lapses in communication which may lead to breaking the rules of linguistic clarity (Ross, 1998).

The language of humour tends to be ambiguous, having both surface and deep meanings that can be deduced from analysing the text to find out how the existing conventions of language have been utilised to express wider possibilities of meanings. Ross (1998) identifies the essence of humour as surprise, innovation and rule-breaking, what may be referred to as a deviation from the norm. However, humour varies according to contexts, cultures, individuals and medium of communication. What may elicit laughter in one context may not, in another. Cultures differ and world views and experiences are perceived from different perspectives. Each culture or social group defines what constitutes humour per time. Also, humour is dependent on the individual; the age, gender and social class of an individual will impact on the variety of humour at play per time. The medium of communication also plays an all important role in determining humour. For instance, with the Internet and its attendant social media, there appears to have evolved a new style of language use, in addition to the complexities in defining the term, 'humour'.

HUMOUR IN THE NIGERIAN CONTEXT

Humour has a seemingly high profile in the Nigerian society, with an array of stand-up comedians and comedy series available on TV and the social media; *Facebook* in particular, attests to Nigerians seeming penchant for jokes on social events and situations. Ross (1998) observes that social context is important in the creation and reception of humour. In addition to this, humour is not static, it changes constantly changing, a joke on Ebola today for example, may not be funny in the next twenty years.

Humour in the Nigerian context spans from socio-cultural and political satire to idle jokes that are told for phatic communication in order to establish relationship and friendship. With the social media, Nigerians have become more innovative in their patterns of communicating humour, ranging from a short conversation between characters in the joke, to absurd graphic pictures of participants and characters. However, it is observed that there are underlying discursive messages in certain humorous communication. Why would people really want to make a joke of a deadly disease as EVD and not cancer? What unintended messages can be derived from such seemingly drastic jokes? Are there identifiable patterns to such humorous communication? This work intends to find answers to these questions by analysing selected humorous posts on *Facebook* by Nigerians on the Ebola epidemic recorded in the country between April and August of 2014.

THEORETICAL FRAMEWORK: KRESS AND VAN LEEUWEN'S SOCIAL SEMIOTICS

Kress and van Leeuwen's (2006) "Social Semiotics" is an approach to multimodal analysis influenced by the works of Michael Halliday (1978). It perceives language as a system of options and meaning potentials. Kress and van Leeuwen (1996, 2006) shift emphasis from written language to multimodality (visual) and explore texts in relation to a socially created network of options that have meaning potential realised in the context of use and perform ideological functions. Thus, association of meanings that a text can connote is in a continuum, and adaptive to different social contexts. In other words, meaning making is seen as an ongoing process relative to specific context and experience; it is a social practice, and every aspect of the multimodal text—linguistic choices as well as visual modes which may include colour, perspective, modality, etc.—is a signifier.

This framework is found suitable for this work because the analysis and interpretation of language use is contextualised in conjunction with other semiotic resources which are simultaneously used for the construction of meaning (O'Halloran, 2004). Kress and van Leeuwen's approach emphasises that signs are not arbitrary, hence, meaning is derived through an integration of all semiotic elements present in a text as, even though these elements are not meanings by themselves, they are meaning potentials realisable in specific social contexts (Jewitt and Oyama, 2001).

Analysis takes into account the integrated use of two semiotic codes – written and visual in interpreting meaning. Drawing upon Halliday's ideational, interpersonal and textual metafunctions, Kress and van Leeuwen (2006) posit three metafunctions or types of meaning realised in semiotic signs or multimodal texts; the representational meaning; interactive meaning and the compositional meaning. Representational meaning is derived from two kinds of images, each of which involves certain processes. Narrative images involve action, reactional, speech and mental, and conversational processes, while conceptual images involve classificational, analytical and symbolic processes. However, these processes within representational meaning potential are streamlined into two processes, conceptual processes which "represent participants in terms of their generalised and more or less stable and timeless essence"; these involve attributive and suggestive meanings. The second set of processes is presentational processes which function as narratives, as they relate to actions and events (Kress and van Leeuwen, 1996:56).

This study explores the ideational or representational meaning in sampled texts, noting that representation is a "scale running from maximum abstraction to maximum representation of pictorial detail, [and that] [a]n image may show every detail of the represented participants: the individual strands of hair, the pores in the skin, the creases in the clothes, … or it may abstract from detail to a greater or lesser degree' (Kress and van Leeuwen, 2006, p.161). Consequently, in the context of a multimodal analysis as this, all modes, both written, graphic, colour and size are studied with the view to identify the underlying messages embedded in each text in relation to the reasons people make semiotic choices and the meaning potential in such choices. It also identifies elements of emphasis and 'de-emphasis' created by the presence or absence of certain features in the texts.

In relation to Halliday's *transitivity process,* Kress and van Leeuwen (2006) suggest that analysis of images in representational terms requires the identification of the represented participants, the process or the activity described, the qualities of the participants and the circumstances in which the action is being developed since "different logics govern the mode of written language and that of visual image: written text is governed by the logic of time or temporal sequence, whereas, visual image is governed by the logic of spatiality, organised arrangements, and simultaneity" (Kress, 2003 cited in Liu, 2013: 1260). Both written language and visual image are therefore significant to meaning making, as they interconnect to create a unified communicative event.

METHODOLOGY

The study is qualitative in nature and it involves descriptive and discursive multimodal analysis of data. Data comprises fifty (50) Internet memes (comic photos, verbal and visual posts, etc.) purposively sampled from the 'Ebola Jokes' community on popular social networking site, *Facebook* during the 2014 Ebola epidemic in Nigeria. Because of similarity among some of these samples however, fifteen (15) are selected for analysis, these are numbered Figures 1 - 15. Analysis focuses on socio-semiotic interpretation of these memes, especially as they serve as meaning making strategies in the Nigerian socio-cultural context.

DATA ANALYSIS AND DISCUSSION OF FINDINGS

Sampled Ebola-themed memes generated by Nigerian users of *Facebook* are classified under six acts, namely: Narrative Acts, Conceptual Acts, Reactional Acts, Speech and Action Acts, Analytical Acts and Classification Acts. These are referred to as acts because it is perceived that the creators of the memes are performing certain acts with the memes. The table below presents the categorisation of sampled memes collected from *Facebook* on the Ebola epidemic in Nigeria.

Table 1 shows the frequency of acts performed by the memes. Narrative acts are the most frequently used, with 26% frequency. These are closely followed by the conceptual acts which occur at a frequency of 22%. The reactional, analytical and classification acts have a frequency of 14% respectively, while the least occurring are speech and action acts, which occurs at 10% frequency. This disparity in frequency could imply that over anything else, Nigerians are quick to relay stories of social threats within very short notice through social media platforms as evident in the narrative acts.

Table 1. Frequency of acts

Types	Frequency	Percentage
A: Narrative Acts	13	26%
B: Conceptual Acts	11	22%
C: Reactional Acts	7	14%
D: Speech and Action Acts	5	10%
E: Analytical Acts	7	14%
F: Classification Acts	7	14%
Total	**50**	**100**

A: Narrative Acts

During the outbreak of the EVD epidemic in Nigeria, several curative suggestions were proposed by novices in the field of virology, religious leaders and people who felt that the virus could be tackled using indigenous methods. One of the most circulated methods that even went viral, especially on *Facebook*, was the addition of cooking salt to bathwater as salt was rumoured to possess antiviral properties that were potent enough to destroy the Ebola virus. It was suggested that people should bathe with such salt water at least three times per day. Figure 1, 2 and 3 are deployed to humorously dramatise the salt-water concoction in different exaggerated perspectives. These memes or posts, though comical in nature, are strategically employed by Nigerian users of *Facebook* to sensitise other Nigerians about the absurdity of such unfounded claims. They attempt to mock the susceptibility of many Nigerians who quickly resorted to alternative measures to prevent themselves from being infected with EVD.

The participant in Figure 1 is a squatted man, the actor, with a blue towel wrapped around his waist, and a lighter shade of blue shower cap worn on his head. His head is bowed and supported with his left hand, this posture symbolically projects dilemma. Foregrounded by the young man are co-participants, transparent jars of salt and red ground pepper, which function as the goal in the narrative. The jar of pepper is placed on top of the jar of salt, perhaps to signify the relational process that exists between them, that is, in hierarchy of usage, the pepper is to be used before the salt. Closely situated by the jars are other participants, a transparent bottle of vegetable oil, and a blue bucket of water, just about two-third filled, with a small blue bowl that has a white tablet of soap, sailing on the water. The man's habit and the scene in general, are carriers of attributive meaning that suggest that he is about to take a bath, while the proximity of the jars and bottle to the bucket of water in relation to the visual texts, are suggestive of a process that involves applying the ingredients to the water. The author of Figure 1 deliberately made the jars and bottles transparent in order to foreground their content.

Figure 1.

Figure 2.

Figure 3.

Within the context of the EVD, the narrative processes suggest that the man attempts to bathe with the concoction in order to prevent EVD. The colour blue, which is salient in this picture, connotes a cold and depressing mood (NAz and Epp, 2004). Hence, the scene is made to appear even more depressing than the Ebola virus. The integration of the elements in Figure 1 as well as its attendant contradiction of what a real bath scene is in the real world helps to portray the fallacy of the salt-water-bath approach to preventing EVD. This contradiction makes the picture all the more humorous since table salt together with pepper (chilli), seasoning cubes and vegetable oil are popular condiments in many Nigerian kitchens, Figure 1 mocks Nigerians and suggests that in addition to salt, these too should be added to the already prepared bathwater in order to make the preventive procedure more effective. It may be assumed that Figure 1 is a central awareness campaign against superstitious anti-EVD claims as the frustration, and or dilemma reflected in the man's demeanour explains that such practices are acts of desperation and only frustrated attempts at seeking for a cure to EVD.

Figure 2 represents three prominent participants, a mean looking/ determined lady, the actor, whose focus of attention follows a vector within a phenomenon to the viewer, her left index finger points at a fully clothed astounded child seated in a stainless pot on a cooker, other prominent participants in the transactional process. In her right hand is an almost empty transparent sachet of salt. Her mean stare and pointed index finger is used to draw attention to the content of the pot. The baby in the pot appears to be a boy; he is dressed in a white over-all which is typically worn for babies in order to prevent cold. In the background are sets of cooking spoons and utensil, hanging on a tiled wall. These attributive processes are symbolic of a kitchen setting. The raised almost empty sachet of salt in the representation is a carrier that suggests that that the woman has emptied most of its content in the goal, 'pot-of-baby'.

The presentational process in the visual images suggests that the woman is about to boil the baby in a pot of salt water in order to protect him from the deadly EVD. The extremity of the visual elements in Figure 2 is foregrounded and evokes surprise, which is one of the features of humour (Ross, 1998). The white colour of the baby's cloth is equally foregrounded to symbolise innocence, the baby stares at his mum in puzzlement and sits still in the pot of water in innocence (NAz and Epps, 2004). The vector in the woman's gaze at the viewer is an attention-drawing strategy. The totality of the presentation is deployed to mockingly suggest that in addition to adding salt to their bath water, Nigerians could possibly go further to boil themselves and their loved ones in the salt water solution for more effective results. The post questions the ludicrousness of such salt-water claims, and depicts through exaggerated humour, the fallaciousness of eradicating EVD through untested methods.

Figure 3 likewise ridicules the eagerness with which Nigerians had begun to experiment anti-EVD practices, even though these had not been institutionalised by health organisations or institutions in the country. The post has two salient images, two men who function together as actors in a transactional process; the two men are by a gas cooker, bent over a blue bucket of hot water. The man in a white shirt is seen turning a kettle of water into the bucket, the goal. It is suggested that this water is boiled as the kettle is in an attributive relationship with the gas cooker which lies at a close social distance with the gas cylinder, the kettle and the man. This proximity shows that the cooker had just been used. The white colour of the shirt worn by the man holding the kettle signifies the ignorance which informs the performance of the acts. The second man in the presentation is scantily clothed. He is holding yet another transparent sachet of salt in his right hand, and is bent over the blue bucket. This implies that he is about to empty or has emptied some of the salt into the bucket. His state of dressing shows that he is about to take a bath with the bucket of water. The conceptual process that informs Figure 4, like other posts is that the constructions are created to mock the salt-water-cure and prevention claim by many Nigerians during the EVD outbreak. Internet memes like this are discursive practices that suggest the ways in which information is quickly spread across the country. One man has heard of the anti-Ebola potency of salt, he swiftly informs another friend, brother, or neighbour who is also eager to 'protect' himself as well. Implicitly, the post may be said to question Nigerians' dispositions towards rumours as well as the speed with which rumours go round.

Figure 4.

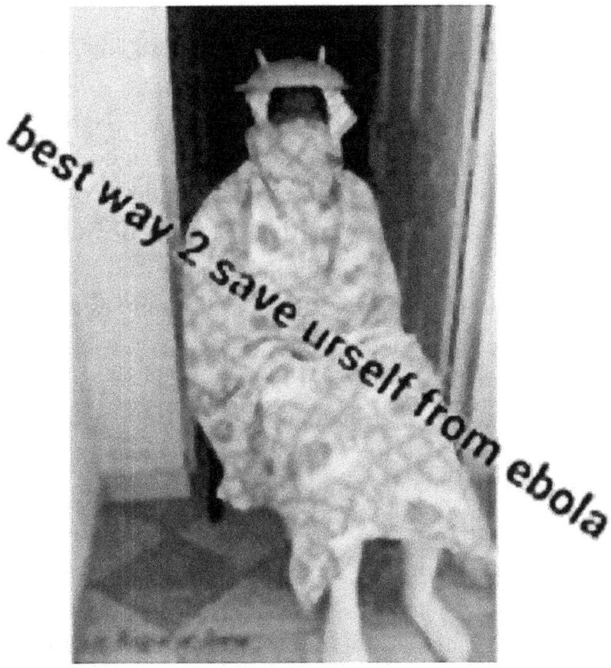

Although these memes elicit laughter at the surface level, at a deeper level, viewers are made to ponder on the possibility of such drastic measures. The surprise and absurdity the pictures portray make the acts unrealistic, thus emphasise the deceitfulness of the claims that salt-water bath is a preventive measure for Ebola.

The visual image in Figure 4 is transactional, it features one actor, who is the focus of attention, an unidentifiable individual whose body is completely covered in a patterned lemon green wrapper, his legs are shielded by a pair of white stockings, and his head is also covered with a piece of towel, held firmly with a metal-like hat. The lemon green colour of the wrapper, which is a principal hue is used to express a kind of calmness, the colour promotes relaxation and helps to douse anxiety (NAz and Epps, 2004). Because only the individual's eyes are visible, and his hands are hidden under the wrapper, there is a relational process which carries a meaning potential of a state of calmness and satisfaction. The text written across the post reads, 'best way 2 save urself from ebola'. The use of short forms; '2' and 'urself', in the inscription shows that there no elaborate measures are needed for the prevention of EVD, the best and easiest way has been depicted by the individual.

In addition, the salience with which the text is written in a slant is a relational process that is directly linked to the foregrounded participant, the individual. It implies within the presentational process, that the person in the picture characterises what the inscription says. The picture is an exaggerated conceptual process that portrays the need for people to wear protective clothing to avoid direct body contact with infected persons. Inasmuch as the intended message is clear, the extremity in the portrayal of the message is more likely an effective attention-getter, and like an advert, it likely serves to increase awareness on the EVD.

B: Conceptual Acts

Nigerians are known to be characteristically courteous and friendly. Greeting is an identifiable element of the Nigerian culture; thus, failure to extend friendly greetings and compliments to one's neighbour is largely perceived as a deficiency in home training and manners (Nwoke, 2013). When relationships with neighbours or acquaintances are closely knit, greetings in Nigeria are usually accompanied by an embrace, a hug, a pat on the back or even a kiss. Consequently, the EVD posed some limitations to the expression of these greetings. These seemingly motivated *Facebook* users to humorously suggest innovative but bizarre ways of getting around the situation.

Figure 5 to Figure 8 each shows two actors exchanging pleasantries while equally taking precautions against EVD. Figure 5 shows one foregrounded participant, a young man in a white vest, who shakes another foregrounded participant (another man) hand, the handshake represents the goal. The first participant has taken great care to shield his feet, hands and face with several layers of nylon sheets. The nylon sheets in this instance are relational attributive processes establishing a relation with the other shielded body parts, hence, a conceptual process is developed to portray an underlying message of the need to take precautions while "doing the needful" (greeting) without necessarily risking one's health. The use of the nylon suggests the ingenuity of Nigerians and their ability to improvise in the midst of needs as Nigeria is a developing nation and most of her citizens would rather buy food and shelter than spend their income on synthetic gloves and other forms of protective measures (Okoroafor and Nwaeze, 2013). The social distance represented in the interactive process between the two men in Figure 5 is unusual in the Nigerian setting. The expectation would have been for the men to be closer than they are.

Figure 5.

Figure 6.

Figure 6 relatedly is presentational process that foregrounds two participants, a lady in black top and a man in white shirt also exchanging pleasantries, with a bold inscription across the picture which reads, 'Ebola greeting...'. One recurring theme in the presentational processes within Figure 5 to Figure 8 is the foregrounded neutral colours; 'black' and 'white', which are carriers of representational meaning, as they are symbolic processes in themselves. The colour black relates to the hidden, the secretive and the unknown which creates an air of mystery and fear, while on the other hand, white represents a new beginning, wholeness, innocence and perfection (NAz and Epp, 2004). There is the saying that what black covers, white uncovers. Thus, Figure 5 to Figure 6 are symbolic processes. It may therefore be inferred that while the characters in black conceal their fear of being infected with EVD, those in white suggest that they are able to relate with the situation and thus, share the same fear. However, the foregrounded participants in the posts still succeed in sustaining a jovial exchange as indicated by their smiling faces. The unusual bow by the characters in Figure 6 is a face saving device, it has interactive meaning potential, as it is deployed to cushion the inner embarrassment of both participants. The social distance between the visual images in the narrative is an element of salience interrelates with other participants to express deliberate avoidance of direct body contact. The ellipsis on the inscription on Figure 6 also suggests that there is more to say but the picture gives all the necessary clues. Such clues may include that Nigerians are innovative, jovial, and health conscious.

Figure 7 is a shift from Figure 5 and Figure 6; the narrative introduces a completely new form of greeting, at the analytical level, it appears to be a deliberate exaggeration of innovative greeting methods, though seemingly unreal, a conceptual process is established to assert that body contact may still be maintained while exchanging pleasantries, even if this means through unusual methods as the two men in Figure 7 humorously hit their buttocks together in place of a hug. This attributive process signi-

Figure 7.

Figure 8.

fies that even if the Ebola virus escapes through protective gloves, it is not likely to pass through thick items of clothing.

The presentational process in Figure 8 is a complete break from the Nigerian politeness norm; the second man bluntly refuses to extend his unprotected hands for a handshake and goes on to inquire if the 'salutee' has not heard of Ebola: 'Hmm! My guy Hang am! You never hear about Ebola?' (Figure 8). The use of Nigerian Pidgin in the conversational process is foregrounded to express the sociocultural identity of the participants in the narrative. While the memes elicit laughter, they provide clues to Nigerians' abilities to retain their socio-cultural practices and still observe EVD preventive measures.

C: Reactional Acts

As a developing nation, Nigerians are known to be very innovative and creative especially in dire situations where they perceive an opportunity to take advantage of a desperate situation in order to make money (Nnadozie, 2002). It is therefore no wonder to find jokes on commercialised Ebola preventive items on *Facebook* as a reaction to the need for prevention.

Figure 9 portrays one foregrounded participant, a sachet of 'Blessed Anti-Ebola Salt: Chineke Punish Ebola', with an inscription on the top right corner, 'Buy 2 Get 1 Free!' in red flash frame. ANTI-EBOLA is written in red upper-case letters, a salient type-face to make it conspicuous and catchy. Also, BLESSED and SALT are written in upper case letters and large typeface to appeal to the religious sensibilities of the viewer, as these texts lie in a frontal vector in relation to the viewer. The representations in this post offer some insights into the Nigerian socio-cultural context. First, the use of the term, "Blessed" presupposes some spiritual sense relations in the brand-name. It tends to suggest that Nigerians have an affinity to religion, and would therefore be more willing to patronise a blessed "Anti-Ebola salt". This is a form of double preventive measure against EVD, the spiritual measure on the one hand, and the use of table-salt on the other hand (as already indicated in the section on 'Narrative Acts'. 'Chineke' is the Igbo term for 'God'; its use on the salt sachet is an attributive process that relates to the Igbo identity of the merchant. Nigerians, especially Igbos who belong to the south-eastern and south-central regions of the country, are known to be perhaps the most enterprising ethnic group in the country; hence, they see business potentials in almost every circumstance (Nnadozie, 2002). The use of the term, 'Chineke' also coheres with the name, 'Blessed Anti-Ebola Salt', as it is a conceptual process of representation which

Figure 9.

suggests a spiritual variable in the packaging of the product. The message flashed in the red frame on the upper left corner reads, BUY 2 AND GET 1 FREE offers additional value to other texts in the image, and this is equally done to draw attention to the commercialisation intent of the producers of such products during that time.

The conceptual meaning deducible by the reader of this representation appears to be a sensitisation to Nigerians on the need to be wary of dubious motives by some individuals who may take undue advantage of the Ebola epidemic in Nigeria.The inscription, 'buy 2 and get 1 free', further suggests a purely commercial intent, as it appears to be another aim at persuasion. Thus, the meme with all of its semiotic features, such as the typeface, the colour, the letter case which appear to be commercial strategies, is deliberately created to discredit the efficacy of any seemingly convincing anti-Ebola measures. All other features in the background such as the small fonts used for the expiry date and trademark are deliberately so done in order to raise attention to such aspects of the product. It is done to conceal the producers and legality of the products. This is the trend with many fake products in Nigeria, the author of Figure 9 by so doing, establish a conceptual meaning that the 'blessed salt' is a fake product.

Figure 10 in like manner shows a black bottle of perfume with the inscription, 'Ebola Perfume Spray'. The undefined of the bottle is significant, as it suggests that its contents are unusual. The choice of black as the colour of the bottle makes it opaque, preventing the content of the bottle from being visible; this has a relational attributive process as it establishes the psychological implication of black as a secretive colour. This again functions as a narrative that suggests that the product and many like it in the Nigerian market are flukes; as a mental process, the mere thought of the possibility of a perfume spray that dispels Ebola is comparable to the possibility of a spray that can make one invisible – which is only seen in magic and myths. Though Figure 9 and Figure 10 reveal Nigerian socio-cultural realities, they also serve as sources of humour in the digital world, that is, the online community.

Figure 10.

D: Speech and Action Acts

In this section, the visual and verbal modes are almost equally integrated to express salient messages. The participants in Figure 11 are four black scantily dressed children smiling excitedly and dancing at the news that "A White Person Got Ebola", consequently, "Cure is on the Wayl. The underpants of the children are 'backgrounded' to emphasise poverty, backwardness, depravity and primitivism that may be associated with the black race. The literal framing of Figure 11 is actually the figurative framing of the black race as a poverty stricken people. In establishing interactive meaning the text, "A White Person Get Ebola", boldly presented in white font, an asymmetry is observed in the contrast between the participants' complexion and the reference to "a white person". The dance style and smile of the children is infectious and humorous, but an underlying message is implicitly passed across through the meme; it implies that developed countries would be more proactive towards seeking a cure for EVD since one of their own (a white) has been infected. For example, the United States of America, a world power, has remained complacent towards fighting a cure for EVD in African nations, as the country's position on the epidemic in Africa may have seemed controversial (Ogundipe, et al., 2014) Figure 11 appears ideological, as it accuses developed nations of complacency in the face of a disease that has resulted in a high fatality rate among Africans. The background of Figure 11 also foregrounds dryness; as the brown sand and dry grass cohere with the representation of the children to depict lack, austerity, depravity, crude, under-development.

Figure 11.

The foregrounded participant in Figure 12 is a monkey in big goggles, comfortably seated on a blue stool as he plays a guitar on a stage. The meme has an inscription that reads, 'i wanna sing a little song about an EBOLA i gave'. In the two instances where the pronoun 'I" occurs in the post, it is written in lower case, in contravention of the writing convention that the personal pronoun, 'I' should be capitalised. This appears to be a deliberate de-personalisation strategy which tends to suggest that the humans generally consider the monkey as an insignificant creature. However, the monkey engages in a reactional process as it resists the belittling attempt by humans. The monkey proudly claims that it is responsible for EVD, the post places emphasis on the magnifying impact of EVD, through the use of upper case letters and bigger fonts—'EBOLA' (Figure 12). The crossed left leg of the monkey and his big goggle combine to project a *laissez-faire* attitude towards every accusation.

Even though the meme is a comical post, it is a presentational process which functions as an awareness strategy. It sends the message that EVD is contaminable through monkeys, and therefore, it is the duty of humans to keep away from monkeys if they must avoid EVD.

E: Analytical Acts

Figure 13 is a presentational process that features two hands, the trademark of Nokia, a technology company, whose products are popular in Nigeria. It likewise has other textual language within its narrative. When a Nokia phone is powered on, two hands briefly engage in a handshake before the phone lights up its home-screen, however, Figure 13 jokingly notes that 'I turned on my Nokia phone for the past one hour but these hands won't hold themselves, that's the fear of Ebola'. This text is presented in black font to connote fear, as the joke on the one hand suggests the hands are held back from each other in fear of the EVD. Though this is likely a conjecture, the meme, on the other hand, is a conceptual process which re-emphasises the awareness campaign against EVD, notifying viewers/readers against unguarded body contact. The message here is similar to that of Figure 5, 6, 7 and 8.

Figure 12.

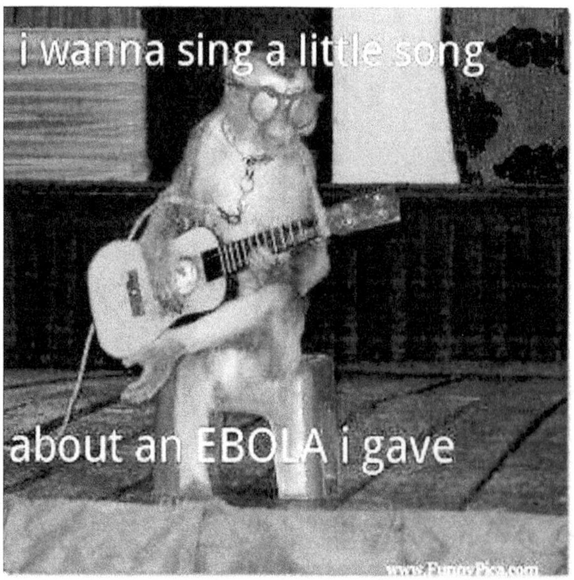

Figure 13.

The freedom of self-expression that *Facebook* users enjoy allows them to impersonate and defame important political personalities and names at will. In Figure 14, President Barack Obama of the United States of America is caricatured as a turbaned Muslim with two Islamic flags hoisted behind him. The meme reads, 'Let me make this perfectly clear...i am not a Muslim i am the ayatolla of Ebola'. While it is rumoured that Obama belongs to the Islamic religious sect (Weeks & Southwell, 2010; Hollander, 2010), Figure 14 presents an antithesis, by dismissing the claim that Obama is a Muslim, but conferring a high

Figure 14.

order Islamic title on him; an 'ayatollah' is a powerful religious leader of Shiite Muslims. Though the meme presents comical visual images through caricature, its verbal text does not create compositional meaning as its information value appears to be in contradiction with the images portrayed. This implies that Nigerian creators of memes may lack visual and media literacy which should underlie the creation of such memes.

F: Classification Acts

Crises are not unusual in human societies. Figure 15 employs the logic of time to reflect of crises bedevilling the Nigerian society. In 2014, there was the popular hashtag, '#Bring Back Our Girls' that raised global awareness on over two hundred school girls kidnapped by terrorist organisation, Boko Haram in Nigeria. The Boko Haram insurgency has continued to attract attention to the country, and is a major concern in the country. The EVD appears to be an addition to Nigeria's already existing problems, hence, the meme has two participants (cartoon characters) performing two goals. One of them carries the placard, #Bring Back Our Girls, and appears to be bewildered (as depicted by the '?' and '!' above his head) with the presence of another, '#Send Back Their Ebola' placard, the goal of the second participant. There is a suggestive conceptual process in the narrative that the latter's hashtag performs a blame game. Though they may be classified as humour, since the verbal and or visual semiotic modes produce both meaning and humour in cartoons (Tsakona, 2009), the images suggest that rather than seeking solution to Nigerian problems, Nigerians are trading blames, as signalled by the determiner, "their" in the expression 'their Ebola'. The question is "whose Ebola?" An 'us'-'them' ideological categorisation is equally brought to the fore by the representational process embedded in the use of 'their Ebola' and '... our girls'.

Figure 15.

FINDINGS AND CONCLUSION

This chapter analysed different humorous online posts on the 2014 EVD epidemic by Nigerian *Facebook* users by noting that these posts (memes), perform different semeiotic acts of representational meaning. The findings reveal that despite the ability of the posts to elicit laughter, the posts combine interrelated meaning-making processes which have significant underlying meanings embedded in the messages. The selected posts all have the features of ambiguity, surprise and deviation; which are qualities that enhance the humour in them. In addition, the semiotic patterns of the humorous posts include excessive exaggeration, salutation, innovation, jubilation, impersonation and blame game, as they reflect the Nigerian society, their usage largely reveal the deceit in some of the unorthodox practices recommended to quell the spread of the virus. The posts further warn Nigerians from falling victim of products designed to take advantage of consumers in desperate situations, such as the EVD. In addition to these, the study notes that Nigerians are able to maintain and sustain their positive socio-cultural practices even in the midst of a threat. Salient in some of the memes is the foregrounding of Nigerians' expectations from developed countries and world leaders; and the memes further reveal the need to evaluate the cause of any form of crises and address it from the right perspective.

However, the conceptual process that spreads across the posts is that they raise the level of awareness on EVD. They were indeed resourceful in combating and winning the fight against EVD in Nigeria. This study establishes that messages are embedded within humour; hence, beyond their abilities to elicit laugher, humorous posts are messages that may be resourceful in tackling social problems. It is however recommended that readers of *Facebook* posts should be more analytic and systematic in their perception of such memes, in order to get the intended message. This calls for improved media and visual literacy among meme producers because literacy has come to refer to the ability to access, interpret, analyse, access and communicate messages in various forms (Hobbs, 1997; Chauvin, 2003).

REFERENCES

Apte, M. (1988). Disciplinary boundaries in humorology: An anthropologist's ruminations. *Humor: International Journal of Humor Research*, *1*(1), 5–26. doi:10.1515/humr.1988.1.1.5

Chauvin, B. A. (2003). Visual or media literacy? *Journal of Visual Literacy*, *23*(2), 119–128.

Denkey, G. K. (2015). *By the time you read this, we'll all be dead: the failures of history and institutions regarding the 2013-2015 West African Ebola pandemic.* (Unpublished B.A. thesis). Trinity College, Hartford, CT. Retrieved May 3, 2015 from http://digitalrepository.trincoll.edu/cgi/viewcontent.cgi?article=1531&context=theses

Ding, Z. (2015). *The internet meme as a rhetoric discourse: investigating Asian/Asian Americans' identity negotiation.* (Unpublished M.A. thesis). Graduate College of Bowling Green State University, OH.

Evrard, F. (1996). *L'Humor*. Paris: Hachette.

Greendhow, C. (2009). *Tapping the wealth of social network for professional development: learning and reading with technology*. New Haven, CT: Yale University Press.

Halliday, M. A. K. (1978). *Language as a social semiotic: the social interpretation of language and meanings*. London: Edward Arnold.

Hobbs, R. (1997). Literacy for the information age. In J. Flood, S. Brice Heath, & D. Lapp (Eds.), *The Handbook of Reservation on Teaching Literacy Through the Communicative and Visual Arts* (pp. 7–14). New York: Simon & Schuster Macmillan.

Hollander, B. A. (2010). Persistence in the perception of Barack Obama as a Muslim in the 2008 presidential campaign. *Journal of Media and Religion*, *9*(2), 55–66. doi:10.1080/15348421003738769

Jewitt, C., & Oyama, R. (2001). Visual Meaning: A Social Semiotic Approach. In T. Van Leeuwen & C. Jewitt (Eds.), Handbook of Visual Analysis, (pp. 134–156). London: Sage.

Kress, G. (2003). *Literacy in the New Media*. London: Routlege. doi:10.4324/9780203164754

Kress, G., & van Leeuwen, T. (2006). Reading images: The grammar of visual design. London: Routledge.

Liu, J. (2013). Visual Images Interpretive Strategies in Multimodal Texts. *Journal of Language Teaching and Research*, *4*(6), 1259–1263. doi:10.4304/jltr.4.6.1259-1263

NAz, K. A. Y. A., & Epps, H. (2004). Relationship between color and emotion: A study of college students. *College Student Journal*, *38*(3), 396–405.

Nnadozie, E. (2002). African indigenous entrepreneurship determinants of resurgence and growth of Igbo entrepreneurship during the post-Biafra period. *Journal of African Business*, *3*(1), 49–80. doi:10.1300/J156v03n01_04

Norrick, N. (1993). *Conversational joking: humor in everyday talk*. Bloomington, IN: Indiana University Press.

Norrick, N. (2003). Issues in conversational joking. *Journal of Pragmatics*, *35*(9), 133–159. doi:10.1016/S0378-2166(02)00180-7

Nwoke, M. B. (2013). Influence of cultural value system and home on child-rearing practices in the contemporary Nigerian society. *Open Journal of Philosophy*, *3*(01), 200–206. doi:10.4236/ojpp.2013.31A033

O'Halloran, K. L. (2004). *Multimodal discourse analysis: systemic functional perspectives*. New York: Continuum.

Ogundipe, S., Obinna, C., Ojeme, V., Mikairu, L., Ewepu, G., & Olawale, G. (2014, August 8). *Ebola Latest: US rejects Nigeria's request for trial drug*. Retrieved February 20, 2015 from: http://www.vanguardngr.com/2014/08/ebola-latest-us-rejects-nigerias-request-trial-drug/

Oketola, D. (2014, December 27). *How social media helped Nigerians win the war against Ebola*. Retrieved March 30, 2015 from www.punchng.com/feature/how-social-media-helped-nigerians-win-war-against-ebola/

Okoroafor, M. O., & Nwaeze, C. (2013). Poverty and economic growth in Nigeria 1990-2011. *The MacrothemeReview*, *2*(6), 105–115.

Shifman, L. (2014). *Memes in digital culture*. MIT Press.

Tsakona, V. (2009). Language and image interaction in cartoons: Towards a multimodal theory of humor. *Journal of Pragmatics*, *41*(6), 1171–1188. doi:10.1016/j.pragma.2008.12.003

Weeks, B., & Southwell, B. (2010). The symbiosis of news coverage and aggregate online search behavior: Obama, rumors, and presidential politics. *Mass Communication & Society*, *13*(4), 341–360. doi:10.1080/15205430903470532

Chapter 15
Contextual Beliefs and Pragmatic Strategies in Online Humour:
An Example of *Akpos* Jokes

Oluwatomi Adeoti
Kwara State University, Nigeria

Ibukun Filani
University of Ibadan, Nigeria

ABSTRACT

The social media in Nigeria provides an avenue where cultural practices are produced and consumed. One of such practices is joking. Specifically, a genre of jokes found in Nigeria social media space is Akpos jokes. The goal of this chapter is to explore the contextual beliefs in Akpos jokes and the pragmatic strategies employed by the writers of Akpos jokes. Akpos jokes are narratives about an imaginary character named Akpos. The study benefited from contextual belief theory (Odebunmi, 2006) while the data comprised jokes randomly picked from a blog and Facebook pages where Akpos jokes are published. The study revealed that the writer(s) of the Akpos jokes manipulate contextual beliefs like shared knowledge of language and shared knowledge of situations and events in Nigeria in order to generate humour. The writers also employ Implicature and stereotyping of the character of Akpos for humorous effects.

INTRODUCTION

Humour is part of cultural universals produced in interactions. Its prototypical form, jokes, is constantly employed in interactions among participants for various purposes. When participants employ jokes in their interactions, they adopt different strategies for their jokes. Specifically, these strategies involve the use and manipulation of existing background information between the joke teller and recipient. This paper is a pragmatic investigation of a genre of Nigerian jokes- Akpos Jokes, which was introduced into Nigerian cultural space through the social media. Akpos jokes are products of the influence of the

DOI: 10.4018/978-1-5225-0338-5.ch015

Copyright © 2016, IGI Global. Copying or distributing in print or electronic forms without written permission of IGI Global is prohibited.

social media platforms like Facebook, blogs and Nigerian virtual communities. This study is interested in how, in the construction of the jokes (an instance of language in use), contextual beliefs are employed and pragmatic strategies are manipulated for the creation of mirth in the recipients.

Akpos jokes are instances of verbal humour. The term verbal humour refers to humorous forms that are produced by the means of language (Dynel, 2009). Verbal humour may come in terms of jokes, which are further divided into referential and verbal jokes. Ritchie (2004, p. 14) posits that "verbal humour is wholly dependent on the language used, and is regarded as not translatable into another language, whereas in referential humour, the amusing substance is in what the jokes say- the events described, the characters, the situations- rather than the details of the language used". Akpos jokes are instances of referential jokes because the humour in the genre is based on what the jokes say, and this draws from background information. This is why a pragmatic approach is adopted in investigating Akpos jokes in this study.

BACKGROUND TO THE STUDY

Jokes are cultural and linguistic innovations.It can consequently be assumed that they are traditionally found in all ethnolinguistic groups of Nigeria. Each culture in Nigeria has its own repertoire of jokes and also certain rules which guide the use of jokes in interactions. With the advent of internet in Nigeria and the social networking sites it offers, new trends were introduced in cultural interactions in the country. One of the areas where innovative trends were articulated is the production and consumption of humour. With the internet, the art and act of joking develop new dimensions, one of which is Akpos jokes.

Akpos jokes are humorous creative narrations which are very popular in the social media space in Nigeria. The social media are cultural spaces that have been used by Nigerians to construct dialogues where their socio-cultural and ideological inclinations are articulated and negotiated. This social space accommodates the mode for joking, what Dynel (2009, p. 1286) calls "humorous mode/frame/key". In this interactional frame, speakers are not held responsible for the sincerity or truth of their propositions. It is this humorous mode in the social media that licenses the creation of Akpos jokes. These jokes are called Akpos jokes because they are created around an imaginary character- Akpos, who is always the major character in the jokes and sometimes the butt of the jokes. Ayakoroma (2013) describes Akpos Jokes as a brand on the social media and as a series of jokes centred on the life of a teenager- Akpos. Akpos is a very predictable character as he is always portrayed as a narrow-minded and one-way thinker who seeks the easiest means to solve a problem. In the jokes, *Akpos'* utterances and actions hold the punchlines.

The word Akpos is clipped from some common names in the Niger-Delta Region of Nigeria. Some of these names are *Akporido*, *Akpofure*, *Onoakporobo*, *Akpororo*, etc. Nigeria's Niger-Delta Region is known for youthful restiveness. The social unrest of the region is not unconnected to exploration of crude oil in the area. The Niger-Delta region of Nigeria is rich in large deposit of crude oil which has been explored and has been the mainstay of the Nigerian economy. The exploration of oil has had adverse effects on the environment, with the inhabitants no longer having their normal means of livelihood, as the oil spillage continues to ravage the waters, killing whatever life that exists in it, and making fishing next to impossible. Rather than providing basic amenities in the region, the government, as well as the oil companies working in the area, has chosen over the years, to neglect the region. The neglect of the region led to restiveness of the occupants. I Go Dye, one of Nigeria's popular stand-up comedians and who is also from Niger-Delta Region of Nigeria notes that one of the ways in which the people of the Niger-Delta Region deal with the degenerating status of the region is by bringing humour into their conversations (Francis Agoda, 2009). Furthermore, Akpos is also the real name of the progenitor of Nigerian stand-up comedy, who is popularly called *Ali Baba. Ali Baba*'s real name is Atunyota Alleluia Akporobomerere. Other stand-up comedians sometimes refer to the name Akpos in their performances.

From the foregoing, it can be seen that the use of Akpos as the major character in these jokes is a reflection of the socio-cultural realities of Nigeria. Akpos is a reflection and an expression of Nigerians' understanding of the happenings around them as it relates to politics, culture, the economy, religion and seemingly mundane everyday occurrences.

Because of its method of propagation, Akpos joke is an instance of public joking genre. Public joking genre refers to jokes which are produced in the public sphere and are easily accessible to people. In this mode of joking, the number and demographic features of the recipients cannot be determined. Usually, in public joking genre, there is no ongoing or previous interpersonal relationship between the producer of the joke and its recipient. Examples of jokes in public mode are jokes published in newspapers, internet platforms and humorous narratives of stand-up comedians. On the other hand, private joking mode exists between participants who have previous or ongoing interpersonal or social relationship. In the private joking mode, the participants are familiar with each other; the number of the recipients of the joke is fixed and well-known to the producer of the joke. Examples of private joking mode include occupational humour (Schmidt, 2011) and cooperative conversational humour, which "is a solidarity-oriented discourse between friends" (Knight, 2008: 482). In private joking mode, outsiders to the conversation may find the jokes inaccessible because the joke text is dependent on the identities and shared values of the participants, who are members of the same community.

It should be noted that in public joking genre too, community membership is also vital in that participants should be aware of language rules and the prevailing culture(s) of the community where the joking exchange is situated. For instance, in stand-up comedy performances, the audience members should be aware of how the stand-up performance begins and how the stand-up activity proceeds. Similarly, in other public joking genres, the recipients should share aspects of the background information which the joke-producer uses in constructing the jokes. These aspects include the knowledge of the language used in conveying the joke and the knowledge of the subject matter in the joke. Shared values and community membership are, therefore, important in public joking. This is why Mintz (1985) notes that in public joking, the context and process of joke telling are as important as the text of the joke because both are crucial to comprehending the humour in the joke. Essential to the success of the jokes in the public mode is public recognition and acceptance. People must accept the joke as a joke- as humorous. The public acceptance of the joke is therefore vital for the sustenance of the genre. Thus, for jokes in the public mode, the joke structure rarely lies in the utterance alone, but it is dependent on what the public will take as humorous. The construction of jokes in the public mode, therefore, depends on shared beliefs between the joke producers and recipients. As an instance of public joking, community membership plays a vital role in the interpretation of Akpos jokes and the ultimate realisation of humour in the joke.

In the next section, we present the methodology adopted for data collection, and after which, we explore the shared beliefs in Akpos Jokes using Odebunmi's (2006) framework of contextual beliefs.

METHODOLOGY

The data for this study were derived from three sources; the Facebook pages- Akpos Jokes and Akpos the comedian and the blog http://www.akposjokes.com/. Although there are other computer mediated avenues where Akpos jokes were published, these three sources were selected because they are deliberately created for the publication of mainly Akpos jokes. Also, the selected social media spaces are quite popular in that they have large followership, for instance, as at the time of collecting data from Akpos the comedian, the Facebook page had 710, 873 likes. Jokes were randomly selected for analysis. The selected jokes were extracted by copying from the web pages. In instances where needed, translations of expressions were provided. Akpos jokes are primarily presented in English language. However, there are instances where Nigerian Pidgin and other Nigerian languages were alternated with the English language.

Contextual Beliefs in Jokes

Odebunmi (2006, p.30) opines that "interactions move on smoothly when participants have common socio-cultural and situational experiences". Odebunmi articulates socio-cultural and situational experiences needed for facilitating linguistic exchanges in terms of beliefs that take place at two levels: language level beliefs and situational level beliefs. As Odebunmi and Alo (2010) note, when shared beliefs exit between participants, collaboration takes place. Collaboration is invaluable for the realisation of humour. Participants must be willing to participate in joking for a joke to be felicitous. Public joking depends on anticipated cooperation of the recipients. As observed by Mintz (1985), public joking is an instance of public affirmation and re-examination of shared cultural beliefs, shared laughter, celebration of agreement on what deserves ridicule and affirmation, and, fostering community and mutual support for common belief and behaviour.

At the language level, it is assumed that participants should speak the same language and operate within the same set of nonverbal codes. At the situational level, it is assumed that participants should have a shared knowledge of the subject topic; word choices, referent and references; and, sociocultural experiences - previous and immediate.

Since this study considers the pragmatics of jokes, there is a need to show how Odebunmi's contextual beliefs framework is relevant for the analysis of jokes. We begin by noting that a joke should be described within the context of its realisation. This context primarily identifies the total speech situation of the joke or what Schmidt (2011, p. 615) described as "performance arena" of the joke. The speech situation or performance arena of a joke is grounded in the contextual beliefs of the joke. First, the language level belief accentuates that for a joke to be felicitous, its producer and recipient should be operating within the same code of communication, both linguistic and paralinguistic. For verbal jokes to be realised, participants depend on language that would be used in conveying the joke. In general theory of verbal humour, language is identified as one of the knowledge resources which participants tap into to generate and interpret a joke. Language is described as containing all the information necessary for the verbalisation of the joke (Attardo, 1994). At the situational level, the participants' shared knowledge of utterances, references, referent and register comes into play. An important aspect of this is the targets found in the joke. The participants should, based on a shared knowledge of the context, be able to identify the referent.

Second, the shared knowledge of discourse topic and socio-cultural experiences are important for interpreting the activity in the joke. Jokes are always about something. The activity in joke is the event, action or doing found in the joke text (Filani, 2015). The activity in the joke could be a mundane or ritual event like crossing the road, having sex, praying, greeting or teaching. The way the activity in the joke is presented may be different from how it should be presented given the participants' shared knowledge of discourse topic and socio-cultural experiences. Shared knowledge of discourse topic and socio-cultural experiences are important for the scripts that would be activated for interpreting the joke. Scripts have been identified as the basis for humour in any joke text. For scripts to activate humour, they must be brought into opposition as described in script theories of humour (Attardo, 1994).

Third and last, the language level and situational level beliefs are important determinants for incongruity. Incongruity is usually weaved into either language- as in the case of verbal joke like puns- or situation described in the joke - as in the case of referential jokes. Incongruity is viewed as a mismatch between two propositions, ideas or scripts found in a joke (Attardo, ibid). Although incongruity is a necessary factor for humour, incongruity in itself does not lead to humour. According to Attardo (2009), factors like fatigue, anger, hunger and/or needed background knowledge for understanding incongruity may impede a participant from finding humour in a joke. As much as incongruity can work for humour, it can also generate other effects. It could create fear, awe or suspense. Attardo (2009) notes the example of detective narratives where incongruity is used in a way to prevent the reader from reconciling the events in the novel with their background knowledge. Attardo (ibid) cites some conditions for incongruity to be perceived as funny: it should not be threatening, too complex or too simple; it should be unexpected or surprising; the participants must have the available scripts or background knowledge to interpret the incongruity; the participant must be in a frame where they can enjoy humour; and, co-occurrence of opposing scripts which should be activated at the same time or closely after each other.

Having discussed the relationship between contextual beliefs and humour, there is a need to identify the contextual beliefs which are employed in the construction of Akpos jokes. This is presented in the next section.

Contextual Beliefs in Akpos Jokes (AJ)

Shared Knowledge of Linguistic Forms

When jokes are performed within a community where communal common ground exists, it is expected that the members of such community or group share certain things such as linguistic forms and socio-cultural expectations. A deviation from this has the potentiality of impeding the creation and realisation of humour. However, when the shared knowledge of linguistic form is exploited or manipulated, as it is found in puns, there is the creation of humour. In AJ, we found that in some instances, linguistic forms are manipulated for the purpose of creating humour. In *Akpos the Porter* for example, Akpos recently resumed as a porter in a five star hotel and the manager expressed to Akpos the need for him (Akpos) to be very observant and give 'personalised services' to every customer. The short excerpt from the joke presents the scenario:

Example 1

... Before the manager could finish, a couple walked through the hotel entrance and the manager quickly approached them, nicely took their baggage and said, "Welcome Mr & Mrs James, it is our delight to have you in our hotel. Please come this way to the reception" and he led them to the reception.

After the couple had been taken care of, Akpos asked the manager, "Has the couple been visiting this hotel before?"

"No" came the reply from the manager.

"So how come you knew their name?" asked Akpos.

"That is why I told you to be very observant. All I had to do was to quickly look at the label on their baggage while I'm taking it from them and see the name on the tag."

"Oh, here comes another couple. Why don't you give it a try?"

"Ok" said Akpos and he hurriedly approached the couple, helped them with their luggage and said, "Welcome Mr & Mrs SUPERIOR HAND MADE LEATHER! We are delighted to have you in our hotel..."

The manager fainted!

Addressing customers by their names is considered to be a very good practice as it gives the customer a feeling of relevance and also gives the impression that the service provider, the hotel manager in this instance is personally interested in the customer. In Ex. 1, the manager exploits this strategy and encourages Akpos, the new staff, to do the same. The manager however uses the name tags used for identification on the suitcase to know the name of the customer without having to ask them. He then challenges Akpos to do the same. Akpos, having been instructed by his manager, attempts to repeat what he saw his manager doing. As another couple enter the hotel, Akpos walks up to them to welcome them. He looks at the bag of the couple and addresses them by the description of the quality of the suitcase (superior handmade leather), rather than using the name on the identification tags. The shared knowledge of the meaning of lexical items 'superior handmade leather' is therefore exploited in generating humour in this joke. It should be noted that naming and references assignment to names are linguistic practices.

A vital aspect of shared knowledge of linguistic forms in Akpos jokes is the knowledge of Nigerian use of English which include the use of Nigerian English coinages and alternating English with indigenous languages like the major Nigerian languages and Nigerian pidgin. Nigerian English terms like *Oga, Madam* and code alternation are commonly found in Akpos jokes. Ex. 2 below illustrates Nigerians' use of the English language:

Example 2

Akpos again!!!

Akpos got to school late on Monday morning and the teacher asked "Akpos, why did you come to school late?"

Akpos answered, "one man lost one hundred naira note at the bus stop."

The teacher said, "oh! That's good of you, seems you were helping the man look for his lost money."

Akpos answered, "No oh! I dey craze??? Na me stand on top of the money."

In Ex. 2, the joke is presented in the English language. However, the writer deliberately code switches to NP in the last line of the joke. The use of Nigerian English features like code-switching is meant to create community bonding and identity in terms of language use between the joke writers and the recipients. On the whole, the writers of AJ deliberately make use of expressions which the recipients – Nigerians - are familiar with. Should they have written the jokes without incorporating features of Nigerian English, the recipient might find the jokes alien to them.

Shared Knowledge of Context

The use of words is usually context bound. As a result of this, language users are expected to be sensitive to the immediate context of language use for a proper understanding of what words are employed to do in any given situation. Given that Akpos is sometimes stereotyped as foolish, the writers of Akpos jokes sometimes exploit this stereotype, combining it with shared situational knowledge to generate humour. Consider the example below:

Example 3

The inimitable Akpos sent the following story from the hospital, where he is currently on admission.

"Today I got knocked out by a woman. I was in the elevator when that busty lady with excellent cleavage got on. I was staring at her boobs, then she said, would you please press 1? So I picked the left one. I don't remember much afterwards."

In Ex. 3, Akpos is presented as being a contextually tactless individual whose lack of knowledge of the use of situation-bound utterances provides the garden path for the creation of humour in this joke. Given the nature of elevators, users could, sometimes, request that another occupant of the elevator punch their destination floors for them, as sometimes, such people are unable to get close enough to the control buttons for space constraints. Akpos in this instance however focuses on the boobs of the lady who just got on the elevator and instead of pressing the elevator button to take her to the 1st floor at the lady's request, Akpos presses one of the lady's two breasts, taking her use of "could you please press one" out of context and literally pressing the 'one' that has his attention. While the 'boobs woman' expected her request for someone close to the elevator to "please press one" to evoke the knowledge of elevator etiquette, Akpos is rambunctious rather than cooperative, generating humour in the process.

The Knowledge of Events and Situations in Nigeria

Shared knowledge of events and situation in Nigeria forms the class Odebunmi (2006) calls shared socio-cultural experiences, previous and immediate. This class thus subsumes shared situational (immediate) and shared experiential (previous) knowledge. Given that Akpos jokes are considered to be a reflection and an expression of the socio-political realities of Nigerians, their social, economic, religious and political experiences form a good source for AJs. The day to day experiences of Nigerians, group peculiarities in terms of linguistic competence, religious activities (such as celebrations) among others are engaged as indicators of shared knowledge of events and situations in Nigeria. Consider the following AJ:

Example 4

Zain to Airtel

Teacher: *Why did Zain change to Airtel?*
Akpos: *Because Yoruba people kept calling it 'Sane'*

The Change in ownership of the Telecommunications Company 'Zain' informed a change in the brand name from 'Zain' to 'Airtel'. This however, was not the first time the company was having a change in name (probably as a result of a change in ownership) as it started out, as one of the first private owned telecommunications companies in Nigeria, in the early 2000's as Econet. The writers of AJs however create a joke out of the name change by attributing it to the Yorubas' problem of phonological interference where they realise the voiced alveolar fricative /z/ as the voiceless alveolar fricative /s/. Understanding this joke is reliant on the knowledge of this interference as a recognised area of weakness in some Yoruba speakers' competence and performance of the English language which, is a target language and thus contrasts with the realisations of such sounds that already exist in their mother tongue (Yoruba). However, the garden path that serves as the set-up for the punchline of the joke is derived from the shared knowledge of the change of ownership of the telecommunication company.

In another AJ, a religious celebration (Eid' Kabir, 'Ileya' in Yourba) and the realities of poor cash flow in Nigeria, which made it difficult for Muslims to buy the 'customary ram' are engaged as a situational experience to create the joke:

Example 5

Akpos and Ileya ram

A conversation ensued between Sule and Akpos about Sule's preparedness for Eid-el-Kabir (Ileya)

Sule: *Na wah for this government people oh! Every thing just tight for man pikin*

[Translation: These government officials are very terrible. They have made life unbearable for one]

Akpos: *Sule, wetin happen na?*

[What is it Sule?]

Sule: *The economy too tight so tey say man pikin no fit buy ram for this Ileya sef*

[The economy is not buoyant and I am not finding it easy. I cannot even buy the ram for Eid' Kabir]

Akpos: *Eiya! But I have two rams na and I fit give you one from the two.*

[I am sorry about that. However, I have two rams, and I can give you one]

Sule excitedly jumped up for joy and began to dance for joy as he follows Akpos to his house. On getting home, Akpos calls to Chuks (his neighbour) to give him a screw driver and Sule (anxious to see the ram he's to be given) excitedly asked, Akpos where you tie the rams na?

[Akpos, where did you keep the rams]

Akpos responds, "they are inside the house na"

Sule: *(surprise but anxious to get his gift) Akpos, why you keep ram inside the house na? The ram go shit full your room oh.*

[Why did you keep the rams in the house? They would have excreted in your room]

Akpos: *Haba Sule! Na my laptop the rams follow come na and na the screw driver wey I go use open the back of my laptop I wan collect for Chuks hand so na.*

[Not at all Sule! I am talking about my laptop rams, and that is why I collected the screw driver from Chuks, so that I can open up my laptop and give you the ram]

Before you could say jack Akpos ended up at the hospital as if he's been hit by a trailer.

In this AJ, preparations for the Ileya celebration are ongoing in the country. However, Sule, a Muslim, laments his inability to buy a ram because of hard economic realities. Akpos offers to give him one of the two that he (Akpos) has. Eventually, we find that Akpos' rams are in his laptop, mere pictures and not life rams. His raising of Sule's hopes and eventual disappointment of that very hope gets Akpos a beating. The knowledge of the importance attached to sacrificing of rams during Ileya by Nigerian Muslims has been exploited for the construction of the joke. This knowledge provides the necessary script derived from the word ram as an animal, which is used to lead the readers of the joke in the garden path needed for the punchline.

We must also note the manipulation of shared knowledge of language in this joke. In the first instance, there is the use of Nigerian Pidgin (NP), which functions as the unofficial lingua franca in the country. NP functions in this instance as an affiliative resource between the joke writer and the recipients.The second aspect of shared knowledge of language in the joke is the pun on the word *ram*. Apart from drawing from shared knowledge of situations and events in Nigeria (Eid' Kabir festival in Nigeria and its importance to Muslims), the writer also drew from shared knowledge of the word *Ram* which is polysemous. In the first use of the word in Sule's statement, it means an adult male sheep while in Akpos' utterances it is referring to pictures of rams in his laptop. It can also be argued that the word ram refers to a part of computer- specifically, the abbreviation for random access memory (RAM). It can be argued that Akpos is referring to RAM and that he needs a screw-driver to access the RAM in his computer. We opine that the use of the ambiguous word- ram, which draws on the shared knowledge of language, events and situations, is a deliberate strategy adopted for humour by the joke producer.

The Existence of the Imaginary and Humorous Character: Akpos

Perhaps, the most obvious assumption in Akpos narratives is the use of the imaginary and humorous character Akpos. Both the composer of the jokes and their recipient must accept, at least in the world of the jokes, that a character called Akpos exists, and that this character, with his actions and utterances, is capable of generating humorous effects. As explained above, Akpos is a clipped name-form from a common first name in the Niger-Delta region of Nigeria. This suggests that the character is representative of youths in the Niger-Delta region of the country. Perhaps, as suggested by I Go Dye, the use of humour by the Niger-Deltans to deal with their daily activities is fully encoded in the character of Akpos. It is assumed that Akpos will either do or say something that is funny. Akpos typifies an utterance which is commonly found in the narratives of Nigerian stand-up comedians: *Warri*[1] *boy/ pako pikin no dey carry last* which translates into "a Warri boy/ an indigent boy is never beaten at his game"; a statement which the comedians use in poking fun at Warri people.

The character of Akpos is synonymous with the use of fools in a number of narratives. For instance, in Shakespearean plays, the fool was adopted as a jester and an individual who mirrors the society. Similarly, fools have been adopted in Nigerian narratives, both in the traditional sense and contemporary sense. In the traditional sense, in a number of cultures in Nigeria, like Yoruba, court fools are found in kings' palaces. According to Adeleke (2006, p. 63), "the fool in court focused on pure entertainment and rhetoric". Similarly, in Nigerian television, film and theatre productions, the use of jesters or fools has become rampant. Starting with Baba Sala who produced comic movies and acted comic roles in the 1980s and early 1990s, comic roles have become a major feature of Nollywood productions. Haynes (1994) describes Baba Sala's comic acting as high watermarks of Nigerian film comedy. The character of Akpos depicts the use of fools in creative narratives like film and drama. Akpos does not only act funnily, he also mirrors the society where his jokes originate from. Like the court fool, in traditional cultures, the character of Akpos focuses on pure entertainment and rhetoric of humour.

Closely linked to the existence of the humorous character Akpos is the expectation of humour from the jokes. As the word joke conjures expectation of funniness, so does the tag '*Akpos*' bring expectation of amusement or funny behaviour.This is not unconnected to the fact that the character has been presented as having a predictable humorous trait, in that the humour in the jokes is woven into the utterances or action of Akpos. Outside the world of the jokes, the name *Apkos* has become a label associated with humorous behaviour. For instance, it is an abusive term for someone who behaves funnily or stupidly. Akpos is the real name of the progenitor of Nigerian stand-up comedy and it is also the stage name of one of Nigerian stand-up comedians.

PRAGMATIC STRATEGIES IN AKPOS JOKES

The Use of Opening and Closing Phrases

The performance of a joke is said to have three parts: the preface, the joke telling and the response phase (Attardo, 1994). Akpos jokes are presented in a similar but different sequence. The variance in AJ is due to the medium through which the jokes are presented. Conversational joking studies have been focused on physical ongoing spoken interaction. On the other hand, AJs are presented in written form in computer mediated interaction. The medium through which the jokes are presented informs the peculiarity of its presentation sequence and the functions of each part.

In the presentation of AJs, the joke producer uses opening and closing markers to signal the start of the joke and its closing. In between these two, there is the actual telling of the jokes. Unlike verbal conversational joking where response phases follow closely after the telling, AJs still have a closing phase which is used to trigger the response from the readers. Ex. 6 below illustrates the sequence of presenting Akpos jokes.

Example 6

Three men in the desert

Akpos, John and Rukewe were stranded in the Sahara desert, when they saw a bottle of wine. They were so happy because they hadn't taken a drink in days. They decided to share the drink equally among themselves. John would take the top one-third, Rukewe would take the second, and Akpos would take the last. Since it was evening, they decided to keep it till the next morning, before drinking. Then they made themselves swear not to steal the wine. The next morning, the bottle of wine was empty. After cross examination, Akpos admitted he drank it.

They asked him why and he said, "I woke up in the middle of the night, and was thirsty. But since my portion was at the bottom of the bottle, I had to drink through yours to get to it"

Please is Akpos at fault?

- **Opening Phrase:** *Three men in the desert*
- **The Joke:** *Akpos, John and Rukewe were stranded… I had to drink through yours to get to it*
- **Closing Phrase:** *Please is Akpos at fault?*

Opening and closing markers are very important aspects of narratives. According to Norrick (2000: 54), these discourse markers are "stock phrases" which announce and close the jokes. The opening markers point to and provide controlling images for what would be found in the jokes while the closing markers are meant to align the responses towards a particular direction like appreciating the joke and appraising the character of Akpos. The opening markers are used to activate background information that would be needed to understand the jokes. They are suggestive of the roles Akpos plays in the jokes and they also position the readers in an interpretive frame grounded in the contextual beliefs activated by the markers. The opening markers also have textual functions in that they indicate the thematic preoccupation of the jokes while the closing markers serve the textual function by indicating the ending of the jokes. In conversational joking, the telling of the joke ends with the presentation of the punchline, but in AJs, the telling of the joke ends with the closing markers. As their primary discourse function, the ending of the AJs invites the recipients of the jokes to give their perspectives on the joke or the character of Akpos.

Some opening markers found in the data are *House boy Akpos* (For a joke where Akpos played the role of a house boy to a family), *Akpos and Ileya ram* (For a joke where Akpos promised his friend a ram for a festival), *In the club* (For a joke in which Akpos went clubbing without his mother's permission) and *Akpos the taxi driver* (For a joke where Akpos played the role of a taxi driver). Examples of closing markers are '*One word for Akpos',' how many LIKE for Akpos'* and '*LIKE if funny'*.

Stereotyping of the Character of Akpos

Adetunji (2013) describes stereotypes as pragmatic phenomena which are employed to position the self and the other in socially meaningfully manner. This is because participants derive their stereotypes about social categories and manners from their cultural background. Stereotyping has been described as a nimble tool for humourists. Gruner (1997, p. 99) observes that "a stereotype is merely a very handy kind of shorthand to provide the essential framework for understanding the content of a joke". Stereotyping elicits humorous response when it involves exaggerating or understating some features which could be an action, a trait or behaviour.

In AJ, stereotyping is crucially employed to typify the character of Akpos. We find two primary ways by which Akpos is stereotyped in the jokes. These are illustrated below:

Akpos as a Trickster

A primary stereotype of Akpos is that the character is a trickster. In some of the jokes, Akpos is presented as manipulative and seeking the easiest means to solve a problem. In a number of instances, his solutions to problems benefit only him. Such solutions are at the expense of the other characters in the joke. An example of this is seen in Ex. 6 above. Two other instances are presented below:

Example 7

A Japanese tourist hailed a taxi in Nigeria and asked to be taken to Ahmadu Bello Airport. On the way, a car zoomed by and the tourist responded, "Oh! Toyota- Made in Japan! Very fast!". Not long afterward, another car flew by the taxi. "Oh! Nissan- Made in Japan! Very fast!" Yet another car zipped by and the tourist said, "Oh! Mitsubishi- Made in Japan! Very fast!"

Akpos, who is 100% Nigerian, was starting to get a little annoyed that the Japanese made cars were passing his taxi when another car passed the taxi as they were turning into the airport. "Oh! Honda- Made in Japan! Very fast!"

Akpos stopped the car, pointed to the meter, and said, "That'll be 5000 naira"

The tourist exclaimed "5000 Naria? It was short ride! Why so much?"

Akpos smiled as he replied, "Meter- Made in Nigeria. Very fast!"

Example 8

In a restaurant yesterday, Akpos and his girlfriend were having dinner. Suddenly, Akpos goes on one knee! Gir friend cries, "Oh my God, I can't believe this is happening. You wanna propose to me.....!??"

Akpos: *Abeg!!! Shut up!! My wife just walked in!*

It is important to note that these jokes draw from the collective knowledge of the participants, specifically, shared situational belief. In Ex. 7, the joke is dependent on the background knowledge that if one takes a taxi, one's fare should be commensurate with the distance. However, this collective knowledge is contradicted in the joke. How the contradiction is achieved is closely knitted to the character of Akpos, which is stereotyped here as manipulative. Because the passenger has been praising the products of his country (the cars that overtook Akpos' taxi), it infuriated Akpos. Akpos, in order to "punish" the Japanese tourist for praising Japanese products while in Nigeria, surcharged him for the service he rendered. This is an instance of Akpos as a trickster, since he did not give the charge that was equal to the service he rendered.

In Ex. 8 too, we see Akpos having two love relationships. Specifically, Akpos was having extramarital relationship. Akpos' action in the joke misleads the other character, his girlfriend, into believing that Akpos is about to propose marriage to her. Akpos is portrayed as a deceptive male who leads a lady into believing that he is interested in marrying her, but who is actually trying to hide his extramarital relationship from his wife.

Akpos as Stupid

Another stereotyping in Akpos jokes is the portrayal of the character of Akpos as stupid. Akpos is commonly depicted as a character who is not capable of logical reasoning and whose intelligence quotient is below average. In some of the jokes, Akpos' statements and actions show that he is a one-way thinker who cannot employ his common sense to solve problems and who runs away from tasks which demand rigorous thinking. In Ex. 9 below, Akpos' utterances show that, as a student, he could not comprehend a scientific formula. The stereotyping of Akpos as stupid is much more foregrounded in Ex 10, where he places his computer in a washing machine in order to clean it.

Example 9

Teacher: *What is the chemical formula for water?..*
Akpos: *H I J K L M N O.*
Teacher: *What are you talking about?*
Akpos: *Yesterday, you said it's H to O.*

Example 10

Akpos: *I cleaned my computer and it's broken!*
Technician: *What did you clean it with?*
Akpos: *Soap and water.*
Technician: *You are not supposed to use water near a computer!*
Akpos: *I don't think it was the water that broke it, I think it is the washing machine.*

The Use of Implicature

AJs are usually composed and structured as conversation between Akpos and other characters, who are, usually, not more than three. When the jokes are structured as conversation, the basis of humour in the jokes follows the flouting of one of Gricean maxims. Akpos' responses to the utterances of other character(s) in the jokes constitute non-observance of the cooperative principles. Since conversations are social events that are built on social actors' collaboration, and since creative narratives like AJs are reflective of real world narratives, the cooperative principles can be evoked to explain how the conversations in AJs lead to humour.

The use of Grice cooperative principle has been employed in accounting for humour in conversations. According to Attardo (1994, pp. 271-272), "a large number of jokes involve violations of one or more of Grice's maxims… the claim that jokes could be viewed in terms of violations of maxims dates back to Grice himself, who considers irony as an example of implicature". We must note that some scholars, most especially relevance theorists, kick against explaining humour in conversations using Grice maxims, for instance Yus (2003). However, some studies like Attardo (1993) and Pan (2012) have shown that Grice maxims account for humour in conversations.

We find that the use of implicature in Akpos jokes closely follows from stereotyping the character of Akpos. Whenever Akpos is stereotyped as manipulative, his utterances generate implicatures which indicate that he deliberately manipulates the maxims to his advantage. In such instances, Akpos's utterances in the jokes depict that he can infer the intentions of other characters. Akpos understands the propositions in the utterances of other characters and the implicature derived from them. Most of the time, such propositions and implicatures place Akpos in the wrong footing, therefore, Akpos chooses to discard the propositions and implicatures in his response to the utterances of other characters. Conversely, whenever he is presented as stupid, Akpos' utterances generate implicatures which indicate that he is unable to carry out the processes of assigning sense and reference, and inference, to the utterances of other characters. In such instances, Akpos does not understand the propositions in other characters' utterances and what he is expected to infer from them. Either way, Akpos' utterances reveal that he is unaware of or he chooses to ignore the set of rules, both social and linguistic, that guide conversations. It might be argued that Akpos is "intuitively" uncooperative; therefore, there is no expectation that he will fulfil the cooperative principles. Such stance suggests that Akpos is not flouting the maxims but only suspending them. Taking this line of reasoning seems unproductive in that the intentions of the producer of the jokes is to create humour, and, a primary way of uncovering humour in the narratives is to evoke the maxims. Moreover, it is expected that participants in conversations, real or imaginative narratives, should cooperate. We illustrate the use of implicature with Ex. 11- 14.

Example 11

Teacher: *What is the chemical formula for water?*
Akpos: *H I J K L M N O.*
Teacher: *What are you talking about?*
Akpos: *Yesterday, you said it's H to O.*

Ex. 11 is an instance where Akpos is stereotyped as stupid. The joke shows that Akpos does not deduce the right proposition from the *Teacher's* interrogative. The first response of Akpos shows that he flouted the maxim of relation, which gives the implicature that, he does not know the answer to the question. In the Nigerian educational context, the chemical formula for water is one of the formulas that students are exposed to at the preceding stage of secondary education; therefore, it is assumed that every student should know the formula. Also, with Akpos' second response, it is expected that he would know the formula. However, because he is stereotyped as foolish in the joke, he is portrayed as incapable of understanding the *Teacher's* proposition which he reported in his second response.

Example 12

Akpos went to an electronic store and he asked the store keeper, "What is the price of this TV?" The storekeeper answered, "We don't sell our products to Akpos."

Akpos went again the next day to the same store after cutting his beard and asked "what is the price of this TV?" The storekeeper replied, "We don't sell our products to Akpos."

The next day, Akpos came with a different disguise and asked "What is the price of this TV?" The store-keeper replied, "We don't sell our products to Akpos."

Finally, Akpos got irritated and asked the shopkeeper, "How do you recognise me every time?" The store keeper replied "because this is not a TV, it is a Microwave Oven"

In Ex. 12, Akpos does not uncover the implicature generated from the proposition of the *storekeeper*. With the statement, *we don't sell our products to Akpos*, the *storekeeper* implies that the gadget is not a TV, which Akpos thought it was. We see Akpos referring to a microwave as a television because the joke producer is portraying him as a stupid individual who cannot differentiate a microwave from a television.

On the other hand, instances where Akpos is portrayed as manipulative and as flouting the maxims so as to influence other characters and circumstances to his advantage is shown in Examples 13 and 14

Example 13

Akpos was lying unconscious in a hospital bed. After a week, he finally regained consciousness. The doctor was immediately summoned.

Doctor: *Your recovery was a miracle.*
Akpos: *Thank God! That means I don't have to pay you.*

Example 14

Girlfriend: *Akpos dear, I'm pregnant, what do you want it to be?*
Akpos: *A joke.*

In Ex. 13, Akpos understands that after his recovery, he would have to pay for the services of the doctor. Since Akpos is seen in this joke as a trickster, he is more particular about paying his hospital bills rather than his health. The doctor's statement is about his recovery from a bad state of health. Rather than making his contribution to be relevant to the proposition of the *doctor,* he chooses to talk about payment of bills. In the same vein, in Ex.14, Akpos flouted the maxim of relevance by saying that he wanted his girlfriend's pregnancy to be a joke. The implicature generated by Akpos' response is that he does not want to be responsible for the pregnancy. This further strengthens the claim that when Akpos is stereotyped as a trickster, the implicatures from his utterances are to the disadvantage of other characters in the narratives.

CONCLUSION

This chapter examined the deployment of contextual beliefs in AJs and the pragmatic strategies employed by the writers of the jokes. The writers of the jokes depend on their knowledge of Nigerian social context. The readers also need to draw from their understanding of Nigeria in interpreting the jokes. The background information needed for the construction and comprehension of the jokes is articulated as contextual beliefs which include the existence of the imaginary character, shared knowledge of linguistic form, events and situations in Nigeria. While the primary goal of AJs is to create humorous effects, the use of Akpos as the main character in the joke mirrors the use of fools like court jesters in traditional cultures in the country. As a form of public joking, AJs are reflective of what the Nigerian society takes as humorous, and in our view, the jokes project more than the humour image of Nigerians. They mirror how Nigerians comment on and reflect on the events happening in their country and their beliefs about their country. For instance, in Ex. 6, Akpos mirrors any Nigerian business man who would play a fast trick on his transactional partner. Thus, an important aspect of AJs is the community bonding and shared laughter between the joke writers and readers which the jokes project.

REFERENCES

Adeleke, D. A. (2006). The Yoruba Fool Paradigm. *Oye: Ogun Journal of Arts*, *7*, 45–66.

Adetunji, A. (2013). The interactional context of humor in Nigerian stand-up comedy. *Pragmatics*, *23*(1), 1–22. doi:10.1075/prag.23.1.01ade

Attardo, S. (1993). The violation of conversational maxims and cooperation: The case of jokes. *Journal of Pragmatics*, *19*(6), 537–558. doi:10.1016/0378-2166(93)90111-2

Attardo, S. (1994). *Linguistic theories of humour*. New York: Waiter de Gruyer.

Attardo, S. (2009). Salience of incongruities in humorous texts and their resolution. In E. Chrzanowska-Kluczewska & G. Szpila (Eds.), *In search of (non)sense* (pp. 164–179). Newcastle upon Tyne, UK: Cambridge Scholars Publishing.

Ayakoroma, B. F. (2013, June). *The rise of stand-up comedy genre in Nigeria: from nothing to something in artistic entertainment*. Paper presented at the Society of Nigeria Theatre Artists Annual Conference, Makurdi, Benue State.

Dynel, M. (2009). Beyond a joke: Types of conversational humour. *Language and Linguistics Compass*, *3*(5), 1284–1299. doi:10.1111/j.1749-818X.2009.00152.x

Filani, I. (2015). Discourse types in stand-up comedy performances: An example of Nigerian stand-up comedy. *European Journal of Humour Research*, *3*(1), 41–60.

Francis Agoda. (n.d.). Retrieved August 12, 2013 from Nigerian Films Magazine Web site: http://www.nigeriafilms.com/artists_profile_details.asp?user_id=1929

Gruner, C. R. (1997). *Thegame of humour: a comprehensive theory of why we laugh*. New Brunswick, NJ: Transaction Publishers.

Haynes, J. (1994). Structural adjustments of Nigerian comedy: Baba Sala. *Evanston, IL: Program of African Studies. Northwestern University*, *8*, 17–20.

Knight, N. K. (2008). "Still cool…and American too!": An SFLanalysis of deferred bonds in internet messaging humour. *Systemic Functional Linguistics in Use: Odense Working Papers in Language and Communication, 29,* 481-502.

Mintz, L. (1985). Standup comedy as social and cultural mediation. *American Quarterly*, *37*(1), 71–80. doi:10.2307/2712763

Norrick, N. R. (2000). *Conversational narrative: story telling in everyday talk*. Philadelphia, PA: John Benjamins Publishing Company. doi:10.1075/cilt.203

Odebunmi, A. (2006). *Meaning in English: an introduction*. Ogbomoso, Nigeria: Critical Sphere.

Odebunmi, A., & Alo, M. A. (2010). Beliefs in GSM text messaging among academics in two Nigerian Universities. In R. Taiwo (Ed.), *Handbook of research on discourse behavior and digital communication: language structures and social interaction* (pp. 468–478). Hershey, PA: IGI Global. doi:10.4018/978-1-61520-773-2.ch029

Pan, W. (2012). Linguistic basis of humor in uses of Grice's cooperative principle. *International Journal of Applied Linguistics and English Literature, 1*(6), 20-25.

Ritchie, G. (2004). *The linguistic analysis of jokes*. Oxford, UK: Routledge.

Schmidt, C. (2011). Prisons, performance arena and occupational humor. *Oral Tradition*, *26*(2), 613–616. doi:10.1353/ort.2011.0023

Yus, F. (2003). Humour and the search for relevance. *Journal of Pragmatics*, *35*(9), 1295–1331. doi:10.1016/S0378-2166(02)00179-0

KEY TERMS AND DEFINITIONS

Contextual Beliefs: Beliefs, propositions, ideas, etc. which are shared by members of a community or group. They are usually instantiated by shared knowledge of context, of situation, of particular linguistic forms among others.

Garden-Path: It refers to the phenomenon in joke through which the recipients of jokes are made to identify the most salient interpretation of the set-up. This salient interpretation is later contradicted when the punchline is presented.

Incongruity: A major mechanism in jokes and other humorous narratives. It refers to existence of a clash or contradiction of propositions found in the set-up and punchline of a joke, which must be resolved for the realisation of humour.

Joke: We view a joke as a piece of discourse aimed at creating mirth in the recipients. It should be made up of two important parts: the build-up/set-up and the punchline.

Punchline: The final part of a joke text. It brings about surprise and it is incongruous with the punchline. The proposition in the punchline usually contradicts the one in the set-up.

Stereotype: Positive or negative biased, rigid and often exaggerated belief that is applied both to an entire social category of people and to each individual within it. Stereotypes form the basis for prejudice, which in turn is used to justify discrimination and attitudes.

ENDNOTE

1 Warri is an oil rich city in Delta State, Nigeria. It is one of the major oil producing cities in the Niger-Delta.

Compilation of References

9 ja Comedy Videos. (n.d.). Retrieved from: https://www. 9jacomedyvideos.com

Aarons, D. (2011). *Jokes and the linguistic mind*. London: Routledge.

Abel, M. H. (1998). Interaction of humor and gender in moderating relationships between stress and outcomes. *The Journal of Psychology*, *132*(3), 267–276. doi:10.1080/00223989809599166 PMID:9540225

Adams, A. C. (2012). *On the identification of humor markers in computer-mediated communication*. AAAI Technical Report FS-12-02. Artificial Intelligence of humor. Retrieved March 6, 2015, from https://www.aaai.org/ocs/index.php/FSS/FSS12/paper/viewFile/5554/5796

Adams, A. (2012). On the identification of humour markers in computer –mediated communication. *Association for the Advancement of Artificial Intelligence.*, *2*, 1–3.

Adejunmobi, M. (2014). Standup Comedy and the Ethics of Popular Performance in Nigeria. In N. Stephanie & O. Onookome (Eds.), *Popular Culture in Africa: The Episteme of the Everyday* (pp. 175–194). New York: Routledge.

Adeleke, D. A. (2006). The Yoruba Fool Paradigm. *Oye: Ogun Journal of Arts*, *7*, 45–66.

Ademilokun, M. (2012). Communicative Imports of Visual Images in the Discourse of Some Nigerian Student Soccer Fans. *IBADAN Journal of English Studies*, *8*, 75–94.

Adetunji, A. (2013). The Interactional Context of Hummour in Nigerian Stand-up Comedy. *Pragmatics*, *23*(1), 1–22. doi:10.1075/prag.23.1.01ade

Adetunji, A. (2013). The interactional context of humor in Nigerian stand-up comedy. *Pragmatics*, *23*(1), 1–22.

Agbenyega, E. (2014, April 10). *Ghana's power crisis: What about renewable energy?* Retrieved from graphic.com.gh

Akinwale, A. A. (2010). Repression of press freedom in Nigerian democratic dispensations. *Africa Development. Afrique et Developpement*, *35*(2), 47–70.

Allan, K. (Forthcoming). What is common ground? In Perspective on Pragmatics and Philosophy. Berlin: Springer Verlag. doi:10.1007/978-3-319-01014-4_11

Allen-Dutton, J., Fasolo, M., Goldstein, D., Green, S., McCallum, P., Root, T., & Senreich, M. (Writers), & Senreich. M. (Director). (2005). Toy Meets Girl [Television series episode]. In M. Senreich & S. Green (Producers), Robot Chicken. Los Angeles, CA: ShadowMachine Studios.

American Mental Association. (2008). *AMA Reports of the Council on Science and Public Health: Substance Use and Substance Use Disorder*. AMA Annual Note.

Annoying Orange. (2013, Nov 23). *Annoying Orange – kitchen intruder (bed intruder spoof) with autotune remix!* [Video File]. Retrieved from https://www.youtube.com/watch?v=pezdRcVe04c.

Apte, M. (1985). *Humor and laughter: an anthropological approach*. Ithaca, NY: Cornell University Press.

Apte, M. (1988). Disciplinary boundaries in humorology: An anthropologist's ruminations. *Humor: International Journal of Humor Research, 1*(1), 5–26. doi:10.1515/humr.1988.1.1.5

Archakis, A., & Tsakona, V. (2005). Analyzing conversational data in GTVH terms: A new approach to the issue of identity construction via humor. *Humor: International Journal of Humor Research, 18*(1), 41–68. doi:10.1515/humr.2005.18.1.41

Aristotle. (1941/ 2001). The basic works of Aristotle. New York: Random House.

Arundale, R. B. (1997). *Against (Grice's) intention*. Paper presented at LSI Preconference on Language and Cognition, International Communication Association Conference, Montreal, Canada.

Arundale, R. B. (2008). Against (Gricean) intention at the heart of human interaction. *Intercultural Pragmatics, 5*(2), 229–258. doi:10.1515/IP.2008.012

Atoye, R. O. (1991). Word Stress in Nigerian English. *World Englishes, No., 10*(1), 1–6. doi:10.1111/j.1467-971X.1991.tb00132.x

Attardo, S. (2007). A Primer for the Linguistics of Humor. Academic Press.

Attardo, S. et al. (1994). The linear organization of jokes: analysis of two thousand texts. *Humor, 7*(1), 27-54.

Attardo, S., & Raskin, V. (1991) Script theory revis(it)ed: joke similarity and joke representation model. HUMOR, the International Journal of Humor Research, 4(3-4), 293-348. doi:10.1515/humr.1991.4.3-4.293

Attardo, S., & Raskin, V. (1991). Script theory revis(it)ed: joke similarity and joke representation model. Humor, 4(3/4), 293-347.

Attardo, S., & Raskin, V. (1991). Script theory revis(it)ed: joke similarity and joke representation model. Humor: International Journal of Humor Research, 4(3), 293-348.

Attardo, S., & Raskin, V. (1991). Script theory revis(it)ed: Joke similarity and joke representation model. Humor: International Journal of Humor Research, 4(3-4), 293-347.

Attardo, S. (1993). Violation of conversational maxims and cooperation: The case of jokes. *Journal of Pragmatics, 19*(6), 537–558. doi:10.1016/0378-2166(93)90111-2

Attardo, S. (1994). *Linguistic theories of humor*. Berlin: Mouton de Gruyter.

Attardo, S. (1994). *Linguistic Theories of Humor*. Berlin: Mouton de Gruyter.

Attardo, S. (1994). *Linguistic theories of humour*. Berlin: Mouton de Gruyter.

Attardo, S. (1997). The semantic foundations of cognitive theories of humor. *Humor: International Journal of Humor Research, 10*(4), 395–420. doi:10.1515/humr.1997.10.4.395

Attardo, S. (2001). *Humorous texts: A semantic and pragmatic analysis*. Berlin: Mouton de Gruyter. doi:10.1515/9783110887969

Attardo, S. (2009). Salience of incongruities in humorous texts and their resolution. In E. Chrzanowska-Kluczewska & G. Szpila (Eds.), *In search of (non)sense* (pp. 164–179). Newcastle upon Tyne, UK: Cambridge Scholars Publishing.

Attardo, S., & Raskin, V. (1994). Non-literalness and non-bona-fide in language: An approach to formal and computational treatments of humor. *Pragmatics & Cognition*, *2*(1), 31–69. doi:10.1075/pc.2.1.02ras

Audrey, A. (2012). *Humor markers in computer-mediated communication.* (M.A. thesis). Texas A & M University. ProQuest document, dissertations & theses - Gradworks. Retrieved January 2, 2014, from http://gradworks.umi.com/15/29/1529858.html

Ayakoroma, B. F. (2013). The Rise of Stand-up Comedy Genre in Nigeria: From Nothing to Something in Artistic Entertainment. *The Rise of Stand-up Comedy Genre in Nigeria*. Retrieved from http://www.nico.gov.ng/features/1008-the-rise-of-stand-up-comedy-genre-in-nigeria.html

Ayakoroma, B. F. (2013, June). *The rise of stand-up comedy genre in Nigeria: from nothing to something in artistic entertainment.* Paper presented at the Society of Nigeria Theatre Artists Annual Conference, Makurdi, Benue State.

B'Ayin. Z. (2015, January 14). This Chronological History Of The Holocaust Was Done Entirely With Legos. *Heeb*. Retrieved from http://heebmagazine.com/chronological-history-holocaust-done-entirely-legos/53985

Bachmann, R. (2015, January 22). Sein Hitler-Selfie kennt jetzt die halbe Welt. *Bild*. Retrieved from http://www.bild.de/politik/inland/pegida/presseecho-ruecktritt-lutz-bachmann-39447360.bild.html

Bai, Y. (2011). Incongruity-resolution in English Humor. *Theory and Practice in Language Studies*, *1*(1), 83-86. Retrieved March 5, 2015, from http://ojs.academypublisher.com/index.php/tpls/article/viewFile/01018386/2468

Bakhtin, M. M. (1981). *The dialogic imagination: Four essays* (C. Emerson & M. Holquist, Trans.). Austin, TX: University of Texas Press.

Balirano, G., & Corduas, M. (2006). Statistical methods for the linguistic analysis of a humorous TV sketch show. *Quaderni di Statistica*, *8*, 1–24.

Ball, H. (1999). *Prosecuting War Crimes and Genocide: The Twentieth-Century Experience*. Lawrence, KS: University Press of Kansas.

Baran, A. (n.d.). *Visual Humour on the Internet*. Retrieved from http://www.folklore.ee/pubte/eraamat/eestipoola/baran.pdf

Baron, N. S. (2003). Language of the Internet. In A. Farghali (Ed.), *The Stanford Handbook for Language Engineers* (pp. 59–127). Standford: CSLI Publications.

Baron, N. S. (2010). *Always on: Language in an online and mobile world.* Oxford, UK: Oxford University Press.

Barrera, M. (2002). Hottentot 2000: Jennifer Lopez and her butt. In B. K. M. Philips & B. Reay (Eds.), *Sexualities in history* (pp. 407–420). New York: Routledge.

Barrett, L. E. (1988). *The Rastafarians*. Beacon Press.

Barthes, R. (2003). Camera lucida. In H. S. Karen (Ed.), *Ways of reading words and images.* Bedford, St. Martin.

Bateson, G. (1953). The position of humor in human communication. In H. von Foerster (Ed.), *Cybernetics* (pp. 1–47). New York: Josiah Macy, Jr Foundation.

Bateson, G. (1972). A Theory of Play and Fantasy. In G. Bateson (Ed.), *Steps to an Ecology of Mind* (pp. 177–193). Chandler.

Baym, N. K. (1995). The performance of humor in computer-mediated communication. *Journal of Computer Mediated Communication*, *1*(2). Retrieved January 2, 2014 from www.ascusc,org/jcmc/vol1/issue2/baym.html

Baym, N. K. (2004). The performance of humor in computer-mediated communication. *Journal of Computer-Mediated Communication, 1*(2).

Baym, Nancy, K. (1995). The performance of humour in computer-mediated communication. *Journal of Computer-Mediated Communication.*

Beam, S. L., Gant, R. W., & Mecham, M. J. (1978). Communication Deviations in Alcoholics: A Pilot Study. *Journal of Studies on Alcohol, 39*(3), 548–551. doi:10.15288/jsa.1978.39.548 PMID:651363

Beattie, J. (1778). *Essays*. Edinburgh, UK: William Creech.

Beeman. (2000). Humor. *Journal of Linguistic Anthropology, 9*(2).

Belz, J. A. (2002). Second language play as a representation of the multicompetent self in foreign language study. *Journal of Language, Identity, and Education, 1*(1), 13–39. doi:10.1207/S15327701JLIE0101_3

Belz, J. A., & Reinhardt, J. (2004). Aspects of advanced foreign language proficiency: Internet-mediated German language play. *International Journal of Applied Linguistics, 14*(3), 324–362. doi:10.1111/j.1473-4192.2004.00069.x

Benjamin, A., & Patton, A., & Sheats, D. (2001). So Fresh, So Clean [Recorded by Outkast]. On *Stankonia* [CD]. New York: NY: Arista, RCA Records.

Bennett, G. A. (2012). Say what? (笑): The representation of laughter as a contextualization cue in online Japanese discourse. *Linguistica, 52*, 187-199. Retrieved December 15, 2014, from www.dlib.si/stream/URN:NBN:SI:DOCMYWF5CHD/...0e5e.../PDF

Berger, A. A. (n.d.). *Signs of Humor: On the Structure of Laughter*. Retrieved from www.culturestudies.pbworks.com/f/Semiotics+of+Humor+AAB.doc

Berger, A. (1995). The Holocaust, Second-Generation Witness, and the Voluntary Covenant in American Judaism. *Religion and American Culture:Journal of Interpretation, 5*, 23–47.

Berger, P. L., & Luckmann, T. (1966). *The social construction of reality: A treatise in the sociology of knowledge*. Garden City, NY: Anchor Books.

Bergson, H. (1928). *Laughter: An Essay on the Meaning of the Comic*. New York: The Macmillan Co.

Berk, R. A. (2005). LAUGHTERPIECE THEATRE: Humour as a Systematic Teaching Tool. *Essays on Teaching Excellence toward the Best in the Academy, 17*(2), 1-8.

Billig, M. (2005). *Laughter and Ridicule. Towards a Social Critique of Humour*. London: SAGE Publications.

Blackburn, R. E. (2013). *Fem and funny: Three women who changed the face of stand-up comedy*. (Unpublished MFA thesis). Virginia Commonwealth University, Richmond, VA.

Blakeslee, S. (2000). *The Death Of American Anti-Semitism*. Westport, CT: Praeger.

Blitt, R. (Writer), & M.D. DiMartino (Director). (2000). Death Is A Bitch [Television series episode]. In S. MacFarlane (Producer), Family Guy. Los Angeles, CA: Fox Broadcasting Company.

Boxer, D., & Cortés-Conde, F. (1997). From bonding to biting: Conversational joking and identity display. *Journal of Pragmatics, 27*(3), 275–294. doi:10.1016/S0378-2166(96)00031-8

boyd, D. M. & Ellinson, N. B. (2008). Social network sites: Definition, history, and scholarship. *Journal of Computer-Mediated Communication, 13*, 210-230.

Breitman, R., & Lichtman, A. (2013). *FDR and the Jews*. Cambridge, MA: The Belknap Press of Harvard University Press. doi:10.4159/harvard.9780674073654

Brest, P., & Krieger, L. H. (2010). *Problem solving, decision making, and professional judgment: A guide for lawyers and policymakers*. New York, NY: Oxford University Press.

Brillenburg, K. (2011). Spitting Image and pre-televisual political satire: Graphics and puppets to screens. *Image and Narrative*, *12*(3), 113–136.

Bro^ne, G. (2008). Hyper-and misunderstanding in interactional humour. *Journal of Pragmatics*, *40*(12), 2027–2061. doi:10.1016/j.pragma.2008.04.011

Brown, P., & Levinson, S. (1987). *Politeness: Some Universals in Language Usage*. Cambridge, UK: Cambridge University Press.

Butler, J. (1990). *Gender trouble: Feminism and the subversion of identity*. New York: Routledge.

Cahill, S., & Densham, R. (2014). *Women, Humour and Power...in the workplace: A Review of the current literature for funny Women*. Accessed in February 10, 2015 from http://www.funnywomen.com

Capone, A. (2001). *Modal Adverbs and Discourse*. Pisa: ETS.

Capone, A. (2005). Pragmemes: A study with reference to English and Italian. *Journal of Pragmatics*, *37*(9), 1355–1371. doi:10.1016/j.pragma.2005.01.013

Carstyn, R., & Noh, E. (1995).A truth-functional account of metalinguistic negation with evidence from Korean. *UCL Working Papers in Linguistics, 7*, 1–26

CBS News. (2013, May 9). *Cleveland neighbor Charles Ramsey's 911 call for missing girls*. Retrieved from http://www.cbsnews.com/news/cleveland-neighbor-charles- ramseys-911-call-for-missing-girls/ May 9, 2013.

Chace, Z. (2010, August 13). 'Bed Intruder Song' climbs the charts. *NPR*. Retrieved from http://www.npr.org/sections/therecord/2010/08/13/129178815/bed-intruder-song-climbs-the-charts

Chandler, D., & Munday, R. (2011). *A dictionary of media and communication*. Oxford. doi:10.1093/acref/9780199568758.001.0001

Chaouat, B. (2013). Anti-Semitism Redux: On Literary and Theoretical Perversions. In A. Rosenfeld (Eds.), Resurgent Anti-Semitism: Global Perspectives (pp. 118-140). Bloomington, IN: Indiana University Press.

Chauvin, B. A. (2003). Visual or media literacy? *Journal of Visual Literacy*, *23*(2), 119–128.

Chiaro, D. (1992). *The language of jokes: analyzing verbal play*. London: Routledge. doi:10.4324/9780203327562

Chik, M. D. Y., Leung, C. S., Benjamin, M., & Geoffrey, N. (2005). Develoment of a Measure of Humour Appreciation. *Australian Journal of Educational and Developmental Psychology*, *5*, 26–31.

Chovanec, J. (2011). Humour in quasi-conversations: Constructing fun in online sports journalism. In M. Dynel (Ed.), The Pragmatics of Humour Across Discourse Domains (pp. 243-264). Amsterdam: John Benjamins Publishing Company.

Chovanec, J. (2012). Conversational humour and joint fantasizing in online journalism. In J. Chovanec & I. Ermida (Eds.), Language and Humour in the Media (pp. 139-161). Newcastle upon Tyne, UK: Cambridge Scholars Publishing.

Chovanec, J. (2009). Simulation of spoken interaction in written online media texts. *Brno Studies in English*, *35*(2), 109–128.

Clarke, A. (2009). *The Eight Patterns of Humour*. Cumbria, UK: Pyrrhic House.

Clark, H. H. (1996). *Using Language*. Cambridge, UK: Cambridge University Press. doi:10.1017/CBO9780511620539

Clark, H. H., & Brennan, S. E. (1991). Grounding in communication. In *Perspective on Socially Shared Cognition* (pp. 127–149). Washington, DC: American Psychological Association.

Clark, H. H., Schreuder, R., & Buttrick, S. (1983). Common ground and the understanding of demonstrative reference. *Journal of Verbal Learning and Verbal Behavior*, *22*, 245–258. doi:10.1037/10096-006

Cole, T. (1999). *Selling the Holocaust: From Auschwitz to Schindler: How History Is Bought, Packaged, and Sold*. New York: Routledge.

Collinson, D. L. (1988). Engineering humour: Masculinity, joking and conflict in shop floor relations. *Organization Studies*, *1*(3), 58–76.

Collins, P. H. (2000). *Black feminist thought: knowledge, consciousness and the politics of empowerment*. New York, NY: Routledge.

Connolly, K. (2015, February 5). Adolf Hitler Novel Tops German Bestseller List But Divides Critics. *The Guardian*. Retrieved from http://www.theguardian.com/world/2013/feb/05/adolf-hitler-novel-german-bestseller

Connolly, K. (2015, January 6). German Leaders Condemn Xenophobia After Pegida Protests. *The Guardian*. Retrieved from http://www.theguardian.com/world/2015/jan/06/germany-pegida-protests-dresden-immigration

Crawford, C. B. (1994). Theory and Implications regarding the utilization of strategic Humour by Leaders. *The Journal of Leadership Studies*, *1*(4), 53–67. doi:10.1177/107179199400100406

Crines, A. S. (2014). Rhetoric and Satire – Spitting Image And Political Comedy. In *Rhetoric in British politics and society*. Basingstoke, UK: Palgrave Macmillan.

Critchley, S. (2002). *On Humour*. New York: Routledge.

Crystal, D. (2008b). 2b or not 2b? *The Guardian*. Retrieved February 2, 2015, from http://www.theguardian.com/books/2008/jul/05/saturdayreviewsfeatres.guardianreview

Crystal, D. (1996). Language play and linguistic intervention. *Child Language Teaching and Therapy*, *12*(3), 328–344. doi:10.1177/026565909601200307

Crystal, D. (2001). *Language play*. Chicago: University of Chicago Press.

Crystal, D. (2006). *Language and the Internet* (2nd ed.). Cambridge, UK: Cambridge University Press. doi:10.1017/CBO9780511487002

Crystal, D. (2008a). *Txting: The gr8 db8*. Oxford, UK: Oxford University Press.

Cutting, J. (2008). *Pragmatics and Discourse: A Resource Book for students* (2nd ed.). New York: Routledge.

Danet, B., Ruedenberg-Wright, L., & Rosenbaum-Tamari, Y. (1997). Hmmm ... Where's that smoke coming from? Writing, play and performance on Internet Relay Chat. *Journal of Computer-Mediated Communication*, *2*(4). Retrieved from http://onlinelibrary.wiley.com/doi/10.1111/j.1083-6101.1997.tb00195.x/full

Davies, C. (1990). *Ethnic humor around the world: A comparative analysis*. Bloomington, IN: Indiana University Press.

de Beaugrande, R., & Dressler, W. (1990). *Introduction to Text Linguistics*. London: Longman.

Deaner, S. L., & McConatha, J. T. (1993). The relation of humor to depression and personality. *Psychological Reports*, *72*(3), 755–763. doi:10.2466/pr0.1993.72.3.755 PMID:8332677

Delise, N. N. (2012). Me, Myself, & Identity Online: Identity Salience on Facebook vs Non-Virtual Identity. *University of New Orleans Theses and Dissertations*. Paper 1431.

Denham, J. (2015, February 5). The Simpsons in Auschwitz: Harrowing aleXsandro Palombo Cartoons Mark 70th Anniversary of Death Camp Liberation. *The Independent*. Retrieved from http://www.independent.co.uk/arts-entertainment/art/news/the-simpsons-in-auschwitz-harrowing-alexsandro-palombo-cartoons-mark-70th-anniversary-of-death-camp-liberation-10025606.html

Denkey, G. K. (2015). *By the time you read this, we'll all be dead: the failures of history and institutions regarding the 2013-2015 West African Ebola pandemic*. (Unpublished B.A. thesis). Trinity College, Hartford, CT. Retrieved May 3, 2015 from http://digitalrepository.trincoll.edu/cgi/viewcontent.cgi?article=1531&context=theses

Denzin, N. K., & Lincoln, Y. S. (2011). The discipline and practice of qualitative research. In N. K. Denzin & Y. S. Lincoln (Eds.), *The Sage Handbook of Qualitative Research* (2nd ed., pp. 1–19). Urbana-Champaign, IL: Sage.

Desilet, G., & Appel, E. C. (2011). Choosing a Rhetoric of the Enemy: Kenneth Burke's Comic Frame, Warrantable Outrage, and the Problem of Scapegoating. *Rhetoric Society Quarterly*, *41*(4), 340–362. doi:10.1080/02773945.2011.596177

Ding, Z. (2015). *The internet meme as a rhetoric discourse: investigating Asian/Asian Americans' identity negotiation*. (Unpublished M.A. thesis). Graduate College of Bowling Green State University, OH.

Dochartaigh, P. (2006). Americanizing the Holocaust: The Case of "Jakob the Liar. *Modern Language Review*, *101*(2), 456–471. doi:10.2307/20466794

Double, O. (2014). *Getting the joke: The inner workings of stand-up comedy* (2nd ed.). London: Bloomsbury.

Double, O. (2014). *Getting the Joke: The Inner Workings of Stand-up Comedy*. London: Bloomsbury.

Drew, P. (1987). Po-faced receipts of teases. *Linguistics*, *25*(1), 219–253. doi:10.1515/ling.1987.25.1.219

Drop it like it's hot. (n.d.). Available atwww.azlyrics.com/lyrics/snoopdogg/dropitlikeitshot.html

Dumitru, D. (2008). The Use and Abuse of the Holocaust: Historiography and Politics in Moldova. *Holocaust and Genocide Studies*, *22*(1), 49–73. doi:10.1093/hgs/dcn002

Durant, A., & Lambrou, M. (2009). *Language and media*. London: Routledge.

Dynel, M. (2011a.) Joker in the pack: Towards determining the status of humorous framing in conversations. In M. Dynel (Ed.), The Pragmatics of Humour Across Discourse Domains (pp. 217-241). Amsterdam: John Benjamins Publishing Company

Dynel, M. (2011b). Pragmatics and Linguistic Research into Humour. In M. Dynel (Ed.), The Pragmatics of Humour Across Discourse Domains (pp. 1-15). Amsterdam: John Benjamins Publishing Company.

Dynel, M. (2009). Beyond a joke: Types of conversational humour. *Language and Linguistics Compass*, *3*(5), 1284–1299. doi:10.1111/j.1749-818X.2009.00152.x

Dynel, M. (2011). *The Pragmatic of Humour aross Discourse Domain*. Amsterdam: John Benjanmin Publishing. doi:10.1075/pbns.210

Eco, U. (1976). *A Theory of Semiotics*. Bloomington, IN: Indiana University Press. doi:10.1007/978-1-349-15849-2

Eder, J. S. (2012). *West German Reactions to American Holocaust Memorial Culture*. Paper presented at the Benelux American Studies Association Conference: American Responses to the Holocaust, Transatlantic Perspectives, Middleburg, The Netherlands.

Edward, C., Bresnahan, K., & Krystal, A. (2008). The influence of humorous positive computer-mediated word-of-mouth communication on student motivation and affective learning. *Texas Speech Communication Journal*, *53*(1), 1–8.

Erickson, D., Yoshida, K., & Meneze, C. (2006). Exploratory Study of Some Acoustic and Articulatory Characteristics of Sad Speech. *Phonetica*, *63*(1), 1–25. doi:10.1159/000091404 PMID:16514273

Ervin-Tripp, S. M., & Lampert, M. D. (1992). Gender differences in the construction of humorous talk. In Hall, K., Buchholtz, E. & Moonwoman, B. (Eds.), *Locating power:Proceedings of the Second Berkeley Women and Language Conference* (pp. 108-117). Berkeley, CA: Berkeley Women and Language Group, Linguistics Department, University of California.

Eshman, R. (2013, February 25). Seth MacFarlane: Not An Anti-Semite. *Jewish Journal*. Retrieved from http://www.jewishjournal.com/rob_eshman/article/seth_macfarlane_not_an_anti_semite/

Evans, S. (2013, May 2). Timur Vermes' Hitler Novel: Can the Führer be funny? *BBC News*. Retrieved from http://www.bbc.com/culture/story/20130417-is-it-okay-to-laugh-at-hitler

Evrard, F. (1996). *L'Humor*. Paris: Hachette.

Fairclough, N. (2006) semiosis, ideology and mediation. In Mediating ideology in text and image: ten critical studies (pp.19-36). Amsterdam: John Benjamins.

Fallace, T. D. (2006). The Origins of Holocaust Education in American Public Schools. *Holocaust and Genocide Studies*, *20*(1), 80–102. doi:10.1093/hgs/dcj004

Fearman, R. J. (2014). *Punchline Predictability Comprehension Speed, and Joke Funningness: Investigating Incongruity theories of humour*. (Honours Psychology Thesis). Department of Psychology, University of West Ontario, London, Ontario, Canada. Retrieved from http://ir.lib.uwo.ca/psychd_uht

Feigelson, S. (1989). Mixing Mirth and Management. *Super Vision*, *50*(11), 6–8.

Filani, I. (2015). Discourse types in stand-up comedy performances: An example of Nigerian stand-up comedy. *European Journal of Humour Research*, *3*(1), 41–60.

Filani, I. (2015). Discourse types in stand-up comedy performances: An example of Nigerian stand-up comedy. *The European Journal of Humour Research*, *3*(1), 41–60.

Filani, I. (2015). Stand up comedy as activity type. *International Journal of Humor Research*, *4*(1), 73–97.

Filani, I. (2015). Stand-up Comedy as an Activity Type. *International Journal of Humour Research*, *4*(1), 73–97.

Finkelstein, N. G. (2000). *The Holocaust Industry: Reflections On The Exploitation Of Jewish Suffering*. New York: Verso.

Francis Agoda. (n.d.). Retrieved August 12, 2013 from Nigerian Films Magazine Web site: http://www.nigeriafilms.com/artists_profile_details.asp?user_id=1929

Freud, S. (1960). Jokes and their relation to the unconscious. New York: Norton.

Funk, T. (2015, April 10). With Holocaust Survivors Aging, Keeping Memories Alive Falls To Their Children, Grandchildren. *Charlotte Observer*. Retrieved from http://www.charlotteobserver.com/living/religion/article18142778.html#storylink=cpy

Furukawa, T. (2011). *Humor-ing the Local: Multivocal Performance in Stand-up Comedy in Hawai'i.* (Unpublished PhD dissertation). University of Hawai'i.

Gallagher, P. (2010, August 14). Antoine Dodson: from local news item to internet sensation. *The Guardian.* Retrieved from http://www.theguardian.com/world/2010/aug/15/antoine-dodson-Internet-sensation

Garber, Z., & Zuckerman, B. (1989). Why Do We Call the Holocaust "The Holocaust?": An Inquiry Into the Psychology of Labels. *Modern Judaism*, *9*(2), 197–211. doi:10.1093/mj/9.2.197

Georgakopoulou, A. (2011). "On for drinkies?": Email cues of participant alignments. *Language@Internet*, *8*, article 4. Retrieved January 2, 2015, from www.languageatinternet.org.urn:nbn:de

Gibbs, R. W. Jr. (1994). *The Poetics of Mind.* Cambridge, UK: Cambridge University Press.

Gilbert, J. (2004). *Performing marginality: Humor, gender, and cultural critique.* Detroit, MI: Wayne University Press.

Gilbert, S. (2010). Jews and the Racial State: Legacies of the Holocaust in Apartheid South Africa, 1945-60. *Jewish Social Studies*, *16*(3), 32–64. doi:10.2979/jewisocistud.16.3.32

Giora, R. (1991). On the cognitive aspects of the joke. *Journal of Pragmatics*, *16*(5), 465–485. doi:10.1016/0378-2166(91)90137-M

Giora, R. (1997). Understanding figurative and literal language: The graded salience hypothesis. *Cognitive Linguistics*, *8*(3), 183–206. doi:10.1515/cogl.1997.8.3.183

Giora, R. (1997a). Discourse coherence and theory of relevançe: Stumbling blocks in search of a unified theory. *Journal of Pragmatics*, *27*(1), 17–34. doi:10.1016/0378-2166(95)00065-8

Giora, R. (2002a). Literal vs. figurative language: Different or equal? *Journal of Pragmatics*, *34*(4), 487–506. doi:10.1016/S0378-2166(01)00045-5

Giora, R. (2003). *On Our Mind: Salience, Context, and Figurative Language.* New York: Oxford University Press. doi:10.1093/acprof:oso/9780195136166.001.0001

Goatly, A. (2012). *Meaning and Humour.* Cambridge, UK: Cambridge University Press. doi:10.1017/CBO9780511791536

Goffman, E. (1981). *Forms of Talk.* Philadelphia: University of Pennsylvania Press.

Goldberg, J. (2015, April). Is It Time For The Jews To Leave Europe? *The Atlantic.* Retrieved from http://www.theatlantic.com/features/archive/2015/03/is-it-time-for-the-jews-to-leave-europe/386279/

Gray, F. (1994). *Women and laughter.* Charlottesville, VA: University Press of Virginia. doi:10.1007/978-1-349-23275-8

Greendhow, C. (2009). *Tapping the wealth of social network for professional development: learning and reading with technology.* New Haven, CT: Yale University Press.

Grice, H. P. (1975). Logic and conversation. In Speech Acts. Syntax and Semantics (pp. 41–58). New York: Academic Press.

Grice, H. P. (1975). Logic and Conversation. In P. Cole & J. L. Morgan (Eds.), Syntax and Semantics:*Speech Acts* (vol. 3, pp. 41–58). New York: Academic Press.

Gross, D. (2013, May 10). Why the web loves Cleveland hero Charles Ramsey. *CNN.* Retrieved from http://www.cnn.com/2013/05/08/tech/web/charles-ramsey-viral

Gruner, C. (1997). *The Game of Humor: A Comprehensive Theory of Why We Laugh.* New Brunswick, NJ: Transaction Publishers.

Gruner, C. R. (1978). *Understanding laughter*. Chicago: Nelson-Hall.

Gruner, C. R. (1997). *The game of humor: a comprehensive theory of why we laugh*. New Brunswick, NJ: Transaction Publishers.

Gruner, C. R. (1997). *Thegame of humour: a comprehensive theory of why we laugh*. New Brunswick, NJ: Transaction Publishers.

Guillemin, M., & Gillam, L. (2004). Ethics, reflexivity, and "ethically important moments" in research. *Qualitative Inquiry*, *10*(2), 261–280. doi:10.1177/1077800403262360

Guzmán, I. M., & Valdiva, A. N. (2004). Brain, brow, and booty: Latina iconicity in U.S. popular culture. *Communication Review*, *7*(2), 205–221. doi:10.1080/10714420490448723

Hall, R. E. (2007). Racism as Health Risk for African-American Males: Correlations Between Hypertension and Skin Color. *Journal of African American Studies*, *11*(3/4), 204-213.

Halliday M. A. K., & Hasan, R. (1989). *Language, Context, and Text: Aspects of Language in a Social-Semiotic Perspective*. Oxford, UK: Oxford University Press.

Halliday, M. A. K. (1978). *Language as a social semiotic: the social interpretation of language and meanings*. London: Edward Arnold.

Halliday, M. A. K. (1978). *Language as social semiotic: the social interpretation of language and meaning*. London: Edward Arnold.

Harrison, C. (2003, February). Visual Social Semiotics: Understanding How Still Images Make Meaning. *Technical Communication (Washington)*, *50*(1).

Hay, J. (1995). *Gender and humour: Beyond a joke*. (Unpublished Master's thesis). Victoria University of Wellington, Wellington, New Zealand.

Haynes, J. (1994). Structural adjustments of Nigerian comedy: Baba Sala. *Evanston, IL: Program of African Studies. Northwestern University*, *8*, 17–20.

He, Y. (2008).Humor in Discourse: A Linguistic Study of the Chinese Dialect Film, *Crazy Stone*, *in* Marjorie K.M. Chan and Hana Kang (Eds.) *Proceedings of the 20th North American Conference on Chinese Linguistics* (NACCL-20), Columbus, OH: The Ohio State University.

Hein, K. (2006). Switching between Estonian Sign Language and Spoken Estonian in a School Environment. *EESTI RAKENDUSLINGVISTIKA UHINGU AASTRAAMAT*, *10*, 91–106.

Heller, A. (2015, April 13). Children of Holocaust Survivors Inherit the Role of Witness. *The Times of Israel*. Retrieved from http://www.timesofisrael.com/children-of-holocaust-survivors-inherit-the-role-of-witness/

Hentemann, M. (Writer), & J. Purdum (Director). (2008). Family Goy [Television series episode]. In S. MacFarlane (Producer), Family Guy. Los Angeles, CA: Fox Broadcasting Company.

Herberg, W. (1960). *Protestant, Catholic, Jew*. Garden City, NY: Anchor Books.

Herring, S. (2012). Grammar and electronic communication. In C. Chapelle (Ed.), *Encyclopedia of Applied Linguistics*. Hoboken, NJ: Wiley-Blackwell. Retrieved June 16, 2012, from http://ella.slis.indiana.edu/~herring/e-grammar.2011.pdf

Herring, S. C. (2010). Computer-mediated conversation: Introduction and overview. *Language@Internet*, *7*. Retrieved from http://www.languageatinternet.org/articles/2010/2801

Herring, S. (2001). Computer- mediated discourse. In D. Tannen, D. Schiffrin, & H. Hamilton (Eds.), *The Handbook of Discourse Analysis* (pp. 612–634). Oxford, UK: Blackwell.

Herring, S. C. (1999). Interactional coherence in CMC. *Journal of Computer-Mediated Communication*, *4*(4). doi:10.1111/j.1083-6101.1999.tb00106.x

Herring, S. C. (2004). Computer-mediated discourse analysis: An approach to researching online behavior. In S. A. Barab, R. Kling, & J. H. Gray (Eds.), *Designing for Virtual Communities in the Service of Learning* (pp. 338–376). New York: Cambridge University Press. doi:10.1017/CBO9780511805080.016

Hilberg, R. (1992). *Perpetrators, Victims, Bystanders: The Jewish Catastrophe, 1933-1945*. New York: Aaron Asher.

Hirsch, M. (2012). *The Generation of Postmemory: Writing and Visual Culture after the Holocaust*. New York: Columbia University Press.

Hobbs, R. (1997). Literacy for the information age. In J. Flood, S. Brice Heath, & D. Lapp (Eds.), *The Handbook of Reservation on Teaching Literacy Through the Communicative and Visual Arts* (pp. 7–14). New York: Simon & Schuster Macmillan.

Hockett, C. F. (1977). Jokes. In C. F. Hockett (Ed.), The view from language (pp. 257-289). Athens, GA: University of Georgia Press.

Holcomb, C. (1997). A class of clowns: Spontaneous joking in computer assisted discussions. *Computers and Composition*, *14*(1), 3–18. doi:10.1016/S8755-4615(97)90035-9

Hollander, B. A. (2010). Persistence in the perception of Barack Obama as a Muslim in the 2008 presidential campaign. *Journal of Media and Religion*, *9*(2), 55–66. doi:10.1080/15348421003738769

Holland, S. P. (2012). *The Erotic Life of Racism*. Durham, NC: Duke University Press. doi:10.1215/9780822395157

Holligan, A. (2014, May 8). Anne Frank Keeps Memory Alive For New Generation. *BBC News*. Retrieved from http://www.bbc.com/news/entertainment-arts-27308964

Holm, N. (2011). Reassessing the Right to Laughter: Humour, Dissent and the Liberal Imagination. *AntePodium: Online Journal of World Affairs*. Retrieved from http://www.victoria.ac.nz/atp/articles/pdf/Holm-2011.pdf

Hookway, N. (2008). 'Entering the blogosphere': Some strategies for using blogs in social research. *Qualitative Research*, *8*(1), 91–113. doi:10.1177/1468794107085298

Horowitz, S. (1997). *Queens of comedy: Lucille Ball, Phyllis Diller, Carol Burnett, Joan Rivers, and the new generation of funny women*. Amsterdam: Gordon and Breach.

Horozitz, S. (1997). But Is It Good For The Jews? Spielberg's Schindler and the Aesthetics of Atrocity. In Y. Loshitzky (Eds.), Spielberg's Holocaust: Critical Perspectives On Schindler's List (pp. 119-140). Bloomington, IN: Indiana University Press.

Huang, C. & Szafir, D. (n.d.). *No joke: Examining the use of humour in computer- mediated learning*. Retrieved January 15, 2015, from pages.cs.wisc.edu/~dszafir/documents/hci- final. pdf

Hubler, M. T., & Bell, D. C. (2003). Computer-mediated humor and ethos: Exploring threads of constitutive laughter in online communities. *Computers and Composition*, *20*(3), 277–294. doi:10.1016/S8755-4615(03)00036-7

Hudak, D. A., Dale, J. A., Hudak, M. A., & Degood, D. (1991). Effects of humorous stimuli and sense of humor on discomfort. *Psychological Reports*, *69*(3), 779–786. doi:10.2466/pr0.1991.69.3.779 PMID:1784666

Idowu-Faith, B. O. (2012). *Hyperfictional Language in Michael Joyce's afternoon, a story and Megan Heyward's of day, of night.* (Unpublished doctoral dissertation). University of Ibadan, Ibadan, Nigeria.

Iedema, R. (2003). Multimodality, resemiotization: Extending the analysis of discourse asmulti-semiotic practice. *Visual Communication, 2*(1), 29–57. doi:10.1177/1470357203002001751

Inya, O. (2012). Defending a Thesis: Pragmatic Acts in Contemporary Christian Apologetics. *Theory and Practice in Language Studies, 2*(10), 2016-2023.

Ivanova, E. (2004). Ukrainian High School Students' Understanding of the Holocaust. *Holocaust and Genocide Studies, 18*(3), 402–420. doi:10.1093/hgs/dch086

Jacquemet, M. (1992, November). Imagining identities: Nation, culture, and the past. *American Ethnologist, 19*(4), 733–748. doi:10.1525/ae.1992.19.4.02a00060

Jaher, F. C. (1994). A Scapegoat. In *The New Wilderness: The Origins and Rise Of Anti-Semitism In America*. Cambridge, MA: Harvard University Press.

Jakoaho, V., & Marjamäki, S. (2012). *"OH MY GOD, THAT NIGGER SAID GUN!": Use of Ethnic Humor in Modern Stand-Up Comedy*. (Masters Thesis). University of Jyväskylä, Finland.

Jensen, K. E. (2009, Fall). Humour. Modern World.

Jepson, K. (2005). Conversations and negotiated interaction in text and voice chat rooms. *Language Learning & Technology*, *9*(3), 79–98.

Jewitt, C., & Oyama, R. (2001). Visual Meaning: A Social Semiotic Approach. In T. Van Leeuwen & C. Jewitt (Eds.), Handbook of Visual Analysis, (pp. 134–156). London: Sage.

Jimmy Wong. (2011, Mar 15). *Ching Chong! Asians in the Library Song (Response to UCLA's Alexandra Wallace).* [Video File]. Retrieved from "White Girls in the Library" https://www.youtube.com/watch?v=PiEvmr3I-Ik.

Johann, A., & Ries, S. (Writers), & B. Iles (Director). (2011). Cool Hand Peter [Television series episode]. In S. MacFarlane (Producer), Family Guy. Los Angeles, CA: Fox Broadcasting Company.

Julian, H. L. (2010). *South Park* Writers Warned Not to Say 'M' Word 'Mohammed'. *Israeli National News.* Retrieved from http://www.israelnationalnews.com/News/News.aspx/137187#.VV_s4qbyBnR

Jungius, M., & Seibel, W. (2008). The Citizen As Perpetrator: Kurt Blanke and Aryanization In France, 1940-1944. *Holocaust and Genocide Studies*, *22*(3), 441–474. doi:10.1093/hgs/dcn040

Kansteiner, W. (2006). Losing the War, Winning the Memory Battle: The Legacy of Nazism, World War II, and the Holocaust In the Federal Republic Of Germany. In R. N. Lebow & W. Kansteiner & C. Fugo (Eds.), The Politics of Memory In Postwar Europe (pp. 102-147). Durham, NC: Duke University Press.

Kansteiner, W. (2003). Entertaining Catastrophe: The Reinvention of the Holocaust In the Television of the Federal Republic of Germany. *New German Critique, NGC, 90*(90), 135–162. doi:10.2307/3211113

Kant, I. (1914). *The Critique of judgment*. London: Macmillan. Retrieved February 5, 2015, from http://oll.libertyfund.org/titles/1217

Kant, I. (1911). *Critique of Judgment*. Oxford, UK: Clarendon Press. (Original work published 1790)

Kantor Center for Study of Contemporary European Jewry. (2014). *Anti-Semitism Worldwide 2014*. Tel Aviv: Dina Porat.

Kaplan, L. (2002). It Will Get a Tremendous Laugh: On the Problematic Pleasures and Politics of Holocaust Humor. In H. Jenkins & T. McPherson & J. Shattuc (Eds.), Hop on Pop: The Politics and Pleasures of Popular Culture (pp. 343-357). Durham, NC: Duke University Press.

Katayama, H. (2008). Humor in Manzai stand-up comedy: A historical and comparative analysis. *The International Journal of the Humanities*, *6*(1), 213–223.

Katayama, H. (2009). A Cross-cultural Analysis of Humor In Stand-up Comedy In the United States and Japan. *JoLIE*, *2*, 125–142.

Kecskes, I. (2010). Situation-bound utterances as pragmatic acts. *Journal of Pragmatics*, *42*(1), 2889–2897. doi:10.1016/j.pragma.2010.06.008

Kecskes, I. (2014). *Intercultural Pragmatics*. Oxford, UK: Oxford University Press.

Keisannen, T., & Karkkanen, E. (2014). Stance. In K. Schneider & A. Barron (Eds.), *Pragmatics of Discourse* (pp. 295–322). Berlin: Mouton de Gruyter. doi:10.1515/9783110214406-012

Khan, M. (2014). *Reflecting On Joan Rivers Rant On Israel Gaza Conflict: Palestinians 'Deserve To Be Dead'*. Retrieved on November 27, 2015 from www.ibtimes.co.uk

Khodasevich, V. (n.d.). *The Debasement of Females in South Park*. Retrieved from Lecture Notes Online Web site: http://www.brooklyn.cuny.edu/pub/departments/bcurj/pdf/khoidasevich.pdf

Kint da Drunk. (2015). Retrieved from: https://www.youtube.com/watch?v=elcxD1sw-dw

Klint da Drunk. (2012). *People don't Understand My Swag*. Retrieved from http://www.nigeriafilms.com/news/16623/13/people-dont-understand-my-swag-klint-da-drunk.html)

Knight, N. K. (2008). "Still cool…and American too!": An SFLanalysis of deferred bonds in internet messaging humour. *Systemic Functional Linguistics in Use: Odense Working Papers in Language and Communication, 29,* 481-502.

Knight, N. (2008). "Still cool…and american too!": An SFL Analysis of Deferred Bonds in Internet Messaging Humour. *Language & Communication*.

Koestler, A. (1969). *The Act of Creation*. London: Hutchinson & Co.

Kofod-Petersen, A., & Wegener, R. (2010). Like a poke on Facebook: Emergent semantics in location-aware social network services. In R. Taiwo (Ed.), *Handbook of Research on Discourse Behavior and Digital Communication: Language Structures and Social Interaction* (pp. 497–512). Hershey, PA: IGI Global. doi:10.4018/978-1-61520-773-2.ch032

Kotthoff, H. (2007). Oral genres of humor: On the dialectic of genre knowledge and creative authoring. *Pragmatics*, *17*(2), 263–296. doi:10.1075/prag.17.2.04kot

Kozinets, R. V. (2010). *Netnography: Doing Ethnographic Research Online*. Thousand Oaks, CA: Sage.

Kress, G., & van Leeuwen, T. (2006). Reading images: The grammar of visual design. London: Routledge.

Kress, G. (2003). *Literacy in the New Media*. London: Routlege. doi:10.4324/9780203164754

Kress, G., & van Leeuwen, T. (2001). *Multimodal Discourse: The Modes and Media of Contemporary Communication*. London: Arnold.

Krikmann, A. (2006). *Contemporary Linguistic Theories of Humour*. Retrieved 20 January 2015 from http://www.folklore.ee/folklore/vol33/kriku.pdf

Laineste, L. (n.d.). Funny or Aggressive? Failed Humour in Internet Comments. *Folklore, 53*. Retrieved on February 10, 2015 from http://www.folklore.ee/folklore/vol53/laineste.pdf

Laineste, L. (2013). Funny or aggressive? Failed humour in Internet comments. *Folklore*, *53*, 29–46. Retrieved from http://www.folklore.ee/folklore/vol53/laineste.pdf

Landsberg, A. (1997). America, the Holocaust, and the Mass Culture of Memory: Toward a Radical Politics of Empathy. *New German Critique, NGC*, *71*(71), 63–86. doi:10.2307/488559

Lanineste, L. (2013). Funny or Aggressive? Failed humour in Internet comment. Electronic. *Journal of Folklore*, *53*, 29–46.

Lanz, M. (Producer). (2015, January 27). *Markus Lanz* [Television Broadcast]. Mainz, Germany: Zweites Deutsches Fernsehen.

Lester, L., & Skousen, R. (1974). The Phonology of Drunkenness. In A. Bruck, R. Fox & M. W. LaGaly (Eds.), *Papers from the Para session On Natural Phonology*. Chicago Linguistics.

Lester, P. M. (2000). Visual Communication: Images with Messages (2nd ed.). Wadsworth.

Levinson, S. C. (1983). Pragmatics. Cambridge, UK: Cambridge.

Li, C. (2014). Two immigrant humor styles of stand-up comedy: A linguistic perspective. In *Proceedings of International Conference on Education, Language, Art and Intercultural Communication (ICELAIC-14)* (pp. 276-279). Atlantis Press. doi:10.2991/icelaic-14.2014.70

Limon, J. (2000). *Stand-up comedy in theory, or, abjection in America*. Durham, NC: Duke University Press. doi:10.1215/9780822380504

Linda Ikeji's Blog. (2013, May 13). *More photos from Linda Ikeji's Mania magazine shoot* [Blog Post]. Retrieved from http://lindaikeji.blogspot.com/2013/05/more-photos-from-linda-ikejis-mania.html

Linda Ikeji's Blog. (2015a, February 12). *ONYX Godwin releases new photos for the holidays* [Blog Post]. Retrieved from http://lindaikeji.blogspot.com/2015/04/onyx-godwin-releases-new-photos-for.html

Linda Ikeji's Blog. (2015b, February 28). *Calvin Klein now saying they never said Lupita's dress was worth $150k... lol* [Blog Post]. Retrieved from http://lindaikeji.blogspot.com/2015/02/calvin-klein-now-saying-they-never-said.html

Linda Ikeji's Blog. (2015c, February 28). *They say this is a job application letter from Ibadan...:-)* [BlogPost]. Retrieved from http://lindaikeji.blogspot.com/2015/02/they-say-this-is-job-application-letter.html

Linda Ikeji's Blog. (2015d, February 28). *Toyin Lawani shows off her custom made Swarovski Stones Bikini* [BlogPost]. Retrieved from http://lindaikeji.blogspot.com/2015/02/toyin-lawani-shows-off-her-cutosm-made.html

Linda Ikeji's Blog. (2015e, February 4). *What is wrong with this photo?* [Blog Post]. Retrieved from http://lindaikeji.blogspot.com/2015/02/what-is-wrong-with-this-photo.html

Linda Ikeji's Blog. (2015f, January 12). *Ronke Oshodi Oke thanks her fans for liking her pics on instagram* [Blog Post]. Retrieved from http://lindaikeji.blogspot.com/2015/01/ronke-oshodi-oke-thanks-her-fans-for.html

Linda Ikeji's Blog. (2015g, January 6). *Guys, if she had the personality of an angel but with skin like this, would you still hit?* [Blog Post]. Retrieved from http://lindaikeji.blogspot.com/2015/01/guys-if-she-had-personality-of-angel.html

Linda Ikeji's Blog. (2015h, March 15). *Laura Ikeji releases hot new photos as she turns a year older today* [Blog Post]. Retrieved from http://lindaikeji.blogspot.com/2015/03/laura-ikeji-releases-hot-new-photos-as.html

Linda Ikeji's Blog. (2015i, March 7). *Wait, there are more people on LIB than Twitter Nigeria? Yay!* [Blog Post]. Retrieved from http://lindaikeji.blogspot.com/2015/03/wait-there-are-more-people-on-lib-than.html

Lipman, S. (1991). Laughter. In *Hell: The Use of Humor during the Holocaust*. Northvale, NJ: J. Aronson.

Lipstadt, D. (1993). *Denying the Holocaust: The Growing Assault On Truth and Memory*. New York: Free Press.

Liu, J. (2013). Visual Images Interpretive Strategies in Multimodal Texts. *Journal of Language Teaching and Research*, *4*(6), 1259–1263. doi:10.4304/jltr.4.6.1259-1263

Lockyer, S. (2011). From toothpick legs to dropping vaginas: Gender and sexuality in Joan Rivers' stand-up comedy performance. *Comedy Studies*, *2*(2), 113–123. doi:10.1386/cost.2.2.113_1

Lopez-Rocha, S. (2010). Nethnography in context: Methodological and practical implications of virtual ethnography. *International Journal of Interdisciplinary Social Sciences*, *5*(4), 291–301.

Loshitzky, L. (1997). Holocaust Others: Schindler's List versus Lanzmann's Shoah. In Y. Loshitzky (Eds.), Spielberg's Holocaust: Critical Perspectives On Schindler's List (pp. 104-119). Bloomington, IN: Indiana University Press.

Loving, M., & Ochoa, M. (2011). Facebook as a classroom management solution. *New Library World*, *112*(3/4), 121–130. doi:10.1108/03074801111117023

Malone, P. (1980). Humor: A Double-edged tool for today's managers?. *Academy of Management Review*, *5*(3), 357–360. doi:10.5465/AMR.1980.4288842

Manolopoulos, K. N., Karpe, F., & Frayn, K. N. (2010). Gluteofemoral body fat as a determinant of metabolic health. *International Journal of Obesity*, *34*(6), 949–959. doi:10.1038/ijo.2009.286 PMID:20065965

Marc, D. (1997). *Comic Visions: Television Comedy and American Culture* (2nd ed.). Malden, MA: Blackwell Publishers.

Markoe, L. (2015, February 28). Anti-Semitism Is A Big Problem At American College Campuses, According To New Report. *Huffington Post*. Retrieved from http://www.huffingtonpost.com/2015/02/28/anti-semitism-college-cam_n_6775238.html

Marone, V. (2015). Online humour as a community- building cushioning glue 3,1. Cognitive Constraints on Communication.

Martin, R. (2007). *The Psychology of Humor: An Integrative Approach*. Academic Press.

Martin, M. W. (1987). Humor and the Aesthetic Enjoyment of Incongruities. In J. Morreall (Ed.), *The Philosophy of Laughter and Humor* (pp. 172–186). Albany, NY: State University of New York Press.

Martin, R. (2007). *The Psychology of Humor. An Integrative Approach*. Burlington, MA: Elsevier.

Mazer, J. P., Murphy, R. E., & Simonds, C. J. (2007). "I'll see you on Facebook": The Effects of Computer-mediated Teacher Self-disclosure on Student Motivation, Affective Learning, and Classroom Climate. *Communication Education*, *56*(1), 1–17. doi:10.1080/03634520601009710

Mc Cann, B. (2015, January). *LOLZ* [Msg 1]. Message posted to https://www.youtube.com/watch?v=gjm8iMRkfFQ

McLaughlin, E. C. (2015, January 21). Anti-Islamization Leader Steps Down Amid Uproar Over Hitler Selfie. *CNN*. Retrieved from http://www.cnn.com/2015/01/21/europe/germany-pegida-hitler-pose-bild/index.html

McLennan, R. (2012). *American and European Representations of Anne Frank*. Paper presented at the Benelux American Studies Association Conference: American Responses to the Holocaust, Transatlantic Perspectives, Middleburg, The Netherlands.

Mcllvenny, P., Mettovaara, S., & Tapio, R. (1992). I really wanna make you laugh: Stand-up comedy and audience response. In M.K. Suijanen & A. Kulkki- Nieminen (Eds.), *Folia, Fennistica and Linguistica:Proceedings of the Annual Finnish Symposium.*

Medoff, R. (2009). *Blowing the Whistle On Genocide: Josiah E. Dubois, Jr., and the Struggle For A U.S. Response To the Holocaust*. West Lafayette, IN: Purdue University Press.

Medoff, R. (2013). *FDR and The Holocaust: A Breach of Faith*. Washington, DC: David S. Wyman Institute for Holocaust Studies.

Meighan, P. (Writer), & G. Colton (Director). (2008). Road To Germany [Television series episode]. In S. MacFarlane (Producer), Family Guy. Los Angeles, CA: Fox Broadcasting Company.

Mellinger, W. M. (1992). Postcards from the Edge of the Color Line: Images of African Americans in Popular Culture, 1893–1917. *Symbolic Interaction, 15*(4), 413-433.

Mey, J. (2009). Pragmatic Act. In Concise Encyclopedia of Pragmatics. Elsevier.

Meyer, J. C. (2000). Humor as a Double-Edged Sword: Four Functions of Humor in Communication. *Communication Theory, 10*(3), 310–331. doi:10.1111/j.1468-2885.2000.tb00194.x

Mey, J. (2000). *When voices clash: A study in literary pragmatics*. Berlin: Mouton de Gruyter.

Mey, J. (2001). *Pragmatics: An Introduction* (2nd ed.). Oxford, UK: Blackwell.

Mills, B. (2011). "A pleasure working with you": Humour theory and Joan Rivers. *Comedy Studies*, *2*(2), 151–160. doi:10.1386/cost.2.2.151_1

Mintz, L. E. (1985). Standup comedy as social and cultural mediation. *American Quarterly, 37*(1), 71-80.

Mintz, A. (2001). *Popular Culture and the Shaping of Holocaust Memory in America*. Seattle, WA: University of Washington Press.

Mintz, L. (1985). Stand–up Comedy as Social and Cultural Mediation. *American Quarterly*, *37*(1), 71–80. doi:10.2307/2712763

Mock, R. (2011). Really Jewish? Joan Rivers Live at the Apollo. *Comedy Studies*, *2*(2), 101–111. doi:10.1386/cost.2.2.101_1

Montgomery, M., Durant, A., Fabb, N., Furniss, T., & Mills, S. (2000). *Ways of reading: advanced reading skills for students of English literature* (2nd ed.). London: Routledge.

Moriarty, M. (2011). Minority languages and performative genres: The case of Irish language stand-up comedy. *Journal of Multilingual and Multicultural Development*, *32*(6), 547–559. doi:10.1080/01434632.2011.604420

Morkes, J., Kernal, H. K., & Nass, C. (1999). Effects of humor in task oriented human- computer interaction and computer-mediated communication: A direct test of SRCT theory. *Human-Computer Interaction*, *14*(4), 395–435. doi:10.1207/S15327051HCI1404_2

Morreal, J. (2012). Philosophy of humor. *Stanford Encyclopedia of philosophy*. Retrieved March 5, 2015, from http://plato.stanford.edu/entries/humour/

Morreall, J. (2001). Humor in the Holocaust: Its Critical, Cohesive, and Coping Functions. In *Proceedings of the Conference on the Holocaust and the Churches, Hearing The Voices: Teaching the Holocaust to Future Generations*. Retrieved from http://www.holocaust-trc.org/humor-in-the-holocaust/

Morreall, J. (1983). *Taking Laughter Seriously*. Albany, NY: State University of New York Press.

Morreall, J. (1987). *The Philosophy of Laughter and Humor.* Albany, NY: State University of New York Press.

Morreall, J. (1997). *Humor Works.* Amherst, MA: Human Resource Development Press.

Morreall, J. (2009). *Comic Relief: A Comprehensive Philosophy of Humor.* Malden, MA: Wiley Blackwell. doi:10.1002/9781444307795

Morris, P. (1994). *The Bakhtin reader: Selected writings of Bakhtin, Medvedev, Voloshinov.* New York: Oxford University Press.

Morson, G. S. (2009). Addressivity. In J. Mey (Ed.), *Concise Encyclopedia of Pragmatics* (2nd ed.; pp. 13–16). Oxford, UK: Elsevier.

Mudler, M. P., & Nijholt, A. (2002). *Humour research: state of the art.* Retrieved February 2, 2015, from wwwhome.ewi.utwente.nl/~anijholt/artikelen/ctit24_2002.pdf

Mulder, M. P., & Nijholt, A. (2002). Humour Research: State of the Arts. Centre for Telematics and Information Technology.

Muller, A. (2012). *Have a Holly Jolly Holocaust: Humor, Genocide, and the Moral Imagination.* Paper presented at the International Network Of Genocide Scholars: Third Global Conference on Genocide, San Francisco, CA.

Munoz, C., & Towner, T. (2009). Opening Facebook: How to use Facebook in the college classroom. In I. Gibson, R. Weber, K. McFerrin, R. Carlsen, & D. Willis (Eds.), *Proceedings of Society for Information Technology & Teacher Education International Conference 2009* (pp. 2623-2627). Chesapeake, VA: Association for the Advancement of Computing in Education (AACE).

Murtagh, K. J. (2013). Mary's Menses and Morality: Blasphemy in South Park. In R. Arp and K. Decker (Eds.), The Ultimate South Park and Philosophy: Respect my Philosophah! (pp. 108-119). West Sussex, UK: Wiley-Blackwell.

Nash, W. (1985). *The language of humour.* Harlow: Longman.

National Fire Prevention Association. (2011, March). *Fatal Effects of Fire.* Retrieved from http://www.nfpa.org/research/reports-and-statistics/demographics-and-victim- patterns/fatal-effects-of-fire

NAz, K. A. Y. A., & Epps, H. (2004). Relationship between color and emotion: A study of college students. *College Student Journal, 38*(3), 396–405.

Ngamsa, J. (2013). Patterns of Intersemiotic Cohesion in the Moving Image Text. *New Media and Mass Communication, 9,* 11–17.

Nigeria Internet Users. (n.d.). Retrieved 23 May 2015 from www.internetlivestats.com/internet-user/nigeria/

Ninalowo, A. (1996). Contradictions of Military Governance and Industrial Democracy. In A. Ninalwo (Ed.), *The Quest for Democratization; Military Governance and Trade Union* (pp. 105–128). Yaba, Nigeria: Friedrich Elbert Foundation.

Nnadozie, E. (2002). African indigenous entrepreneurship determinants of resurgence and growth of Igbo entrepreneurship during the post-Biafra period. *Journal of African Business, 3*(1), 49–80. doi:10.1300/J156v03n01_04

Norrick, N. R. (1993) Repetition in canned jokes and spontaneous conversational joking. HUMOR, The International Journal of Humor Research, 6(4), 385-402.

Norrick, N. R. (2001). On the conversational performance of narrative jokes: Toward an account of timing. *Humor, 14*(3), 255-274.

Norrick, N. R. (2004). Non-verbal humor and joke performance. *Humor, 17*(4), 401-409.

Norrick, N. R. (2005). *Saarbrücken Corpus of Spoken English (SCoSE): Jokes*. Retrieved from http://www.uni-saarland.de/fak4/norrick/index2.htm

Norrick, N. (1984). Stock conversational witticisms. *Journal of Pragmatics*, *8*(2), 195–209. doi:10.1016/0378-2166(84)90049-3

Norrick, N. (1986). A frame-theoretical analysis of verbal humor: Bisociation as schema conflict. *Semiotica*, *60*(3-4), 225–245. doi:10.1515/semi.1986.60.3-4.225

Norrick, N. (1993). *Conversational joking: humor in everyday talk*. Bloomington, IN: Indiana University Press.

Norrick, N. (2001). On the conversational performance of narrative jokes: Towards an account of timing. *Humor: International Journal of Humor Research*, *14*(3), 255–274. doi:10.1515/humr.2001.003

Norrick, N. R. (1982). In K. Detering, J. Schmidt-Radefeldt, & W. Sucharowski (Eds.), *On the semantics of overstatement. Sprache erkennen und verstehen* (pp. 168–176). Tübingen: Niemeyer.

Norrick, N. R. (1989). Intertextuality in humor. *Humor: International Journal of Humor Research*, *2*(2), 117–139. doi:10.1515/humr.1989.2.2.117

Norrick, N. R. (1993). *Conversational Joking*. Bloomington, IN: Indiana University Press.

Norrick, N. R. (1993a). Repetition in canned jokes and spontaneous conversational joking. *Humor: International Journal of Humor Research*, *6*(4), 385–402. doi:10.1515/humr.1993.6.4.385

Norrick, N. R. (2000). *Conversational narrative*. Philadelphia: Benjamins. doi:10.1075/cilt.203

Norrick, N. R. (2003). Issues in conversational joking. *Journal of Pragmatics*, *35*(9), 1333–1359. doi:10.1016/S0378-2166(02)00180-7

Norrick, N. R. (2010). Humor in Interaction. *Language and Linguistics Compass*, *4*(4), 232–244. doi:10.1111/j.1749-818X.2010.00189.x

North, S. (2007). 'The voices, the voices': Creativity in Online Conversation. *Applied Linguistics*, *28*(4), 538–555. doi:10.1093/applin/amm042

Novick, P. (2003). The American National Narrative of the Holocaust: There Isn't Any. *New German Critique, NGC*, *90*(90), 27–35. doi:10.2307/3211105

Nuefeld, M. J., & Berenbaum, M. (2000). *The Bombing of Auschwitz: Should the Allies Have Attempted It?* New York: St. Martin's Press.

Nwana, E. (2013, August 13). The Business of Comedy in Nigeria. *Economic Financial Times*.

Nwoke, M. B. (2013). Influence of cultural value system and home on child-rearing practices in the contemporary Nigerian society. *Open Journal of Philosophy*, *3*(01), 200–206. doi:10.4236/ojpp.2013.31A033

O'Halloran, K. L. (2004). *Multimodal discourse analysis: systemic functional perspectives*. New York: Continuum.

O'Halloran, K. L. (2011). Multimodal discourse analysis. In K. Hyland & B. Paltridge (Eds.), *Companiontodiscourse analysis* (pp. 120–137). London, New York: Continuum.

Obadare, E. (2009). The Use of Ridicule: Humour, 'Infrapolitics' and Civil Society in Nigeria. *African Affairs*, *108*(431), 241–261. doi:10.1093/afraf/adn086

Obour, S. K. & Gamor, E. (2015, January 21). *I've been named 'Mr Dumsor' in Ghana – Prez Mahama tells Ghanaians in Germany*. Retrieved from graphic.com.gh

Ochwada, H. (2012). From Kamiirithu to XYZ-Show: Between cultural "flaws" and democratic change in independent Kenya. In A. Agwuele A (Ed.), Development, modernism and modernity in Africa (pp. 196-211). New York: Routledge.

Odebunmi, A. (2006). *Meaning in English: An Introduction*. Ogbomoso: Critical Sphere.

Odebunmi, A., & Alo, M. (2010). Belief in GSM Text Messaging Among Academics in Two Nigerian Universities. In Handbook of Research on Discourse Behavior and Digital Communication Language Structures and Social Interaction (vol. 1, pp. 468-478). New York: Information Science Reference. doi:10.4018/978-1-61520-773-2.ch029

Odebunmi, A. (2006). *Meaning in English: an introduction*. Ogbomoso, Nigeria: Critical Sphere.

Ogas at the Top. (n.d.). Available at http://buni.tv/shows/ogas-at-the-top/; http://www.youtube.com/ogasatthetop

Ogundipe, S., Obinna, C., Ojeme, V., Mikairu, L., Ewepu, G., & Olawale, G. (2014, August 8). *Ebola Latest: US rejects Nigeria's request for trial drug*. Retrieved February 20, 2015 from: http://www.vanguardngr.com/2014/08/ebola-latest-us-rejects-nigerias-request-trial-drug/

Oke, B. O. (2004). *Language and creative freedom in cyberspace*. (Unpublished Masters Thesis). University of Ibadan, Ibadan, Nigeria.

Oketola, D. (2014, December 27). *How social media helped Nigerians win the war against Ebola*. Retrieved March 30, 2015 from www.punchng.com/feature/how-social-media-helped-nigerians-win-war-against-ebola/

Okoroafor, M. O., & Nwaeze, C. (2013). Poverty and economic growth in Nigeria 1990-2011. *The MacrothemeReview*, *2*(6), 105–115.

Ong'onda, N. A., Oketch, O. & Ongarora, D. (2013). Prosodic features in facebook communication. *International Journal of Academic Research in Progressive Education and Development*, *2*(2), 166 – 180. Retrieved February 2, 2015, from http://www.hrmars.com/admin/pics/1884.pdf

Oren, M. (2002). *Six Days Of War: June 1967 and the Making Of the Modern Middle East*. Oxford, UK: Oxford University Press.

Orhiunu, W. (2007). *Tribal stereotypes in Nigerian comedy: The Calabar example*. Retrieved on August 2, 2009 from http://www.nigeriansinamerica.com/articles/1951/1/Tribal-Stereotypes-in-Nigerian-Comedy-TheCalabar-Example/html

Orr, A. J. (2003, October). Black-white differences in achievement: The importance of wealth. *Sociology of Education*, *76*(4), 281–304. doi:10.2307/1519867

Ozick, C. (1997, October 6). Who Owns Anne Frank? *The New Yorker Magazine*, 76-88.

Page, R. (2014). Blogs. In M-L. Ryan, L. Emerson, & B. J. Robertson (Eds.), The Johns Hopkins Guide to Digital Media. Baltimore, MD: Johns Hopkins University Press.

Palombo. (2014, March 3). *What Kind Of Man Are You?* [Web log comment]. Retrieved from http://humorchic.blogspot.it/2014/03/humor-chic-art-social-campaign.html

Pan, W. (2012). Linguistic basis of humor in uses of Grice's cooperative principle. *International Journal of Applied Linguistics and English Literature, 1*(6), 20-25.

Panksepp, J. (2000). The Riddle of Laughter: Neural and Psycho Evolutionary Underpinning of Joy. *Current Directions in Psychological Science*, *9*(6), 183–186. doi:10.1111/1467-8721.00090

Parker, T. (Writer), & Stough, E. (Director). (2001). Scott Tenorman Must Die [Television series episode]. In T. Parker & M. Stone (Producers), South Park. Ft. Worth, TX: Braniff Productions.

Parker, T., & Stone, M. (Writers), & Parker, T. (Director). (2008). Major Boobage [Television series episode]. In T. Parker & M. Stone (Producers), South Park. New York, NY: Comedy Partners.

Parker, T., Stone, M., & Stark, P. (Writers), & Parker, T., & Stone, M. (Directors). (1997). Pinkeye [Television series episode]. In T. Parker & M. Stone (Producers), South Park. Denver, CO: Celluloid Studios.

Parkinson-Morgan, K. (2011, March 18). Alexandra Wallace apologizes, announces she will no longer attend UCLA. *Daily Bruin.* Retrieved from http://dailybruin.com/2011/03/18/alexandra_wallace_apologizes_announces_she_will_no_longer_attend_ucla/

Parkinson-Morgan, K. (2011, March 18). Alexandra Wallace apologizes, announces she will no longer attend UCLA. *Daily Bruin.* Retrieved from http://dailybruin.com/2011/03/18/alexandra_wallace_apologizes_announces_she_will_no_longer_attend_ucla/

Parsa, S., & Parsa, A. F. (2002). *GöstergebilimÇözümlemeleri.* İzmir: Ege Üniversitesi Basımevi.

Partington, A. (2006). *The Linguistics of Laughter: A corpus-assisted study of layghter-talk.* New York: Routledge.

Peacock, L. (2011). Joan Rivers—reading the meaning. *Comedy Studies, 2*(2), 125–137. doi:10.1386/cost.2.2.125_1

Personally. (n.d.). Available at www.azlyrics.com/lyrics/psquare/personally.html

Peters, M. (2010, August 19). Gregory Brothers take Antoine Dodson to Hot 100. *Billboard.* Retrieved from http://www.billboard.com/articles/news/956772/gregory-brothers-take-antoine-dodson-to-the-hot-100

Peterson, E. E. (2011). How conversational are weblogs? *Language@Internet, 8.* Retrieved from http://www.languageatinternet.org/articles/2011/Peterson

Picca, L. H., & Feagin, J. R. (2007). *Two-faced racism: Whites in the backstage andfrontstage.* New York, NY: Routledge.

Pinnock, S. (2007). Atrocity and Ambiguity: Recent Developments in Christian Holocaust Responses. *Journal of the American Academy of Religion, 75*(3), 499–523. doi:10.1093/jaarel/lfm038

Pogrebin, M. R., & Poole, E. D. (1988). Humor in the briefing room: A study of strategic uses of humor among police. *Journal of Contemporary Ethnography, 17*(2), 183–210. doi:10.1177/089124188017002003

Polander, E., & Shallin, V. L. (2013). An analysis of Narrative and Figurative Language within Online Alcoholism Discussion Forum. *International Journal Mental Health Association, 11*(4), 458–473. doi:10.1007/s11469-013-9431-8

Popescu, C. (2003). Understanding ethnic humour in Romanian jokes. In M. Dynel (Ed.), *The pragmatics of humour across discourse domain* (pp. 173–190). Amsterdam: John Benjamins Co.

Postman, N. (1985). *Amusing Ourselves to Death: Public Discourse in the Age of Show Business.* New York: Viking Press.

Potts, A. (1996). Sign. In R. S. Nelson & R. Shiff (Eds.), Critical Terms for Art History. London: University of Chicago Press.

PriceWaterhouseCoupe. (2011, Mar 15). *Asians in the Library (UCLA's Alexandra Wallace).* [Video File]. Retrieved from https://www.youtube.com/watch?v=yBxgtYfDgwM.

Provine, R. (2000). *Laughter: A Scientific Investigation.* Penguin.

Puppets take on politicians in South Africa. (n.d.). Retrieved 15 May, 2015 from https://informationactivism.org/en/puppets-take-politicians-south-africa-za-news

Radcliffe-Brown, A. R. (1952). *Structure and Function in Primitive Society: Essays and Addresses.* New York, NY: Free Press.

Rahman, J. (2007). An Ay For an Ah: Language of Survival in African American Narrative Comedy. *American Speech, 82*(1), 65–96. doi:10.1215/00031283-2007-003

Rappoport, L. (2005). *Punchlines: the case for racial, ethnic, and gender humor.* Westport, CT: Praeger Publishers.

Raskin, V. (1984). *Semantic Mechanisms of Humor.* Dordrecht: Reidel. doi:10.1007/978-94-009-6472-3

Raskin, V. (1985). *Semantic mechanism of humor.* Dordrecht: Reidel.

Raskin, V. (1985). *Semantic mechanisms of humor.* Dordrecht: Kluwer Academic Publishers.

Raskin, V. (1985). *Semantic Mechanisms of Humour.* Dordrecht: Reidel.

Reich, W. (2006). Unwelcome Narratives: Listening to Suppressed Themes in American Holocaust Testimonies. *Poetics Today, 27*(2), 463–472. doi:10.1215/03335372-2005-014

Ritchie, G. (1999). Developing the Incongruity-Resolution Theory. In *Proceedings of the AISB'99 Symposium on Creative language: Humor and Stories* (pp. 78-85). Retrieved March 5, 2015, from http:www.informatics.ed.ac.uk/

Ritchie, G. (2004). *The linguistic analysis of jokes.* Oxford, UK: Routledge.

Rivers, J. (1992). *Still talking.* New York: Avon Books.

Rogers, R. (2009). *TV puppet satire torments Kenyan elite.* Available at www.theguardian.com/world/2009/nov/22/xyz-kenya-tv-puppets-satire

Rosen, A. (2005). *Sounds of Defiance: The Holocaust, Multilingualism, and the Problem of English.* Lincoln, NE: University of Nebraska Press.

Rosenberg, B. A. (1970). *The Art of the American Folk Preacher.* New York: Oxford, University Press.

Rosenfeld, A. (2011). *The End of the Holocaust.* Bloomington, IN: Indiana University Press.

Ross, A. (2009). *The Language of Humour.* London: Routledge.

Ruch, W., Attardo, S., & Raskin, V. (1993). Toward an empirical verification of the General Theory of Verbal Humor. *Humor: International Journal of Humor Research, 62*, 123–136.

Rutter, J. (1997). *Stand-up as interaction: Performance and audience in comedy venues.* (Unpublished doctoral dissertation). University of Salford.

Rutter, J. (1997). *Stand-Up as Interaction: Performance and Audience in Comedy Venues.* University of Salford.

Sackett, R. (2002). Memory by Way of Anne Frank: Enlightenment and Denial Among West Germans, Circa 1960. *Holocaust and Genocide Studies, 16*(2), 243–265. doi:10.1093/hgs/16.2.243

Sack, H. (1974). An analysis of the course of a joke's telling. In R. Bauman & J. Sherzer (Eds.), *Explorations in the ethnography of speaking* (pp. 337–353). Cambridge, UK: Cambridge University Press.

Said, E. (1975). The text, the world, the critic. *The Bulletin of the Midwest Modern Language Association, 8*(2), 1–23. doi:10.2307/1314778

Saint-preux, S. (2013). *Can't believe how awful that was. C'est terrible! le journal d'Ann Frank* [Msg 20]. Message posted to https://www.youtube.com/watch?v=gjm8iMRkfFQ

Salal, F., Krupat, E., & Roter, D. (2002). 'Satisfaction and the Use of Humour by Physicians and Patients'. *Psychology & Health*, *17*(3), 269–280. doi:10.1080/08870440290029520

Samuels, J. (Writer), & B. Iles (Director). (2015). Fighting Irish [Television series episode]. In S. MacFarlane (Producer), Family Guy. Los Angeles, CA: Fox Broadcasting Company.

Schegloff, E. (1986). The routine as achievement. *Human Studies, 9*, 111–51.

Schmidt, C. (2011). Prisons, performance arena and occupational humor. *Oral Tradition*, *26*(2), 613–616. doi:10.1353/ort.2011.0023

Schmidt, J. (2007). Blogging practices: An analytical framework. *Journal of Computer-Mediated Communication*, *12*(4), 1409–1427. doi:10.1111/j.1083-6101.2007.00379.x

schmoyoho. (2010, Jul 31). *Bed Intruder Song!!! (now on iTunes)* [Video File]. Retrieved from https://www.youtube.com/watch?v=hMtZfW2z9dw.

schmoyoho. (2013, May 7). *Dead giveaway!* [Video File]. Retrieved from https://www.youtube.com/watch?v=nZcRU0Op5P4.

Schnurr, S., & Rowe, C. (2008). The 'dark side' of humour. An analysis of subversive humour in workplace emails. *Lodz Papers in Pragmatics*, *4*(1), 109–130. doi:10.2478/v10016-008-0010-6

Schopenhauer, A. (1995). *The world as Will and Idea*. London: Everyman.

Schultz, T. R. (1976). A cognitive-developmental analysis of humor. In A. J. Chapman & H. C. Foot (Eds.), *Humor and Laughter: Theory, Research and Applications* (pp. 11–36). London: Wiley & Sons.

Schwarz, J. (2010). *Linguistic Aspect of Verbal Humour in Stand-up Comedy*. Dissertation.

Schwarz, J. (2010). *Linguistic aspects of verbal humor in stand-up comedy.* (Unpublished doctoral dissertation). University of Saarland.

Schwarz, J. (2010). *Linguistic Aspects of Verbal Humor in Stand-up Comedy*. (Unpublished PhD Dissertation). Universität des Saarlandes.

Schwarz, J. (2010). *Linguistic Aspects of Verbal Humour in Stand-up Comedy*. (PhD Dissertation). Department of English, University of Saarland.

Seewoester, S. (2011). The role of syllables and morphemes as mechanisms in humorous pun formation. In M. Dynel (Ed.), *The pragmatics of humour across discourse domain* (pp. 71–104). Amsterdam: John Benjamins Co. doi:10.1075/pbns.210.07see

Sen, A. (2012). Humour Analysis and Qualitative Research. *Social Research Update*, *63*, 1-4. Accessed from http://sru.soc.surrey.ac.uk/

Shadow Subscribe!. (2014, Jul 9). *9 + 10 Vine.* [Video File]. Retrieved from https://www.youtube.com/watch?v=BzVXbeASRiQ.

Shandler, J. (1999). Aliens in the Wasteland: American Encounters With the Holocaust on 1960s Science Fiction Television. In H. Flanzbaum (Ed.), The Americanization of the Holocaust (pp. 33-45). Baltimore, MD: Johns Hopkins University Press.

Sharp, H. J. (2011). *Semiotics as a Theoretical Foundation of Information Design' Conference for Information Systems Applied Research 2011 CONISAR Proceedings*. Wilmington, NC: Academic Press.

Shaw, J. (2010). Philosophy of Humor. *Philosophy Compass*, *5*(2), 112–126. doi:10.1111/j.1747-9991.2009.00281.x

Sheridan, C. (Writer), & Scott, S. O. (Director). (2000). If I'm Dyin', I'm Lyin' [Television series episode]. In S. MacFarlane (Producer), Family Guy. Los Angeles, CA: Fox Broadcasting Company.

Shifman, L. (2014). *Memes in digital culture*. MIT Press.

Shifman, L., & Thelwall, M. (2014). Internet jokes: The secret agents of globalization. *Journal of Computer-Mediated Communication*, *19*(4), 727–743. doi:10.1111/jcc4.12082

Simpson, P. (2003). *On the discourse of satire: Towards a stylistic model of satirical humour*. Amsterdam: John Benjamins. doi:10.1075/lal.2

Skovholt, K., Grønning, A., & Kankaanranta, A. (2014). The communicative functions of emoticons in workplace e-mails:-)*. *Journal of Computer-Mediated Communication*, *19*(4), 780–797. doi:10.1111/jcc4.12063

Sobell, L. C., & Sobell, M. B. (1972). Effects of Alcohol on the Speech of Alcoholics. *Journal of Speech and Hearing*, *15*(4), 861–868. doi:10.1044/jshr.1504.861 PMID:4652408

Sperber, D., & Wilson, D. (1986). *Relevance: Communication and Cognition*. Oxford, UK: Blackwell Publishing.

Spiardi. (2013, August 18). *Heil, Heil, Rock-n-Roll. What's with Brit Rockers and the Third Reich?* [Web log article]. Retrieved from http://hipquotient.com/heil-heil-rock-n-roll-whats-with-brit-rockers-and-the-third-reich-part-two/

Sports, B. B. C. (2014, June 25). *World Cup 2014: Ghana Sends $3m Cash To Players In Brazil*. Retrieved from http://www.bbc.com/sport/0/football/28021131

Stain, D. R. (1966). Linguistic Analysis of the Speech of a Selected Group of former alcoholics: A research note. *Quarterly Journal of Studies on Alcohol*, *27*, 106–109. PMID:5907517

Stalnaker, R.C. (2000). Common ground. *Linguistics and Philosophy*, *25*, 701-721.

Stalnaker, R. C. (1978). Assertion. In C. P. Pragmatics (Ed.), *Syntax and Semantics 9* (pp. 315–332). New York: Academic Press.

State Department. (1944). *Department of State Bulletin*. Washington, DC: Government Printing Office.

Stoll, B. A. (2015). The Effects of Humorous *Facebook* Posts on Messenger Credibility and Social Attractiveness. *The Hilltop Review*, *7*(2), 3–18.

Storey, R. (2003). Humor and Sexual Selection. *Human Nature (Hawthorne, N.Y.)*, *14*(4), 319–336. doi:10.1007/s12110-003-1009-x PMID:26190269

Street, J. (1986). *Rebel Rock: The Politics of Popular Music*. New York, NY: Blackwell.

Suls, J. (1972). A Two-Stage Model for the Appreciation of Jokes and Cartoons: An Information-Processing Analysis. In J. Goldstein & P. McGhee (Eds.), *The Psychology of Humor* (pp. 81–99). New York: Academic Press. doi:10.1016/B978-0-12-288950-9.50010-9

Suls, J. M. (1983). Cognitive processes in humour appreciation. In P. McGhee & J. Goldstein (Eds.), *Handbook of humor research: Basic issues* (pp. 39–58). New York: Springer-Verlag. doi:10.1007/978-1-4612-5572-7_3

Sunday, A. (2010). The Suprasegmental of Bilingual Nigerian Adult Aphasics. *SKASE Journal of Theoretical Linguistics, 7*(2). Retrieved from http://www.skase.sk/volumes/JTL16/pdf_doc./03.pdf

Sypher, W. (Ed.). (1991). Comedy. The Johns Hopkins University Press.

Tabe, C. A. (2011). *A study of e-mail messages in Cameroon English.* (Unpublished doctoral thesis). University of Yaounde I, Cameroon.

Taiwo, R. (2007). Satirizing Politicians and Public Officers in Nigerian Newspapers. *The International Journal of Language Society and Culture*, (22), 19 – 28.

Taiwo, R. (2011). Emerging Trends in English Language in the New Media: A Case Study of Satire in Nigerian Text Messages, *Journal of Nigeria English Studies Association Journal, 16*, 58-73.

Taiwo, R. (2013). Emerging Trends in English Language in the New Media: A Case Study of Satire in Nigerian Text Messages. *Journal of the Nigeria English Studies Association, 16*(1), 58–73.

Takagi, D. Y. (1993). Asian Americans and racial politics: A postmodern paradox. *Social Justice, 20*(1-2), 115-128.

Taylor, C. (2009) 'Laughter' in L2 computer-mediated discourse. In Advances in discourse approaches. Cambridge Scholars Publishing.

Taylor, C. (2009). 'Laughter' in L2 Computer-Mediated Discourse. In M. Dynel (Ed.), *Advances in Discourse Approaches* (pp. 174 - 200). Cambridge, UK: Cambridge Scholars Publishing. Retrieved March 5, 2015, from http://www.academia.edu/426141/Laughter_in_L2_Computer_Mediated_Discourse

theparodyfactory1. (2012, Apr 13). *Sweet Brown – Ain't nobody got time for that (autotune remix)* [Video File]. Retrieved from https://www.youtube.com/watch?v=bFEoMO0pc7k.

Thompson, E. G. (2010). Addressing institutional structural barriers to student achievement. *Race, Gender, & Class, 17*(1/2), 51–57.

Tisljar, R., & Bereczkei, T. (2005). An Evolutionary Interpretation of Humor and Laughter. *Journal of Cultural and Evolutionary Psychology, 3*(3), 301–309. doi:10.1556/JCEP.3.2005.3-4.6

Trojan, F., & Kryspin-Exner, K. (1968). The Decay of Articulation under the Influence of Alcohol and Paraldehyde. *Folia Phoniatrica, 20*(4), 217–238. doi:10.1159/000263201 PMID:5671974

Tsakona, V. (2009). Language and image interaction in cartoons: Towards a multimodal theory of humor. *Journal of Pragmatics, 41*(6), 1171–1188. doi:10.1016/j.pragma.2008.12.003

Tsang, W. K., & Wong, M. (2004). Constructing a shared 'Hong Kong Identity' in Comic Discourses. *Discourse & Society, 15*(6), 767–785. doi:10.1177/0957926504046504

Tyrnka, P. (2014). *Brian Jones: The Making Of the Rolling Stones.* New York, NY: Viking.

USC Shoah Foundation. The Institute For Visual History and Education, 2007-2015. (2015). Retrieved from http://sfi.usc.edu/

Van Dijk, T. A. (1986). *Text and Context: Explorations into the Semantics and Pragmatis of Discourse.* London: Longman.

Vandergriff, I. (2010). Humor and play in CMC. In R. Taiwo (Ed.), *Handbook of Research on Discourse Behavior and Digital Communication: Language Structures and Social Interaction* (pp. 235–251). Hershey, PA: IGI Global. doi:10.4018/978-1-61520-773-2.ch015

Vandergriff, I., & Fuchs, C. (2009). Does CMC promote language play? Exploring humor in two modalities. *CALICO Journal*, *27*(1), 26–47. doi:10.11139/cj.27.1.26-47

Veale, T. (2004). Incongruity in Humour: Root Cause or Epiphenomenon?. *Humor: International Journal of Humor Research*, *17*(4), 419–428.

Veatch, T. (1998). A theory of humor. *Humor: International Journal of Humor Research*, *11*(2), 161–215. doi:10.1515/humr.1998.11.2.161

Vereen, L. G., Butler, S. K., Williams, F. C., Darg, J. A., & Downing, T. K. E. (2006). The Use of Humor when Counseling African American College Students. *Journal of Counseling and Development*, *84*(1), 10–15. doi:10.1002/j.1556-6678.2006.tb00375.x

Viener, J. (Writer), & Z. Moncrief (Director). (2006). Untitled Griffin Family [Television series episode]. In S. MacFarlane (Producer), Family Guy. Los Angeles, CA: Fox Broadcasting Company.

Vlahovic, T. A., Roberts, S., & Dunbar, R. (2012). Effects of duration and laughter on subjective happiness within different modes of communication. *Journal of Computer-Mediated Communication*, *17*(4), 436–450. doi:10.1111/j.1083-6101.2012.01584.x

Waisanen, D. (2011). Jokes inviting more than laughter… Joan Rivers' political-rhetorical world view. *Comedy Studies*, *2*(2), 139–150. doi:10.1386/cost.2.2.139_1

Weaver, S. (2011). Definitions of the Humorous in Chris Rock and Russell Peters Fan Blogs: A discussion of the Problem of Incongruity. *Participations Journal of Audience and Reception Studies*, *8*(2), 257–275.

Weeks, B., & Southwell, B. (2010). The symbiosis of news coverage and aggregate online search behavior: Obama, rumors, and presidential politics. *Mass Communication & Society*, *13*(4), 341–360. doi:10.1080/15205430903470532

Weinstock, M. (2013, April 17). Anne Frank, Belieber? *The New Yorker Magazine*. Retrieved from http://www.newyorker.com/books/page-turner/anne-frank-belieber

West, A., Lewis, J., & Currie, P. (2009). Students' Facebook 'friends': Public and private spheres. *Journal of Youth Studies*, *12*(6), 615–627. doi:10.1080/13676260902960752

Wiesen, J. (2009). Service Above Self? Rotary Clubs, National Socialism, and Transnational Memory in the 1960s and 1970s. *Holocaust and Genocide Studies*, *23*(1), 1–25. doi:10.1093/hgs/dcp017

Wild, W. (Writer), & B. Iles (Director). (2008). McStroke [Television series episode]. In S. MacFarlane (Producer), Family Guy. Los Angeles, CA: Fox Broadcasting Company.

Wild, W. (Writer), & D. Polcino (Director). (2008). Long John Peter [Television series episode]. In S. MacFarlane (Producer), Family Guy. Los Angeles, CA: Fox Broadcasting Company.

Wilson, M. (2001). Community without others. *Mots Pluriels, 18.* Retrieved from http://www.arts.uwa.edu.au/MotsPluriels/MP1801mw.html

Wisse, R. R. (2013). *No Joke: Making Jewish Humor*. Princeton, NJ: Princeton University Press. doi:10.1515/9781400846344

Wolfgram, M. A. (2006). The Holocaust Through the Prism Of East German Television: Collective Memory and Audience Perceptions. *Holocaust and Genocide Studies*, *20*(1), 57–79. doi:10.1093/hgs/dcj003

Wolf, J. (2004). Harnessing the Holocaust: The Politics of Memory. In *France*. Palo Alto, CA: Stanford University Press.

Wyche, S. P., Schoenebeck, S. Y. & Forte, A. (2013). Facebook is a Luxury: An Exploratory Study of Facebook Social Use in Rural Kenya. *CSCW, 13.*

Wyman, D. (1968). *Paper Walls: America and the Refugee Crisis, 1938-1941.* Amherst, MA: University of Massachusetts Press.

Wyman, D. (1984). *The Abandonment of the Jews: America and the Holocaust, 1942-1945.* New York: Pantheon.

Xuyah. (2011, Mar 13). *White Girls in the Library.* [Video File]. Retrieved from https://www.youtube.com/watch?v=zulEMWj3sVA.

Yarbrough, B. (2014, July 31). Rialto Unified Panel Wrestles With Accountability For Holocaust Essay Assignment. *San Bernardino Sun.* Retrieved from http://www.sbsun.com/social-affairs/20140731/rialto-unified-panel-wrestles-with-accountability-for-holocaust-essay-assignment

Young, J. E. (1999). America's Holocaust: Memory and the Politics of Identity. In H. Flanzbaum (Ed.), The Americanization of the Holocaust (pp. 68-83). Baltimore, MD: Johns Hopkins University Press.

Young, W. (2013). Flatulence and Philosophy: A Lot of Hot Air, or the Corruption of Youth. In R. Arp & K. Decker (Eds.), The Ultimate South Park and Philosophy: Respect my Philosophah! (pp. 7-19). West Sussex, UK: Wiley-Blackwell. doi:10.1002/9781118607442.ch1

Yule, G. (1996). *The Study of Language* (2nd ed.). Cambridge, UK: Cambridge University Press.

Yus, F. (2002). Stand-up comedy and cultural spread: The case of sex roles. *Babel AFIAL, 10,* 245–292.

Yus, F. (2003). Humour and the search for relevance. *Journal of Pragmatics, 35*(9), 1295–1331. doi:10.1016/S0378-2166(02)00179-0

Zaimov, K. (1969). Die Sprachtorungen als Kriterium der Bewußtseinstrubungen Psychiatrie. *Neurologie, und Medizinische Psychologie, 21,* 218–225.

Zebrowska, E. (2014). Multimodal Messages. *Journal of Multimodal Communication Studies, 1,* 8–15.

Zelizer, B. (1998). *Remembering to Forget: Holocaust Memory Through the Camera's Eye.* Chicago: University of Chicago Press.

Zéro, E. T. (2013). *Firts et last je crois?* [Msg 19]. Message posted to https://www.youtube.com/watch?v=gjm8iMRkfFQ

Zoglin, R. (2008). *Comedy at the edge: How stand-up in the 1970s changed America.* New York, NY: Bloomsbury.

About the Contributors

Rotimi Taiwo (Ph.D.) is a professor of English at Obafemi Awolowo University, Ile-Ife, Nigeria. He was a post-doctoral fellow at University of Freiburg, Germany (September, 2008 - August, 2009). His research focus has been on the application of (critical) discourse analytic and text-linguistic theories to a wide range of discourse, such as those of the media, religion, students' compositions, hospital interaction, politics, and popular culture and of recent, the Internet and telecommunications. *Handbook of Research on Discourse Behavior and Digital Communication: Language Structures and Social Interaction Volumes I & II* (IGI Global, New York, 2010); *Perspectives on African Studies, Essays in Honour of Toyin Falola* (LINCOM Europa, Munchen, Germany); *Collocation in Non-native English: A Study of Nigeria ESL Writing* (VDM Verlag, Saarbrucken, Germany, 2010); *Computer Mediated Discourse in Africa* (Nova, New York, 2012), *Language and Mobile Telecommunication in Nigeria: SMS as a Digital Age Lingual-cultural Expression* (OAU Press, 2012). His most recent edited book *The Discourse of Digital Civic Engagement: Perspectives from the Developing World* (co-edited with Tunde Opeibi) is published by Nova Science Publishers, New York, USA. He was at different times the editor of the journal *Ife Studies in English Language* and the coordinator of the Use of English program at Obafemi Awolowo University, Ile-Ife. He also serves as a consulting editor for *Linguistik Online* (Berne, Switzerland, *Journal of Language Studies* (Covenant University, Ota, Nigeria).

Akinola Odebunmi (PhD) is a specialist in pragmatics, and professor in the Department of English, University of Ibadan, Nigeria. His papers have appeared in *Pragmatics, Linguistik Online, Intercultural Pragmatics, Review of Cognitive Linguistics, Pragmatics and Society, Pragmatics and Cognition*, California Linguistic Notes, *Marang* and *Multilingua*. His contribution entitled, "*Ọmọlúàbí*" appeared in the 2015 edition of the *Handbook of Pragmatics* edited by Jef Verschueren and Jan Ola Ostman. He is co-editor (with Arua E. Arua and Sailal Arimi) of *Language, Gender and Politics*, published by the Centre for Black and African Arts and Civilisation. His reviews of Mira Ariel's *Defining Pragmatics* (published by Cambridge University Press), and Ulrich Busse and Axel Hubler's (eds) *Investigations into the Meta-Communicative Lexicon of English* (published by John Benjamins) have appeared in *Discourse Studies*. Between 2010 and 2011, he was an Alexander von Humboldt Georg Forster experienced fellow at the Freiburg Institute for Advanced Studies, University of Freiburg, Germany.

Akin Adetunji holds a PhD degree in English (Linguistics) from Texas A&M University-Commerce, USA. He has published in peer-reviewed journals, most notably, *Pragmatics, Discourse and Society, World Englishes, MARANG, Ibadan Journal of English* and *Ife Studies in English Language*. He has co-edited two international volumes, *Perspectives on Media Discourse* (2007) and *Studies in Slang and*

Slogans (2010). His areas of research interest are pragmatics, sociolinguistics, stylistics and discourse analysis. He is at present a Chief Lecturer at the Department of General Studies Education, Emmanuel Alayande College of Education, Oyo, Nigeria.

* * *

Oluwatomi Adeoti (PhD) teaches at the Kwara State University, Malete. Her research interests include Pragmatics, Applied Linguistics and Style in language use.

Esther Ajiboye is a doctoral candidate of English at Covenant University, Nigeria, and a member of the RC 25 (Language and Society) of the International Sociological Association. Her research interests include Critical Discourse Analysis, (New) Media Discourse, Crisis Discourse, Language in Society, as well as Language and Identity.

Simeon Ajiboye teaches Use of English at the Centre for Continuous Education, Federal University of Technology, Akure. His interest lies in pragmatics, discourse analysis, semantics and stylistics. He is currently a PhD student in Pragmatics at the Department of English, University of Ibadan.

Lily Chimuanya is a doctoral candidate of English in the Department of Languages and General Studies of Covenant University, Ota, Nigeria. Her research interests span Nigerian English, Discourse Analysis, Stylistics and Semantics.

Wincharles Coker is a member of the Communication Studies Department of the University of Cape Coast, Ghana, and is at present a doctoral candidate of Rhetoric, Theory and Culture at Michigan Technological University, United States. His dissertation interrogates and explores structural, theoretical, and political constraints of communication education in African countries south of the Sahara, using an interdisciplinary approach to theorizing communication practice. He has published extensively in computer-mediated communication, mass and critical communication theory, language and critical discourse studies, and rhetorical studies. His current works have appeared in *African Journal of Rhetoric, Discourse & Communication, Media Dialogues, Language, Society & Culture,* and *Journal of Interdisciplinary Studies in Education.*

Stephen Kwame Dadugblor is currently an MS student of Michigan Tech's Rhetoric, Theory and Culture program. He holds a Bachelor of Arts degree (*summa cum laude*) in English and Sociology from the University of Ghana. In 2012, he was an exchange student at the University of Giessen, Germany, as a member of a research team on the codification of the *International Corpus of English, Ghana.* His research interests meet at the intersection of discourse analysis, rhetoric, and communication.

Jeffrey Demsky (PhD) is a historian of politics and culture. His research agenda focuses primarily on American Holocaust memory. Professor Demsky has authored numerous peer-reviewed articles and book chapters. He has presented his research at conferences convened in Britain, France, Canada Holland, as well as across the United States. In addition to his teaching duties, Professor Demsky has served as a manuscript referee for the *International Journal of Press and Politics.* He is also a historical consultant who helps secondary schools to design and implement their Holocaust and Genocide Studies curriculum. Dr. Demsky's current project examines British rock and roll stars' artistic appropriations of Nazi icons during the 1960s and 1970s.

James Oladunjoye Faleye has a doctorate degree in English language from Obafemi Awolowo University, Ile-Ife, Nigeria. His research interest is in the areas of Phonetics and Phonology in particular and Applied Linguistics in general. He has been researching into the pronunciation and speech styles of Nigerians as users of English as a Second Language (ESL). He has published in reputable referred national and international journals and has contributed chapters to books.

Ibukun Filani is a PhD student in the Department of English, University of Ibadan. He is a recipient of the University of Ibadan Postgraduate School's Teaching and Research Assistantship Award. His research interests include humor, pragmatics and Applied linguistics. He is currently working on language use in Nigerian stand-up comedy.

Fredrick W. Gooding Jr. is a faculty member in Ethnic studies at Northern Arizona University, Flagstaff, Arizona, USA. His research interest and teaching focus on African American History, Critical Race Theory as well as Media Movies and Mainstream Sports. His recent publications include ''The Emperor's New Clothes: Identifying Racism in Obama's Racial Society'' in the edited volume *Revitalizing the American Dream: Essays on Barack Obama* and ''You mean There's RACE in My Movie? The Complete Guide to Understanding Race in Mainstream Hollywood''.

Bimbola Oluwafunlola Idowu-Faith (PhD) was a 2014/2015 Postdoctoral Fellow of the African Humanities Project (AHP) of the American Council of Learned Societies (ACLS), New York, USA. During the fellowship period, her research focused on the multimodal dimensions of semiotic codes in digital literary texts. She currently teaches in the Department of English, Bowen University, Iwo, Nigeria. Her interests are in the areas of (digital) stylistics, digital discourse analysis, women studies and film studies.

Onwu Inya has Bachelor and Masters of Arts in English Language from Ahmadu Bello University, Zaria and University of Ibadan, Nigeria. He lectures in the General Studies department of the Federal University of Technology, Akure and is a PhD candidate in the Department of English, University of Ibadan. His current research interest is on using corpus-based methodology to investigate contextual features of legislative debates in the Nigerian Senate.

M. T. Lamidi is an associate professor in the Department of English, University of Ibadan, Nigeria. With about two decades of teaching in the University, he has developed research interests in generative syntax (involving discussions of the theory and application of generative grammar to the Nigerian linguistic environment and for pedagogical reasons), contrastive linguistics (involving comparison and contrast of English and some Nigerian indigenous languages structures), contact linguistics (where morphological and syntactic structures of Yoruba-English code-switching/code-mixing as well as social applications of the varieties are discussed) and computer-mediated communication (dealing with the varieties and use of language, especially English on the social media). He has published widely in these areas in both local and international journals; and has presented papers on them at different conferences.

Ibrahim Esan Olaosun (PhD) is a Senior Lecturer in the Department of English, Obafemi Awolowo University, Ile-Ife. He teaches and carries out his research in the areas of Stylistics and Semiotics. He also teaches Semantics at post- graduate level.

Funmi Olubode-Sawe is a Senior Lecturer in English at the Federal University of Technology, Akure, Nigeria. Her PhD in Linguistics was earned working on terminology development for the Yorùbá language. Her research interests include pragmatics (metaphors and Yorùbá proverbs), terminology development, translation, and small group collaborative computer-mediated learning. Her recent publications include 'Digital Communication in Indigenous Languages' (In R. Taiwo (Ed.) *Handbook of Research on Discourse Behavior and Digital Communication: Language, Structure and Social Interaction Volumes I & II,* Hershey, PA: IGI Global) and Negotiating Politeness in SMS Text Messages of Yoruba-English Bilinguals' (In I. Chiluwa, P. Ifukor, and R. Taiwo, (Eds.) *Pragmatics of Nigerian English in Digital Discourse,* Munich: LINCOM GmbH).

Camilla Arundie Tabe is senior lecturer of English language in the Department of English language and Literatures of English Expression at the Higher Teacher Training College (Ecole Normale Supérieure) of the University of Maroua. Her research centres on several aspects of Internet linguistics with focus on Cameroon, Socio-linguistics and the use of ICTs in language education. Some of her publications include "The integration and use of ICT tools for English language instruction in Cameroon: assessing challenges and evaluating benefits" that appeared in *Syllabus Review* 4 (1), 2013 and "The Print Media as a Resource in the Development of Cameroon English" that was published in *Research Journal of English Language and Literature (RJELAL)* 3 (3), 2015. Her teaching fields include aspects of English and applied linguistics: Academic writing, the Structure of English, Teaching and Testing language skills.

Index

G

H

I

J

L

M

N

O

P

R

S

T

U

V

W

Y

IRMA INTERNATIONAL

Information Resources Management Association

Become an IRMA Member

Members of the **Information Resources Management Association (IRMA)** understand the importance of community within their field of study. The Information Resources Management Association is an ideal venue through which professionals, students, and academicians can convene and share the latest industry innovations and scholarly research that is changing the field of information science and technology. Become a member today and enjoy the benefits of membership as well as the opportunity to collaborate and network with fellow experts in the field.

IRMA Membership Benefits:

- **One FREE Journal Subscription**
- **30% Off Additional Journal Subscriptions**
- **20% Off Book Purchases**
- Updates on the latest events and research on Information Resources Management through the IRMA-L listserv.
- Updates on new open access and downloadable content added to Research IRM.
- A copy of the Information Technology Management Newsletter twice a year.
- A certificate of membership.

IRMA Membership $195

Scan code to visit irma-international.org and begin by selecting your free journal subscription.

Membership is good for one full year.

www.irma-international.org

www.ingramcontent.com/pod-product-compliance
Lightning Source LLC
LaVergne TN
LVHW060421300926
849162LV00006B/1495
* 9 7 8 1 5 2 2 5 0 3 3 8 5 *